D1382819

Preserving South Street Seaport

Preserving South Street Seaport

The Dream and Reality of a New York
Urban Renewal District

James M. Lindgren

NEW YORK UNIVERSITY PRESS
New York and London

NEW YORK UNIVERSITY PRESS
New York and London
www.nyupress.org

References to Internet websites (URLs) were accurate at the time of writing.
Neither the author nor New York University Press is responsible for URLs
that may have expired or changed since the manuscript was prepared.

Library of Congress Cataloging-in-Publication Data
Lindgren, James Michael, 1950–
Preserving South Street Seaport : the dream and reality of a New York urban
renewal district / James M. Lindgren.
pages cm
Includes bibliographical references and index.
ISBN 978-1-4798-2257-7 (hbk. : alk. paper)
1. South Street Seaport Museum (New York, N.Y.) 2. Maritime museums—
Management—Case studies. 3. Historic preservation—New York (State)—
New York. 4. Historic buildings—New York (State)—New York.
5. Historic ships—New York (State)—New York. 6. City planning—
New York (State)—New York—History—21st century. 7. Land use, Urban—
New York (State)—New York. 8. Harbors—New York (State)—New York—
History—21st century. 9. South Street (New York, N.Y.) I. Title.
V13.U52N4824   2014
387.1074'7471—dc23   2014001723

ISBN 978-1-4798-2257-7 (cl.)

New York University Press books are printed on acid-free paper,
and their binding materials are chosen for strength and durability.
We strive to use environmentally responsible suppliers and materials
to the greatest extent possible in publishing our books.

Manufactured in the United States of America

10 9 8 7 6 5 4 3 2 1

Also available as an ebook

Furthermore:
a program of the J. M. Kaplan Fund

*Preserving South Street Seaport: The Dream and
Reality of a New York Urban Renewal District* was
made possible in part through the generosity of
Furthermore, a program of the J. M. Kaplan Fund,
and the J. Aron Charitable Foundation. Their
thoughtful support helps to ensure that this work is
widely disseminated, and affordable to individuals,
students, scholars, libraries, and other institutions.

With deep gratitude to mentors who inspired me to unfurl my sails:
Edwin "Sandy" King, George Rudé, and Edward P. Crapol

CONTENTS

Preserving South Street Seaport is part of a larger history that began in a 1981 doctoral seminar at the College of William and Mary under William Appleman Williams. Setting a framework for South Street Seaport,* that larger study examines the origins and development of the nation's leading maritime museums—in Salem, MA; New Bedford, MA; Mystic, CT; Newport News, VA; San Francisco, CA; and New York, NY. With over two decades of research on a topic that few historians have assessed, I owe so much to those who have helped in each segment of the forthcoming book, which will be titled "Preserving Maritime America: Public Culture and Memory in the Making of the Nation's Great Marine Museums." But *Preserving South Street Seaport* is about much more than a maritime museum. As I did in writing *Preserving the Old Dominion* (1993) and *Preserving Historic New England* (1995), I use a wide-angle lens to view my subject, in this case the Seaport, in the context of Gotham's debates over preservation, cultural identity, and public policy over the past half century. I am a historian, but *Preserving South Street Seaport* is premised on what anthropologist Clifford Geertz called a "thick description." South Street was enmeshed in what he saw as "webs of significance" that need to be unraveled, many of which philosopher Michel Foucault called "relations of power," whereby its meaning was continually reshaped—internally and externally—in the larger society.[1]

With South Street, I have encountered some typical research problems. As a private institution, the Seaport was under no obligation to open its files to me. When I started my research, president Peter Neill opened the

---

* South Street Seaport is the trademarked name of the South Street Seaport Museum. It lies within the South Street Seaport Historic District, which once included the Fulton Fish Market and now includes residences, businesses, and a shopping mall. Much confusion has arisen because of the mall's appropriation of the name and the Internet URL South Street Seaport. I will use the terms "Seaport," "Seaport Museum," "South Street," and "South Street Seaport" to refer to the museum, as did its founders and makers. The term "seaport" (in lower case) will refer to the district in general.

files that preceded his hiring in 1985. I am grateful to the J. Aron Charitable Foundation for allowing me to use materials collected by long-serving trustees Jack and Peter Aron, which precede and follow Neill's hiring. I supplemented them with public records and interviews. Many Seaport administrators and employees were reluctant to help; few said much that could detract from its image, fundraising, or prospects. Former staff, trustees, and friends, however, were most helpful.

Even within the nation's maritime-museum community, there has been a reluctance to talk about South Street. As one curator told me, "It's not a pretty story." Within the Council of American Maritime Museums, there was, said one director, "an unwillingness to publicly criticize a friend; . . . an interest in showing a unified, non-controversial public face; and concern about a stinging public response." What is interesting is that a vast majority of Americans regard museums as "a more trustworthy source of objective formulation than books or television," but museum managers are hesitant to allow an independent researcher to know what goes on in the boardroom, in the craft shop, or on the poop deck.[2]

A few words are also in order about this book's construction. Those who have written about ships have customarily been past or present sailors whose attitudes were shaped by personal experience and tradition. Hence, those men (and it has been a masculine pursuit) have used the feminine pronoun for ships. I have, however, followed the course of *Lloyd's List* in using neutral pronouns, except in quoted matter, for those vessels. Also, the article *the* has been deleted from ship names, as in *Wavertree*, except again in quoted matter. And lastly, as is the case in writing about organizations, abbreviations have been often substituted for long titles. A short list follows this section.

Besides the many comments made at various presentations of this research, I have been helped (often considerably) by many Seaporters, museum friends, interested parties, consultants, and historians and preservationists (public and academic). Their kind assistance made this book possible. Besides those who requested anonymity, they are Peter A. Aron, Joseph Baiamonte, Kent Barwick, Debbie Swift Batty, Bronson Binger, Jonathan Boulware, Richard Brandt, David Brink, Peter H. Brink, Norman Brouwer, Briton C. Busch, Kathleen Condon, Michael Creamer, Wayne De La Roche, Paul DeOrsay, Charles Deroko, Nicole Dooskin, Richard Dorfman, John Doswell, Joe Doyle, Gary Fagin, Jarrett L. Feldman,

Robert Ferraro, Richard Fewtrell, Susan Fowler, William M. Fowler Jr., Alan D. Frazer, Ileen Gallagher, Thomas Gochberg, Lee Gruzen, Ingo Heidbrink, Paul Heller, John B. Hightower, Sharon A. Holt, Ada Louise Huxtable, Steve Hyman, Jakob Isbrandtsen, Kenneth T. Jackson, Steven H. Jaffe, Shari Galligan Johnson, Paul F. Johnston, Susan Henshaw Jones, Stephen Kloepfer, Amy Krakow, Michael Kramer, Robert LaValva, Michael E. Levine, Philip Levy, Christine Lilyquist, Phillip Lopate, Marie Lore, Christopher J. Lowery, Philip Marshall, George Matteson, Nora McAuley-Gitin, Barbara Mensch, William J. Murtagh, Michael Naab, Peter Neill, Dennis A. O'Toole, Naima Rauam, Paul Ridgway, Warren Riess, Walter P. Rybka, Charles L. Sachs, Allon Schoener, Pete Seeger, Whitney North Seymour Jr., Yvonne Simons, Howard Slotnick, J. Kellum Smith, Rebecca Smith, Michael Sorkin, Peter and Norma Stanford, Jennifer Stanley, Erin Urban, Thomas Walker, Terry Walton, Thomas E. Wilcox, Jeanne Willoz-Egnor, Philip Yenawine, Sally Yerkovich, and John Young.

In addition, photographs and/or their publication rights have been graciously provided by many individuals and institutions, including Peter Aron, Norman Brouwer, Nelson Michael Chin, Morton Dagawitz, Anthony Dean, Charles Deroko, Robert Ferraro, Joel Greenberg, Skeeter Harris, Shari Galligan Johnson, the Library of Congress, Brian Lindgren, Andrew Moore, Jeff Perkell, the South Street Seaport Museum, Peter Stanford, Anthony Venti, Thomas Walker, Terry Walton, and John Young. Naima Rauam kindly permitted the use of one of her paintings as well. In acquiring archival materials, my appreciation also goes out to Norman Brouwer and Carol Clarke of the South Street Seaport Museum, David Hull and Ted Miles of the San Francisco Maritime National Historical Park, Nancy Adgent of the Rockefeller Archive Center, and SUNY Plattsburgh's interlibrary-loan staff. At NYU Press, I have been especially helped by my editor, Steve Maikowski, whose interest in the Seaport facilitated this project, and by my supportive copyeditor, Andrew Katz. Over the years, I have been financially assisted by SUNY Plattsburgh, the NYS UUP/PDIA Program, and the Nina Winkel Fund. My special thanks go out to my family—spouse Mary Ann (who read and improved the text) and sons Brian and Charlie—for reminding me that this book is just one small sail in life's full-rigged ship.

ABBREVIATIONS

AAM	American Association of Museums (later, the American Alliance of Museums)
ASTA	American Sail Training Association
BBB	Beyer Binder Belle
CAMM	Council of American Maritime Museums
CB1	Community Board 1, New York City
DCA	Department of Cultural Affairs, New York City
D-LMA	Downtown-Lower Manhattan Association (later, Downtown Alliance)
EDC	Economic Development Corporation, New York City (preceded by PDC)
FFM	Fulton Fish Market
HABS	Historic American Buildings Survey, Library of Congress
HHC	Howard Hughes Corporation
JACF	J. Aron Charitable Foundation, New York
LMDC	Lower Manhattan Development Corporation
LPC	Landmarks Preservation Commission, New York City
MAS	Municipal Art Society of New York
MCNY	Museum of the City of New York
MoMA	Museum of Modern Art
NEH	National Endowment for the Humanities
NMHS	National Maritime Historical Society
NPS	National Park Service
NTHP	National Trust for Historic Preservation
NYFD	New York Fire Department
N-YHS	New-York Historical Society
NYPL	New York Public Library
NYSCA	New York State Council on the Arts
NYSE	New York Stock Exchange
NYSMM	New York State Maritime Museum

NYYC	New York Yacht Club
PDC	Public Development Corporation, New York City (later EDC)
PJV	Peking Joint Venture
SCC	Seaport Community Coalition
SFMM	San Francisco Maritime Museum
SFMNHP	San Francisco Maritime National Historical Park
SSSC	South Street Seaport Corporation
SSSM	South Street Seaport Museum
UDAG	Urban Development Action Grant
UDC	Urban Development Corporation, New York State
ULURP	Uniform Land Use Review Procedure
USCG	United States Coast Guard
VAF	Vincent Astor Foundation
VISOSSSM	Volunteers in Support of South Street Seaport Museum
WTC	World Trade Center

Introduction

"Salvation on the East River":
How a Clever Editor Saw Jehovah's Light

In the midst of Lower Manhattan's corporate high-rises, the Brooklyn Bridge, and the archaic Fulton Fish Market, South Street Seaport Museum regularly hosted concerts on Pier 16 to attract New Yorkers to its urban renewal district. One July evening in 1971, a folk singer drew a mixed audience who sat on blankets and newspapers at the East River dock. Mellowing in a warm summer breeze, they listened in the shadow of *Wavertree*, the world's largest iron-hulled square-rigger, while an old-time schooner "swayed in time, like a silent metronome." As the audience joined in a chorus, a *New York Times* editor had an epiphany. He was like many who worried that Gotham was being smothered in the boom of soulless skyscrapers and hemorrhaging with racial, class, and generational battles. Across the river in Brooklyn, he saw a neon sign on the Jehovah's Witnesses building flickering "The Dead shall rise." "As the sky darkened in the east and turned pink in the west," he glimpsed his "Salvation on the East River." "For a fleeting hour," he wrote, "one small segment of this great, troubled city was in harmony with itself, and with nature. It was the kind of experience that can help make New York more human and livable again."[1]

Bringing the city together, the Seaport was offering programs by 1971 that featured the likes of maritime adventurer Alan Villiers, folk singer Pete Seeger, and local colorist Joseph Mitchell. But when the museum was launched in 1966, it faced strong currents. Downtown's square mile, which included Wall Street, City Hall, and the old port and markets, was fast changing before the City Planning Commission issued its *Lower Manhattan Plan* (1966), a futuristic design that erased everything in the seaport. Its driving force, David Rockefeller, was determined to stem a perceived exodus of downtown banking and corporate headquarters that was ironically begun by his father's midtown construction of Rockefeller Center.

To remake downtown, he built its first modern skyscraper. His sixty-story Chase Manhattan Bank (1955–61) was, said critic Ada Louise Huxtable, "a desperately needed act of confidence when Lower Manhattan was at its most economically depressed." The journalist Robert Caro regarded that bank as the world's most powerful financial institution. Rockefeller ambitiously proposed building a $355 million World Trade Center to replace the East River's stinking fish market. Speculators scrambled to raze nearby structures, build high-rises, and win quick profits. But New Jersey's governor forced him to move the World Trade Center a mile westward toward the Hudson River. Shocking New Yorkers at first, the 110-story, twin towers long defined the skyline. They symbolized downtown's rebirth, but little did Rockefeller realize that, like the yin and yang of life, an opposite, but complementary, force was rising at the other end of Fulton Street.[2]

The Seaport was one wave in a new preservation movement that ignited after the failure to stop the demolition of midtown's Pennsylvania Station that began in 1963. As scores of elite architects, distinguished humanists, and everyday New Yorkers protested, they argued that buildings, high style and low, deserved protection for more reasons than being the home of a great American or the site of a famous event. Reasons included not only refined aesthetics and symbolism, as at Penn Station, but buildings' practical function and ordinary history, as in the case of the seaport's Schermerhorn Row. These preservationists, more than their forebears, challenged capitalism's precept that "history meant old, old meant decrepit, and decrepit meant you should tear it down." They built a popular-based movement, but their cries were drowned out by bulldozers. Calling Penn Station's demolition a "monumental act of vandalism," the *Times* warned, "We will probably be judged not by the monuments we build but by those we have destroyed." In 1965, city leaders tried to empower the Landmarks Preservation Commission, whose power was limited in stopping the frenzy of demolitions for high-rise construction.[3]

Penn Station's demolition took three years, but as its façade was stripped of sculpture in 1966, an ad hoc committee was forming downtown to save Schermerhorn Row, a Fulton Street block of countinghouses built in 1811–12. Art historian James Van Derpool once called it "the finest example of Federal commercial architecture surviving in America," but its dignity was buried in decrepitude. Committee head Peter M. Stanford recalled that Penn Station's demise was "a warning" that New York's "simple, vernacular buildings were in imminent peril of being wiped off the map." Meanwhile, state senator Whitney North Seymour Jr., past president of the Municipal Art Society of New York (MAS) and acting independently of Stanford, persuaded Albany to establish the New York State Maritime Museum (NYSMM) at the Row. After downtown's real estate and banking interests denounced the bill, however, it was not funded.[4]

Ushering in a new phase of the nation's preservation movement, whereby citizen-activists confronted vested interests over vernacular buildings, Stanford and his wife, Norma, organized the Friends of South Street Maritime Museum to jump-start Seymour's project. But they envisioned much more than his State Maritime Museum at the Row. Besides preserving blocks of the old seaport, they most wanted a fleet of historic ships. Inspired by the San Francisco Maritime Museum, the Stanfords were impressed by its director, Karl Kortum, the major American advocate of a small worldwide group determined to save the last commercial sailing ships. Like the 1960s movements, the Friends included a diverse sort: activists, college students, retirees, small businesses, artists, and lovers of the port. The latter included the novelist Joseph Mitchell and his friend Joe Cantalupo, whom a later museum president called the local "Mafia Capo." Stanford also learned from his own election campaign against Tammany Hall's machine in 1963 that a united front could challenge Goliath. Dynamic and visionary, he was backed by the Friends, was encouraged by Huxtable's newspaper columns, and rode a wave of anger against urban renewal.[5]

Creating a "Street of Ships" on the East River, the Friends wanted to evoke the 1850s port that had handled more passengers and cargo than all other US ports combined. They appealed to a swath of New Yorkers who remembered, as late as the 1950s, its day-and-night activity and regretted its being surpassed by transatlantic jets, skyscrapers, and service-sector jobs. After the Friends incorporated as the South Street Seaport Museum in 1967, two organizations—the State Museum and the Seaport Museum —existed side by side, as was the case in San Francisco. While NYSMM only existed on paper, the Seaport became a vibrant movement. Yet this was Gotham, which, according to a high-level federal planner, was "the only major city in the country planned exclusively for profit and built to that pattern by its businessmen with the city easing the way." Thinking instead that the city's principal purpose was to improve its citizens' lives, the Seaport ameliorated that profit motive. After a bumpy start, the Friends succeeded in 1968. They lined up impressive support, and City Hall reversed itself by designating the Row a landmark to stave off its demolition. But its ownership was left hanging.[6]

By then, the Downtown-Lower Manhattan Association (D-LMA), a corporate alliance led by Rockefeller, also endorsed the Friends. Both City Hall and the D-LMA adopted the Seaport as their proxy, thinking it would draw tourists and future residents to downtown. As the city implemented the *Lower Manhattan Plan*, it privatized a public function by naming the Seaport Museum as the official urban renewal sponsor for a twelve-block, thirty-eight-acre district. More significant than either a 1950s federal grant awarded to Providence, Rhode Island, for preserving some of its old buildings, or federal moneys in the 1960s to selectively restore Strawbery Banke in Portsmouth, New Hampshire, the Seaport was the nation's first museum charged with developing an urban renewal district. That arrangement was, said Mayor John V. Lindsay (1966–73), "the most complex ever entered upon to establish a cultural institution in this city." But in a novel move, City Hall designated the Seaport an *un*assisted sponsor: no public funds would be used to acquire its property. Being cast as an unassisted sponsor meant, moreover, that conservatives could champion this neo-liberal model. The MAS nonetheless said that the Seaport "was forging new ground in halting the City's long-standing policy of self-evisceration." Achievements such as this led an authoritative architectural study to conclude, "The rapid development of the historic preservation movement into a major political as well as cultural force in New York was one of the principal 'success stories' in the city's evolution from the mid-1960s on." Money, however, would always be the issue: how could the Seaport raise funds to purchase those valuable lands and acquire a flotilla of historic ships, which would soon number eleven and was billed as "the largest historic fleet ever assembled by any museum anywhere at any time."[7]

From the start, Stanford envisioned the Seaport as a mix of old and new, where commerce and history would meld and the former would underwrite the latter. Spurning traditional art museums, where rarefied collections were idolized, as well as open-air museums such as Colonial Williamsburg with its reconstructed district, he told the *Times*, "We imagined it as the sort of place where someone would say, 'Let's go down for dinner,' not 'Dammit, it's Sunday, let's take the children to the museum for

some culture.'" He wanted commerce to be lively, profitable, and therapeutic. A romantic, he questioned much of Progress—its mindless race
forward, its destructiveness overseas and at home, and its severance from
nature and the sea—but he held to its central tenet that the future could
be better. For too many people, Gotham had become "an alien and difficult
place" with its tall buildings, giant corporations, and indifferent people. As
Stanford's friend Kent Barwick said, the museum fostered the idea that we
"could recapture ourselves as people and a city."[8]

Stanford called himself "a conservative, rational, and outraged American." Building bridges between classes and generations, many of which
had been burned not only by intransigent elders but by baby boomers
challenging the prevailing injustices, his museum would pioneer successful community programs. He reflected the 1960s culture wars. A disillusioned advertising executive, he said that his Seaport would *not* be like
the traditional stone-columned institution with its "pseudo-experts, flagwavers, Bible thumpers, and . . . bureaucrats" who bred "alienation and
boredom and cruelty." Instead, its programs in music, the arts, history, and
the environment would be salted throughout the district, and his museum
would appeal to those who cared about "life and children and adventure."
Peter Neill, a later Seaport president, acknowledged that museum founders wanted "to counter the debilitating aspects of city life . . . [and] to
advance the cause of civilization by serving the needs of the larger society
through good works." With social reform as the Seaport's agenda, it could
become, as the *Times* editorialized in 1971, "Salvation on the East River."
Aided by Jakob Isbrandtsen, a maverick shipping tycoon who acquired
Wavertree and property for the Seaport, Stanford's remedy for the ever-
visible dilemma was, therefore, a strange brew: aspects of social liberalism and cultural conservatism, mixed with grassroots activism, based on
neoliberal economics, and imbued with a riveting sense of a lost but more
meaningful past. All the while, they favored small-scale development.[9]

Had the story developed along those lines, the Seaport would be
remembered today as the first museum ever charged with the task of redeveloping an urban renewal district, a momentous task that would not only
dramatically shape the organization but save a neighborhood from being
bulldozed for high-rises. It would be also cited as acquiring the largest fleet
of historic ships in the nation, an action that entailed enormous responsibilities. The Seaport would be credited as well with becoming Gotham's

largest historical society, with 25,000 members, and creating one of the city's three major history museums. Moreover, it would be highlighted by policy analysts as perhaps the most significant example of the difficulties museums have in forming partnerships with both city agencies and private corporations. But 9/11 was the turning point. Though the Seaport had faced financial challenges since its founding, the 2001 terrorist attacks exposed its deeply rooted weaknesses, which led to fiscal insolvency, dysfunctional management, and ultimately deathbed negotiations before City Hall arranged a temporary takeover by the Museum of the City of New York in late 2011. Hopes for the Seaport under MCNY management initially ran high. But after Superstorm Sandy devastated the area in late October 2012 and city authorities only seemed willing to accommodate the district's commercial mall, the MCNY pulled out in the following July. Once designated "America's National Maritime Museum," the Seaport's future seemed bleak in the face of politically powerful developers interested only in greater profits.

Most New Yorkers know little of the Seaport's history. Writers have overlooked the Friends and their museum. Some have also misrepresented the neighborhood's development. Since the Seaport's founding, its preservationists have faced powerful developers who wanted to grab these valuable, waterfront blocks. The museum's struggles to preserve the port and its history represented, according to the National Trust, "one of the most complex, controversial and protracted efforts in the history of American preservation."[10] While the district became the city's number-one tourist attraction in the late 1980s, the home of rising professionals in the 1990s, and now the staging ground for the spectacular East River Waterfront Esplanade, it was all to the Seaport's credit and, ironically, its undoing. Focusing on how it could engineer so much change but falter, *Preserving South Street Seaport* is as much about Gotham from the 1960s to today as it is about the Seaport Museum.

1

"Eloquent Reminders of Sailing and Shipbuilding"

How the Seaport and World Trade Center (Re)made Fulton Street

In 1966, as Penn Station's debris was hauled to a landfill, historic preservation seemed to be going against the grain of Gotham's advance. As
the city expanded, it rebuilt itself every generation. Perhaps that "creative
destruction" could be attributed to capitalism, as Karl Marx and Joseph
Schumpeter claimed. *Harper's Magazine* lamented in 1856, "New York
[Manhattan] is notoriously the largest and least loved of any of our great
cities. . . . Why should it be loved as a city? It is never the same city for
a dozen years altogether. A man born in New York forty years ago finds
nothing, absolutely nothing, of the New York he knew." But that growth
had been the city's success. By 1800, New York's population and shipping
tonnage were America's largest; its port grew with the Fulton Fish Market (1817) and the reclamation of what was to become Water, Front, and
South Streets. Its launch of the packet trade to England (1819), the completion of the Erie Canal (1825), and the expansion of the city's financial,
industrial, and commercial sectors boomed it further. The port's share of
US trade leaped from 5.7 percent in 1790 to 57 percent in 1870. However,
South Street's East River traffic declined after 1865 because larger ships
of steam and steel, mostly foreign owned, required the Hudson River's
deeper waters and newer terminals. Overall, New York surpassed London
as the world's greatest port by 1914. That success brought so much conges-
tion to the narrow and ancient streets that Lower Manhattan became "an
intolerable place to do business."[1]

The construction of shoreline elevated highways, including the East
River Drive (later, FDR Drive) was supposed to solve the problem. Begun
in 1934 by Robert Moses using Works Progress Administration crews, the
roadway was later extended by using ship ballast from England's bombed-
out buildings. The last section of FDR Drive, which was completed in 1954,
descended to street level at Old Slip, allowing the fish market to operate

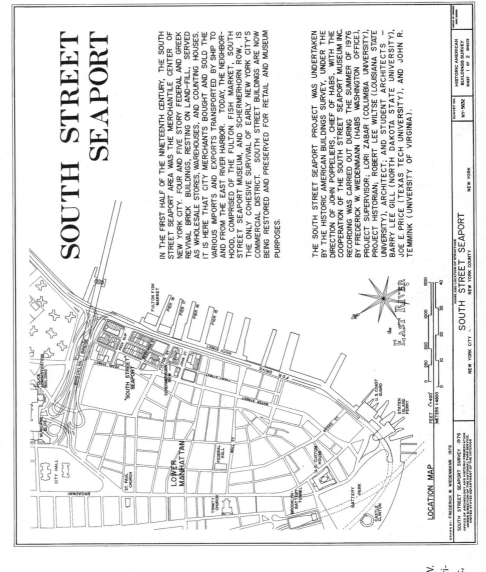

SOUTH STREET SEAPORT

IN THE FIRST HALF OF THE NINETEENTH CENTURY, THE SOUTH STREET SEAPORT AREA WAS THE MERCANTILE CENTER OF NEW YORK CITY. FOUR AND FIVE STORY FEDERAL AND GREEK REVIVAL BRICK BUILDINGS, RESTING ON LAND-FILL, SERVED AS WHOLESALE STORES, WAREHOUSES, AND COUNTING HOUSES. IT IS HERE THAT CITY MERCHANTS BOUGHT AND SOLD THE VARIOUS IMPORTS AND EXPORTS TRANSPORTED BY SHIP TO AND FROM THE EAST RIVER HARBOR. TODAY, THE NEIGHBORHOOD, COMPRISED OF THE FULTON FISH MARKET, SOUTH STREET SEAPORT MUSEUM, AND SCHERMERHORN ROW, IS THE ONLY COHESIVE SURVIVAL OF EARLY NEW YORK CITY'S COMMERCIAL DISTRICT. SOUTH STREET BUILDINGS ARE NOW BEING RESTORED AND PRESERVED FOR RETAIL AND MUSEUM PURPOSES.

THE SOUTH STREET SEAPORT PROJECT WAS UNDERTAKEN BY THE HISTORIC AMERICAN BUILDINGS SURVEY, UNDER THE DIRECTION OF JOHN POPPELIERS, CHIEF OF HABS. WITH THE COOPERATION OF THE SOUTH STREET SEAPORT MUSEUM INC. RECORDING WAS CARRIED OUT DURING THE SUMMER OF 1976 BY FREDERICK W. WIEDENMANN (HABS WASHINGTON OFFICE), PROJECT SUPERVISOR; LORI ZABAR (COLUMBIA UNIVERSITY), PROJECT HISTORIAN; ROBERT LEE WILTSE (LOUISIANA STATE UNIVERSITY), ARCHITECT; AND STUDENT ARCHITECTS — BARRY LEE GILL (NORTH DAKOTA STATE UNIVERSITY), JOE E. PRICE (TEXAS TECH UNIVERSITY), AND JOHN R. TEMMINK (UNIVERSITY OF VIRGINIA).

the EAST RIVER

LOCATION MAP

FEET 1"=400'
METERS 1=4800

DRAWN BY: FREDERICK W. WIEDENMANN 1976

SOUTH STREET SEAPORT SURVEY 1976
OFFICE OF ARCHEOLOGY AND HISTORIC PRESERVATION
UNDER DIRECTION OF THE NATIONAL PARK SERVICE,
UNITED STATES DEPARTMENT OF THE INTERIOR

NAME AND LOCATION OF STRUCTURE

SOUTH STREET SEAPORT
NEW YORK CITY   NEW YORK COUNTY

SURVEY NO.
NY-5632

HISTORIC AMERICAN
BUILDINGS SURVEY
SHEET 1 OF 2 SHEETS

NEW YORK

Fig. 1.1. Lower Manhattan map, 1976. (HABS NY-5632; drawing, Frederick W. Wiedenmann; American Memory Project, Library of Congress)

with fewer obstructions. The nearby piers still handled bulk shipments, while the Port of New York "handled nearly as much cargo as all the other Atlantic and Gulf Coast ports combined." That activity supported almost 25 percent of New York's economy in 1967. But as skyscrapers walled off Manhattan, as travelers used international airports, and as container ships docked at out-of-sight terminals, New Yorkers forgot that their city was one of the world's great ports.[2]

The growth of Gotham itself threatened the port's viability. As early as 1929, the tristate Regional Plan Association proposed moving maritime operations to New Jersey. A dearth of investment, too little space in Manhattan, and a clash between intransigent shipping executives and corrupt longshoremen posed severe problems, ones that were magnified by Hollywood. *On the Waterfront* (1954), which won eight Oscars, portrayed the port as dangerous and sinister. Yet that same year, *National Geographic* celebrated the world's busiest harbor with its one thousand vessels departing each month. More significant for the city's four hundred finger piers was the waning of break-bulk cargos and waxing of containerization, a trend that was pushed by the Port Authority of New York and New Jersey. After the City of New York refused to relinquish control over its finger piers, the Port Authority built the world's first container port at Elizabeth, New Jersey. While 18 percent of the port's general cargo was containerized in 1968, it leaped to 70 percent by 1977, with three-quarters of the containers offloaded in New Jersey. Transatlantic travel also changed. Beginning in 1958, most travelers chose air over sea, and the wharves slowly became ruinous.[3]

Remnants of Manhattan's nautical history were still evident downtown. The Cunard Building (1921) included superb oceanic murals, and the Beaux-Arts Custom House (1907) featured twelve statues representing history's great seafaring powers. A proposal to convert the Custom House into a marine museum aired in 1957. The Seamen's Church Institute, which itinerant Jack Tars called "the doghouse," hosted a museum of ship models and paintings, but its curator admitted to a chagrined Karl Kortum that he "personally detest[ed] all sailing ships other than yachts" and thought that a floating ship museum such as Kortum's *Balclutha* "couldn't be made a go" in Gotham. He warned that "very few of the visiting public are 'ship minded.'" The institute eventually lost interest and sold much of its collection in 1968. Perhaps the most dazzling space was India House (1853),

Fig. 1.2. Carter Fish Company, 4 a.m., Fulton Fish Market, 1993; watercolor painting by Naima Rauam.

a private club founded in 1914 by Wall Street mogul James A. Farrell Sr., president of US Steel Corporation. He developed what James Morris called a "shrine of nautophilia, as polished and spanking as a ship itself."[4]

The most authentic maritime operation was the world's largest open-air fish market half a mile away. In addition to first-floor shops in Schermerhorn Row and on nearby streets, the Fulton Fish Market (FFM) district centered around South Street's Tin Building (1907) and New Market Building (1939). The FFM attracted uptown curiosity seekers who, afflicted with the bourgeois blues, had come, since the 1880s, to observe the "incautious, unguarded, unfettered life of the working classes." Their "brawling, foul-mouthed, hard-working, fish-slinging, fun-loving" ways, said Peter Stanford, "kept it alive." Born on South Street, New York Governor Alfred E. Smith worked there as a basketboy. Later, the governor and presidential candidate paid tribute and boasted of his FFM degree. Gradually its iconic Gloucester fishing schooners were being displaced by newer methods of transportation, distribution, and sale. By 1958, only 6–7 percent of the catch arrived by sea. As Stanford recalled, four or five ships still tied up there in the early 1960s, but they were not "the graceful, elliptical-sterned schooners" of his childhood. What remained of the FFM was its archaic culture, including vendors whose discarded scraps the poor retrieved for fish soup.[5]

"Cities Need Old Buildings So Badly":
The Clash between Robert Moses and Jane Jacobs

Meanwhile, three giants by the names of Moses, Jacobs, and Rockefeller were shaking Manhattan to its bedrock. Over the previous decades, Robert Moses left a massive footprint in public works, but there was, noted Ada Louise Huxtable, "the 'good' Moses versus the 'bad' Moses." The latter ravaged the old port. To funnel traffic into Wall Street, he built the Brooklyn Battery Tunnel (1950), which undercut the city's pedestrian ferries. Clearing out Sailortown, which ran inland from the East River's shipyards, he also built the Alfred E. Smith Houses (1953), a dozen high-rises wedged between Chinatown and the FFM. They became what the museum called a "massive belt of waterfront public housing." He also hawked construction of a river-to-river Lower Manhattan Expressway, which the city prematurely placed on its map in 1960. Then came Jane Jacobs. With a blend of humanism, urbanism, and libertarianism, she, more than anyone else, made Americans think differently about cities. The duel between Jacobs and Moses defined Gotham's development. Since Moses's proposed ten-lane, elevated expressway would destroy neighborhoods from Chinatown to SoHo, including Jacobs's West Village, she thundered, it would "LosAngelize New York!" Her masterpiece, *The Death and Life of Great American Cities* (1961), became, said the *Atlantic*, "the most influential American book ever written about cities." She even suggested retaining "plain, ordinary, low-value old buildings." Yet urbanists such as Lewis Mumford scoffed at her notion that "cities need old buildings" for their vigorous growth.[6]

David Rockefeller hoped to prove Jacobs wrong. While his family was becoming "the leading promoters of urban renewal in America," and even maneuvered Moses out of office in 1968, his Downtown-Lower Manhattan Association (D-LMA, 1958) issued plans to remake the area south of the Brooklyn Bridge. At the time, Lower Manhattan had a working population of four hundred thousand but only four thousand residents. With such words as "erosion, decay and exodus," the D-LMA called it a wasteland.

Fig. 1.3. Proposed World Trade Center on the East River (*center*), with World Trade Mart (*far right*) and hotel (*left*), D-LMA, January 1960. (Courtesy of Rockefeller Archive Center)

It proposed leveling the land between Old Slip and the bridge; eliminating cramped and crooked lanes; widening Fulton, Water, and South Streets; building a loop to connect to the proposed expressway; moving the FFM to the Bronx; and constructing residential high-rises for Wall Street employees. Welcoming the project, a *Times* editorial predicted "a great future" for downtown. Yet *Times* columnist Meyer Berger reminded readers that "almost all of the properties . . . were handsome dwellings a little over 100 years ago." All told, those 564 acres downtown included 2,776 buildings, of which 52 percent were at least a century old, while 17 percent had been built between 1858 and 1883. With the possible exception of Federal Hall, Fraunces Tavern, and City Hall, old Lower Manhattan was doomed.[7]

In 1960, City Hall and the D-LMA amplified a proposal for a tract from Old Slip to Fulton Street (and South Street inward to Pearl and Water Streets) to include not only a seventy-story hotel, an exhibition hall, and a new stock exchange but a five-million-square-foot World Trade Center for a workforce of up to forty thousand. Paired with a proposed World Trade Mart on the FFM site, the WTC would be 20 percent larger than Chicago's Merchandise Mart, the world's biggest building. The D-LMA approached the Port Authority, which, as a quasi-independent agency, could bypass local regulations. The city pushed through zoning changes in 1961 to pave the way for high-rise construction. Skyscrapers would be set "back in plazas, inside property lines, and at a greater average height and bulk," thus altering streetscapes that had defined cities for over a millennium.[8]

Though historian Samuel Zipp has suggested that urban renewal "was undone by the experiences and critiques of those living in the places it left in its wake," the question was, who even lived there? Much of it was, alleged the *Times*, "a ghost town" with few residents. You "could count the population on your hand," said planner Richard Weinstein. Yet some of the invisible inhabitants were squatters or poor folk; others were bohemians and artists chased out of Greenwich Village by high rents. Artists Jasper Johns, Robert Rauschenberg, and Mark di Suvero, for example, lived there but laid low because of building-code violations or their unconventional lifestyle. Johns mined the garbage of its "narrow and filthy streets" for his mixed media. The "decrepit structures" were "good for nothing at all," said the *Times*, as their $20-per-foot tax valuations paled compared to those at "$700 a foot in skyscraper country." If the plan was approved, the area would become "a city of vistas, of promenades, and greenery along the waterfront."[9]

Opposition soon arose. Businessman Edmund (Ted) A. Stanley Jr. was president of Bowne & Company Stationers (1775), a family-owned firm that employed 150 in a soon-to-be-demolished, Front Street building. When he started working downtown in 1949, his "father set his watch at noon by the ball dropping on the Titanic Memorial atop the Seamen's Church Institute." Photographing buildings before they fell to the wreckers, he led a businessmen's group opposing the D-LMA. Many in the arts and business communities criticized the D-LMA plan to demolish Wall Street's impressive New York Stock Exchange (1903). Jacobs called the entire plan "an exercise in cures irrelevant to the disease." If Rockefeller wanted to correct downtown's imbalance between peak and off-hours populations, she suggested that the only reasonable solution would be to draw outsiders to the area. In late 1961, the governor of New Jersey forced a change of venue. Because the Port Authority required his assent, the proposed WTC was moved one mile west to a site whose Hudson Tubes served New Jersey. The three hundred businesses along the West Side's Radio Row were no match, moreover, for the Rockefeller juggernaut.[10]

Thinking that a maritime museum could draw outsiders, the D-LMA's executive director, L. Porter Moore, approached Moses in the late 1950s about converting the ferry terminal building at the foot of South Street to a museum. Moore wanted to move the galleries of the Marine Room at the old-fashioned Museum of the City of New York, at Fifth Avenue and 103rd Street, and create an exhibit using its paintings, models, and evocative diorama of the mid-nineteenth-century "street of ships" along South Street. Moses warned that private monies would be required because the city's budget was strained. More ambitiously, Jacobs proposed a "great marine museum" like Kortum's in San Francisco, with "the best collection [of ships] to be seen and boarded everywhere."[11]

Of all critics, Ada Louise Huxtable best articulated the changing scope of preservation. She had worked as a freelancer critiquing preservation, architecture, art, and technology, but Penn Station's demise was a turning point for her, the movement, and for the *New York Times*, which hired her as its first full-time architecture critic. "It's time we stopped talking about our affluent society," she wrote in an editorial denouncing Penn Station's destruction. "It is a poor society indeed that . . . has no money for anything except expressways to rush people out of our dull and deteriorating cities." Though Mumford had written brilliant essays for the *New Yorker*, Huxtable turned "consistently bold and forthright" criticism into a public art that crossed disciplines and quickly gained fame. She angered many people but noted that there were "no constraints, ever, on anything" she wrote, "inside or outside of the *Times*."[12]

With Huxtable's interests in preserving vernacular buildings, conserving streetscapes, and emphasizing their authenticity and humanity, she shifted the movement. As with New York's Municipal Art Society (1893) and the American Scenic and Historic Preservation Society (1895), preservationists had mostly supported the connoisseur and patriotic traditions by restoring architectural masterpieces or the homes of patriotic leaders. New Englanders had preserved everyday structures, but they privileged certain traditions and, except in rare cases such as Boston's Beacon Hill, did not save their streetscapes. Challenging the National Trust for Historic

Fig. 1.4. Front Street, looking southwest at Blocks 96W (*right*), 74W (*center*), and 74E (*left*), with Chase Manhattan Bank towering over the ten-story Green Coffee Exchange, 1968. (Photo, John Young and Urban Deadline)

Preservation (1949) and Colonial Williamsburg (1926), Huxtable also embraced the then-derided architectural eclecticism and technology of the nineteenth century. Mainstream architects and planners resisted her thinking, as they were "often openly hostile to historic buildings and districts." As a result, John Young, a student in Columbia University's graduate preservation program in 1968, realized that his quest for authentic streetscapes was "a marginal even subversive activity."[13]

Remarkably, Huxtable cut her preservationist teeth in Lower Manhattan, where planners, bureaucrats, and developers were obliterating the landscape from the Brooklyn Bridge to the Battery. After reading the D-LMA's plans in 1960, she mocked the planners' "occupational insanity" and their "uncontrollable urge for . . . the crashing roar of bulldozers clearing away the past." That led to her 1961 feature story, "To Keep the Best of New York," in the *Times*'s Sunday magazine. Walking the seaport, one of the city's few areas with an intact early nineteenth-century flavor, she saw "eloquent reminders of sailing and shipbuilding, of schooners and spices, of a fascinating, vital chapter of New York's early commercial life." Alluding to John F. Kennedy's endorsement of preservation, she called for judiciously mixing the old and new.[14]

After chiding the modernism-addicted American Institute of Architects that "the art of architecture has died," Huxtable again toured what was called the Brooklyn Bridge urban renewal districts. To the north of Pearl Street, the " 'total clearance' philosophy" had already erased blocks. To the south, the rows of four- and five-story buildings, some with cast-iron fronts, were next. Walking the FFM's Peck Slip with its former countinghouses, warehouses, and provision stores, she found that her personal favorite had been leveled. Then she discovered an "amazingly homogeneous" block at Fulton and South Streets—Schermerhorn Row. In 1964, she urged readers of her *Classic New York* to see the neighborhood without delay and warned that their visit would be "tinged with fear and concern" since these buildings were "living on borrowed time." Her timely book, said essayist Russell Lynes, was "required reading for the city fathers."[15]

"Plea to Curb the Bulldozer": Seymour's Campaign and Legislation

Whitney North ("Mike") Seymour Jr. was also familiar with the fish market. Raised in a Greenwich Village row house, he had taken the two-mile trek to South Street with his father, a distinguished lawyer who, as MAS president, had instigated a "Landmarks of New York" listing program in 1957. That budding interest intersected Albany's passage of the Bard Act (1956), which empowered cities to protect aesthetically and historically important landmarks. However, 10 percent of MAS's "highly selective list" was gone by 1958. Reflecting the connoisseur tradition, the MAS, moreover, spurned a request in 1957 to preserve the Peck Slip block so loved by Huxtable; it ruled that the "outworn structures" lacked "historic or architectural importance."[16]

After graduating from Yale Law School in 1950, Mike Seymour worked as an assistant US attorney and Wall Street lawyer. There he strolled the old port, often eating lunch at Sloppy Louie's in Schermerhorn Row. Though a waiter joked that "it was really a dump," Mike recalled it as "a lovely experience." He was dismayed that buildings were being razed to create parking lots. Moving beyond his interest in creating pocket parks, and shortly before Penn Station's demise in 1963, he issued a "Plea to Curb the Bulldozer" in the *Times* magazine. Though limited by a connoisseur's belief that a building "must have a potential for giving pleasure and instruction" to warrant action, he listed ten Manhattan sites for consideration, beginning with Schermerhorn Row, which, he said, could house a maritime museum. Becoming MAS president in 1965, he called it the "one remaining block in this area that is still a legitimate landmark." While the Real Estate Board of New York resisted, City Hall granted more power to its newly established Landmarks Preservation Commission (LPC) in April 1965. But because of what Huxtable called "one of the nastiest little loopholes ever devised," demolitions continued. Moreover, the designated watchdogs, LPC chairman Geoffrey Platt and later chairman Harmon Goldstone, were "terrified that if they made the wrong move the new landmarks law could be easily invalidated by the courts before a believable body of action and precedent had been established." The LPC held hearings on the Row but, fearing Rockefeller's anger, took no action.[17]

Seymour took to politics, and in what was "almost a fluke," he was elected in 1965 as a Republican to the state senate, where he worked on preservation issues. At the same time, US mayors were issuing a major report on preservation, but it addressed few of Huxtable's concerns regarding economic viability, historical authenticity, and cultural vitality. It called for a greater federal role, which led to the watershed Historic Preservation Act of 1966 and the establishment of the National Register of Historic Places. "One of my very first projects" was South Street, Seymour said; on February 22, 1966, he introduced a bill to establish a state maritime museum at the Row. He asked for help from John Hightower, director of the New York State Council on the Arts (NYSCA), which joined with the MAS to fund a feasibility study.[18]

Once Seymour's bill "unanimously passed the senate without debate," he logrolled votes with the Assembly leader from Brooklyn, and the approved legislation went to Governor Nelson Rockefeller for his signature. Suddenly, Seymour remembered, it "met with strong opposition from a real-estate group headed by powerful banking interests led by the governor's own brother," David, whose D-LMA eyed the land for a "huge insurance complex." The Museum of the City of New York also urged the governor to veto the bill. Seymour brashly sent Huxtable a copy of the D-LMA letter. "The violence of the attack," she wrote in the *Times*, surprised all. But she was most flabbergasted by Rockefeller's idea of creating, in the family tradition of Colonial Williamsburg, an outdoor museum of old buildings around Fraunces Tavern, which even the MAS favored over the Row.[19] Coincidentally, both David Rockefeller and Seymour faced a public relations problem. For the banker, who received the courts' go-ahead in March 1966 for the WTC construction on the Hudson, the Row, although a minor matter, could exacerbate negotiations for his larger East River development. Seymour, for his part, did not want to alienate those interests that controlled downtown and perhaps his seat. The original concept was premised on fifty-fifty funding between government and private monies, but Seymour was forced to defer indefinitely any state funding to buy the block and set up the New York State Maritime Museum. After his bill was amended, the governor signed it on August 2, 1966.[20]

Seymour knew that the D-LMA had the support of LPC chairman Platt and his colleague Goldstone, who also sat on the Planning Commission. The sharpest opponent of the Fraunces Tavern project was Huxtable. As she recalled, the D-LMA "was totally archaic in its viewpoint and real-estate oriented in its programs." Her criticisms later framed the debate on the Seaport. She was continuing the century-long battle against architect Viollet le Duc's practice of reconstruction that was launched by England's John Ruskin and William Morris, which Stanford portrayed as a contest between "the [Colonial] Williamsburg school and the Huxtable school" of preservation.[21]

Huxtable opposed the Rockefeller project because, for one, Fraunces Tavern had been reinvented in 1907. Someone who saw it in 1965, she explained, "is looking at a 20th-century fabrication on a few 18th-century remains. 'It's fun to be fooled' is no motto for preservation." Second, she opposed the proposed park because it would include not only old houses to be forced off their original sites but a multimillion-dollar replica of New Amsterdam's first government building, the Stadthuys (1642). Reconstructing an edifice, she cried, was "so fallacious, so insidious and so dangerous" as to be utterly reprehensible. Third, she knew that, as Platt said, the downtown community "feels it cannot afford both preservation projects." Huxtable retorted that "on-the-site preservation of existing buildings has the highest priority." As the contest unfolded, her column became the most timely expression of the rapidly evolving notion of historic preservation. As she tore into the D-LMA proposal, she was laying out her own conditions for Stanford's work. In the meantime, he said, she was able "to disarm Rockefeller our most dangerous opponent."[22]

"A Seadog since the Age of Two": Peter Stanford's Lifelong Cause

If Huxtable helped shift attitudes and Seymour authored the legislation, Peter Stanford made the Seaport Museum happen and served as its first president for a decade. His father, Alfred, was a yachtsman who, as commodore of the Cruising Club of America, sailed with the likes of US Ambassador Chester Bowles. For Alfred, sailing was "an intensification of life, a great affirmation of human connection with the stars, the wind, and the wide sea." With the outbreak of World War II, he even volunteered his club for submarine watch, an offer that the inveterate sailor at 1600 Pennsylvania Avenue accepted. After the war, he became vice president for advertising at the *New York Herald Tribune*. Born and raised until age thirteen in Brooklyn Heights, which later became the city's first historic district, Peter was schooled in Greenwich Village. His mother's Connecticut home enabled him to boat on the Saugatuck River and Long Island Sound. In the late 1930s, his father took him to meet Carl Cutler, the founder of what was to become Mystic Seaport. Peter also met the adventurer Alan Villiers, who came to their Brooklyn home in 1935 while *Joseph Conrad*, in which he had circumnavigated the globe, was laid up in Gowanus Creek. Attending an experimental high school at Columbia University, Peter met Joan Kaplan, whose father established a foundation focusing on Gotham's civic betterment. Peter was "a very romantic, ethereal creature with his eyes always on the far horizon," Joan Kaplan recalled, "and he walked around with a copy of *Jane's Fighting Ships* under his arm." Featuring him in 1943, *Time* magazine crowed that he had been "a seadog since the age of two" who knew "naval history backward and forward." Writing more than half a dozen articles for the Naval Academy's *Proceedings*, starting at age fifteen, he was "the youngest contributor in the magazine's history."[23]

Peter walked the fish market with his father, who had authored *Men, Fish & Boats* (1934); they mingled with crews and boarded their vessels. Though too young for the wartime draft, Peter joined the naval reserve through his Bowles connection. Matriculating at Harvard College in 1947, he earned a B.A. in history in 1949 but skipped the ceremony in order to sail a forty-two-foot cutter to England. There he earned a master's degree in English literature in 1951 at King's College. Afterward, he found a niche in advertising, married Eva Franceschi in 1957, and, unlike the one million middle-class residents who fled Gotham from 1950 to 1960, settled in the city. Inspired by John F. Kennedy's liberalism, he marched for civil rights and was arrested in the South. In 1963, at the urging of the Rutgers Democratic Club, he ran in the primary against Tammany Hall in a working-class district of the old seaport. The *Times* noted that he stood out and "could have passed for a professor of English at an Ivy League college." He campaigned in housing projects that resembled a "concentration camp," but his grassroots effort was beaten by the machine.[24]

As a result, Stanford became active in and a trustee of the City Club of New York, a good-government group attracting a civic vanguard. To remedy a list of ills—the middle-class exodus, inferior public school and housing systems, alienation of the citizenry, and "leaders who lack the capacity to understand and master these problems"—he called for establishing more "self-help organizations." He pinned his hopes on John Lindsay in the 1965 mayoral election. Historic preservation was not, however, on his agenda. Even as he explored the FFM on a Sunday walk with his children, he was depressed that "the whole place was run-down." With a divorce, his brother's death, and job dissatisfaction, his own life was also depressing; an old forty-three-foot Alden schooner became his "refuge and a source of reassurance and delight." He emulated his father, who thought that a sailor's "contest against the sea" could help an individual recover the "daring, fortitude, sacrifice, and endurance that have been bred in us."[25]

Peter envisioned his own recovery in October 1965 when he traveled to San Francisco on a business trip. He also fit in a honeymoon, for he had just married Norma Franceschi, the younger sister of his ex-wife, Eva. They walked Fisherman's Wharf and the bustling Ghirardelli Square, the prototype festival marketplace. They were most impressed by Kortum's San Francisco Maritime Museum (SFMM). Before long, Stanford became his loyal student and "worshiped him," said a colleague. Karl

Crouch Kortum was a seminal figure in maritime preservation. Passionate about sailing ships, particularly square-riggers, he opened the SFMM in 1951 and acquired *Balclutha* in 1955. With volunteer labor and business philanthropy, he restored it, outfitting its tweendeck with memorabilia about the ship, port, and trade. Though the SFMM was private, its waterside building, which resembled an ocean liner, was city owned, and Kortum was on the city payroll. Of Kortum's many gifts, his ability to inspire others was strong, and he convinced Sacramento to establish the adjacent California State Maritime Historical Park in 1963 because his SFMM was overstretched.[26]

Stanford was entranced by the park's schooner *Charles A. Thayer* and dreamed "of taking an old sailing ship to sea." Boarding the Cape Horner *Balclutha*, he admitted, "We were swept off our feet." The "brilliant display work . . . made her old frame live for people." He told Kortum, "I had never realized how a museum ship could *live* till I saw her." That "shoved Norma over into active interest in the idea of a New York sea museum." The Stanfords wondered if the idea would work in New York, whose World's Fair in 1964 had introduced Operation Sail to Gotham. Europeans had begun an annual nautical race in 1956, but Op Sail 64 was simply an assembly with tall ships. It was regarded, he said, as "a last gathering of the elephants before they became extinct."[27]

While Seymour was being sworn in as a state senator in January 1966, Norma wrote to Kortum's museum about New York's potential. Though the FFM was odorous and gritty, she called it "the last enjoyable bit of New York waterfront" but said it was slated to be closed and replaced with luxury high-rises. Hoping to establish "an historical marine park," her first concern was the organizing and financing of what they called their East River Seaport. As the bulldozers approached, they knew "exactly which buildings [they] would attempt to save" on Fulton and South Streets. In the Peabody Museum's journal, the *American Neptune*, and England's *Mariner's Mirror*, she announced their plan to form a maritime museum that would acquire, recondition, and display old sailing ships, particularly a square-rigger. Seymour's bill to establish NYSMM, Peter recalled, "caught Norma and me by surprise." On August 10, they met in Seymour's Wall Street office. Seymour spoke of establishing a traditional museum, but he needed help with publicity, promotion, and donors. He did not mention what the Stanfords already knew—that the Rockefellers were opposed.

Protecting his NYSMM, Seymour warned them that if they made "an ill-considered request for money [they] could kill a major prospective gift, and that such fumbles could doom the project by giving it a name as amateurish and disorganized."[28]

Privately, the Stanfords acknowledged their differences with Mystic Seaport, an invented whaling town in Connecticut that they called "a Disneyland of artificial reconstructions," and with Seymour's proposed state museum, which they regarded as "a mere array of materials indoors." Instead, their East River Seaport would use existing early nineteenth-century buildings and stone streets. In all, it would "be a sound commercial operation" that would "clear all its operating expenses by letting space in exhibition buildings to retail and institutional operations." That lively commerce "would reduce the musty feeling one gets in viewing objects long since passed out of use." Hoping to ride NYSMM's coattails, Peter formed a grassroots citizen committee, the Friends of South Street Maritime Museum, on November 15, 1966. Joined by Robert Ferraro, who had returned from the Peace Corps as a community organizer, they pitched in a dollar each, set up a bank account, and recruited members. Swift action was critical because, to Huxtable's consternation, the city was clearing the Brooklyn Bridge Southwest Urban Renewal District, a twenty-seven-acre site of nineteenth-century structures across Pearl Street.[29]

Focusing on the thirty-eight-acre Brooklyn Bridge Southeast Urban Renewal District, the Friends held their first meeting in a cold FFM shop. Their ambitious goal was not simply to help the State Museum but to save five blocks and a fleet of ships. With 149 members by the end of 1966, the Friends grew despite a lack of what a consultant called the requisites for success, including major political and financial support. Their organization included, they said, "first, rank-and-file citizens, second, scholarly advisors, and third, the men of substance and civic leaders who are finally responsible for the project as trustees." Those movers and shakers included tycoon Jakob Isbrandtsen, publisher Eric Ridder, *Yachting*'s Richard Rath, arts advocate Kent Barwick, and FFM garbageman Joe Cantalupo. From the start, the question was, could those movers and shakers win the political and financial support of the city?[30]

Speaking at the first meeting was the soon-to-be-chairman of the Friends, Joseph Cantalupo. Said John Hightower, who later headed the Seaport, "He drove a maroon Mercedes and wore a classic Italian

Borsalino. Were he to have fancied wearing a cape, he would have given Rodin's monumental sculpture of Balzac in MoMA's garden uneasy pause. His position as Mafia Capo for the South Street area was prominence enough." Though Hightower understandably (but mistakenly) called him a caporegime, which Captain Jeremiah Driscoll rejected as "an ethnic slur," Cantalupo was by necessity connected to the Family but not part of it. Born in Brooklyn, his Cantalupo Carting Corp. operated for half a century at the FFM, where "he owned the exclusive carting contract." Said his friend and writer Joseph Mitchell, his trucks were decorated with the sign, "A load on this truck / Is a load off your mind." He was liberal minded, cultured, and generous. With a framed photo of Eleanor Roosevelt in his office, he held little regard for those who denigrated the neighborhood's tenement kids, street people, and fishmongers. "With Joe's benediction," the fishmongers "didn't hinder us at all" in the project, said Ferraro. After reading about the Friends in Bennet Cerf's column in the *Saturday Review of Literature,* Cantalupo offered his help. As an antiquarian, he had joined the MAS years before and with Mitchell had rescued terra-cotta statuary when the fish market's grand cast-iron 1880s building was razed for a garage in the 1950s. In mid-1967, Stanford desperately needed $10,000. While Ridder suggested closing down the Friends, Cantalupo said the Mafia would help but warned against it. He gave $1,000 himself, "no strings attached," he said, because "you're doing a good thing here."[31]

Cantalupo told Stanford that the FFM's capo was Joseph "Socks" Lanza, so called because he socked those who refused to do business with him. Founder of the United Seafood Workers, Lanza extracted income from every fish transaction and even ran his racketeering ring while in Sing Sing. After he died in 1968, USW Local 359 president Carmine Romano of the Genovese family stepped in. Meanwhile, Cantalupo "bought the museum protection," said Stanford, "by simply writing an extra check" to the mob-operated Fulton Market Watchmen's and Protective Association. That made the museum "complicit in the rackets." The Mafia headquarters above Carmine's Restaurant at the corner of Front and Beekman was owned by relatives of Romano, whose union office was next door. Romano "held court" on the restaurant's second floor, said a US attorney.[32]

Cantalupo loved the seaport's "ethnic bouillabaisse," as its housing projects had, he said, "the same ethnic mix as we had here in the 1800s." Stanford thought that his Rutgers Democratic Club campaign helped by giving the museum "a firm footing" there. The seaport's grit was evident as Cantalupo waxed about that "beautiful odor" emanating from diverse workshops, "that salt air-fish-leather-printer's ink-coffee-tobacco combination." Wanting to preserve its authenticity, Cantalupo resisted both the fish dealers willing to replace the market with high-rises and romantics intent on making the old buildings, he joked, "like a lady with too much makeup." Little did he know that his declaration—"This Museum *Is* People"—was to become the Seaport's motto and build the city's largest preservation movement. Moreover, it was a concept ahead of its time. Revolving less around artifacts and more around community, "This Museum *Is* People" vitalized the Friends but created tension as developers eyed the district's valuable land.[33]

"It's Politics All the Way": Finding Friends in the Metropolis

Stanford needed help to beat the odds. Until recently, he had been an account executive for Ogilvy & Mather, the tenth-largest advertising firm in the world. He knew that the Friends' organization, sales pitch, and rapport were crucial for success. "David Ogilvy used to try to teach me," he told Kortum, "*facts move people*," so he developed a prospectus modeled on the SFMM. Ogilvy also taught the necessity of building a "flat organization" that stressed decentralization, cohesion, and team loyalty. In the 1960s movements, those qualities, said the Friends' Terry Walton, gave Stanford an "almost messianic" appeal. Emulating Kortum's museum, he presented his battle plan at a City Club lunchtime assembly on January 20, 1967. After Kortum's assistant, Anita Ventura, suggested constructing an "irresistibly charming" model of the plan, Stanford showed architect Leevi Kiil's mock-up of the old buildings around a new open square; the Stanfords carved the model's miniature ships themselves. Thereafter, Ventura warned, "it's politics all the way." By then, the NYSCA-MAS study authored by Frederick L. Rath Jr., first director of the National Trust, had been released. The *Sunday News* followed with a three-quarter-page story. Endorsed by two Gotham congressmen, the plan would restore the Row to its 1811 appearances, "place historic furnishings in vacant lofts, outfit clipper ships in the harbor and lease space to restaurants, marine and arts stores and bookshops." Predicting a million visitors per year, Stanford said it "would give people a sense of belonging, a place of enjoyment where they would be enriched with visible reminders of the city's past." It would be "a recreational activity with a social good."[34]

Shifting with the preservationist tide, the City Club's board unanimously approved Stanford's plan. Offering a start-up grant was Raymond S. Rubinow, executive director of the J. M. Kaplan Fund, which, said critic Paul Goldberger, unlike the Ford, Carnegie, Mellon, and Rockefeller foundations, would be the principal friend of people most "concerned with historic preservation, city planning and the quality of life in New York City." Courting Jacob Kaplan personally, Stanford met him in a Lower East Side slum, and they walked the seaport. "I hear a lot about it from Joan and I've talked it over with your friend Jakob [Isbrandtsen]," Kaplan said but then bluntly asked, "How is it really going to help the city?" Once persuaded, he endorsed the project, as did Moulton Farnham, editor of *Boating*, and Critchell Rimington, editor and publisher of *Yachting*. Bennet Cerf, the Random House publisher best known as the witty TV celebrity on *What's My Line?* gave a thumbs-up. Also offering support was Emory Lewis, editor of the weekly entertainment guide *Cue*. After scolding Gotham for its "appalling lack of civic pride and awareness of our architectural heritage," he joined Stanford's Advisory Board.[35]

Surprisingly, the preservation and museum communities were divided. MAS president Harmon Goldstone, a defender of connoisseurship who became LPC chairman, had snubbed the Row in 1963 and did again in October 1968, thus opening the door to demolition. That tired not only Huxtable but Stanford, who frustratingly told Kortum in early 1967, "Norma and I are going to a dreary little arty meeting to get to know some of this floating population of snobs and belle lettristes who make up the social base of the city's planning process." Yet preservationism was changing. One ally was Margot Gayle, who "almost single-handedly" won landmark status for SoHo's cast-iron architecture. For Gayle, politics and preservation were intertwined. As a leader of the Samuel J. Tilden Democratic Club, "her campaign manager" in 1957 was none other than Stanford, who took his experience to the Rutgers Democratic Club. Its one-dollar membership taught each person, she said to Stanford, "that he or she has an actual share in your venture."[36]

Mystic Seaport, which was a day trip from New York, looked askance at this upstart. Founded in 1929 as a small museum, it expanded in 1941 by acquiring the nation's oldest whaling ship, *Charles W. Morgan*, and after

World War II by creating a make-believe village that extolled Yankee virtue. Its principal benefactor was the Mallory family, who made their initial fortune in shipping. Clifford D. Mallory Jr. regarded South Street as a rival that could, said Stanford, undermine its funding and its ties to the New York Yacht Club (NYYC). Mystic was then facing significant problems, and its fleet was a mess. Said Isbrandtsen, who was dropped from Mystic's board after funding South Street, there was a lot of "jealousy in those days," and "none of them cooperated."[37]

Stanford was able to attract the Smithsonian's Howard Chapelle, the University of North Carolina's John Lyman, and Harvard University's Robert Albion as maritime advisers. Also joining was Kortum, who laid out what became "the essential Seaport plan." MCNY director Ralph C. Miller joined because he expected to take over the project once it failed. Combing the NYYC library, Stanford read about Frank O. Braynard, who became "the dean of ocean liner history, the commodore master, the high priest." That expertise was strengthened by his failing his Ph.D. history exams at Columbia University because, he admitted, "All I knew was ships." Once a maritime reporter for the *Herald Tribune*, he led a troika that staged Op Sail 64. As publications director for Moran Towing and Transportation, the port's largest tug company, he had ample time to sell the Seaport "to shipping magnates, bankers, labor unions, the whole downtown community." Doing "more than anybody to get the word out," he became the Seaport's program director in 1970.[38]

Stanford also read about Eric Ridder. A gold medalist in yachting at the 1952 Olympics and coskipper of *Constellation*'s successful defense of the America's Cup in 1964, Ridder published and managed the *Journal of Commerce*, a trade, shipping, and transportation newspaper owned by the Knight-Ridder Company. He invited Stanford to India House and offered to convene a small meeting of potential backers, but Stanford feared that they, like his consultant, would damn the project. Ridder said bluntly, "No matter how you slice it, this venture is going to take a lot of money." He arranged for Stanford to meet a senior executive of the Standard Oil Company of New Jersey, Melvin Conant, who had a keen interest in clipper ships. When they met, Conant said, "Peter showed up" in his "busted down Volkswagen, . . . one of the worst heaps that continued to be licensed in New York."[39]

Luckily, Stanford asked Ridder about Jakob Isbrandtsen, whose

Danish-born father, Hans, had single-handedly built and controlled the Isbrandtsen Steamship Company. Hans forced his son to work for the company, but Jakob bolted to enlist in the wartime Coast Guard, listening for submarines in New York Harbor with the Cruising Club of America. After Hans died, Jakob formed American Export-Isbrandtsen Lines in 1964. Amid the intense competition and unstable markets of the 1960s, he became a maverick. Because his ships were sailing in red ink, he proposed and later built an intermodal container facility on Staten Island. Stanford, Ridder, and Conant met Isbrandtsen, who was worth, according to *Forbes*, "as much as $125 million" but "held sway over $900 million worth of assets." Both Stanford and Isbrandtsen had joined the NYYC in 1953 but never met. Isbrandtsen's office at 26 Broadway included an array of sea memorabilia. Pushing Isbrandtsen to support Stanford was their mutual friend Charles J. Lundgren, a forty-year veteran sailor, NYYC member, and marine painter. Isbrandtsen embraced Stanford's plan because his firm had used those piers adjacent to the FFM. Isbrandtsen agreed to serve as the project's chairman, beginning in June 1967, while Ridder became its treasurer. In the midst of Isbrandtsen's modernizing his business and fighting off his creditors, he found psychological relief through not only Stanford's museum but competitive North Atlantic sailing.[40]

Stanford, having hooked his big fish, wanted Isbrandtsen in 1967 "to move in now and buy up" all the land they could get "at reasonable prices," to "1. Prevent demolition. 2. Bargain from a strong base for State and Federal monies for the Museum," and "3. Secure remaining land at leisure, wielding long-range threat of condemnation." Though the second and third step never happened, the principal question was, could his project fit into Lindsay's plan? While Huxtable suggested that City Hall learn from tiny New Bedford, the Massachusetts port that regarded the area around its whaling museum "as a living 'continuum,'" Gotham was tied to the *Lower Manhattan Plan*. As a small counterpoint, city planners sketched an area for historic ships, but it was on the Hudson opposite the planned twin towers. One bureaucrat called Stanford's proposal "the weirdest thing I've ever heard of." The backing of Richard Buford was crucial, and in early 1967, Stanford met him at the NYYC. After working for the city of Philadelphia, Buford was hired by Mayor Lindsay and served (1967–69) as the executive director of the Department of City Planning and as director of the Office of Lower Manhattan Development, which Lindsay established

Fig. 1.5. Schermerhorn Row (Block 74E), 1974. (Photo, Norman Brouwer)

to implement the *Lower Manhattan Plan*. Stanford played the district's booster, accepting the plan's high-rises and commercial spaces, but only for its outer blocks. Focusing on the pricey inner blocks around the Row, he wanted to finance their purchase by selling air rights, a practice that Gotham would copy from Chicago, so that space above four- and five-story buildings could be sold to developers who would be permitted to build larger high-rises nearby. Those sales would become, he predicted, "a 'dowry' for the Seaport Museum of many millions." Stanford expected no commitment from Buford, who was hindered by developers, the D-LMA, and a tortuous review process.[41]

Surprisingly, Buford supported the plan, but he warned, "there are tremendous developmental pressures, . . . and it would be quite an expensive proposition." He also realized that the city's plans were undergoing forced revision. For one, an urban renewal plan to the south had just collapsed, prompting the New York Stock Exchange (NYSE) to retain its 1903 building. Second, four antique houses that Rockefeller had wanted for his Fraunces Tavern park were demolished by Atlas-McGrath because of the city's delay. Third, what sociologist Robert Fitch called the city's "real estate stalinism" had led to open revolt. Not only did the city blink after fishmongers resisted their eviction, but anti-superblock forces were coalescing behind the Seaport because its Row seemed to be the last hope for saving a contiguous patch of the old-time port.[42]

"We're Mostly Youngish, Not Overly Influential People": Building a Community in a Ghost Town

Unlike Kortum's museum, the Stanfords were building a people-oriented organization. Despite the list of impressive supporters, they were not what sociologist C. Wright Mills called the "power elite." Said Peter, "We're mostly youngish, not overly influential people who have agreed to form a public for this project in the public interest." With Peter as president and Norma as secretary, the Friends ironically held their first formal meetings at and listed their address as 37 West Forty-Fourth Street, the NYYC's Beaux-Arts palace, which "goodnaturedly" tolerated the unusual scene, said Walton, "until that became too trying." While Peter was not yet ready to quit his advertising job, the museum hired Norma full-time, and she handled the behind-the-scene logistics. That included their first newsletter in January 1967. Designed to create a movement, the *South Street Reporter* was appreciated by all but Seymour, who resigned as honorary chairman because he feared his NYSMM would be threatened.[43]

As volunteers walked into the Seaport's new headquarters in the Row at 16 Fulton Street, they created a unique community identity. The contrast with Greenwich Village or Brooklyn Heights is telling. In the Village, for instance, residents had so coalesced around an inherited (but debated) architectural tradition that they were "preoccupied, indeed obsessed," with their identity. The Seaport, however, had been described as a ghost town. While some residents from the new Mitchell-Lama high-rise across Pearl Street lent a hand, the Seaport mostly relied on outsiders who worked nearby, prized old ships or buildings, or felt a need to become involved. In so doing, the Seaport created a civic identity. As Stanford told *Smithsonian* magazine, "The museum *is* the volunteers. It exists not just *because* of them, but *for* them, so they can look at a little piece of New York and say, 'Something of my hands and head, something of *me* is here.'" Ironically, the National Trust was heading in the other direction. Lamenting that preservation had been shaped by amateur volunteers, it had joined forces with Colonial Williamsburg a few years earlier to encourage professionalization and paid staff.[44]

More volunteers joined. One group, said craftsman Richard Fewtrell, was looking for something "in their lives to sustain them when not at work or school." But his favorites were "the retired or laid-off professionals who suddenly had time on their hands and needed to feel useful again." Val Wenzel, a retired architect, for example, was "free to haunt the riverfront, which had always fascinated" him. At the Seaport, he said, "I found something to fill my entire life." As he gave a tour in 1970 to actress Helen Hayes, she recognized, "There's nothing so precious as a good, strong, healthy obsession." Others were committed to the Seaport's ideals. Joining in 1967 was Edna Fitzpatrick. Raised without a television or radio in Gulfport, Mississippi, she was entertained by yarns spun by sailors and fishermen there. As a black woman and a ship interpreter, she rekindled her Gulfport tradition by telling stories about African Americans, one about a frequent visitor, a black nonagenarian who reputedly was the last harpooner on *Charles W. Morgan*. In 1972, Jennifer Berger Stanley arrived from Vermont and became the Seaport's first education director. "Everyone was working for an exciting idea and it was infectious," she said; there were "lots of little communities within the Seaport staff but we were all believers." Architect William C. Shopsin loved "the street façades—the pitched roofs, the narrow fronts, the brick chimneys and walls." Active in the MAS, he later headed the city's American Institute of Architects.[45]

The Seaport, publicizing its cause, staged a Riverboat Ball in May 1968. Held aboard the Circle Line's paddlewheel steamer *Alexander Hamilton*, it attracted the everyday sort, a thousand of whom bought $15 tickets, and some high-enders who paid the $100 admission. Organized by Lundgren and Howard Slotnick, a car dealer, it included a music-filled cruise on the Hudson. The high-enders also assembled "in a private cabin suggestive of Edwardian naughtiness," thus showing, said Stanford, that the Seaport could "appeal to the monied levels of society." Yet they were few in number compared to the Friends, who, said Ferraro, "were a ragtag army that took every warm body, so grizzled graybeard or sweet young thing, Upper East Side swell or Lower East Side project dweller, all worked side by side."[46]

One early volunteer was Kent Barwick. Raised on Long Island, where his parents were "fierce opponents of Robert Moses," he relished his summers in the fabled village of Cooperstown. There the teen worked under Fred Rath at the New York State Historical Association (NYSHA) and loved the "intellectually exciting place." At Syracuse University, while his date enjoyed the opera, he surreptitiously read Joseph Mitchell's Lower East Side tale *McSorley's Wonderful Saloon* (1943). Graduating in 1962, he moved to Gotham and visited McSorley's in the East Village, an all-male pub serving patrons from Abe Lincoln to Woody Guthrie. Hearing that developers wanted to raze the 1854 saloon, he called Mitchell at the *New Yorker*, and they testified before Mayor Robert Wagner Jr. The saloon was later spared. Becoming an ad-agency director, Barwick was shocked by Penn Station's fall and took action by volunteering for the Friends in 1967; he did everything from painting the men's room to working on the archaeology of the Dutch ship *Tigjre* at the WTC site. In 1969, he moved to the MAS, where he built coalitions to protect art and architecture.[47]

Linking the museum to sea-minded readers were the editors of *Boating* and *Yachting* magazines. *Boating*'s Richard L. Rath first met Stanford in 1964. Rath was then the skipper of a small freighter out of Puerto Rico, and his gruff manner masked a passion for schooners. As associate editor of *Boating*, he solicited scores of one-dollar memberships for the museum, building "a roster of fellow magazine editors, boatbuilders, marina operators and engine manufacturers to such an extent that South Street was becoming a boating industry project." Besides his editor, Moulton ("Monk") H. Farnham, Rath enlisted managing editor Terry Walton, who said, Monk "let Dick and me do lots of [Seaport] stuff on *Boating* time." *Yachting*'s editor and publisher, Critchell Rimington, also knew Alfred and Peter Stanford well.[48]

When the Seaport Museum was chartered by the state on April 28, 1967, the Friends of South Street Seaport provided its grassroots base. Coalition was "too grand a term for what we had," joked Ferraro. "A witches brew is more like it." Yet, by May, their cauldron was a little fish stall at 16 Fulton Street that became their museum. That one-room exhibit started with a model of the British *Cutty Sark*, which was built from a "large Revell kit" and "doubled for an American clipper." Still in a space "no larger than Helen [Hayes's] double parlor in Nyack," it held "records of two centuries of waterfront activity." Getting people there was the trick. As a taxi driver told Walton, "Lady, you really shouldn't be down in a place like this at night." Other Friends worried about the nearby housing projects. In response, the Friends staged weekend shows and walking tours, said Michael Levine, to "put eyes on the street" à la Jane Jacobs. "The whole mélange of New York hoi polloi" came to see and even volunteer, said

Ferraro. But "the true extent of the formidable obstacles and roadblocks were kept hidden from us mainly to keep morale up." Stanford told them, "Everything was 'terrific!' "[49]

It was not. In 1967, while the *Journal of Commerce* helped by placing a large ad asking NYSE members to join and attend the museum's May 22 opening, financier John H. G. Pell, whose largesse funded Fort Ticonderoga, bluntly told Stanford that downtown businessmen cared little for maritime history. Four hundred souls did attend the festive opening, at which Marine & Aviation Commissioner Herbert B. Halberg promised to remove the obsolete sheds, which covered Piers 15 and 16, to open up rare vistas and spaces on the river. By mid-1967 membership reached one thousand, but money was scarce. The board was reorganized to speed up fundraising, and Isbrandtsen went "around knocking on doors." Stanford, who quit his advertising job, admitted difficulties. "I am not good either at getting money or at lining up help," he confessed to Kortum. "I've tried to encourage big men to play a role but it's not my game, I don't know how to make them feel secure and happy." Discouraged, he warned in late 1967, "My hunch is we'll have to give the Seaport development away, wholly or partly." Kortum's assistant suggested contacting the James Rouse Company as a sympathetic developer.[50]

Meanwhile, the State Maritime Museum existed only on paper. Charged by the legislature with preserving and displaying the city's and state's history as a "ship-building center and a major world port," NYSMM was responsible for restoring the Row, which Stanford expected to be the district's central feature. Because nothing was moving in Albany, he offered to absorb NYSMM in his own budget, despite an $11 million price tag for the Row and the district's restoration, an estimate that was to triple by 1969. NYSMM's chairman, Admiral John M. Will, USN (Ret.), called Stanford's operation "a mess." Compromised by "commercial slickness," it lacked any "real feeling for the old working waterfront of New York." Besides Ridder, Will's trustees included the popular author Walter Lord and the brewer-yachtsman Rudolph J. Schaefer III. Stanford in turn called the state's proposal "just another musty little museum in a corner."[51]

Challenging the status quo, Seaporters were establishing a civic sphere, actually a counterculture, to revive mythical values. Though Stanford conceded that the museum did not attract a stream of volunteers "out of public housing to pick up paintbrushes and go to work," the Seaport reflected his notion of a participatory society at an earlier Fulton Market. Joan Kaplan Davidson thought that it was "so genuinely democratic an effort" that volunteers from all walks of life felt free to debate its implementation. That connectedness and openness were unique for historical societies, then and later. NYSHA's Fred Rath, for one, knew "of no project whose plans are more publicly discussed, or whose decisions are more openly arrived at." With scores of volunteers and only a three-person paid staff, it resembled "a political campaign headquarters at election time." Yet volunteers can be "a spacey, fractious and disorderly lot," Ferraro admitted, and Stanford pushed "everyone hard to make sure [a project] was done." That led a prankster to create a broadside, *South Street Seepage*. In its "First and . . . Final Issue," a half-page cartoon showed a smiling Stanford, with his trademark pipe, coming into the office and saying, "Here's a simple job —shouldn't take any time at all!" But volunteers were frazzled: one had collapsed at her desk and another on the floor, while a third was shooting himself with a revolver. Stanford confessed, "I am a difficult person to work for," but there were one hundred regular volunteers by 1970. Some who helped "with the dirty work," said collector Barbara Johnson, "were from well-to-do families." Reflecting that "pretty extraordinary" mix, polar opposites—William F. Buckley Jr. and Pete Seeger—visited with their boats to show support.[52]

The Seaport created a diverse coalition in behalf of its plan to restore some five blocks and piers near Schermerhorn Row, winning support from three of Manhattan's four congressmen and over a third of the City Council by 1967. But the fate of the outer blocks of the Brooklyn Bridge Southeast Urban Renewal District was on shaky ground. It was hardly what Mayor Ed Koch later called a "forgotten, and not very promising corner of lower Manhattan." While some in the Friends wanted to re-create the old seaport in the whole district, the city's power brokers had other plans for the outer blocks. They were similar to those Huxtable called a casebook of errors that thrust the new Beekman-Downtown Hospital, Pace College, and high-rise apartments into the southwest renewal district. That gentrification was, said a scholar, the "knife-edge" of a neoliberal urbanism.[53] Thus, the question became, could the Friends pose a people-oriented alternative? Their success would hinge on a program that would bring people to the waterfront, build bridges between them, and put life into the decaying fish-market district.

2

"The Kind of Civilized Vision That New Yorkers Are Not Supposed to Have"

How Historic Preservation Shaped
Lower Manhattan's Development

The two megaprojects developing at opposite ends of Fulton Street, the only street in Lower Manhattan then running uninterrupted from river to river, dramatically reshaped Manhattan after 1966. The World Trade Center and South Street Seaport were the yin and yang of 1960s development. Conceived separately but adopted by the nation's most powerful family, each complemented the other. Port Authority director Austin Tobin characterized the twin towers as a "vertical port," while the Seaport depicted how the World Trade Center "will carry out the mission started at South Street." Said Robert Fitch, there would have been "No South Street Seaport. No World Trade Center" without the Rockefellers.[1]

When built in 1811–12 to house merchants and countinghouses, Schermerhorn Row was "the first and largest of its kind" in New York. The *Times* later called it "the city's original world trade center." The twin towers, whose construction ran from 1966 to 1973, eclipsed any other skyscraper in the world. While the old Row was integrated into its neighborhood, the paired monoliths so overwhelmed theirs that they even had their own zip code. Bankrolled by the Port Authority, they were in 1974 "hurting for tenants," while the Rockefellers' proposed residential complex across West Street, called Battery Park City, was begging for funding. The Seaport's fate was different as it had to answer these questions: What was its mission? Who would come to its aid? Why was it important for New York? All the while, the district became intertwined with the economic and cultural meaning of New York.[2]

More significant than the battle over Penn Station, whose sentence of execution was summarily announced and commenced, the three-year battle for Schermerhorn Row set the context for much of Gotham's attitudes about historic preservation. The debate was heightened as the city was socially, racially, and economically fracturing. And because Albany failed to fund the state museum, the Row's fate was shaped by the highest bidder—the partnership of Sol Atlas and John McGrath. Ambitious and brash, Atlas had submitted in 1958 the high bid for Ellis Island, which had closed in 1954; he proposed demolishing the site and creating a resort, but the bid was rejected. Atlas-McGrath's profit-driven speculation resembled that of Peter Schermerhorn 160 years earlier. Son of a Knickerbocker father and Huguenot mother, Schermerhorn was a merchant, chandler, and developer. He filled in a six-hundred-foot section of the river and, instead of letting the land settle after building a story, hurriedly finished the four-story Row to attract tenants. As a result, the leaning walls, out-of-plumb floors, and skewed lintels still reveal improperly settled fill. But renters were easy to find; within the next decade, the Brooklyn ferry landing, the Fulton Market, and the nation's first packet lines for transatlantic and coastal shipping located nearby. It was the heart of the port.[3]

Lower Manhattan most dramatically changed when zoning revisions in 1961 set off a building boom. Except for a few landmarks, "the old building mortality rate," Huxtable wrote in 1962, was "running dangerously close to 100 per cent." By 1967, a dozen skyscrapers and superblocks were being built by Atlas-McGrath, Emery Roth, and Uris Brothers, the latter of which bulldozed "one of the city's best preserved rows of early 19th-century Greek Revival buildings" on South Street. Huxtable wondered if Uris had a conscience, and others if the LPC had a spine. Uris erected 55 Water Street, whose 3.2 million square feet made it the world's largest commercial office building. Yet, like other binges, significant space remained vacant until the late 1970s. Frustrated by the unregulated growth, Huxtable wrote, "It isn't just that New York has had no muscle; it has had no vision." Thinking that the Seaport did, she encouraged Stanford "to use her name" and approach her editors. But Kortum feared he was "slow to grasp this cosmic strategy."[4]

Reflecting a changing climate, John V. Lindsay, a Republican-Liberal, became mayor in 1966. He was "the darling of the Municipal Art Society," said Barwick, and he later told LPC chairman Goldstone in 1968, "When in any doubt on landmarks, I say designate." The LPC was slow to move

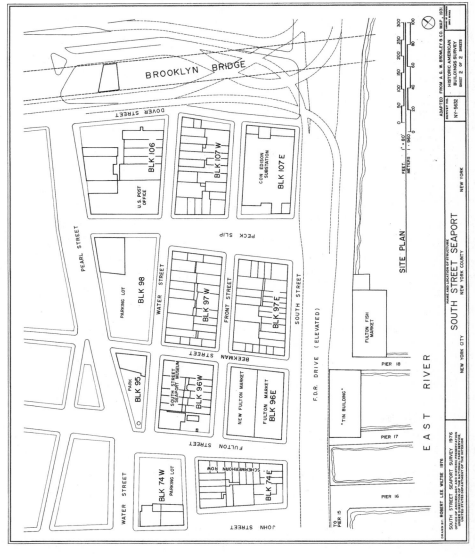

Fig. 2.1. South Street Seaport map, 1976. (HABS NY-5632; drawing, Robert Lee Wiltse; American Memory Project, Library of Congress)

on the Row. After the US Conference of Mayors endorsed preservation as a tool for economic development, Lindsay moved. By designating the Seaport Museum as the unassisted sponsor of the Brooklyn Bridge Southeast Urban Renewal District, which would be approved in 1969, he capitalized historic resources and recognized changes in urban renewal. By then, numerous streams of criticism were converging—including those of conservatives such as Martin Anderson, libertarians such as Jane Jacobs, and emerging preservationists—in condemning large-scale clearing. Though federal dollars were available in 1966 for big projects in hardcore areas like the Bronx, the seaport district would be a profit-oriented, market-based project. It was, said Richard Weinstein, Lindsay's director of Lower Manhattan Development from 1969 to 1973, "perceived as a business area" ripe for redevelopment.[5]

City Hall asked Stanford to systematize his thinking. After Seaport trustees endorsed Fred Rath's feasibility study, they released the twenty-seven-page Seaport Plan, *Proposal to Recreate the Historic "Street of Ships,"* in July 1967. Focusing on the area and piers near Schermerhorn Row, the Seaport planned to introduce shops, restaurants, and museum space. A later City Planning Commission (CPC) chairman cautioned that the "ultimate vitality" of the Seaport Plan required "careful fitting into the whole plan for Lower Manhattan." With that advice, the Seaport Plan accepted removing the FFM, razing the John Street half of Block 74E, and erecting some seven thousand dwelling units. Outpacing San Francisco, "the heart" of the plan consisted of three square-riggers at the piers. Fishing schooners and vintage vessels, including a floating restaurant à la Anthony's Pier 4 in Boston, would also dock there. Stanford even added a marina for yachts, but Kortum scoffed that it would be as classy "as a parking lot full of Chevrolets and Ford Falcons." Landside, the *Proposal* pictured a plaza displacing the 1953 garage on Block 96E. Select buildings would be restored, and the remainder razed. The proposal was later incorporated in the city's Manhattan Landing plan, which envisioned residential towers nearby, FDR Drive submerged under a seventeen-acre East River landfill, and the Seaport's fleet at its piers.[6]

Prior to an April 1968 CPC hearing, City Hall released a revised eleven-block scheme for an " 'old New York' neighborhood of museums, restored historical buildings and apartment houses." CPC chairman Donald H. Elliott stressed that it would not receive "any grants of public funds." The

Seaport then publicly released its "three basic principles," which had been vetted at Colonial Williamsburg:

> First, the Seaport will be a mixed community of museum, craft and commercial activities. . . . Second, the restoration will cover a wide sample in time—from the 1790s through the 1870s. Each building will be restored as nearly as possible to its original state. . . . Meyer's Hotel of 1873 may be accepted as the terminus date. Third, . . . typical activities not found in this sample will be brought in to complete the Seaport presentation. This will include, for instance, Bowne's Printing Shop, which was located several blocks outside the Seaport area in 1851. A *central restoration date* has been chosen within these guidelines to control street decor, craft activities and other variable factors. The date now chosen is the year 1851, a high-point for American commerce at sea, for New York port, and for South Street specifically.

At the CPC hearing, the proposal "drew many bravos and a few blasts," with ten of thirty-four speakers opposing the project. That same April, the LPC designated the Row a landmark, over a year before Grand Central Terminal's selection. But the Row was, said architect Jonathan Barnett, "what any real-estate man" regarded "as a group of useless, rundown buildings, ripe for demolition." Its designation did not preclude demolition if okayed by the Board of Estimate, which, said a later commissioner, was often subverted by private interests. Still, Huxtable applauded the victory, thinking that the Friends had "the kind of faith, hope and civilized vision that New Yorkers are not supposed to have." She also aired her reservations. Disappointed by the Williamsburg-style terminus date, she emphasized that "the full range of styles, sensations and references that record the city's history" should be preserved. "Give us the best of contemporary style, life and uses in the old buildings," she added. "Now that we have won the battle, let's not lose the war."[7]

Through a contract under Jack Aron, the Seaport commissioned a newer, more sophisticated model that showed attractively restored buildings on South Street, minus the twentieth-century fish-market structures, with the 1950s garage replaced by a reconstructed Fulton Market. When Helen Hayes visited, she took it as a "scale model of an early colonial settlement, complete with old Dutch houses and cobblestone streets, dotted

Fig. 2.2. Seaport Architectural Model, 1968. *Left to right, Wavertree* at Pier 15; *Lettie G. Howard* and *Moshulu* at Pier 16; *America, Ambrose (ex-Scotland)*, and *Alexander Hamilton* at Pier 17; and *Pioneer* at Pier 18's shipyard. Note the reconstructed Fulton Market in Block 96E. (Constructed for architect Thomas Van Arkel by Theodore Conrad and Lionel Forrest; ship models by William Hitchcock, William Zaroske, Alan Frazer, and George Demmy; photo, Tony Venti)

with horse-drawn vehicles." As Val Wenzel explained, the project was "to reconstruct the entire South Street waterfront as an enormous out-of-door museum," including "the fine old Dutch houses." Since they had been long erased, he noted, "we'll be able to reproduce them from engravings of New York when it was Nieuw Amsterdam." That image whetted Hayes's appetite, as it did many in the Williamsburg school. "Let's not curb our memories," she said. "Those old days were so gay, so undisturbed by world chaos."[8]

An exasperated Huxtable asked, "Where Did We Go Wrong?" Fearing another fake in the making, she tore into the practice of restoration, which was "a horrendous process of faking the chosen period by removing all subsequent accumulations of time and history." Even worse, she thought, was reconstruction, as it meant "putting up brand new 'old' buildings." Instead, New Yorkers should emphasize preservation. Credit was due to those who got the Seaport moving, but their model reflected "the standard picturesque baloney of gas lamps and horse-drawn cars." Almost pleading, she closed, "The challenge is to make the city's heritage a working part of the dynamic vitality and brutal beauty of this strange and wonderful town. And above all, to make it New York." At Stanford's urging, Kortum sent a rebuttal to the *Times*, but it went unpublished. Though ships were his passion, he repeatedly fought developers who ran roughshod over San Francisco's heritage. Huxtable's rules fit "a quiet game played in an ivory tower," he suggested, but not as preservationists battled "the triumvirate of wrecking ball, insensitive politicians, and insufficient funds." Endorsing restoration, he suggested that she should "be more tolerant." But it was for such analysis that Huxtable received the American Institute of Architects' medal for criticism. Most architects, however, did not follow her advice.[9]

Stanford faced other critics in his Advisory Committee. Even his friend Joan Kaplan Davidson questioned "whether it might not be wiser to adopt a policy of saving old buildings where they existed, and building frankly new ones where you had to start with nothing of the old." One whose model set off the debate, Seaport restoration director Thomas Van Arkel of the Philadelphia firm of Van Arkel & Moss, rebutted that "any new design . . . would compromise our intent to recreate" the 1851 seaport. In Philadelphia, one of his re-creations had gained much attention. There he had ripped off the entire façade of a block in Headhouse market because he wanted to create a mirror image of the colonial row across the street. On Richard Buford's recommendation, Jacob Kaplan, who was subsidizing the museum at $10,000 a month, hired Van Arkel for the Seaport's planning. He concluded that the project would cost $11.25 million. Hoping to sway City Hall with an attractive architectural model, he split the district so that the southern half near the Row would be restored or reconstructed, while the area beyond Peck Slip and Water Street would be high-rise apartments and offices. The proposal raised questions about gentrification, a concept sensitive to the Kaplan Fund, because, as Huxtable complained, the city's artists were being evicted from their lofts. That prompted Seaport advisers to debate "the social implications of high-rent, full taxpaying housing proposed in the northern area." Stanford, hoping to gain City Hall's consent for his Seaport Plan, wanted to bring "monied people into residence in the central city." The Seaport's location would be, said Walter Lord, "the catalyst for the transformation of an entire neighborhood, the way Lincoln Center transformed the [Upper] West Side." As disputes broke out over gentrification, the Kaplan Fund's Raymond Rubinow urged the museum to explain its rationale before any public confrontation occurred, while others feared that developers would accrue a windfall.[10]

"South Street Changes People's Heads": Finding Hope in the Seaport's Preservation and Redesign

In 1953, a terrifying threat confronted South Street, but only cinematically. In *The Beast from 20,000 Fathoms*, a monster surfaced at the FFM and ravaged the area. The threat in 1966 was more insidious—the bulldozer—but preservationists did not have a radioactive isotope to fell this beast. Instead, they used community programs, documentary cameras, museum exhibits, and consciousness raising, as demonstrated by photographer Danny Lyon, NYSCA's Allon Schoener, and Columbia University's striking graduate students.

NYSCA's director, John Hightower, recognized the Seaport's huge potential and wanted to help, but funding was limited, as his state appropriation was "less than the cost of 120 yards of the Cross-Bronx Expressway." He hired Schoener as his Visual Arts Program director in 1967. Schoener was more radical in his thinking than Hightower and was, said his assistant Philip Yenawine, willing to "to take chances." That led him to fund a photographic exhibit by Lyon, who had just made a splash with a book about a motorcycle club. The "Destruction of Lower Manhattan (Nov. 1966–Nov. 1967)" shocked many people as it focused on the "architectural suicide" committed by City Hall, especially in the Brooklyn Bridge Southwest Urban Renewal District. Its best Victorian structures, said Pulitzer Prize–winning historian Talbot Hamlin, were "delicate in detail." Tagged for demolition, they were occupied by "bums and pigeons." As the exhibit became a popular dollar book, Schoener hoped that "South Street changes people's heads."[11]

So, too, did Urban Deadline. A crew of activists, who included John Young, a graduate student in architectural preservation, was both appalled by the urban destruction and energized by Columbia's ferment. In April 1968, Young told a meeting of his striking "Avery Commune," which occupied the architecture school, that they "should talk to people on the outside" about their beliefs and hopes. Supporting the strike was his mentor, James Marston Fitch. Founder of the university's historic preservation program and a Seaport adviser, he urged students to invest their energies in the Seaport. Working pro bono, a dozen students in Urban Deadline "set out to cure the ills of the urban world," and Young hoped to "foster land-based museum activities." But, he said, "that was a hard sale" because of the power of commercial developers. Helping an array of progressive organizations elsewhere, Urban Deadline won the Albert S. Bard Award in 1969 from Citizens Union of the City of New York, as did Stanford in 1970. Most significantly, it was not Urban Deadline's vision but that of Beyer Blinder Belle that later won the right from the Seaport to develop the Museum Block (96W). With this first major institutional commission, the architectural firm was rising as the city's specialist in historic preservation.[12]

Defending the Seaport Plan to reconstruct the old market, Stanford met with Huxtable on several occasions but admitted to his trustees that it was "too bad that the first critical evaluation of the Seaport to appear in the *N.Y. Times* should reflect so much of Mrs. Huxtable's reservations and so little of the positive feeling about the project." He nonetheless assured them that he would weigh "carefully the Williamsburg school and the Huxtable school" in the process. Yet she recalled that he considered the buildings mostly as a backdrop because ships were "his chief love and . . . he thought of the Seaport primarily in those terms." Other aspects were mutually acceptable, such as his hope of fitting modern conveniences into the shells of old buildings. Hearing that, *Daily News* columnist Glenn Loney, who disdained Williamsburg-style "candle and wig-makers," applauded the plan, noting that new residents needed practical facilities, including an A&P, because "the closest supermarket was a subway ride away in the West Village." "And what a thought," he joked, "to buy your bagels and cream cheese from an 18th century deli!" As the Row once "housed the earliest grocers" in Manhattan, a new one would complete the circle. But with waves of criticism, Stanford knew he had to reballast his ship.[13]

"You Should Not Call Yourself a Museum": A Planning Conference Debates the Options

The Seaport held a conference on November 6–7, 1968, that was initiated and underwritten by the Kaplan Fund. Most critics had challenged either Stanford's architectural plan or land acquisitions, but two keynote speakers reaffirmed the Seaport's role in remaking Gotham. Daniel P. Moynihan spoke at the luncheon. Raised in a poor, broken home in Hell's Kitchen, he had risen to serve in the Kennedy and Johnson administrations and headed an urban think tank remaking liberalism. Stressing the cultural and spiritual dislocation of city dwellers, he endorsed the Seaport movement and restoration. Not only would it offer New Yorkers a sense of continuity and stability, but it would give them future direction. In a widely distributed testimonial, he affirmed that it was "not just a matter of cultural interest but of a potent, responsible concern for social stability, to be involved in the efforts that are building South Street Seaport." James Biddle was the keynote dinner speaker at India House. An old-style connoisseur, he had left the Metropolitan Museum in 1967 to begin a twelve-year presidency of the National Trust, which to the dismay of some critics was still oriented to aesthetics and landmarks. Yet the Historic Preservation Act of 1966 began a shift, prompting the Trust to recognize vernacular sites as potentially valuable resources. Calling up a mythical past, Biddle predicted the Seaport would "weave back into the fabric of New York's life some of the warmth and accessibility that have been lost over the years. The social value of this kind of restoration in a highly urbanized setting is enormous."[14]

More substantive questions were addressed in the workshops. One probed aspects of "the basic question" set by Huxtable: "Should South Street Seaport represent a frozen time in history . . . or a fluid progression of beginning, growth, and continuation?" With separate panels discussing the Seaport's relationship to the city, its architectural legacy, and its ships program, a contentious discussion ensued, sparked by personal agendas. Participating was not only Edwin Kendrew, a Colonial Williamsburg vice president, but Giorgio Cavaglieri, who won kudos for his conversion of the city's Jefferson Market Courthouse and Astor Library into prized public spaces. Jim Fitch headed the architecture panel. The debate over Stanford's proposed reconstruction of the fish market rambled between spurning the 1950s garage, critiquing Colonial Williamsburg, and erecting an obviously modern building. The latter was particularly unacceptable to Stanford. With no consensus, the proposed reconstruction stalled.[15]

The discussion turned to the physical remaking of the district. Recently appointed LPC chairman Harmon Goldstone defended the connoisseur tradition and found no building there "of great quality" and certainly no grounds for a historic district. Recognizing the drive to capitalize history, he added, it should not become "a dead place for antiquarians" but instead should be "imaginatively tied into the economy and the cultural life of the city." Mystic Seaport's Waldo Johnston bristled at the jab against antiquarians. While City Parks Commissioner William Ginsberg also dismissed Mystic as "the Williamsburg model," Hightower was more blunt. Showing his hand, he quipped, "How do I know what I think until I see what Ada Louise Huxtable has written." Lambasting "the Williamsburg concept of museum," he praised San Francisco's Ghirardelli Square, the former factory converted into a festival marketplace. When Kortum objected to Hightower calling Ghirardelli Square a museum, the future Seaport president shot back, "I think it is a museum" as it was "preserved for contemporary use" and created "a much more involving situation" than most museums. He also disdained kitsch. Seeing a Fulton Street pirate shop, he warned, "if there's a Ye Olde Pirate sign there next year, I've known [the Seaport] failed."[16]

Another workshop revealed a battle over the soul of museums. Since the 1930s, critics such as New York University's Thomas R. Adam had argued that museums reflect their era's turmoil and should address society's needs, whether civic education or aesthetic appreciation. Most curators generally preferred what would be regarded as professional pursuits. The panel included Kortum, the Smithsonian's Howard Chapelle, and the Mariners' Museum's Howard Sniffen, all devoted collectors. At a time when the national focus was shifting to public education, Ginsberg suggested, for example, that the Seaport should teach teachers about the environment and containerization. Yet Rubinow wanted even more — "something beyond a museum" — and referred to psychologist Eric Fromm, who feared that men were becoming machines. "This great interest in the sea," said the Kaplan director, could be explained because it was where a man still "has some control over his destiny." Along those lines, Stanford wanted the Seaport to emphasize "discipline, initiative, hard work and comradeship." Kortum, despite his sea spirit, rebutted that museums should not be "getting into the educational field." That was too much for Hightower. Like those who criticized the MAS for being disengaged from society, he believed that art museums were obsolete, history museums were worse, and they caused alienation, fragmentation, and rebellion. They were "terribly hung up on a nineteenth-century concept of what a museum is." He ridiculed Kortum, saying, "The last thing that New York State needs is another museum." Of the state's five hundred museums, only one hundred performed a public service. They had to be "much more socially responsible and responsive" to modern concerns such as pollution and racial strife. That applied to Gotham, whose economic and social tensions were "seething at every faucet." The Seaport "should not be a club or warehouse for the wealthy or for scholars to . . . study and fondle the objects."[17]

A pioneering historian in the relatively unstudied field of small craft, Chapelle was perplexed and wondered, how did his scholarship relate to society? While he innocently replied that "the social aspect of the museum is something relatively new," he was caught up in the daily turmoil over professionalization at the Smithsonian. Irritated, Chapelle said that "an air of unreality" had shaped the discussion, and he lacked any expertise on those social ills. "A great many people," he said, "can tell you what a museum should be, but there are damn few who can do it. And this is a big headache." He was referring to his Smithsonian collection, but Hightower retorted, "I get a bigger boot out of seeing a maritime hardware store than I do frequently a display in a museum of maritime hardware." Chapelle was offended, but the moderator decided that conviviality was in order and broke the discussion for lunch.[18]

Stanford faced an impasse. While he believed in a flat organization and participatory decision making, his conference had drifted into a raucous debate and provided little direction. Resorting to his belief in experiential learning, he pictured the Seaport as an arena for self-discovery, which also fit newer educational models and adult education. "The citizen of today" who visits, he predicted, will "find his own message and his own dream." Fearing that too many people had become a "dependent population," he wanted them to shape their identity around the Seaport's social and historical environment. Because the Seaport was so unique, Schoener told Stanford, "You should not call yourself a museum," which was "a box to put things in." Suspicious that many institutions were developing collections simply "to enhance the egos and bank accounts of the people who collect them," Schoener was directing more NYSCA moneys to neighborhood programs. As in Joseph Cantalupo's motto, Stanford defined his project as a "place where men may reflect and talk upon the things that matter to them, and, particularly, upon those things it takes more than one

Fig. 2.3. Seaport Museum meeting, March 1969. *Clockwise from foreground*, Moulton Farnham, Alan Frazer, Peter Stanford (standing), Joe Cantalupo, Jakob Isbrandtsen, and Thomas Van Arkel. (Photo, Morton Dagawitz)

generation to learn." Stanford tried to explain that unconventional position in the journal *Curator*. As other city museums were facing identity crises and the Metropolitan Museum was being called "the enemy" for a daring exhibit on Harlem, he lashed out in *Cue* in 1969, "To hell with . . . the mass of pseudo-experts, flagwavers, [and] Bible thumpers" at those stodgy, elite institutions, as well as their "bureaucrats, empire builders, and cashers-in on piety's easy tears." As Seaporters voiced their dismay with the Establishment, they were ironically relying not only on the movers and shakers of Manhattan's foundations but on kingpins such as Rockefeller and Lindsay in the daily battle to protect the physical remains of the nineteenth-century port.[19]

"The Dreamers Have Turned Out to Be Realists":
Saving Schermerhorn Row

With Lindsay and Rockefeller's nod, the LPC designated the Row a landmark in 1968. If then approved by the Planning Commission and Board of Estimate, any demolition or façade change would require LPC approval.

Atlas-McGrath resisted, as they had paid a premium of $100 a square foot for the Row (or $3 million) and were buying nearby properties. Offering to buy an island as an alternative site for the Seaport, John McGrath, a former city corporation counsel, demanded demolition and warned, "I am not accustomed to losing." In turn, Huxtable called their actions "a sordid commentary on the values and morality of men." So, before the Board of Estimate hearing, said Stanford, the Seaport "used every damn trick we knew to get that designation." The Friends gathered one thousand letters of endorsement, which they separated by borough to show each president the support. Just as Rubinow had done in his campaign to save Washington Park, they collected high-profile endorsements, including John Kenneth Galbraith, Arthur Schlesinger Jr., and Pete Seeger, and listed them in a full-page advertisement in the *Times*. There were sympathetic television interviews and editorials. While the *Times* called Atlas-McGrath's actions a "sabotage of the public interest," the *Journal of Commerce* called the Seaport "one of the most ambitious declarations of faith in the future of New York as a liveable city."[20]

The Seaport's campaign was restrained, however, when compared to the near riot over the proposed demolition of the West Village, which, Goldstone claimed, did not "accomplish very much." His dismissive attitude led critics such as journalist Roberta Brandes Gratz to regard the LPC as "the worst enemy of the work it professed to do." Goldstone was also wrong about the publicity, as the pendulum swung toward preserving the Row. While the Friends generated momentum, the Establishment testified for the Row, including the D-LMA, the Chamber of Commerce, and Roger S. Starr. A cautious preservationist, Starr had criticized the movement's "misguided enthusiasm" for dilapidated buildings but detested modern highrises as "cereal boxes." At the Citizens Housing and Planning Council, he gained notoriety by calling for Gotham's planned population shrinkage. One of the founding generation of neoconservatism, he supported the Seaport because it could help unify a city warring against itself.[21]

Greasing the museum's skids, the Board of Estimate voted unanimously to uphold the landmark designation of Block 74E and the Row. Said a *Times* editorial, the vote showed "that New York is beginning to subscribe officially to values that make a city civilized as well as great." Though preservationists were dismissed as bleeding hearts, "the dreamers have turned out to be realists." Challenging the legality of the landmarks legislation,

Atlas-McGrath filed suit. A settlement was reached when Atlas learned that the Row's air rights could be transferred, and he bought the adjacent (74W) block, thus dooming its handsome ten-story Coffee Exchange and five partially preserved early nineteenth-century buildings. After Atlas "wished us good luck with our hysterical buildings," Jakob Isbrandtsen joked, the partnership withdrew its suit but kept ownership of the Row. Ten years later, in *Penn Central v. City of New York* (1978), the US Supreme Court affirmed the LPC's constitutionality, ruling in behalf of Grand Central Terminal's preservation.[22]

"One of the Most Complex Real Estate Deals in the History of the City": Isbrandtsen Buys a Neighborhood, the Museum Makes a Historic District

Though Stanford had hoped to lure the marine industry's millionaires, as Kortum had done, he was forced to rely on Isbrandtsen, who approached David Rockefeller for a credit line in the Seaport's name. Rockefeller stipulated that a consortium, including his own Chase Manhattan Bank, would make the loan, said Isbrandtsen, to "a subsidiary of my company." In 1968, Isbrandtsen formed Seaport Holdings, which he secretly controlled. With his portfolio as collateral, Seaport Holdings had a $12 million line of credit through six banks by March 1969. It bought lots in Blocks 96 E-W at boomtown prices and, at the urging of megadeveloper William Zeckendorf Sr., scattered properties in Block 97 to stop rivals from building a superblock high-rise. Yet Zeckendorf warned that their goal of letting to restaurants and shops would be difficult, particularly during winter. All in all, Isbrandtsen "personally advanced the $16.5 million required" for the land, whose reimbursement he expected from the sale of air rights to developers in the outer blocks. While Seaport Holdings would retain some lots for income, Isbrandtsen intended to transfer the rest to the Seaport for one dollar. Intrigued by that strategy of buying lands and reusing them in the marketplace, the National Trust invited Isbrandtsen to make a keynote address at its annual meeting. His purchases represented, said Stanford, "80 percent" of the land that the Seaport itself wanted. Robert Graham, senior vice president of First National City Bank, directed the strategy, which was called "one of the most complex real estate deals in the history of the city." The National Trust praised the Seaport for "the kind of financial ingenuity and leverage that preservationists everywhere must learn to emulate."[23]

Grabbing the spotlight, the museum staged a ground-breaking ceremony at 236 Front Street on May 15, 1969. Though the decrepit building later collapsed, it served an immediate purpose for a photo op for Lindsay, borough presidents, comptroller Mario Proccacino, and Congressman John Murphy. With a hemorrhaging budget and an increasingly polarized city, and forced to abandon the Lower Manhattan Expressway, Lindsay was in trouble as a Republican and lost its primary. Symbolically driving a nail in the 1820s building and his Liberal Party reelection plank, he predicted that the Seaport's restoration through private, not public, funding would "serve as a model for creative urban planning." He also included the Seaport Plan in the city's master plan. With some four and a half blocks destined for restoration, the rest of the district was earmarked for modern apartments, up to thirty stories tall, and four blocks of commercial offices. But that master plan, laughed Huxtable, was "out of date the moment it was printed."[24]

City Hall's planning was left to Richard Weinstein, who replaced Buford as director of the Mayor's Office of Lower Manhattan Development (1969–73). By 1969, Weinstein said, "it was unthinkable to put high-rises in the seaport district." The Seaport found itself in a catch-22 as it was negotiating the terms of its ninety-nine-year lease and its air-rights sales, both of which were little-understood devices but critical for the Seaport's necessary income. At the same time, it faced mounting expenses for lawyers and Isbrandtsen's bank loans. Thinking that the lease agreement was nearing completion in early 1970, one staffer credited "our friend Ada Louise Huxtable," while Frank Braynard optimistically said the air rights would earn the Seaport $27 million. To the Seaport administrators' consternation, the negotiations took four years to complete. Early on, Stanford admitted, "I honestly don't think our own people understood" the details, so he placed Chase Manhattan's executive vice president for real estate on his board. Then, the WTC began to come on line in 1970 and swamp the market with nine million square feet of floor space. The building boom fizzled, and air-rights buyers disappeared.[25]

The Seaport quaked in mid-1971 when Isbrandtsen's corporate empire imploded; a share of American Export-Isbrandtsen Lines, which sold for seventy dollars in 1968, plunged to under six dollars by early 1972. Forced out in June 1971, Isbrandtsen was devastated. Auditors asked about the "various loans and advances made upon his instructions" for real estate. He had even "pledged a family trust" as collateral, leaving his four children in a quandary for decades. By July 1971, one $10.7 million loan had leaped by $3.5 million with 9.5 percent interest. *Forbes* asked, "Was Isbrandtsen siphoning off money from Export?" With that quake, a tsunami hit the Seaport, which had acquired some fifty-six buildings, or about three blocks, through Isbrandtsen. His $11 million for Block 96 bought what the *Times* called "the most valuable commercial property in the world," but his IOUs ran to $17 million. Stanford was pressed to explain the collapse. "The anonymous benefactor," he said, "had purchased about half the property in the seaport area"; Stanford begged the banks to "buy the air rights as an investment for resale." Now the Seaport, which the *Times* had called the city's "salvation," was facing doom. Moreover, cash-strapped Atlas-McGrath put the Row up for sale.[26]

The banks and city seized the moment. Led by Graham and Weinstein, they worked to save the $1.2 billion Manhattan Landing project, a Rockefeller-supported concept that superseded the *Lower Manhattan Plan* and included a towered complex surrounding a plaza of restored buildings and ships. With Manhattan Landing, said the *Daily News*, the Seaport, which was "now a minor attraction, would become a major tourist and cultural center." While later scholars missed the Seaport's key role, Weinstein told the *Times* that "social ecology" made it a magnet for stores, hotels, and residential high-rises. Stanford knew the Seaport was a pawn because his "bureaucratic and banking support" stemmed from the project. Arguing for culture and the arts and the riches they generated, he said, "we speak with people who hardly know our tongue." Similarly, Weinstein used the Seaport as "a hunting license to go after Federal funds" for the Bicentennial.[27]

In a highly complex deal, the city, half a dozen banks, New York State, and the telephone company took their slices of the bankrupt venture. City Hall purchased the Row from Atlas-McGrath, while the banks and city worked on Seaport Holdings' debt. In a complicated repayment scheme, the Seaport agreed to pay $6 million to the banks "as it realized income from its real estate," which would be a difficult promise to keep. The banks also purchased the air rights in what Stanford called "a deal very favorable to them." In all, Isbrandtsen suffered major losses, for he had paid at

Fig. 2.4. South Street Seaport, from the Brooklyn Bridge, 1981; New Market Building and Tin Building (*foreground*). (HABS NY-6072-1; photo, Walter Smalling Jr.; American Memory Project, Library of Congress)

least $12 million for the relinquished properties, and his Seaport Holdings had loaned the museum $2.9 million. Chase Manhattan Bank insisted that this loan, which was due in twenty-five years, be subordinated to its own. Because the public knew few details, Seaport trustees voted disingenuously that the "land held by Mr. Isbrandtsen for Museum use, and further land purchased by the banks, will be donated to the City of New York." Yet, with more strings than the New York Philharmonic, the so-called donation put a positive spin on the bailout. In early 1973, the *Daily News* editorialized that the acquisition would "not cost the taxpayers a penny." But that was contingent on many "ifs." After issuing $8 million in bonds and getting the telephone company to agree to buy Block 74W and build on it ten years later, the city purchased Blocks 74 E-W, 96 E-W, and portions of 97 E-W.[28]

Most importantly, the museum became a lessee, not a landowner, in its own district. With the city in control, a two-inch-thick agreement, which had been repeatedly revised since 1969, was finished. Signed in a June 1973 ceremony at Pier 16 by Stanford and Lindsay, it was, said Weinstein, "a legal miracle." Lindsay admitted to Stanford that it "was the most complex lease he had to sign during his administration." The Seaport retained its designation as sponsor of the district's development. The city leased back to the museum the "Uplands" (Isbrandtsen's Blocks 96 E-W and eight parcels in 97 E-W) and the "Waterfront" (Piers 16–18, the north side of Pier 15, and a portion of South Street) for ninety-nine years. In return, the Seaport agreed to pay 13 percent of its income from the properties, private tenants, and retail sales to the city. The lease also included demapping parts of Fulton, Water, and Front Streets so that a pedestrian mall could be developed and the banks could sell their air rights for nearby high-rises. Because the deal was so convoluted, the museum hired Buford, then a Uris executive, as its planning consultant.[29]

Though the Row was listed on the National Register in 1971, and part of the district followed in 1972, the Seaport was pulled further into the plans for Manhattan Landing. Planners expected to clear Blocks 106, 107 E-W, and most of 97 E-W. The *New York Post*, whose offices were nearby, noted the LPC's dismal record, as the city's 360 landmarks did not amount to "a grain of sand in the desert." Yet these plans were revised again and again. While the Post Office saved Block 106 for its own use, Borough President Percy Sutton protected Block 98 from any high-rise construction so that Southbridge Tower residents could keep their vistas and sunlight. City Hall, as it did elsewhere, established a special zoning district, coterminous with the urban renewal area. Within the South Street Seaport district, the city could demap streets, sell their air rights, and create pedestrian malls. Accordingly, the Seaport's historic blocks (74E, 96E, and 96W) were expected to sell their air rights within six designated peripheral areas in the urban renewal district, including Blocks 106, 107 E-W, 71 and 72, and the waterfront south of Pier 14.[30]

Manhattan Landing set off a hot debate. As the *Times* warned, it was "a plan for the haves, not for the have-nots." Three borough heads objected, and the Seaport took the heat. Its architect, Bronson Binger, conceded that the sale of air rights would have eased the museum's $11 million debt. In the *Times*, museum volunteer Marie Lore asked, however, "Is South Street Seaport being sold down the (East) River?" Other critics claimed that the *South Street Reporter* had become a "mindless, maudlin propaganda sheet" to sell the plan. Even the Seaport's director of history, Frank Braynard, wrote privately and called it "a profit-oriented, anti-people project."

Stanford felt the rebuke but thought the city desperately needed the project. Yet he wondered if "a miracle may occur and our part go forward even if the rest bogged down." That is exactly what happened when Manhattan Landing collapsed by 1976 with the city's fiscal crisis.[31] The D-LMA and the LPC then relented on the designation of the South Street Seaport Historic District in 1978. That designation perhaps deflected some criticism from LPC connoisseurs who were, as sociologist Herbert J. Gans charged, denigrating the present. The Seaport's designation was only made possible by Goldstone's retirement because he was, said Barwick, simply "uninterested in the whole idea of historic districts."[32]

Since 1966, the Seaport had created a grassroots movement that was beginning to change one small, important corner of Manhattan. Reflecting the era's idealism, the Friends had instituted a sea change in both historic preservation and history museums. But the takeover of Isbrandtsen's holdings by the banks and City Hall was a major setback that left the Seaport with huge funding problems. Most Friends and observers, however, did not know of either the financial cancer within or City Hall's hidden agenda. To them, South Street Seaport was one of the few public spaces in Lower Manhattan that offered choice vistas, a refuge from a troubled city, and the experiences that Stanford thought necessary to rebuild a civic culture. But he was beginning to reconsider Kortum's earlier warning that, as preservationists focused on buildings, "the ship end of things comes out second." That happened in Mystic and San Francisco, where the ships had become "a kind of fringe of not too consequential character." By the mid-1970s, those buildings were financially starving Stanford's raison d'être, his East River fleet.[33]

3

"Ships, the Heart of the Story"

How Tall Ships Became Big News

By the mid-1960s, fewer commercial ships were navigating the waters off Manhattan. Once omnipresent, their sights and sounds—broad sails, plumes of smoke, fog horns, passenger decks, churning tugs—had given way to transatlantic jets, tractor trailers, commuter bridges, container ships, and the ascent of rival ports near and far. Recognizing the change, Seaporters worried that the city and nation were less sea minded, that another character-making frontier had been closed, and that the present generation would forget from whence it came. While ships from their target date of 1851 had largely passed from the scene, they hoped to save sailing craft from the late nineteenth and early twentieth centuries. They regarded those vessels as representatives of an era that seemed better than their own and could teach Americans about their failings and prepare them for the rough seas ahead. Myths, nostalgia, and wishful thinking partly shaped Seaporters' perspectives, but they were as much concerned about bettering their own world as lamenting the lost past.

It took Kortum four years to acquire the square-rigged *Balclutha* and Carl Cutler twelve years for the whaler *Charles W. Morgan*, but the Seaport's first resolution in 1967 was "to bring historic ships to the waterfront." Yet some Seaporters claimed that such permanently docked museum ships were "an alien thing" because a ship's purpose was "to live and travel through unquiet waters . . . and do battle with untamed sweeping forces." As a result, the Seaport amended its resolution to require its ships to "be regularly exercised at sea, if humanly possible, in order to keep the gear in working order, and to keep alive the skills and sailorly culture of the ship's people." That is what the famed seafarer Captain Irving Johnson called "the religion of sail," but its implementation was difficult. Because of the dangers involved, Stanford acknowledged in 1968, for one, that "only reconstructed ships, with ballast keels, Diesel auxiliaries, and other [Coast

Guard—required features] should sail from the Seaport." For another, Howard Chapelle was "philosophically opposed" to acquiring old hulls and preferred building replicas. Some Seaporters were even landlubbers. While Joan Davidson said "she didn't 'give two figs' for old ships," Joseph Cantalupo admitted that his seasickness was no fun. Even so, identities could be forged with keen imagination, as Terry Walton made "the deep-water experience" found in Conrad and Melville her own.[1]

Fitting for Gotham's towering stature, Stanford wanted to be the unri-valed collector of old ships. Pushing him "to recreate the street of ships with bowsprits lining South Street," Kortum was the most determined of a small cadre scrambling to save the fast-disappearing survivors of the square-rigged era. As a later Seaport president put it, "We owe these people a great debt of gratitude. Without their passion and their com-mitment, we would have simply lost it all." Kortum wanted New York to quickly acquire "at least three large, deepwater, square-rigged ships." When Stanford mentioned fishing schooners, Kortum rejoined that Stanford's yachting experiences were compromising his wisdom. One whose life was defined by a half-year sail aboard the 231-foot, square-rigged *Kaiulani* (1899), Kortum cautioned, "Schooners are just spear carriers for square-riggers, which are divas."[2]

But, as in Greek mythology, those divas sang the sirens' song that drew ship savers to dangerous shoals because preservationists slowly realized that the bigger the ship, the bigger the headache. Ship committee chair-man Monk Farnham, for one, wanted money in the treasury before acquir-ing a ship, but, as Stanford charged ahead, he felt like "a small boy on the back of a bull." While almost all vintage, wooden tall ships had been lost to the elements, the last iron or steel commercial square-riggers, which once numbered in the thousands, were "rusting away in quiet corners of the world." As their numbers declined to fewer than two dozen in the 1960s, the National Trust's vice chairman, Peter Manigault, warned that the 1970s would be the last decade to save any of them. But most Americans knew little about those vessels. While the English sage John Ruskin had called them "the most honorable thing that man . . . ever produced," his disciple Frank Carr, who saved *Cutty Sark*, pictured them as "cathedrals of the sea." Thinking that America suffered from amnesia and dissipation, Stanford lamented that the world of sail was "almost inconceivable to youngsters today." When the Seaport of 1851 was re-created, he predicted, "the bored suburbanite, or the child of the urban slum" would see "the pride men took in their work" and appreciate "the danger, the uncertainty, and the cost of it all." While schooners would depict the fish market, other ships would represent the port's halcyon days. But he rejected those many cheaply built cargo carriers of World War II, the Liberty ships, that were passing from the scene because their bulk was overwhelming. Like Kortum, the Seaport "planned nothing for naval vessels in this commercial port," though some, such as the experimental submarine *Intelligent Whale* (1863) in Brooklyn, were begging for a home. The Seaport Plan even proposed creating a shipyard to build replicas and preserve the "archaic skills and expertise."[3]

Stanford and Kortum would be far more successful as ship savers than earlier Americans, whose failures were daunting.[4] Though descended from robber barons, Cornelius Vanderbilt IV was unable in 1922 to persuade New Yorkers or Bostonians to save shipbuilder Donald McKay's famed clipper *Glory of the Seas* (1869). "She stood for things," said seafaring author Lincoln Colcord, "the world cannot afford to lose." Lost it was, but James Farrell bought the figurehead for India House. Meanwhile, Felix Riesenberg, a prolific maritime writer, prodded Farrell and a band of Gotham literati to purchase an 1883 full-rigged Scots ship, which they christened *Tusitala* ("Teller of Tales"), as Samoans called Robert Louis Stevenson. But it proved burdensome, and Farrell consigned it to his shipping line. Sailing last in 1932, *Tusitala* became a Hudson River exhibit before being scrapped after World War II. Moreover, the full-rigged *Benjamin F. Packard* (1883), which was called "a glorious work of man's mind, spirit and hand," was acquired by Theodore Roosevelt Pell, a wealthy New York yachtsman. But he failed to create a Manhattan museum, and it was auctioned to an antiques dealer in 1929 for $1,000, which was less than half the price of some auctioned ship models. Though *Packard* had once been a notorious "Hell ship" run by miserly Maine masters, it ironically became an attraction at Playland Amusement Park in Rye, New York. Like *Pacific Queen* (ex-*Balclutha*), it was fitted with wax pirates and gimmickry. After nine years of "rowdys coming aboard and destroying things sacred to all sailing men," lamented a mariner, it was scuttled in 1939. Cutler declined to purchase it but salvaged the captain's aftercabin and stateroom, while its binnacle and compass later went to South Street. It was only with *Charles W. Morgan* and *Balclutha* that preservationists found success.[5]

"An Important Part of a Vital and Growing Lower Manhattan": Assembling a Fleet at Pier 16

After meeting with Seymour in August 1966, Stanford began looking for ships. His holy grail was a square-rigger like *Kaiulani*, but the Maine-built vessel, which was included in the museum's architectural model, was wrecked on a Filipino beach. His quest for schooners met a similar fate. The seventy-three-foot *Alice S. Wentworth* (1863), for example, was "in terrible shape" at its Boston dock. Kept afloat by polystyrene foam stuffed into its hull, it served as, said Robert Ferraro, "a carney come-on" for the popular Anthony's Pier 4 restaurant. Thus, the Seaport's first ship was more by chance than design, as it did not fit its 1851 ambience. Still, *Ambrose, LV-87* (1908) had been a New York Harbor fixture since the Ambrose Channel was dredged for *Lusitania*'s maiden voyage in 1907. Becoming the first lightship to use a radio fog beacon in 1921, it was replaced by automation in 1964 and displayed at the New York World's Fair. Isbrandtsen wanted its big generators and compressors and asked the Coast Guard to donate the stubby red hull in 1968. Though Stanford waxed eloquently about a sailor's fight against the sea, the USCG crew of the tethered *Ambrose* ironically fought claustrophobia and boredom. But that contrast was difficult to convey, and the ship confused a visiting Helen Hayes. Touring what she called the "ancient" vessel, which was actually younger than herself, she assumed Pier 16 was "restored as in colonial days." Entering *Ambrose's* cabin, she thought the bunks "were certainly built to fit some very portly married couples." Meanwhile, the ward room, which she called a spacious lounge, could accommodate "a dozen or more easy chairs where voyagers could while away the hours, spinning tall tales of the sea"—as she did too.[6]

The Seaport touted *Ambrose*, but the press only paid attention when a "derelict" committed suicide by jumping from its sixty-five-foot mast. That publicity changed when it was opened to the public in February 1970 and the Seaport pulled a rabbit out of its hat—David Rockefeller. Though Isbrandtsen and Eric Ridder had tried to win his support, he remained aloof until L. Porter Moore of the D-LMA glimpsed the project's potential. Rockefeller agreed to cochair the reception and serve as a featured speaker, thus giving the D-LMA's imprimatur. He called the Seaport "an important part of a vital and growing Lower Manhattan." Socially shy, he was uncomfortable in its tight ward room because the hoi polloi

—museum volunteers and supporters—"were completely unknown to him." Soon after, the Seaport reciprocated by participating in his World Trade Week.[7]

Also acquired in 1968, and headlined at the Seaport's planning conference, was the 125-foot schooner *Caviare*. Schooners once had been the mainstays of coastal commerce and fishing, but most were abandoned, scuttled, or burned in harbor cleanups. Gloucester preservationists partially restored this vessel, but when they failed to find funding for a fisheries museum, the Seaport purchased it, thus leaving them "stricken with regret." Stanford called it "a remarkably graceful survivor of the vanished schooner fleet that used to dry their canvas" at the FFM. Soon, however, the Seaport had doubts about its identity. As the recognized expert on Gloucester schooners, Chapelle discovered that the real *Caviare* had sunk off Yucatán. This vessel's lineage was traced to *Lettie G. Howard*, built in 1893 in Essex, Massachusetts. Holding a record for some seventy-five years of fishing in cold and warm waters, *Lettie* was "the last surviving" example of Fredonia schooners, whose "slender hulls, sharp lines, and graceful bows" made them, said ship historian Norman Brouwer, "almost yacht-like." Its silhouette contrasted with the East River's corporate high-rises. Forbidden by insurers to sail, *Lettie* was nonetheless able to evoke voyages of the past through the Seaport's sail-drying exercises. "We invited morning visitors on the pier to join us," Stanford said, "and people in city clothes would cheerfully come aboard to do that, shedding their jackets to roll up their sleeves." The cash-strapped museum jury-rigged operations in other ways. *Lettie* was moved about, not by a tug but "up, down and across the slips with my old Volkswagen bus," recalled dock manager George Demmy. Promoting the FFM, the Seaport displayed the crew's quarters, the bins for the catch, and photographs from *Men, Fish & Boats*. But, starved of maintenance funds, *Lettie* soon became derelict.[8]

A second schooner, the 102-foot *Pioneer* (1885), arrived from Gloucester in 1970. Built as a sloop for a Delaware River iron works, it was rerigged as a schooner in 1895. Later owners stripped the rigging, added an engine, created concrete compartments in the wrought-iron hull, and operated it as a barge and oil tanker. Much disfigured, it was abandoned in 1966 on a Woods Hole beach until Russell Grinnell Jr. stepped in two years later. Descended from a New Bedford family that had amassed wealth through shipping, including its spectacular clipper *Flying Cloud* (1851), and textile

Fig. 3.1. *Pioneer* on the North River. (Photo, Norman Brouwer)

mills, he began its refurbishment, spending $250,000. After his acciden-
tal death, the Seaport expressed interest, and an unusual deal was struck.
Because the estate could make no gifts, Grinnell's nephew, George A. Matteson III, asked his parents to anonymously donate $65,000 to enable the
Seaport to purchase it in 1970. They also stipulated that it be used for sail
training. As such, *Pioneer* was "the only remaining American-built iron
sailing vessel." The schooner's small engine was inadequate in squalls, but
museum volunteers vied with one another to sail it, prompting the ship
committee to rule that *Pioneer* was "certainly not a luxury yacht to provide
'boat rides' as a reward to deserving volunteers." Certified by the USCG

in 1974 to carry passengers, it became, said Matteson, "one of the very few, perhaps the only, museum-owned historic vessel in the United States, consistently able to support herself."[9]

An opposite case was that of *Charles Cooper* (1856), "the last American packet ship to sail out of South Street." Built in Black Rock, Connecticut, it was "the only surviving wooden square-rigged American merchant ship," out of some seventeen thousand that antiquarian John Lyman counted as US built. But it was a world away. Damaged while rounding Cape Horn in 1866 and then condemned, it had been incorporated into a jetty in the Falklands. Still, after seeing it in 1966, Kortum told Stanford, "There is more of the original *Charles Cooper* to be seen than there is of the original *Charles W. Morgan*," which had been designated a National Historic Landmark. After the *Journal of Commerce* donated $5,000, the Seaport acquired *Cooper* in 1968 but backed off from its planned restoration in New York because critics warned it would destroy the artifact. By 1970, the Seaport wondered if it was "practical (or desirable) to remove the ship from the preservative chill of the South Atlantic." Marine archaeologist Peter Throckmorton admired its craftsmanship. Glimpsing "the beauty of the shapes created by the broad-axe and the adze," he knew that similar authenticity was "only visible today in the country in the tweendecks of the *Constitution* and the *Charles Morgan*." Cherishing "this last remainder of the real thing," he compared it to the Parthenon and wanted *Cooper* "returned to her home port of New York."[10]

"A *Real* Ship with a *Real* History": Focusing on *Wavertree*

Pushing Stanford to acquire three large square-riggers, such as *Kaiulani* (1899), *Champigny* (1902), and *Wavertree* (1885), Kortum predicted that their crossed yards would show "South Street as it exists in legend." For Kortum, they represented the epitome of manly sailing. If Irving Johnson proselytized "the religion of sail," Kortum evangelized the cult of the square-rigger. Whether it was its crew's life-or-death responsibilities, its sails harnessing powerful winds, or its age-old traditions, it was a world apart from modernity. After Stanford and famed Australian adventurer Alan Villiers inspected the abandoned *Ville de Mulhouse* (1899) in the Strait of Magellan, Kortum proposed acquiring *Wavertree*, which he found when searching for old hulks in the backwaters of Buenos Aires in 1966.

Coming upon a much-disfigured vessel with faint lettering, he boomed, "I felt the elation a paleontologist must feel when he has triangulated where early man left his jawbone in the Olduvai Gorge." Though *Wavertree* was shorn of its rigging, its hull seemed sound as it was moored near a slaughterhouse and floated in a sea of lanolin. He began looking for the right institution to adopt it. Always his willing pupil, Stanford worried that he would disappoint Kortum by failing to catch *Wavertree*. Retorting that it was "a *real* ship with a *real* history," Kortum stressed that it was full of "the stuff of which sea romance is made." He warned that Gotham deserved more "than a worn-out and over-exposed cadet bark discarded by some European training ship association."[11]

When launched as *Southgate* in Southampton, England, the 279-foot *Wavertree* was an anachronism that was labor intensive and dangerous to operate. It not only was fitted with single, not double, topgallants on its three masts, thus making it cumbersome for its crew, but was built of wrought iron, not steel, and its sails were raised by hand, not steam winches. Sailing between Scotland and India before new owners renamed it after a village near Liverpool in 1888, it eventually visited ports on six continents. Like *Balclutha*, it seemed destined as a stationary museum ship. Kortum and Stanford agreed with Barclay H. Warburton III, who established the American Sail Training Association (ASTA) in 1973, that large square-riggers were unsafe for the inexperienced. Moreover, *Wavertree* was rare. More than three thousand similar iron-hulled British vessels had been built between 1838 and 1907, but only seven survived. Even more rare, the steel-hulled *Kaiulani* was the last of thirteen US-built iron or steel square-riggers. Determined to berth it next to *Wavertree*, Stanford said, "No *Kaiulani*, no Seaport."[12]

Knowing that such square-riggers had become nameless or lost in the record books, Stanford said they represented "a unique seafaring culture." *Wavertree*, *Balclutha*, and other merchant ships had "made history at the most basic level, moving the cargoes and people, and ultimately the ideas that shaped the world we know today." He even believed that a prime rule had developed within their "own small societies" at sea. Unlike the individualism that defined, say, the western settler, the priority of sailors was, he said, "the ship comes first," and that determined their "loyalties and standards of behavior." This culture "transcended national boundaries and developed its own language, ethos and continuities across changing generations." While Stanford's emphasis on maritime culture was war-ranted, his story sidestepped sailors' radicalism, their often utter des-peration, and the ways they challenged capitalist authority. In praising this mythical past, he was criticizing his own generation's individualism and narcissism.[13]

Displacing over two thousand tons, *Wavertree* fit Stanford's idealized globetrotter. As a tramp, it had scoured distant ports for bulk cargo. On its only visit to New York, *Wavertree* arrived in 1895 with Chilean nitrate and left with kerosene for Calcutta. Essential for sail's profitability, Chile salt-peter was carried to Europe by *Wavertree* and many other ships. As such, it was a cog in prewar tensions as European militarists turned nitrates into explosives. Later the museum's guidebook and Stanford depicted them as fertilizer for French and German farmers. With 31,495 square feet of canvas and a 140-foot-high mainmast, said Villiers, *Wavertree*'s "ghastly deep top-gallant sails, that brute of a great mainsail, and the enormous foresail were hell to set and murder to take in again." That became evident in 1910 on a westbound voyage two hundred miles south of Cape Horn, where storms with one-hundred-mile-per-hour winds and sixty-foot waves could take out the mightiest vessel. An August gale ripped away most of its sails, but *Wavertree* was able to limp back to Montevideo for repairs. Three months later, it tried again, only to be dismasted, leaving several crew members with broken ribs and legs. Towed to Port Stanley in the Falkland Islands, it was condemned. Afterward, *Wavertree* served as a storage hulk anchored in the Strait of Magellan and then as a sand barge and clandestine gam-bling house in Buenos Aires in 1958.[14]

Arriving in New York in 1970, *Wavertree* flew the US flag for the first time. Headlining *Wavertree*'s publicity campaign was Villiers. With six Cape Horn passages to his credit and his own sail-training program aboard *Joseph Conrad*, he earned a four-decade-long byline at *National Geographic*, even penning its popular *Men, Ships, and the Sea* (1962). Describing real men and exotic natives, his essays intrigued Stanford and Kortum. In 1957, he sailed a replica of *Mayflower* to Massachusetts and then New York, receiving a Gotham ticker-tape parade, and later navigated a replica of *Santa Maria* to the West Indies in 1963. Putting wind in the Seaport's sails, he spoke at the New York Yacht Club, Overseas Press Club, India House, and Chamber of Commerce. But Stanford's admitted unfamiliarity with fundraising left few spinoff dollars. Such deepwater vessels as *Wavertree*,

Fig. 3.2. *Wavertree* entering New York Harbor, with schooner *America* (*left*), 1970. (Photo, Robert Ferraro)

Villiers wrote in the *Times*, should inspire all. While many Americans were decrying militarism and ecocide, he suggested, "These ships sailed in peace under God. They consumed nothing they did not carry with them; they destroyed nothing; they polluted nothing." As the Seaport tried to preserve its district, he further hoped that the contrary "schemes of real estate operators" would fail. "I knew your traditions in South Street as a boy," he told New Yorkers, expressing admiration for "the 'quiet men' who sailed the ships."[15]

With a mix of awe, respect, and longing, those "quiet men" described their experiences in almost spiritual terms. James E. Roberts, who at fifteen signed on to *Wavertree*, told a Seaport audience that there was something about a square-rigger "that makes you feel she is a thing of life." At age eighty-eight and retired at Sailors' Snug Harbor on Staten Island, he showed up at Pier 16 in 1970 and recounted the ship's original details. Returning at regular intervals, he was happiest, Stanford imagined, as children gathered around for questions. When the Seaport brought other "old salts" together, Captain Archie Horka recalled his own transformation. As work shifted from sail to steam, he chased after the few sailing jobs, thinking that the "hard and inhuman" work aboard the likes of *Wavertree* "drew men to it, real men." Still, the passage of time erased many hard memories.

As a Brooklyn sailor admitted, "All the hardships have slowly faded from my mind, leaving the proverbial 'Romance of the Sea' as a legacy from those far-off days." Experiences varied. Stanford was a yachtsman, but the term had a "very negative" ring in Kortum's mind. Stanford thought, however, that Kortum gave him "a kind of parity" because they both could tell tales of "the man-against-the-sea experience" and Stanford recognized the square-rigger's mysticism. That was partly explained by a square-rigger's beauty—its lines, silhouette, and massing—but Isbrandtsen knew not to be deceived by beauty after witnessing the horrible dismasting of the full-rigged *Seven Seas* in a 1934 storm.[16]

Saying that the Seaport "didn't have a pot to piss in," Isbrandtsen funded the purchase. Though the scrap market usually set values for old hulls and only offered $7,000, *Wavertree*'s price tag was $37,000. An Argentine appraiser reported a sound hull, but Brooklyn surveyor Charles Deroko later wondered how, because "considerable hull structure" was removed when it was converted into a barge, making the ship "deficient in vertical stiffness" for sailing. Stanford quickly accepted the deal, however, when a last-minute "secret bid" was made by a San Franciscan. Thinking of the "$160,000 gross receipts" that *Balclutha* collected yearly, he expected *Wavertree* to be the Seaport's "greatest earner." But, while Isbrandtsen gave $90,000 to the *Wavertree* fund before the ship left Buenos Aires, the yard bill alone was $290,000. When the Seaport failed to reimburse $60,000 to the Argentine navy, whose yard made the repairs, the US ambassador warned that "there would be an international lawsuit embarrassing to the national interest" if the bill was not paid.[17]

Footing the bill was a syndicate of philanthropists who joined Isbrandtsen, including Brooklyn brewer Rudolph Schaefer, New York banker George F. Baker III, and Jack R. Aron, a Manhattan commodities dealer who particularly befriended the museum. J. Peter Grace also joined. Following Kortum's advice, Stanford solicited the help of prominent shippers such as Grace who not only headed a shipping firm but was a yachtsman. He helped the museum in a pinch, but his family's dedication to shipping was debatable. Pushing modernization, W. R. Grace and Company first purchased a fleet of British-made steel steamers and later, like Isbrandtsen, containerized vessels. Grace abandoned shipping for chemicals in 1969. Ironically, the Grace Line newsletter had just praised the Seaport because it would "bring people something they need now as ever before: roots and pride." Like many who romanticized the past, Grace relentlessly pushed ahead to the future. Yet, deep in arrears, *Wavertree* almost went aground before its arrival. To boost its fundraising, Isbrandtsen and Davidson organized a luncheon for two hundred select guests aboard *Victoria*, a stately 1936 cruise ship. Harvard economist John Kenneth Galbraith spoke about the Seaport and asked Gotham's merchant princes for support. But, Stanford recalled, "there were no major contributions," partly because "we had no organized follow-up plan for the visit." The giving by corporations, foundations, and wealthy individuals had also stalled because of the city's delay in writing the Seaport leases. Distraught, Stanford slammed his fist into a brick wall, ending up with a broken bone and a cast. Difficulties with his board also intensified. As he told Kortum, "I'm far beyond my depth in bringing [*Wavertree*] in, but I know I can do it with 'a little help from my friends.' "[18]

"The Largest Museum Artifact Ever Brought to New York in One Piece": Gotham Returns to the Square-Rigged Era

By mayoral proclamation, August 11, 1970, was "*Wavertree* Day." After a six-thousand-mile, thirty-three-day tow through gale-force winds and waves, *Wavertree*, which lacked its yards and main mast, was front-page news across town. Escorted into port by Schaefer's schooner *America* (1967), the Chinese junk-yacht *Mon Lei* (1939), USCG cutters, fireboats with water fountains, and smaller vessels, it passed office windows jammed with cheering people. Pier 16 was full of "moist and choked-up" celebrants whose revelry had been prepped by two days of partying. Its arrival seventy-five years earlier was unnoticed, but now a drove of dignitaries welcomed it. Mrs. Lindsay stood in for her out-of-town husband, and Whitney North Seymour Jr., who had been appointed the city's US attorney, welcomed what the mayor called "the largest museum artifact ever brought to New York in one piece."[19]

Realizing that what visitors saw was either inscrutable, inaccurate, or off message, the Seaport began what Isbrandtsen (under)estimated as a $1 million, three-to-five-year restoration. Seaporters then debated what kind of restoration. First, they asked if it should "go slow and have every fitting authentic to sailing standards or go faster" and use "modern lighter weight, cheaper or more durable substitutes" so as "to achieve a better visual display, with an inevitable sacrifice of quality." The ship committee unanimously voted for authenticity. Second, it chose to use salvaged equipment. And third, it resolved that "the ship should be correctly restored and rerigged as if she were to sail again." After rejecting Stanford's attempt to hire Kortum to direct the restoration, the board adopted Stanford's "*Wavertree*: A Plan for 1973." Instead of adapting "the central tweendeck and lower cargo hold for use as museum display space and central exhibition hall," as on *Balclutha*, it was decided that the tweendeck, which had been largely removed to create sand bins, should be returned to its initial configuration. That would "result in a longer and more costly job," but "the benefits in real understanding" justified the expense.[20]

In 1972, at Kortum's urging, the Seaport hired Norman J. Brouwer as ship historian. "Fascinated by ships since grade school," he graduated in 1962 from the Maine Maritime Academy. He then served as a deck officer voyaging the Indian Ocean, what he called "an adventure right out of the stories of Joseph Conrad." Later on an Antarctic research vessel, he saw beached ships doomed by the Cape Horn passage and heard yarns about *Wavertree*, including one about "a sealed-up storeroom in the ship's stern" that revealed "the wife of a captain, murdered and hidden there." His career choice was influenced by a 1965 visit to Kortum's museum, whose exhibits were, he said, "exactly what a maritime museum should be." After earning a master's degree at the Cooperstown Graduate Program, he interviewed at South Street. As he recalled, Stanford occupied "a tiny unrenovated corner office with a broken window" in the Row, so he was taken to the Square Rigger, a "grungy, . . . atmospheric, waterfront bar" where Stanford retreated "nearly every afternoon around 2 or 3 o'clock." "The craziest part of this scene," he said, was that the bar's television set was "showing the film *Captain Hornblower*. While we were discussing sailing ships, they were exchanging broadsides over our heads!" With Kortum's endorsement of Brouwer as "one of the most thorough maritime historians at work today," he was hired. He built the Seaport's library, advised its restorations, and, as an internationally recognized writer, filled its publications.[21]

Also in 1972, the Seaport hired Richard A. Fewtrell to manage the restoration. Raised near London on a surplus war craft, he played among discarded sailing ships that became his "dream chariots," he said. At age thirteen, he was sent to a two-year Shaftesbury Homes school for needy boys aboard *Arethusa* (formerly and later, *Peking*). He served eight years

Fig. 3.3. Norman Brouwer, 1984. (Photo, Jeff Perkell)

in the Royal Engineers, playing in the Corps Band. Later, sailing near the Galapagos Islands, he was chief mate aboard a schooner chartered by a travel agency, but he got "tired of people reliving the adventures of Captain Cook," especially those who "got very upset if we ran out of ice" for their cocktails. In July 1972, he introduced himself to Kortum, who "seemed mesmerized" by his tales and telephoned Stanford "to let him know that he, Karl, had the answer to Peter's prayer."[22]

Fewtrell discovered that *Wavertree*'s earlier work had been spotty. Under Isbrandtsen, it consisted mostly of, he said, "the copious application of 'fish oil,' " which was "a metal preservative much favoured by pinchpurse ship owners as all one does is pour it on. No chipping, no red lead, no enamel." Yet more had been done by Capt. William J. Lacey, who provided his own barge and crew in return for free docking for his repair business. One of the River Rats, a band of old salts who frequented his barge, Lacey was a war hero whose Liberty ship was torpedoed on the Murmansk run. He was a good friend of NYSMM chairman Admiral Will. Said fellow River Rat Capt. Jeremiah Driscoll, "Lacey's crew labored as if [*Wavertree*] was their own." Now in charge, Fewtrell trained his own small crew, bunked aboard *Ambrose*, and was paid minimum wage. He became, said the Seaport's Walter Rybka, "one of the most versatile craftsmen I have ever met," one who was "equally good at rigging, or carpentry, or metal working or engine mechanics, and particularly good at problem solving." Seeing absolute disarray, Fewtrell most appreciated the chance to put "order in the place of chaos." The *National Fisherman* called him "an extraordinary man who hums Bach while rigging ships," for Bach, Fewtrell said, "put things together in a way that was not subject to decay." Whether aboard *Wavertree* or at the Square Rigger, said craftsman Michael Creamer, Fewtrell had a "fine voice, knew all the chanteys and ballads, [and] played concertina, violin and ukulele."[23]

Even more important was Fewtrell's commitment to the original ship. His concern differed dramatically from that of Lacey, who added such features as "a fake bowsprit" and an inauthentic access door that exposed the Seaport's problematic approach to restoration. Yet Fewtrell's crew lacked any blueprints or detailed photographs, thus clouding the issue of authenticity. Within the ship committee, he sparred with Stanford and marine architect George Campbell, who had restored *Cutty Sark*. Fewtrell warned them that "inauthentic work" would lead to "unintended difficulties and unplanned expenses." When Campbell argued that *Wavertree* would never sail again, Fewtrell admitted, "no other ship I know of has been this far dismantled and brought back to sailing condition." He pushed back any thought of sailing or USCG certification, saying, "We'll worry about watertight bulkheads and auxiliary engines after we've got her back in the shape she was in in 1885." He quipped, "I was not yet 30 yrs old and it was easy for me to determine that I would outlive the opposition." Removing Lacey's fakery and championing authenticity, his work became time-consuming and expensive. Beside a small crew, he used volunteers such as Axel Ekstand, a lifelong seaman. When "we'd do some back-breaking work," crew member Charles Deroko joked, "his exhortation was the standard Norwegian donkey call, Eeee-orrr, eeee-orrr!" Just one of a tight-knit crew, Ekstand stood for an old New York way of life that was quickly passing.[24]

"Too Much Planning Can Kill Anything": Filling Up Piers 15, 16, and 17

By 1972, *Wavertree* had been joined by the propeller-driven, double-ended ferry *Maj. Gen. William H. Hart*, the paddle-wheeler *Alexander Hamilton*, and the square-rigged *Moshulu* at Piers 15, 16, and 17. As the museum raced ahead, it acted as a shelter of last resort or experimented with partners to keep ships from the breakers. As trustee Dick Rath remembered, the piers were full, but if another ship was available, "Peter would get it anyway." In 1970, for example, the USCG announced that *Maj. Gen. Hart* would be scrapped. On this occasion, said George Matteson, Seaport volunteers approached the Coasties and asked for its donation "without any formal consent from the museum leadership or administration." The ferry arrived during a Seaport festival so that Lindsay, who was decked out in yachting gear, found a photo op. The unbudgeted acquisition led Monk Farnham to resign as ship committee chairman.[25]

Controversy also ensued over the ship's name. Christened *John A. Lynch* (1925) and named for a Richmond borough president, it was renamed *Harlem* during Mayor LaGuardia's campaign of "throwing the rascals out" of office. With the opening of the Verrazano Narrows Bridge in 1964, the ferry became obsolete. The Seaport worried that using its original name would be seen as endorsing a corrupt politician, while using *Harlem* could be viewed as "fashionably 'liberal'" and create a backlash. That was a possibility because in the racially polarized city, the Metropolitan Museum was still reverberating from protests over Schoener's exhibit *Harlem on My Mind*. The USCG name, *Maj. Gen. William H. Hart*, was inconsistent with its Fulton Street service, but the Seaport kept it.[26]

Another victim of the automobile age, the elegant 338-foot *Alexander Hamilton* (1924) last cruised in 1971. As the Atlantic coast's sole surviving sidewheel steamer, it evoked the era of leisurely Hudson River cruises. Passengers, who numbered up to three thousand, were intrigued by its triple-expansion inclined engine, whose movement was, said an old-timer, "a sight never to be forgotten." Unlike a diesel, its moving parts were, Brouwer explained, "almost fully visible. The interaction of well-oiled, finely polished iron, steel, and brass was remarkably quiet, the major sounds being ponderous whishes and clicks suggestive of the mechanism of a giant clock." Encouraged by Lindsay's Public Development Corporation (PDC), Stanford hoped that it would, like Boston's *Peter Stuyvesant*, become a floating restaurant. Yet *Hamilton* was owned by California-based Specialty Restaurants, which also managed *Queen Mary* in Long Beach, and the three-party deal confused the press and the public. The agreement would have allowed Specialty to dock two ship restaurants at the Seaport for $50,000 a year, but it was problematic from the start. Specialty failed to deliver on promised repairs because, as the son of the firm's president told the press, "I think this boat's a wreck." Driscoll asked with alarm, if it sank on top of the subway tunnel, could explosives be used to remove the hulk? An angry supporter wanted it "scuttled at sea, so she could die proudly" rather than "go slowly with rot and rust." When Specialty backed out, City Hall refused to act. After a "stay of execution" at the former Brooklyn Navy Yard, *Hamilton* migrated to New Jersey, where it was listed as a state historic site, placed on the National Register, and partially repaired by a new owner for a Hudson River restaurant. Then the National Trust allegedly failed to deliver on promised monetary help, and the ship partly sank in a gale in 1977. Rotting at a navy pier in sixteen feet of water, it was, Stanford told the *Times*, "in the hands of God and the Navy." But when the navy refused the $250,000 salvage, he angrily said, "We have been flimflammed."[27]

Hamilton's demise, said Stanford, illustrated a sad fact: "Empty promises sink ships." A frustrated Peter Spectre, editor of *WoodenBoat* magazine, ripped into would-be ship savers. The saga showed how "politics, not logic, rules all too many" of their decisions. Like *Kaiulani*, *Hamilton* required better planning, funding, and implementation. But as Rybka acknowledged, "most ship saves are started by ardent preservationists with little grasp of the technical problems." If they knew everything beforehand, "they would be too discouraged to make the attempt." He admitted, "You win some and you lose some." Spectre was asking too much, said David Hull of San Francisco's maritime museum. He characterized his position as "let's-have-everything-in-order-and-all-the-funds-and-skills-lined-up-before-we-take-the-first-step." If others had taken that perspective, there would have been no *Balclutha*, whose initial efforts were unstructured and unfunded. As Hull warned, "Too much planning can kill anything."[28]

Still hoping to profit from the shipboard dining fad, Specialty Restaurants bought the four-masted *Moshulu* (1904) from the Walt Disney Company and partnered with the Seaport in 1972. First proposed in 1967 by Kortum, the plan called for bringing a restaurant and shops aboard. In 1970, Stanford reportedly "had a tentative 20-year lease" that bankers told them "would be cashable for $750,000," especially for "one of the world's best known sailing ships." Outfitted with inauthentic rigging in Holland and arriving by tow to much hoopla in 1972, *Moshulu* (335 feet) occupied an entire side of Pier 16. A former captain called it "the supreme development of man's use of the wind as a means of propulsion." Built in Scotland as *Kurt*, the barque was active in the Chile saltpeter trade. Operating out of Hamburg, it was confiscated by the USCG in 1917 and renamed *Moshulu*, the Seneca word for "fearless," by President Woodrow Wilson's wife, Edith. After hauling lumber and grain, it was confiscated during World War II by the Germans.[29]

Yet *Moshulu* arrived at an inauspicious moment. Though backed by the PDC, Specialty was unable to secure a restaurant license because city regulators quarreled over jurisdiction, as they asked, "Was it a building or a vessel?" Regardless, teetotaling sailors said it was a sacrilege to install a bar. When the firm could not get financing during the city's own fiscal crisis, the lease fell through. "Many wept when she left" in 1975 for Philadelphia, where Specialty cut windows in its tweendeck and remade the interior as an ocean liner. It became, joked one craftsman, a "four-masted salad barque." As a consolation prize, the Seaport got its eatery when Lacey, who operated the fast-food Galley on Pier 16, purchased *Lloyd I. Seaman* (1935). Formerly a floating hospital, the four-deck, motorless barge docked at Pier 16. Renamed *Robert Fulton*, its fake stacks were painted at Frank Braynard's behest to imitate a United States Lines steamer.[30]

"The Largest Sailing Vessel in the World": *Peking* Takes Pier 16

The museum lost one four-masted, steel-hulled barque, but it gained another in 1975. Though in 1972 it had plans to berth as many as a dozen ships, the museum experienced a setback with Isbrandtsen's fiscal collapse and its own insolvency. Then, trustee Jack R. Aron made an offer that could not be refused—to purchase *Peking*. A navy officer in World War II, he developed, said his son Peter, "a life-long interest in everything maritime." Becoming a discriminating collector of marine and Oriental art and an avid yachtsman, he headed the firm J. Aron & Company, which dealt in commodities such as gold and "ranked number one in the world as an importer of unroasted green coffee." By the 1970s, Aron focused more time on his charitable foundation, whose work included the Seaport. Peter A. Aron sailed in his father's wake. He said, "I grew up around all sorts of boats," including Jack's forty-four-foot Alden sloop. After graduating from Tulane University in 1969 through its ROTC program, he served a tour in Vietnam with the army's Transportation Corps. Working for J. Aron & Company at the nearby New York Coffee Exchange on Pine Street, he joined the Seaport's board in the late 1970s. Becoming one of its most committed trustees, he chaired the board from 1987 to 1999. Like Isbrandtsen, the Aron family contributed mightily to the Seaport.[31]

After seeing a classified ad in the *New York Times* for a square-rigger in 1974, the Seaport's managing director, Robert Bonham, whom the board hired to offset Stanford, contacted Peter Aron. *Peking* (1911) was built for Ferdinand Laeisz & Company of Hamburg. It had forty-four thousand square feet of canvas in thirty-two sails, which amounted to more than an acre. Its sister ships in the German Flying P Line were the great *Passat*, *Preussen*, and *Pamir*, the last of which sank in a hurricane in 1957 and ended square-rigged commerce. *Peking* was confiscated during World War I but was repatriated by Laeisz and carried nitrates until 1932, when the trade was no longer profitable. It was sold to the British charity Shaftesbury Homes, which renamed it *Arethusa*, disposed of unnecessary gear, and converted its hull into a stationary school for needy boys, including Fewtrell. During World War II, the British navy used it as a barracks and removed the yards from the main and mizzen masts. As such, it was, said Villiers, "a waste of good rigging." After cutting down the royal masts, the school moved ashore in 1974 and consigned it to Savills of London for auction. In Britain, Jack Aron excitedly inspected the ship. With the 1976 Bicentennial celebration approaching in the United States, he knew that a second square-rigger would raise the Seaport's profile. Bonham recognized that his board was "scared to death of taking on another vessel" and asked the J. Aron Charitable Foundation (JACF) to intercede. Doubting "that the museum staff was going to handle the funds correctly," Aron created a subsidiary to fast-track the process. Although the Seaport's board was not consulted, said Isbrandtsen, its Executive Committee approved the deal.[32]

Governed by Jack Aron and board chairman Robert McCullough, the subsidiary Peking Joint Venture (PJV) stipulated that *Arethusa's* management would initially "be outside the framework" of the Seaport. It was given "the principal berth" at Pier 16, and, to the shock of *Wavertree's* friends, the Seaport agreed not to "berth other ship exhibits in such a way as to detract" from it. The JACF provided $480,000, with one-third as an interest-free loan, for its purchase, restoration, towing, and upkeep. The Seaport held the title, contributed $100,000, and agreed to share control over its restoration. Thus, with a budget of $580,000 and a satisfactory hull survey, the PJV made the sole bid of £70,000 ($165,000). A German association had raised money but made no bid.[33]

Placed in drydock at Blackwall on the River Thames, *Arethusa* was readied for its tow to New York by Harold A. "Hap" Paulsen, retired commander of USCG *Eagle*. While removing the school's 125 portholes and installing twelve thousand hull rivets and many steel plates, the shipyard did a very good job, said Deroko. Attracted to the throwback, as riveted ships had been obsolete for a quarter century, Britain's Prince Philip visited the yard. After a seventeen-day tow, *Arethusa* arrived in late July 1975 at a Staten Island drydock for what Peter Aron called "a good deal of cosmetic work." As he was paying the piper, Jack Aron called the tune. Towed on November 22, 1975, to Pier 16, *Peking* was ceremoniously welcomed by the city's fireboats, press corps, dignitaries, and a band playing "Anchors Aweigh." "It was an event," said the *Times*, "roughly equivalent to the Metropolitan Museum of Art's finally acquiring a passionately sought-after Rembrandt." Rembrandts numbered in the thousands, but there were "perhaps 10 sailing ships [*Peking's*] size left in the world." Befitting Gotham's ambition, claimed Jack Aron, *Peking* was "the largest sailing vessel in the world." Like *Wavertree*, its restoration cost much more than expected.[34]

The PJV and museum staff debated *Peking's* restoration and future. Brouwer recalled being assured that it "was going to be restored accurately." While in London, Jack Aron brought in engineers from its German builder, Blohm & Voss, to assess if the barque "could be brought to sailing condition." When it had been launched in 1911, less strict standards prevailed, as builders had usually placed collision bulkheads only forward. As

Fig. 3.4. *Peking* approaching Manhattan, 1975. (Photo, Peter Aron Collection)

Peter Aron admitted, those early ships "were pretty much expendable." But the USCG wanted watertight doors and more bulkheads if it was to sail. The engineers said it "would have to be entirely rebuilt at a cost of tens of millions of dollars, and it would have to be modified to install transverse bulkheads (to keep the ship from totally flooding if holed)." Not willing to fund that expense, Jack Aron hired Paulsen, not Fewtrell, to work on the stationary museum vessel.[35]

The rigging also reflected budgetary considerations. *Peking* was out-fitted in Staten Island with controversial yards. Remembering that some critics derided the work as a "Hollywood rig," Peter Aron explained that its upper masts and yards were fabricated by a company named Flagpoles Inc., but that "gave the nay-sayers a chance to criticize and make fun of the project." In addition, they "were welded as opposed to being riveted" because of the cost and lack of skilled riveters. Fewtrell resented those cost-cutting measures, as he did the fixed rudder and the speculative re-creation of the staterooms and fo'c'sle. He railed that *Wavertree* was "the only ship down here." Yet *Wavertree* was a derelict with no rig, what Peter Aron called "an iron box with paint put on it." *Peking* stood out, as its 320-foot length and towering masts dominated the waterfront.[36]

When *Peking* arrived, Deroko recalled, a lot of sniping occurred between the two ships. While Isbrandtsen "felt put out," Fewtrell thought that the Seaport's $100,000 contribution "had the effect, and maybe also the intention, of causing a sudden and permanent halt to almost all" of his funding. Stanford initially supported the PJV but was excluded from its committee. He was, said Peter Aron, "a naysayer," not only thinking of *Peking* as *Wavertree*'s competitor but realizing that its restoration would be tightly managed by Jack Aron, who regarded his critics as purists. Jack Aron reasoned that "the *Cutty Sark* isn't restored completely correct and very few people know the difference." As trustee Howard Slotnick admitted, *Peking* was "never meant to be historically accurate." The fallout radiated to programs on shore. As education director Jennifer Stanley recalled, *Peking* became "a drain on already existing ships, buildings and programs." Those trustees "who had an interest in the 'Museum' had very little weight," she thought, because "the Board was too heavily weighted with Fortune 500 business types" who favored the big show at the pier.[37]

Though stationary, *Peking* became best known as the star of a thrilling film shot by Irving M. Johnson while rounding Cape Horn in a fierce gale in 1929. Inspired by Jack London, Johnson signed on as a tourist for the eleven-thousand-mile voyage. Edited to ten minutes, which included a taped commentary, *The* Peking *Battles Cape Horn* was continuously shown aboard the ship after 1980. Seeing it was "a must," said a reviewer, as it "makes all other kinds of sailing look like child's play." Johnson was mobbed by admirers when he came to visit; he was not only a living legend who sailed the globe seven times but a popular writer in *National Geographic* and author of a dozen adventure books, including *The* Peking *Battles Cape Horn* (1977). Preaching his "religion of sail" to a flaccid age, Johnson knew that sailing a square-rigger, especially in foul weather, converted everyday men into heroes who showed extraordinary "feats of strength, effectiveness and daring" as they focused solely on "the extreme need of the ship." What he learned from them was "to lean forward into life." A septuagenarian in 1977, he found a sense of permanence at the Seaport. "Can you imagine greater satisfaction to a sailor than having his old Cape Horner saved from the ship breakers?" he asked. He even took his son and grandsons to help bring *Peking* to Pier 16, gratified that it would last centuries more.[38]

"If You Brought It In, God Would Provide": Rounding Out the East River Fleet

More prosaic acquisitions, but essential for the port's history, were every-day tugs and lighters. According to one estimate, there were more than 750 tugs in New York Harbor in 1900, each having a distinguishing whistle. But when the McAllister Brothers Towing Company donated the seventy-two-foot steam tug *Mathilda* in 1970, it stuck out like a red maple leaf, as it was built in Quebec in 1899, spent seventy years working in fresh water, and lacked saltwater equipment. Its tattered Canadian flag was even saved "by patching its frayed edge with a remnant of the perfect color red underwear." After Canadians protested, a suitable ensign was raised. Yet *Mathilda* was neglected and sank at its berth in January 1976. Adding to the Seaport's embarrassment, *Maj. Gen. Hart's* engine room had flooded a week earlier. With *Mathilda* settling in twenty-five feet of muck and with its smokestack almost submerged, it became the wrong kind of photo op. Some people blamed Stanford, as did Peter Aron, who described his attitude as "If you brought it in, God would provide." God came via the Port Authority, whose crane lifted *Mathilda* onto a barge. Its hull had been extensively damaged, but the Seaport chose not to scrap it because the publicity would have hurt its "fund raising campaign for ship maintenance and restoration." The McAllisters were irate and later persuaded the Seaport to give *Mathilda* to the Hudson River Maritime Museum in Kingston, where it became a shore exhibit.[39]

A bittersweet fate also met *Aqua*, the last operating steam lighter. Built in 1918 as *New York Central #29*, it was donated in 1973. Lighters were once ubiquitous in the harbor as they connected east-west railroad traffic to and from New England. Although replaced by intermodal transport and ignored by maritime museums, they showed the real grit of the harbor, as artist John Noble barked, "Welcome Aqua! Thou ain't scrimshaw." Yet "thou ain't seaworthy" was the case because of galvanic deterioration. Fearing it would join *Matilda* below, the Seaport removed its prized high-pressure Scots marine boiler and put *Aqua* in Brooklyn storage in 1977. Stanford even proposed encasing *Aqua's* hull, as well as those of *Hart* and *Mathilda*, in ferro-cement, so that while floating, their inner steel frame could be seen by visitors, but the logistics would have been a nightmare.

Fig. 3.5. Aerial view, looking northwest, with Piers 16, 17, and 18, seaport district (*center*), Alfred E. Smith Houses (*top right*), 1981. (HABS NY-6072-1; photo, Celia Orgel; American Memory Project, Library of Congress)

With the Seaport lacking $80,000 for repairs, *Aqua* was unceremoniously scrapped.[40]

As the heart of the story, these ships—eleven at one time—were planned as a representative sample of New York's harbor in the late nineteenth and early twentieth centuries. Brushing aside the setbacks, the Seaport's ship modeler, Michael Creamer, described the Seaport's impact. "The most significant thing SSSM was doing in the early '70's," he said, "was saving ships. Period. Public awareness of the city's history right in your face; not hidden away in a glass display case uptown somewhere." Though it was "the largest historic fleet ever assembled by any museum anywhere at any time," it was the largest headache too. While Jack Aron controlled and helped finance *Peking*, the rest of the fleet was in disarray, as the ships had been acquired quickly and were generally in poor repair. Moreover, Seaport leadership was overwhelmed by the tide.

By 1976, Stanford confessed to Isbrandtsen, "I am quite ready to step aside from what I regard as a deteriorating and sadly unseamanlike scene." Those ships were the Seaport's raison d'être, but its leaders believed that their financial wherewithal would come from members, philanthropists, and programs.[41]

4

"Look at Our Waterfront! Just Look"

How Earth Day Boomed the Seaport

The tempest of the Sixties and Seventies set the Seaport's context as racial tensions flared, construction workers beat antiwar protestors, countercultures blossomed, minorities and women spoke out, pollution became visible, and cultural alienation, political corruption, and physical degradation were palpable. Crises were everywhere. Movements flourished in behalf of civil and equal rights, the environment, peace, and youth. As the city's old liberal coalition broke apart, it polarized. If the Seaport proclaimed itself as *the people*, the question now was, which people? While Rockefeller dedicated *Ambrose*, Lindsay lunched aboard *Wavertree*, and Galbraith spoke at a fundraiser, Pete Seeger sang at the Seaport, the Friends of the Earth established a headquarters there, and Allen Ginsberg read poetry on Pier 16. As the Seaport's membership approached twenty-five thousand, it became the largest historical society of its kind in America. Two-thirds were regular members (five dollars or more), while the rest were introductory one-dollar members. Stanford estimated that "four out of five dollars [in membership] came from sources that had never before had anything to do with ships or with history." As the Seaport spoke to multiple constituencies, it experimented with programs and policies still debated today.[1]

Rejecting crusty curators and haughty historians, and initially including a staff that proudly had no "prior museum experience," the Seaport redefined the concept of a museum. It rejected rarefied institutions such as Colonial Williamsburg whose "pre-programed 'lessons'" left visitors smug and uncritical. As in the innovative theory of the open classroom, Seaport visitors would encounter its buildings, ships, and artifacts in a "casual, ordinary, almost accidental" manner. Carrying that message in 1970 to the annual meeting of the staid American Association of Museums (AAM), Stanford "met a wall of apathy." But Lindsay's City Hall endorsed the Seaport's role as a stage where city dwellers could build a community.

By then, even landmarks commissar Goldstone championed preservation as "an enormously stabilizing force in a city and in a society that's increasingly rootless and in a state of flux." But, as in any movement, ideas varied. Joan Davidson believed the Seaport was important in a "mass society that threatens to crush us all," while Roger Starr, who as a *Times* editor called for the city's "planned shrinkage," narrowly viewed the Seaport's mission as one to teach the present about the port's harsh past. Radically different was John Young, whose reform agenda opposed commercialism. While acknowledging disparate voices, Robert Ferraro still thought that they "could sing along in perfect harmony with Peter Seeger" because their "motivations and goals were the same."[2]

Personal politics ran the gamut. While a volunteer wanted a haven to "dream of voyaging," a retired mariner who was lost on shore admitted that he needed the Seaport and was soon designated *Wavertree*'s honorary captain. Staff and volunteers also built their own community. Craftsman Michael Creamer recalled "late night gams at the Square Rigger," as others sang chanties. There even was the lonely biologist who placed an ad in the *New York Review of Books* hoping to find a mate who "likes [the] South Street Seaport kind of thing." With many budding waterfront romances, Ferraro jested, "It was as romantic an urban setting as could possibly be imagined, and it *was* the Sixties after all!" Yet prospective mates should worry because, Helen Hayes retorted, "they'll always be competing with ships and had better learn to be satisfied with second place."[3]

To Starr's dismay, the Seaport community included nearby projects whose population he wanted to downsize. In addition to hosting a Girl Mariner troop and Sea Scout Explorers from Chinatown aboard *Ambrose*, the Seaport worked with the Hamilton-Madison Settlement House and the Lower East Side Neighborhood Association. The latter's director especially wanted children to see old-time craftsmen in action. Like NYSCA's Allon Schoener, who berated museums for dodging social issues, Stanford believed that handcrafts would "generate pride and respect too often missing in deprived families." Yet Thomas Hoving, who as director of the Metropolitan Museum hired Schoener to curate its controversial *Harlem on My Mind* exhibit, admitted that his attempt to democratize knowledge backfired. Having none of the Met's cultural baggage, the Seaport, said Philip Yenawine, struck NYSCA as "wonderful, possible, idealistic and crazy."[4]

Fig. 4.1. Block 74E, Schermerhorn Row, looking southeast toward *Peking* at Pier 16 (*left*) and *Wavertree* at Pier 15 (*right*), and Baker, Carver & Morrell Building (*far right*), 1981. Note the still-active Brooklyn piers in the background and the ongoing demolition of Block 74W in the foreground. (HABS NY-6072-2; photo, Walter Smalling Jr.; American Memory Project, Library of Congress)

Evoking "This Museum *Is* People," the Seaport attracted attention. "In an age frequently characterized by alienation and irrelevance," *History News* noted in 1971, "it is rewarding to learn of museums that involve their neighbors and relate their programs to people." *Museum News* likewise encouraged museums to meet the needs of the working class, poor, and minorities. Yet black writer June Jordan bluntly asked if those museums were "another sop to the niggers" to cool the cities during riot-prone summers. A South Street restaurateur sang the praise of the tiny community whose diverse members were "rich in love for one another." Meanwhile, the poor were obvious. "A lot of homeless were living under the anchorage of the bridge," said photographer Barbara Mensch, who moved to a Front Street loft in the late 1970s. The fishmongers gave them scraps, which they cooked on open fires. But one's perspective shaped everything in what Stanford called his "industrial slum," as his telephone calls to prospective supporters played on the authenticity of screeching seagulls fighting for those remains.[5]

"Visitors Looked Down at the Oily, Garbage-Strewn East River": Raising Consciousness by Bringing People to the Waterfront

The environmental movement was another community-building opportunity. Encouraged by the White House Conference on Natural Beauty (1965) and Mike Seymour's role in a "David-and-Goliath victory" over a plan to build a hydroelectric plant on the Hudson, New York shifted. For too long, Manhattan Borough President Percy Sutton noted, the waterfront was a dumping ground where access was blocked by busy highways and rotting piers. Even the regional planning authority wanted people to enjoy the strand, but bureaucratic in-fighting over the waterfront followed. Controlling the piers, the Department of Ports and Terminals was an anachronism. In 1968, its commissioner, Edgar C. Fabber, refused to issue a permit for a visit by the USCG *Eagle*. Inviting reporters to watch and crowds to cheer, Stanford took the ship's lines at Pier 16 in what he proudly called an act of civil disobedience. Some critics felt that Fabber was acting like *Eagle*'s former owner, the Nazis. Launched as *Horst Wessel* and named after a Nazi street thug, it was confiscated in 1946. The barque's gold-painted eagle figurehead was shorn of its swastika before being consigned to the USCG Academy. Soon after, Lindsay issued invitations to other training ships. Visiting often, *Eagle* benefited from the Seaport, as the USCG sought to ensure future sail training.[6]

Pier 16 was difficult to enjoy because of its pollution. The water in New York Harbor, said Joseph Mitchell in 1951, was so fouled that "you could bottle it and sell it for poison." Fulton Street was as bad, with gutters full of everything from beer cans to dead fish. In 1967, Stanford told a reporter that the city was "the most scandalous case" that he knew of "in waterfront neglect." The US government discovered in 1967, for example, that the polluted Arthur Kill, a tidal strait between Staten Island and New Jersey, suffocated test cages of crabs, clams, and fish after a brief submersion. Too many New Yorkers accepted filth as an everyday sight. Urging action, Stanford told the AAM in 1970, "We must learn to live with our natural environment, or it will destroy us through accumulated poisons of our own making." That year, the Seaport published his pamphlet *Look at Our Waterfront! Just Look*, but it was Earth Day in 1970, which was celebrated on either the vernal equinox or April 22, or both, that took the spotlight. In "the largest single demonstration by Americans since V-J Day in 1945," over twenty million Americans celebrated or protested, or did both, and that included the Seaport. In April, volunteers swept streets, the museum mounted an exhibit on pollution, and it held a workshop for teenagers aboard *Caviare*. Because Earth Day gave one youngster optimism, he admitted, "Last year I . . . figured I didn't have very long to live. But now I'm beginning to think maybe I won't die so soon." Appearing twice, Pete Seeger was the honorary chairman of the Seaport's Environment Week.[7]

A friend of Dick Rath, Seeger first sang at South Street to three thousand people in August 1967. Becoming a regular, the folk singer was passionate about the Seaport, calling it "a nice informal place" with enthusiastic people. Known for his progressive politics, he was blacklisted during the McCarthy era, but Stanford extended an open invitation. Seeger had a complex agenda. Maligned in his hometown of Beacon, New York, he was shifting his focus by building the seventy-five-foot *Clearwater*, a USCG-approved replica of a nineteenth-century river sloop. His Hudson River Sloop Restoration would bring "together people who normally don't speak to each other," he said, to clean up the river and rebuild communities. That included conservatives whose funds were needed for *Clearwater*'s $181,933 cost. "There was more acceptance of countercultural types," Stanford recalled, "as the ecology movement caught hold," and Seeger drew diverse audiences to the Seaport. His critics claimed, however, that environmentalism was holding down workers and blacks. Disbelieving friends chided, "Pete's a playboy with a yacht," particularly as he associated with Laurance Rockefeller, an environmentalist who was one of the largest shareholders in the city's major air polluter, Consolidated Edison. Appearing in August with singer Don McLean at the Square Riggers '68 festival, his antiwar songs drew unprecedented crowds. Another Seaport friend and popular folk singer, Burl Ives, sang chanties to children aboard *Caviare* in 1969. Ives donated unreleased audio tapes, and the Seaport issued a record album,

Fig. 4.2. Pete Seeger sings to a lunchtime crowd on Pier 16. (Photo, South Street Seaport Museum)

Songs They Sang in South Street. In a separate fundraising letter noting the Seaport's "severe challenge," Ives asked "people like you" to lend a hand. Yet his differences with Seaport friend Seeger were long and bitter, as Ives told the House Committee on Un-American Activities in 1952 that Seeger was a communist.[8]

On *Clearwater*'s fundraising maiden voyage, it arrived in New York on August 1, 1969, stopping at the Statue of Liberty to pick up Mayor Lindsay, who took the tiller. Singing chanties with Seeger, they docked at Pier 16 alongside the Argentine navy's square-rigged trainer *Libertad*. While David Rockefeller was attending an on-board dinner and Isbrandtsen was speaking to *Libertad*'s crew, Argentina's military junta was crushing liberty-minded protestors. Separating politics from sailing, Stanford and the Seaport also held a dinner for the ship's captain at the NYYC. Without missing a beat, the Seaport hosted *Clearwater*, and the AAM praised Seeger's program. *Clearwater*'s crew held four songfests one August weekend at Pier 16. First mate Gordon Bok led the chanties, while civil-rights leader Rev. Frederick Douglass Kirkpatrick sang "Everybody's Got a Right to Live." Besides the Woody Guthrie favorite "This Land Is Your Land," Seeger sang, "My Dirty Stream," about the million toilets and Glens Falls paper mill spoiling the Hudson. The crew sailed up the Hudson but abandoned ship briefly in mid-August to attend the festival at Woodstock.[9]

In April 1970, Seeger docked at Pier 16 on his way to Washington, D.C. Carrying a jug of polluted East River water, he knew that only the federal government could address the problem. Reformers succeeded in creating the Environmental Protection Agency and passing clean-water legislation, but the harbor would long remain "among the most toxic in the nation." Not surprisingly, "sewage odors intruded harshly" at the Seaport's Waterfront Festival in 1970, the *Sunday News* noted, and "visitors looked down at the oily, garbage-strewn East River from the deck of *Clearwater*." The festival included the Seaport-sponsored Mayor's Cup race. Before Lindsay's arrival, Joseph Cantalupo gathered seventy-five volunteers for a cleanup, stating that the streets belonged to the people. Later, other crews wielded hoses and brooms to scrub the FFM's paving stones, as in 1973 when George Plimpton led a brigade. Not only was he a sports celebrity and *Sports Illustrated* essayist, Plimpton was "the public face of the New York intellectual." In the spirit of a public-private partnership, Economic Development Administrator D. Kenneth Patton joined the cleanup, while Lindsay cheered from the sidelines.[10]

The Vietnam War was on everyone's mind, and in every Seeger songfest. "If You Love Your Uncle Sam (Bring Them Home)" was his most popular tune, as it melded social justice, patriotism, and a stay-at-home policy. While two-thirds of Americans supported Nixon's war policy in late 1969, one of the most notorious prowar rallies was held in 1970 near City Hall by rowdy hard hats who attacked demonstrators. Though South Street gave Seeger "a very warm welcome," he remembered, "the business people objected" to his antiwar songs and did not want him to come back. However, he said, "once after I'd sung a 'controversial' song about peace, Joe Cantalupo came up and shook my hand warmly." Cantalupo told the troubadour, "We mustn't ever forget such things around here."[11]

As the museum sought the succor of wealthy businessmen, any advocacy of hot topics was problematic. In May 1970, two weeks after Nixon's invasion of Cambodia, Stanford expressed his outrage, writing Kortum, "American imperialism in Indochina sickens me to the heart." Invited to speak at the AAM in New York soon after, Stanford flew into a hornet's nest as protesters broke up the first day's meeting. They forced John Hightower, who headed MoMA, to revise his session to examine "War, Racism, and Repression: What Can and Should Museums Do?" Stanford challenged "our technological masters, the McNamaras and Kissingers" who even considered nuclear war. Comparing ancient Athens to modern America, he said,

> The Greeks of Athens were so proud of their technology, which was superb, that they tried impossible things, terrified all their friends until they had none left, destroyed their democracy and their very strong economy which had been the world's wonder, and ended up fighting vainly with bare hands to defend their city. They were up against a brutal, dirty little dictatorship that beat them by outlasting them, while they defeated themselves.
>
> I do hope we can learn in time the things it takes more than a generation to learn. We can't go swashbuckling round our world like Vikings anymore, or we'll destroy both it and ourselves. We've got to stop being stupid and provocative. We must listen carefully to young people who see things we do not, to think of other men, and be resolute in proportion as we decide who we really are and what we really want—which, I submit, we're some way yet from soundly deciding.[12]

At the Seaport, Stanford provided a platform for Seeger and his troupe to voice that critique. *Clearwater* came to port for an entire week in 1971 and helped organize a Memorial Day festival, which was traditionally a day of military remembrance but was being redefined by dissenting veterans and *Clearwater* singers. Eliciting "mass participation in choruses," Thom Parrott, for example, sang his "Hudson's Name Was Henry, but the River Is a John" along with a song based on A. J. Muste's "There Is No Way to Peace; Peace Is the Way." Pier 16 concerts were at times rehearsals for Greenwich Village, as in June 1971, when a weekend included Seeger, McLean, and David Bromberg. During the week, said Creamer, Pier 16 goers "could mingle with the masters of the universe and listen to Don McLean busking 'Bye, Bye Miss American Pie' at lunch time." Those buskers were keeping *Clearwater* afloat, as its yearly upkeep was $100,000.[13]

"One of the Few Places Where Pedestrians Could Enjoy NY's Island-ness": Earth Day as Everyday at Pier 16

With *Clearwater* and the Seaport facing a money crunch, they added loca-vore to their strategy by marketing Hudson Valley victuals, such as shad in the spring and pumpkins in the fall. Seeger gradually drifted away from *Clearwater* because of differences with his trustees, as was the case with Stanford. Seeger still voiced his belief that a concerted effort was neces-sary for social change. "Old-time sailors knew," he wrote in *Sea History*, "that some mighty heavy jobs could be done if enough people hauled in rhythm upon a rope. And we know that the strongest ropes are only made up of tiny fibers which are only strong because they are in close contact with each other. May our four billion humans get in ever closer contact with each other, knowing our common past. Then we, and history, will have a future."[14]

Pier 16's events, which boosted attendance to over a million people in 1972, spurred Lindsay to propose programs for unused wharfs. A few had once included recreational facilities, but they closed with World War II. There were thirty-six city-owned piers on the Hudson, reported Mitchell Moss in 1976, but none handled ship cargo and more than two-thirds were vacant or used for parking. Lindsay's proposal, which Albany approved in 1970, angered those who wanted a working, not a recreational, water-front. The International Longshoremen's Association did not picket the Seaport, but it did other docks, charging that the city was undercutting jobs in the world's second-busiest port. Partisanship ensued as prominent Democrats supported the pickets. While Lindsay had privatized Piers 15 and 16 by requiring that the Seaport lease and repair them, he spent mil-lions rebuilding Upper West Side docks "to appease the longshoreman's union." Ann Satterthwaite, an urban planner, later criticized the Seaport, telling the National Trust that US waterfronts were artificial places with Pete Seeger sing-ins and embalmed museums. Philip Yenawine countered that the Seaport was "one of the few places at the time where pedestrians could enjoy NY's island-ness, its port life."[15]

The city's 578-mile shoreline, which Mayor Ed Koch noted was "longer than all the waterfronts of Seattle, San Francisco, and Boston combined," developed within that tension between work and recreation. Though Pier

16 lacked railings, thus alarming insurers, it was a centerpiece for Earth Day in the early 1970s. Its vibes were groovy. Even in its ban on smoking (anything), which it could not enforce, the Seaport wanted its directives to "be phrased in a friendly, non-dictatorial manner." It was the venue for concerts, featuring folk artist Odetta singing in 1972 on the "pollution of the spirit of man," and speakers, such as anthropologist Margaret Mead, who asked her audience in 1973 "to give the Earth the same kind of loving care a mother gives to a new born baby." There were exhibits on geodesic domes and electric cars, displays by the Sierra Club and Zero Population Growth, and if the weather was good, "youths in Army surplus gear" and "the chant of 'Hare Krishna' mingled with conga drums and bagpipes."[16]

David Brower, who became a top environmentalist, moved to the district in 1972. Three years earlier, he had been forced out as the Sierra Club's first executive director by lumber, chemical, and oil interests. After he turned down Seymour's offer to head the Natural Resources Defense Council, which Seymour had conceived and focused on public-interest litigation, he founded Friends of the Earth and rented space from the Seaport for his New York branch. Though the district was four miles distant from his UN campaigning, he hoped to build it into an environmental center. His motto, "Think globally, act locally," fit to a tee that of Stanford and Seeger. John McConnell also briefly headquartered his Earth Society at the Seaport and served as "ecological specialist for the museum." A founder of Earth Day, designer of the Earth Flag, and organizer (with Frank Braynard) of Sea Citizens, McConnell was also campaigning on behalf of Earth Day at the UN.[17]

At the Seaport, Earth Day and National Maritime Day shared a similar focus by the early 1970s. Set on May 22 by Congress in 1933 to honor the nation's sea heritage and the Atlantic crossing of SS *Savannah* in 1819, National Maritime Day had been celebrated by advocates of trade and shipping. In 1968, the Seaport had mourned the decline of US-flagged and US-built vessels, but in 1970 its focus shifted to environmentalism. While its second Riverboat Ball attracted a "really unusual amalgam" of people and music, it recast National Maritime Day as Sea Day with "a protest against seaborne pollution and waterfront decay." The Seaport's activities included a sail to its auxiliary project, the Alice Austen House on Staten Island, a 1690s Dutch farmhouse that the photographer turned into a Victorian cottage. For the voyage, Stanford assembled a small flotilla around the Army Corps of Engineers' cleanup vessel *Driftmaster*. Aboard were not only MAS president Mrs. Louis Auchincloss and Margot Gayle but parks commissioner August Heckscher, who acquired the house for the public. Thereafter, Sea Day promoted maritime culture, ecology, and sail training.[18]

"No Pink Bermuda Shorts or Boat Neck Sweaters in This Crowd": Taking Drug Addicts and Wayward Youth to Sea

One spinoff of the Seaport's activism was the Pioneer program, whose meteoric rise in 1971 mirrored the Seaport's promise and pitfalls. Earlier marine schools had varied remarkably. While a state training ship had evolved into the State University of New York at Fort Schuyler in the Bronx, the city relocated its maritime-trades high school in 1946 to the Liberty ship *John W. Brown* at Pier 42 on the Hudson. Organized labor maintained its own schools. Kortum suggested that the National Maritime Union send a group of students to the Seaport, but they "wouldn't take orders" from its foreman, a former union president. Dick Rath then spawned a unique program for *Pioneer* in 1970. With him on an eight-day *Pioneer* voyage was George Matteson, whose mother made *Pioneer's* donation possible. Rath told him of his dreams. "An ardent believer in the Kipling story *Captains Courageous* and the sail training disciplines of Irving Johnson," Rath envisioned *Pioneer*, said Matteson, "as an opportunity to apply his faith in the sea as a social curative to the problem of inner city drug addiction and the racial biases which he understood to be their root cause." The details were sketchy, he added, but "the idea was compelling." Stanford hesitated to support it because he worried that the Seaport's more conservative backers would be disturbed by including inner-city youth.[19]

In 1971, Rath's idea became the Pioneer Sail Training School. It was "a first-of-its-kind educational program sponsored by a maritime museum working in cooperation with an agency of city government." Funded partly by the Vincent Astor Foundation, Rath entered into an agreement with the Addiction Services Agency (ASA). Relying on "a very potent doctrine of drug abstinence, peer pressure, and mental discipline to combat inner city heroin addiction," the ASA used encounter groups to psychologically reform addicts. Tacking in support, Stanford predicted it would teach

them not only discipline but "their own place in the succeeding generations." Shari Galligan Johnson, a Vermont teacher who joined the crew at
twenty dollars a week, also felt she "could change the world," but her role
as cook "didn't speak to the [era's] women's liberation."[20]

Matteson took command of *Pioneer* but, being close to Greenwich Village, had to first reclaim the ship from half a dozen squatters. Joined by
two counselors and fifteen young men, the group's sail in June was hardly
the Love Boat, as the crew had a plastic bucket for a toilet, pipe-frame
bunks in the hold, and a meal plan of pasta or rice and beans. Matteson
was terrified by the experiment, but there were lighter moments, as when
their "spontaneous jam session" with pots, pans, and wooden spoons
prompted curious boats off Nantucket to circle around. Sailing in 1971
on six two-week cruises, they were joined by deckhand Walter Rybka.
Born in Brooklyn and raised in the suburbs, he returned after graduating
from Macalester College in 1972. With the cheerful optimism of so many
people, he relished his "adventure in urban homesteading, living by 19th
century standards of pay and working conditions." An adventure it was,
because after four or five days, Matteson said, "the atmosphere on board
would be allowed to become quite poisonous until everyone could see
that something had to be done, at which time the counselors would call
for an 'encounter group' and everybody would set to yelling, shrieking,
and crying until things got resolved. Some would say that the experience
reminded them of being in jail."[21]

But Matteson saw another problem. While sail-training programs and
Kurt Hahn's Outward Bound strove to polish the virtues of manliness, initiative, and responsibility of their young participants, "it was Dick Rath's
conception to apply those middle class canards to the inner city." What followed was, said Johnson, "boredom, loneliness and depression," which led
counselors to teach them how to deal with those emotions without drugs.
A nineteen-year-old, first-time sailor from Brooklyn admitted, "Our big
therapeutic is telling each other what it is like. We talk about our problems
and how to solve them to help each other and those that come after us."
Working on board, they learned, said Pioneer School head David Brink,
"to pull their own weight." The program even included an all-female voyage, which, Matteson thought, proved more satisfactory because they were
"much more receptive to organizing themselves into a cooperative group."
Running three years, each voyage included a new batch of ex-offenders,

Fig. 4.3. Capt. George Matteson (*left*) and first mate Walter Rybka (*right*) aboard *Pioneer*, 1973. (Photo, Shari Galligan Johnson)

counselors, and Matteson, Rybka, and Johnson. Described as blond and beautiful, Johnson was treated like a lady, but "it didn't hurt" that she "had a 130 pound German Shepherd who slept next" to her bunk. Still, her total lack of privacy was trying.[22]

Other conflicts occurred over the ship's role. The ship participated in various festivals to publicize the Seaport, but Matteson disliked the public-relations scheduling, recognizing, he said, "a constant low level friction between our mission, our passengers, and the general public." Since the program was composed of approximately "50% black, 25% Hispanic, and 25% Caucasian," the "afros, scars, funky inner city clothing (no pink Bermuda shorts or boat neck sweaters in this crowd!) stuck out like a sore thumb under any conditions." Though the young adults were willing to speak to audiences about their former addiction and the curative powers of meaningful work, he wanted nothing to do with events where they would be "embarrassed by either sanctimonious appreciation or (once in a very great while) overt hostility." There was conflict, as when a vacationing family in a cabin cruiser came on board and the husband bluntly told him, "I work two jobs, I pay my taxes, I take a week off once a year so I can take my family on vacation on my little boat over there; and these guys here walk out of jail and get a free two week cruise? I just don't get it." Matteson and Stanford also had differing perspectives—what Stanford called a "sit down" strike in 1971 "because the crew refused to face the indignity of hard, drilled labor to get [Pioneer] under way," Matteson remembered differently. Attempting to make "a fund raising cocktail party" that Stanford had arranged on Martha's Vineyard, he realized that contrary winds made an on-time arrival impossible except by an all-night sail. Not wanting his tired crew to be "inspected like animals in a zoo," he arrived a day late, but "the prospective benefactress . . . cold shouldered the whole event" because "there were negroes on board." Stanford's strike was a captain's decision not to subject his crew "to gawkers."[23]

The Pioneer program received lavish media praise. With a photograph on the front page of the *Times* and the center page of the *Daily News*, as well as accolades on radio and television, the program generated publicity and donations. As a promotion, the Seaport commissioned a half-hour documentary, *Pioneer Lives* (1974), narrated by actor Stacy Keach with music by Richard Fewtrell. A local TV program dispatched "a young, driven, budding reporter," Geraldo Rivera, for a piece on the schooner. Along with generating publicity, Brink courted philanthropist Roberta Brooke Astor, who headed the Vincent Astor Foundation (VAF). In a late-season sail around Manhattan, she was joined by a Vanderbilt, a Rockefeller, and other aristocrats. With Matteson at *Pioneer*'s helm and Rybka as his first mate, Creamer and the crew were disparaging their "underpowered Lister engine" as Matteson navigated treacherous waters. "The cream of NY's 400 were enjoying their champagne and shrimp and remarking on the bracing effect of the weather and its salubrious effect on one's appetite." Yet, pulled toward broken pilings near Sputen Duyvil, said Creamer, Matteson had to retreat and try again. By the third try, even Astor noticed something was amiss.

> As the splintered piling loomed up I knew we were going to catch our bowsprit between two of them and be opened up like a tin of tuna, drowning

all our benefactors, the Museum and the School in one fell swoop. Terror struck, I heard a calm voice say in a most relaxed tone, "Walter, back the fore stays'l, please!" Walter shook off his paralyzing fears and took three giant steps to make the 60 feet from his post at the Main Sheet to perform the order and we slid by the fatal piling by inches.[24]

Astor gave a $250,000 grant for three years. Often emphasizing self-help community development, her VAF, said Brink, became "the mainstay of our unrestricted programs." Her interest was familial, as John Jacob Astor had lived at the seaport and worked for Bowne & Company before becoming America's first recognized millionaire. Quoting a Thornton Wilder character, she joked, "Money is like manure; it's not worth a thing unless it's spread around." Becoming the doyen of high society, who contributed $195 million to Gotham projects before closing the VAF in 1997, she was so highly regarded that she gave "a special imprimatur" to causes she favored. Soon after, Brink redefined the Pioneer program, however. As Matteson explained, its youth were drug-free, but "had criminal records, little or no education, and no employment history or job skills." If they did not have work, the ghetto and its drugs "would inevitably reclaim them." With the help of Astor, who visited the Seaport "dressed to the nines, complete with hat and gloves," Brink shifted to a pier-based, vocational program aboard *Maj. Gen. Hart.*[25]

"It Bears Out the Plain Truth That Jobs Work Better than Jails": Retraining Addicts for the Modern Sea Trades

The Pioneer Sail Training School was phased out by mid-1973 and replaced by the Pioneer Marine School (PMS), which opened in September 1972. As *Boating's* editor, Rath often heard of manufacturers' need for tradesmen to service their engines. Helped along by Peter Smyth, editor of *Motor Boating and Sailing*, who himself was "a very committed recovering alcoholic," Rath began PMS, a technical school that would help inner-city former addicts, aged seventeen to thirty-one, become self-reliant citizens by learning marine repair and construction. After a plan failed to convert *Maj. Gen. Hart* into an ice cream parlor, PMS students refitted the empty ferry's automobile bays into work areas. The Seaport also acquired two steel-covered barges for welding and woodworking shops, with equipment donated by the marine industry. Its first class graduated at the National Boat Show in January 1973 and was featured on NBC's *Today Show* and in the syndicated press. While the unemployment rate for recovering addicts elsewhere stood at 60 percent, PMS consistently found jobs for its graduates at East Coast marinas because of its pre-screening and industry help.[26]

Hired by Rath, David C. Brink headed the school. Described in the press as "a young, bearded, pigtailed, sharp-eyed man who dresses mainly in jeans and a denim shirt," he graduated from Hobart College and worked nine years in public relations for a yacht manufacturer. He had, said Creamer, "a New Age outlook" and carried in his bag what he needed for "a trip round the world," including "a copy of Wilhelm's 'I Ching.'" He was a masterful communicator, very imaginative, and a good problem solver, added Matteson, and "he was no hippy." Hoping to help ghetto youth escape gang culture, he thought that marine jobs would allow them to relocate out of the city. The PMS saved young men such as a twenty-three-year-old veteran who drifted after six years in Vietnam and was repeatedly jailed. "Unlike a lot of the half-baked job training programs," opined the approving *Daily News*, "this one has a waiting line of employers eager to hire graduates." Anxious for a photo op, Lindsay visited the school to shake hands.[27]

With this success, the PMS established the Pioneer Restoration Program under the Addiction Services Agency, which was administered by the nonprofit Wildcat Service Corporation. With students on methadone maintenance or on parole, each received a sixty-dollar weekly stipend from the federal Office of Economic Opportunity. The PMS expanded its curriculum with sixteen weeks of carpentry, boat repair, and welding, including work aboard *Wavertree*, and with twelve weeks on small boat repair. Though criticized as costing as much as an Ivy League tuition, it was still half the cost of prison. Boasted Lindsay, it "bears out the plain truth that jobs work better than jails." Without it, said a Harlem man, he would be on the street still on drugs. The program faced rough seas in 1974 as more students enrolled through the federally funded, city-run Comprehensive Employment Training Administration. Though CETA's annual $500,000 to $700,000 funding was more reliable revenue, it brought in some "middle class slackers and edgy single moms who were," said Matteson, not interested in marine jobs. Problems also followed when Wildcat failed to screen applicants. Smyth objected because "students were taken 'right off the street,' [and] given free methadone and $100 for a 35-hour work-study week." He alleged that "on the street Wildcat is known as the Plantation, . . . a WPA for junkies." Unlike the sail-training school's abstinence regimen, Wildcat's program led to a high rate of absenteeism, quitting, or even relapse into heroin.[28]

A rift occurred between the Addiction Services Agency, Wildcat, and the Seaport. After the school's staff—who were craftsmen, not social workers—were physically threatened in the classroom, chief instructor Don Archer complained but found no resolution, saying, "It was harder to fight the [city] bureaucracy than teach school." Smyth blamed the students. Thinking that they preferred a government handout over education and lacked discipline and motivation, he claimed, "They act like they're doing you a favor to sit in the classroom." Yet Rybka noted that behavior problems were aggravated by the fact that "too many of the students couldn't read the engine manufacturer's shop manuals," which were "written on a third grade reading level." With the Seaport facing its own financial and leadership crises, it initiated staff layoffs, leading others to resign. Conditions improved after the school changed the composition of applicants by requiring them to be free of drugs for six months and to pass reading, math, and mechanical tests. Finally, after the social experiment ended and the school was opened to any city resident, it achieved a 70 percent graduation rate. As such, Brink told the *Times*, it was "one of the most successful manpower training centers in the city." But that was still below CETA's required 75 percent. Ignoring CETA's "arbitrary quota," Brink "fudged the numbers." Though fearing jail himself, he felt vindicated that more than half of PMS's graduates were "viably employed" five years later.[29]

Brink's challenge-the-Establishment idealism characterized much of the Seaport's public program—the Seeger songfests, the environmental consciousness-raising, the open-classroom experiments, and the Pioneer School. But its success depended on winning the necessary friends and philanthropists to support its programs. Melding unconventional backers, such as City Hall's antidrug campaign and *Clearwater*'s concertgoers, with more traditional supporters, such as Brooke Astor and the *Times* editorial board, the Seaport revealed how the spirit of the late 1960s was redefining America. The museum became a platform for reformers who demanded major changes in the nation's society, economy, and foreign policy. In so doing, the Seaport pushed the boundaries of what history museums did, and it encouraged others to follow suit.

5

"A Million People Came Away Better Human Beings"

How the Past Mended the Present

As the Pioneer program made national news, the Seaport drew New Yorkers to the district, taught them their history, and linked the city's past and present. Even before the twin towers topped off at 110 stories in 1971, the two ends of Fulton Street were symbiotically joined. As the Seaport swelled, its captains made sky-high predictions that its membership would reach one hundred thousand, thereby rivaling the National Trust, and would berth two dozen ships at six piers. Ordained by Lindsay, blessed by the Rockefellers, and featured as Lower Manhattan's tourist draw, it was visited by a million people in 1971. The *Times* wrote, they all "came away better human beings." The Seaport predicted that they would put their "own lives in better perspective—understanding the progress that has been made; appreciating what it has cost us; glad that we have cast some things out of our way of living; and, perhaps, striving to retrieve some other things lost along the way."[1]

Meanwhile, the Seaport was facing centrifugal forces within its coalition. While its supporters were going in different directions with architectural, ship, or neighborhood preservation, and often doing so with a single-minded purpose, the nucleus was Stanford, who most wanted public involvement in these initiatives to revive the city. Yet the Seaport had contradictory responsibilities to develop the land and preserve its neighborhood. Its proximity to Wall Street and City Hall ensnared it in their agendas. In 1968, Urban Deadline had proposed noncommercial uses, but the Seaport turned to architect Thomas Van Arkel for help. First articulated in *A Proposal to Recreate the Historic "Street of Ships"* (1967), the Seaport Plan envisioned museum facilities, restored buildings, and ships near the Row. In 1968, Van Arkel introduced an architectural model that showed the Seaport's restored area as Blocks 96W and 97E, half of 97W and 74W, and Piers 15, 16, and 17 (see figs. 2.1 and 2.2). While Block

96E would encompass a reconstructed FFM, half of 74E would hold NYSMM in Schermerhorn Row. Atop an enlarged Pier 18 would be a shipyard. In 1969, however, the Board of Estimate only approved the Seaport's plan for Blocks 74E, 96E, and 96W, which the Port Authority called the "costliest real estate on earth." City Hall still wanted to transfer the air rights of those restored blocks to the rest of the urban renewal district and build residential high-rises. Stark contrasts resulted. On Block 96W, an attractive 1840s row would be preserved on Water Street, but opposite on Block 75 a monotonous thirty-two-story office tower (1969) was erected at 200 Water Street by Emery Roth. Directly to the east was Block 74W. Eminently worth saving were its five partly preserved structures on Front Street, dating from 1806 to 1818, and the ten-story Green Coffee Exchange, a turn-of-the-century Romanesque. Yet, when the Atlas-McGrath deal was struck to save Schermerhorn Row, museum architect Bronson Binger admitted, "none of us paid [74W] much attention." After most of Block 74W was leveled for a tall office tower, whose construction was planned for 1980, he said, "parking lots are more profitable than old buildings."[2]

Again, when the museum accepted the city's 1969 development plan, the west side of Water Street in Block 98 was written off. Charles Evans Hughes III volunteered to survey the block. A former MAS president and grandson of the famous chief justice, he was a Skidmore, Owings & Merrill architect. While preserving a Block 96W row, he knew that "an almost identical building waiting for the wrecker's ball" stood catercorner in Block 98. Chock-full of intact, worthy buildings, Block 107E became more controversial. A row on Peck Slip, which the *Times*'s Ada Louise Huxtable prized, had mostly fallen in 1962. While Seaport architectural adviser Jim Fitch wanted to restore a row of eight antebellum buildings fronting the river, Consolidated Edison bought the block for a substation. Shamed by the 1965 blackout, Con Ed needed good PR. On Stanford's initiative, a deal was reached in which it gave the last Peck Slip building (the Ward house) to the Seaport and preserved remote Dover Street but demolished the rest. What followed was either a farce or a face-lift. On the substation's wall, Richard Haas painted a one-hundred-foot trompe l'oeil of an antebellum house and a Brooklyn Bridge arcade. Huxtable preferred "reality over illusion." Thinking that the mural represented the Seaport's sellout, she insisted, "there is never any substitute for the real thing."[3]

Fig. 5.1. Filling a row demolished in 1962, Con Ed contracted artist Richard Haas to paint a trompe l'oeil on the wall of its substation at Peck Slip; the sole survivor of the Row, the Jasper Ward house, is at the far right, 2006. (Photo, author)

Public appreciation of the *real* Seaport was slow in coming. With its decay, odor, and trash, the *Post* called it "one of the rattiest looking sections remaining on Manhattan island." But shabby appearances could be deceiving, Huxtable warned, because even "a diamond can be passed over easily in the dirt." Relishing the juxtaposition of eras and forms, she thought that Schermerhorn Row was one of the "few places left where classical red brick stands against a theatrical backdrop of towering steel and glass." Even within museum ranks, perspectives varied. Ship lovers such as Jack Aron could be "the knock 'em down, build 'em up" type. Yet antimodernism was deeply rooted in the preservation movement. Terry Walton, the *Reporter*'s editor, confessed her fondness for "old bricks warmed by sunlight" or a building's "ghost markings." She asked, "How do you confess to a stranger that you've always loved the grass growing up out of Schermerhorn Row eaves?" But volunteer Marie Lore discovered more. "There was one dark night when I opened a door of one [portable toilet], and heard a noise within, so [I] apologized to the occupant, and waited outside for my turn," she told Karl Kortum. But, lo and behold, the "door opened and a pier rat scurried out!" That was the *real* Seaport, for as Lewis Mumford said of

Jane Jacobs's perspective, "the sidewalk, the street, and the neighborhood, in all their higgledy-piggledy unplanned casualness, are the very core of a dynamic urban life."[4]

"To Introduce the Ordinary Person of Today to His Predecessor": Putting Everyman in a Vernacular Landscape

Initially the Seaport Museum conceived of the district as a collection of small museums working to attract the resources necessary to reclaim the endangered buildings. Hoping to sign on affiliated museums that would focus individually on city fires, family shipping, folk art, whaling, or ocean-ography, Stanford thought the district would become a collective where, if necessary, a two-thirds vote of the museums would enforce the common will. But that did not happen. In addition, Stanford wanted to introduce modern commerce into most of the district, especially restaurants that prompted visitors to "engage in revelry." Such gaiety would "help wipe out that funereal reverence for the past which enables you to bury it without ever having understood it."[5]

The Seaport's presentation of history was slow in developing. While praising Kortum's "1st class scholarship . . . about things that happened to real people," Stanford criticized "the Eminences Grise" of Mystic Sea-port. He called their idealized architectural landscape and waterfront a "Disneyland-by-the-Sea" and their program a lot of phony "rhetoric about Americanism, the Flag, and the Sea." He regarded Colonial Williamsburg's re-created town and educational program in the same vein. However, Stanford cast earlier South Streeters in larger-than-life terms because he thought that "words and deeds were bolder" in an earlier day as people "talked with a salt savor to their words, a wholeness and bite in discourse." But as the era's new social history was mining neglected sources to show "history from the bottom up" to include workers, blacks, and women, Stanford stood with the old guard. "We thought little of social historians who took self-indulgent pleasure in pitying the seamen of the day as vic-tims of an oppressive society," he wrote, as he urged that those historians be pushed "back into the gutter [they'd] been muckraking in." Favoring empiricism, Stanford "rejected most 'interpretive' wisdom" as unsound.[6]

Because Stanford was absorbed by endless crises, the Seaport hired Ellen Fletcher Rosebrock as a historian in 1972. Authoring articles in the

Reporter, booklets, and walking tours that explored the area's largely forgotten history, she brought to bear her historic-preservation training at Columbia University and her work on the LPC. She regarded the worn stone steps, faded signs, and rusty doorknobs as "the frame on which history is hung," and, to tell the district's history, she searched little-used written records. In *Counting-house Days in South Street* (1975), she focused on merchants, tradesmen, and craftsmen, about which, a reviewer noted, "practically nothing has been written." Unlike elite histories, Rosebrock focused on "people going about everyday lives . . . in buildings left for us to use today." As the Bicentennial of the American Revolution approached, her success led to more ambitious tasks. She wrote *Farewell to Old England: New York in Revolution* (1976), whose text and exhibit focused on the elite loyalist merchant Isaac Low, the radical patriot Isaac Sears, and Captain Joseph Rose, a merchant who "was more interested in the details of his life and work than he was in politics." Unlike in Virginia, New York's great diversity, noted Rosebrock, "earned it a reputation for political instability." Her intent was to see not so much "what happened" but how it led to "the magnificence of the 19th century seaport."[7]

The Seaport showed that through its innovative Sidewalk History Project, becoming "a museum without walls," whereby the entire district was its canvas. Rooted in Stanford's belief that the Seaport should be "broken into manageable bits that can be encountered and entered into casually," the Seaport would be so unlike "overwhelming collections that generate awe but little relevance to life today." Through posters and placards using nineteenth-century materials and styles, it introduced pedestrians to everything from "Waterfront Dives" to "Warehouse Cats." Highlighting the 1815–65 era, curators developed a two-dollar portfolio that included a thirty-two-page booklet, an 1850 boardinghouse census, and a Mariner's Church minister's diary entry. As it melded professional and public history, historian Thomas Bender found the portfolio "extremely interesting and well done," as "it presents local and urban social history to young people (and adults) in what seems to be just the right way." Indeed, it was a world apart from the Irving Trust's glossy magazine, which informed readers that South Street's earlier residents "had little in common with the good-humored sailors created by Gilbert and Sullivan or the swashbuckling heroes of movie sagas." Instead, they were, like the 1960s hippie stereotype, "ignorant, unshaven, dirty and ragged, [and] they lounged around in

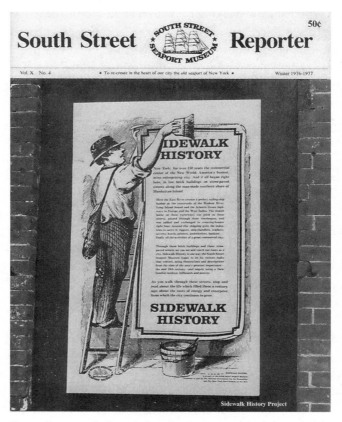

Fig. 5.2. "As you walk through these streets, stop and read about the life which filled them a century ago, about the roots of energy and enterprise from which the city still continues to grow" (Sidewalk History, *South Street Reporter* [Winter 1976–77]). (Photo, Anthony Dean)

small groups on corners." In contrast, Sidewalk History broke stereotypes by making those sailors real.[8]

With the Seaport's success, it was designated a centerpiece of the Bicentennial celebration in New York City. Speaking to dignitaries aboard *Wavertree* on September 28, 1972, David Mahoney, chairman of the national commission, was impressed by the sight of "Wall Street office workers chipping paint" on *Ambrose* and "young people from the city's ghettos" hauling *Pioneer's* halyards. It was "truly a model to the nation." Aboard *Wavertree*, Mary Lindsay hoisted the signal of the colonial independence struggle, "Unite or Perish." Ironically, on that day American diplomats in Paris were opposing a united and independent Vietnam. The Bicentennial celebration kicked off on April 22, 1974, with a re-creation of the New York Tea Party. In December 1973, Bostonians had reenacted theirs with an impressive, albeit fake, ship, but the show was stolen by the Peoples' Bicentennial Commission, an unaffiliated grassroots group. Protesting Nixon's imperial presidency, they dumped empty oil barrels into the water, shouting "Down with King Richard." Because New York State's Bicentennial corporation had no funds for programming, the city was forced to stage a low-budget affair. Visiting schoolchildren said that protestors in 1774 had thrown "a lot of garbage into the water," and they should call it "the New York garbage party." The Seaport brought in Pete Seeger to sing revolutionary songs; students aboard *Clearwater* threw "Tea" crates into the river, but they were tied to lines for easy retrieval. Woody Guthrie's "This Land Is Your Land" was poignantly sung at Federal Hall, opposite the New York Stock Exchange. The *Times* quipped that the song "might seem revolutionary on Wall Street," but passersby paid little attention. Another musical protest followed in 1975 when the Sierra Club staged its "Teaparty: Save the Whales!" at Pier 16. Saving global profits was David Rockefeller's mission, however, as he celebrated "the men and the spirit of South Street" that forged "the bonds of commerce" across the seas. So the exhibit, "Farewell to England," asked visitors to ask themselves "what stand they might have taken in these years, two centuries ago, when the outcome of rebellion and war was far from certain."[9]

The Mafia asked the same question when the mob-controlled fish workers union and its head, Carmine Romano, organized the Fulton Fish Market Bicentennial Committee. The committee held a street fair during Op Sail 76, but it required vendors to buy a permit, costing up to $450, to operate on city-owned streets. As the US district attorney discovered, reluctant vendors were threatened with physical violence. While a Mafia soldier boasted that the heads of uncooperative vendors "would be 'crushed like watermelons,'" another drove a truck over the stand of a seller without a permit. That vendor was an undercover police officer. Museum workers felt "intimidated by hoodlums." Usually the Mafia operated at night, and in the morning their enemies might be "found in cars with a bullet through the head." Yet, said Stanford, "the district was VERY safe" for civilians.[10]

During the Bicentennial, tourists roamed the "museum without walls." Their guidebooks were Rosebrock's *Walking Around in South Street* (1974) and *South Street: A Photographic Guide to New York City's Historic Seaport* (1977). Both reflected the author's strength in everyday architecture and interest in social history. Some visitors preferred the museum's *South Street: The Story of the "Street of Ships" in Pictures and Words* (1977) by Lynne Waller, which was short on the "rootless and impulsive" sailors, except to say that they showed "team work, brute strength, and sheer courage." In a typical top-down story, Waller ranked nineteenth-century shipmasters "among the grand figures in all history." Nudging downtown business leaders lacking civic-mindedness, Waller applauded earlier merchants as "the pillars of society" who "were well aware of their stature in and responsibility to the community." They inspired their clerks, who, as in "the days of Horatio Alger," followed in their footsteps.[11]

Tour guides highlighted forgotten buildings. Some were five-story Greek Revival commercial edifices, such as three warehouses (1835–36) at 207–11 Water Street, where the Seaport placed its model shop and Bowne Printing Shop. They were "among the best buildings of their type left in New York." Tours included the Abiel Abbot Low & Brothers building at 167–71 John Street, which NYSMM had planned to demolish. The Low Building (1849–50), once strikingly handsome but long shorn of its brownstone, was left with, said Stanford, "a cheap-looking stucco façade." The Lows not only brought "the finest silks, porcelains, spices and teas" from the East but also traded opium in China. The building became a photo op for New York's modern China connection. In 1980, historian Marshall Davidson optimistically noted that US trade with China began favorably, but a tally of freighters entering the harbor from China soon revealed a trade deficit. In 1984, China's ambassador boarded *Peking* to celebrate the two hundredth anniversary of US-China trade, which began with the departure of *Empress of China* from New York.[12]

Once abutting Schermerhorn Row, Codwise Row had stood at the corner of South Street and Burling Slip but was demolished for a parking lot and gas station (1956). Across the slip at 170 John Street was Baker, Carver & Morrell Row (1840), named for a ship chandler firm whose own Water Street building had fallen to street widening. Declared a city landmark in 1968, the row boasted a granite façade, a feature that became "virtually extinct" with urban renewal. To set a dramatic contrast, Rosebrock's guidebook urged visitors to see 127 John Street, a behemoth built in 1969–71 on the edge of the urban renewal district. Besides its being "fun to look at," visitors could walk though its "blue-lighted tunnel of corrugated metal," which suggested *2001: A Space Odyssey*, and "check watches against the billboard-size digital clock" on the façade. Old-timers felt Alvin Toffler's "future shock."[13]

Located at 273 Water Street, the Captain Joseph Rose house (1773) was the third oldest in Manhattan. One block south of the long-ago-demolished first presidential mansion of George Washington, the Rose house was earmarked for high-rises, but Stanford realized it was worthy of preservation. After its sale in 1807, the house declined in what became Sailortown. Left unmentioned in the walking tour was its later history, when Kit Burns, a founder of the Dead Rabbits gang, set up Sportsman's Hall in the 1860s and hundreds wagered in his amphitheater on animal fights. Opportunistically, Burns also rented the building for a religious revival in 1868, attended by uptown voyeurs intrigued by "the wickedest ward in the city." The neighborhood burned in an 1878 fire, with some storytellers blaming rats gnawing on matchsticks, but the Rose house survived to become a reformatory for waterfront magdalenes. Jacob Riis used the ward's tenements to illustrate *How the Other Half Lives* (1890). In 1976, however, the empty house was inadvertently burned by squatters but, unlike Sailortown, was later rebuilt. Those omissions in the guidebook set a pattern of sidestepping much of the district's lurid history; Rosebrock said in *Walking Around in South Street*, "a kind of raffishness replaced earlier commercial opulence, and . . . parochial somnolence began to replace the bustle and world-wide outlook of an earlier age."[14]

The Seaport, capitalizing on its setting within the FFM, recruited raconteur Joseph Mitchell. Beginning an eight-year term on the Seaport's restoration committee in 1972, he emphasized the district's recent history. Author of *Bottom of the Harbor* (1959) and many short stories in the *New Yorker*, he captured the "the fringes of life" in the 1940s neighborhood. Though he worried that the museum was romanticizing the district, he spoke at Seaport meetings and collected curios with Joseph Cantalupo for the museum. As John Hightower recalled, "Each had a fascination for the bottom of the harbor. . . . Mitchell was the acute, sensitive observer; Cantalupo knew the territory and its motley denizens like a chess master knows his board and its pieces." The Seaport cemented their bond. Mitchell's

fictional account "Old Mr. Flood" set the human scene with an endear-
ing story of a nonagenarian who lived in a residential hotel on Peck Slip
and frequented the fish market. Said the essayist Phillip Lopate, Mitchell
became "one of the gods of American nonfiction" but was "largely forgotten." The Seaport proposed gentrifying his Meyer's Hotel but did not mention the poor Mr. Floods living in the district's last SRO hotel.[15]

Fun, Diversity, Excitement, and Life Downtown: Making the Seaport Groovy

As Jakob Isbrandtsen told the National Trust, the Seaport welcomed busi-
nesses. Evoking the halcyon days of 1851, the Bowne Printing Shop on
Water Street, for example, was its first landside project. It was privately cre-
ated, funded, and maintained by trustee Ted Stanley, president of Bowne
& Company Stationers, "the oldest incorporated business in the country."
The shop became a convenient prop. Celebrating its own bicentennial,
it opened in 1975 with NBC's *Today Show* staging a live broadcast with
Mayor Abraham Beame. For a 1976 CBS television special, *Song of Myself,*
Rip Torn depicted Walt Whitman, whose original Brooklyn printing shop
had been demolished. In other business ventures, the Seaport published
a friendly booklet for Exxon on Alaska's North Slope, whose Northwest
Passage was a vital issue. Driven by "the needs of Europe, the wealth of the
East and the politics of Islam," said the Seaport pamphlet, Exxon tankers
penetrated the passage in 1968 because, like Bartolomeu Dias in 1488, the
nation needed to "be independent of Islam." Meanwhile, Exxon's refineries
were polluting Staten Island waters.[16]

A Gotham firm that topped the Fortune 500, Exxon gave $200,000 in
1975 to establish a pocket park at Water and Fulton Streets (Block 95E).
The plot of land had been set aside for an airshaft for the long-delayed Second Avenue Subway, whose cancellation by Mayor Beame prompted critics to attribute the district's poor draw to its aborted subway connection.
David Rockefeller, whose high-handed grandfather had founded Exxon's
parent, dedicated the park, and the Seaport created the Titanic Memorial
Lighthouse in 1976. When *Titanic* went down in 1912, some people interpreted it as "a punishment for those devoting their lives to the pursuit of
wealth and power." The lighted cupola ("lighthouse") that topped the Seamen's Church Institute from 1913 to 1967 almost went to the scrap heap, as

did its giant illuminated cross, when the edifice was demolished. In 1968, preservationist Frederick Fried asked the wreckers to donate it but was told "to go to hell." He threatened a seaborne protest around the company owner's yacht. When he mentioned a $10,000 tax deduction for the gift, he succeeded.[17]

City Hall and the D-LMA strove to enliven Lower Manhattan using the Seaport as their proxy. "Downtown has been suffering a lot of bad press with talk about riots, strikes, muggings, dullness, decay and the rest," the D-LMA observed in 1970. Recommending that the area "needs to make itself more fun to live in, work in, shop in and visit," it lamented that it "has been notoriously weak in attracting the young." But as they "quickly tire of the dull suburbs," they would discover that downtown was "groovy" and "the 'in' place." Praising the Seaport, the D-LMA suggested, "Get out Petula Clark's recording of 'Downtown.' Listen to it and you'll get the message again." Many audiences were targeted. Funded by the Kaplans, the Seaport had staged its first free Arts Festival in June 1967. The pier was jammed, but a *Times* reviewer, more accustomed to Carnegie Hall, complained about the "environmental sounds of boats plying the river [and] gulls wheeling overhead" and "the primitive sound system" that made the music sound like a "trans-Atlantic wireless reception." But the format and audience adjusted to the setting, prompting a later critic to call it "the best of all the New York outdoor concert spaces." In 1970, the Seaport tried a sound and light show, but it was hardly the psychedelic hip of Greenwich Village. Jazz concerts by great artists such as saxophonist Charles McPherson became a regular and usually free feature.[18]

During the week, the Seaport staged folk arts and music. Beginning in 1968, a frisky foursome named the Seamen's Institute sang chanties and drinking songs on the pier or aboard *Lettie*. Because they were cavorting like the real sailors the Seaman's Church Institute was trying to reform, the institute was pushed by conservative shippers to take legal action. So the quartet's leader, Bernard Klayman, renamed it the X Seamens Institute. A Brooklyn-born civil engineer who managed the city's school buildings, Bernie Klay, as he was called, regularly drew audiences by the hundreds, further convincing City Hall of the Seaport's pull. Inspired by chanties at the Newport Folk Festival, his lusty voice and Brooklyn chutzpah created authenticity. He later contributed folk music to the Country Dance and Song Society at Pinewoods, which also sponsored concerts on the pier,

Fig. 5.3. Chanteyman Bernie Klay sings aboard *Wavertree*, 1970. *Left to right*, Bernie Klay, D. Kenneth Patton, Peter Stanford, Joe Cantalupo, John Lindsay. (Unknown photographer; *South Street Reporter*, Nov. 1970)

and he founded the Sea Heritage Foundation. During the summer, the Seaport staged chanties on Tuesdays, folk dancing on Wednesdays, and square dancing on Fridays. Thinking that most Americans "lead aimless lives, waiting for the television, the newspaper, for someone else to plea-sure them," Klay taught the joys of singing, macramé, and square dancing. Joining Klay was John Townley on mandolin and accordion. After studying gospel guitar in the South Bronx and singing with folkster David Crosby aboard the derelict *Charles van Damme* in Sausalito, Townley worked ten years running the Seaport's music program. They also sang, said Stanford, "a good mix of black liberation stuff which we welcomed as expressing the concerns of the day—AND because it was great music." Others included Oscar Brand, who hosted a TV broadcast from the pier and gained notori-ety with his 1976 campaign song for President Gerald Ford, who had told the city to drop dead.[19]

The Seaport also hosted art, such as the Ninth Annual Avant Garde Festival held in 1972 aboard *Alexander Hamilton*. With eight thousand attendees, the two hundred artists included Yoko Ono, who showed a "Conceptual Sculpture," while the so-called rainbow artist, Ay-O, replaced the signal flags on its rigging with "hundreds of pairs of women's lavender panties." As Norma Stanford recalled, "I blew my stack!" Frank Braynard, who had okayed the show, assured her that "the controversy would blow over." Open-minded, Braynard often embraced people who were "offbeat or different." That was the case with cellist Charlotte Moorman, notorious for a bare-breasted concert elsewhere. Donning a Day-Glo diving suit and as photographers yelled "Push her down," she played her cello submerged in a tank on the pier. Annette Kuhn of the *Village Voice* bashed "the mostly hollow, shallow avant-garde scene," although the Moog synthesizer and light show in the engine room, as well as the ship itself, thrilled her.[20]

Avant-garde art was hardly the pier norm. After *Clearwater* arrived with one thousand pumpkins for sale on the previous day, an Autumn Pumpkin Festival included a carving contest and a concert by Seeger's Sloop Singers. Seeger had also packed the place on July Fourth. Mixing old and young audiences, as well as the East Village and Madison Avenue, the Seaport cast a wide net. In the early 1970s, through a handbill written in Chinese, it invited residents of nearby Chinatown to attend a two-day Thanksgiving celebration with "a lot of free food" aboard *Pioneer*. Seaports had long been, said its program director, "a place for a person with a devil-may-care attitude and a love for people. We hope the feeling carries over."[21]

"An Ad Man in the Midst of Sophisticated Museologists": Stanford, *Kaiulani*, and a National Movement

The Bicentennial opened other opportunities, including saving *Kaiulani*, stranded on a Filipino beach. Owned by the National Maritime Historical Society (NMHS), which was formed to save it and wanted it berthed in Washington, D.C., Kortum worried that it would be lost there in a sea of "politicians, public relations people and special pleaders." But the NMHS was broke and about to dissolve, so Stanford agreed to serve as its president only if headquartered at the Seaport and if *Kaiulani* would be moved to New York. That plan depended on money, which was, he confided to William F. Buckley Jr., "a big if." Still, the Bicentennial raised his hopes, and he thought that the Nixon administration, which had been "selling off rather than building up the national honor and heritage," could use

Kaiulani politically. To build his coalition, Stanford first helped establish the Sea Museums Council of nine maritime museums in 1971. Second, with Braynard as editor, he published the first issue of *Sea History* in April 1972. Yet Salem's Peabody Museum and Mystic Seaport balked because, said Stanford, they regarded the NMHS as "an arriviste organization" and him as "an ad man suddenly plunked down in the midst of a bunch of sophisticated museologists." In late 1972, his critics forced the NMHS to separate from the Sea Museums Council (which later folded) and in 1974 formed the Council of American Maritime Museums (CAMM). Through Kortum's efforts, *Kaiulani* was designated "the flagship of the Maritime Bicentennial Fleet." Once restored, it would sail the East Coast from Pier 16. As the $2.5 million fundraising drive stalled, Kortum demanded action and angrily pressed Stanford, who became, said Isbrandtsen, a "pain in the neck" as he tried to find the money. As the ship deteriorated, Helen Delich Bentley, chairwoman of the Federal Maritime Commission, endorsed cutting it into pieces and reassembling the ship in Gotham with a new hull, rigging, and engines, but nothing happened.[22]

With the NMHS broke and facing the demise of *Kaiulani* and many other ships, Stanford proposed establishing the American Ship Trust. He was inspired by Britain's National Maritime Trust, founded in 1970 by Frank G. G. Carr. A longtime director of the National Maritime Museum in Greenwich and protector of *Cutty Sark*, Carr also later formed the World Ship Trust, modeled on the World Wildlife Fund. Along with Kortum, Villiers, and Stanford, he was at the helm of the ship-preservation movement. While Stanford authored a pamphlet on Carr, Prince Philip, an aficionado and honorary head of the Trust, praised Carr's "great work." Yet Stanford had no helpful prince, until he found Sen. Edward Kennedy (D-MA). An inveterate sailor like his brother John, Kennedy was most worried about *Alice S. Wentworth*, America's oldest schooner, which was buoyed by polystyrene foam in Boston. Encouraged by their mutual friend Barclay Warburton, Kennedy asked Stanford in March 1974 to draft a bill creating an American ship trust, which he then introduced in the Senate "without changing an essential provision." Its House of Representatives version was proposed by John M. Murphy (D-NY), whom the Advisory Council on Historic Preservation called "the best and most forward congressional friend of maritime preservation." The bill, however, kicked up a storm at the National Trust. William J. Murtagh, the first Keeper of the

National Register and a two-time National Trust executive, said that it simply "didn't want another trust" competing for scarce funds. Indifferent to ship preservation, the National Trust emphasized meritorious buildings and structures, as did the National Register of Historic Places, whose guidelines discouraged the nomination of ships. As a result, only forty-six vessels were listed by 1976, a full decade after the register's creation; a mere 1 percent of federal grants for historic properties went to maritime projects between 1969 and 1978.[23]

Earlier, National Trust chairman Carlisle Humelsine had allegedly threatened to ruin Stanford's career if he set "up a bill in opposition to the National Trust." Facing pressure from Seaport trustees and recognizing his own lack of power, Stanford backed off, angering Kennedy, who then introduced a revised bill in 1975 to establish and initially fund a National Trust for the Preservation of Historic Ships, to rescue ships such as *Kaiulani*, *Wentworth*, and *Alexander Hamilton*. The National Trust, CAMM, and the National Park Service resisted. While the NPS had a limited grants-in-aid program for ships, the others resented Stanford's gambit, feared their own losses, or wanted to influence the agenda. The National Trust created an ad hoc committee, which included Seaport trustee James Shepley, to consider adding ships to its programs. As a result, it amended its 1949 charter and established a Maritime Preservation Office in 1976. Mystic Seaport's Waldo Johnston, who led the fight against Kennedy's bill, admitted to CAMM that the National Trust knew "*nothing* about ships" and the "special problems" of ship museums. As Kennedy's bill was torpedoed, *Wentworth* sank in Boston Harbor. The National Trust's halfhearted maritime program later joined it.[24]

"The Focal Point of the American Revolution Bicentennial": Operation Sail and the Restoration of Sea Culture

Op Sail 76 defined New York's Bicentennial. For Op Sail 64, Braynard and two friends assembled a regatta as "the last hurrah" of tall ships. After Prince Philip and President Kennedy joined as founding patrons, and David Rockefeller and IBM's Thomas Watson agreed to pony up, the twenty-four-ship Op Sail 64 was a stunning success. Kennedy predicted that it would "remind us that strong, disciplined and venturesome men still can find their way safely across uncertain and stormy seas." The

Seaport launched its own Schooner Race in 1967. Though the NYYC had held annual regattas since its founding in 1844, a race of this grandeur had not been held in the crowded harbor since 1870. The advent of containerized vessels using Kill van Kull opened the Upper Bay and made the race possible. The fifteen entrants in 1967 made it "the largest gathering of schooner-yachts in New York waters in this century." Watching aboard Rudie Schaefer's *America*, honorary chairman John Lindsay ordained it the Mayor's Cup. Celebrants gathered on Fulton Street "to sing sea chanties and swap sea tales" in what seemed a new Gotham tradition. The winner received a century-old silver trophy, which had been purchased for $150 by Norma Stanford at "an old junk shop" on Fulton Street. The last boat also received an award: a box of corn flakes and a bottle of Beefeater gin.[25]

The race became a tradition, but it was not always smooth sailing. In 1985, for example, it attracted eighteen schooners which, said a New England observer, "formed a picture almost ghostly and otherworldly —a sad reminder that the heyday of such boats is now just a memory." Otherworldly was almost the case, as they veered to avoid USS *Boulder*, a 522-foot ship that bolted though the course "like a Manhattan bus barging through an intersection." They also encountered "a violent thundersquall" that registered eighty knots and capsized three vessels. Fortunately no one drowned, though many celebrants afterward downed the free-flowing Foster's Lager, which sponsored the race. That Yankee observer admitted, "New England sailing was never like this!" Imitated elsewhere, including Mystic starting in 1968, the Mayor's Cup brought life to the commodious harbor.[26]

As the Seaport's program director, Braynard agreed to don a second hat in 1971 as Op Sail 76's general manager to solicit moneys, recruit participants, and stage what would be the Bicentennial's signature event. Headquartered at the Seaport, Op Sail 76 moved its offices in 1974 to One World Trade Center, where the Port Authority provided gratis the entire north side of the seventy-second floor. Seaport lieutenants, including Howard Slotnick, Jakob Isbrandtsen, and Robert McCullough, worked under the task-force head, Emil Mosbacher, winner of the America's Cup race in 1962 and 1967. While Mosbacher stressed the sea's importance, Op Sail critics noted that the worlds of a square-rigger and a container ship—one mythical, the other routinized—were far apart. There amid "a forest of masts"

Fig. 5.4. Seaport during Bicentennial, July 1976. Visible are *Robert Fulton* (center foreground at Pier 16), *Winston Churchill* (to its right), *Ambrose* (opposite *Fulton* at Pier 16), *Peking* (opposite *Churchill*), *Danmark* (left center at Pier 15), *Christian Radich* (to its right and behind *Peking*), and *Eagle* (opposite *Danmark*). *Pioneer* is across the end of Pier 16, and *Clearwater* across the end of Pier 15. (Photo, Terry Walton)

of real sailing ships and the one hundred thousand Seaport visitors in the week after July Fourth, *Peking* and *Wavertree* seemed like poor cousins. Beginning at the Verrazano Narrows Bridge and parading up the Hudson River, the eighteen-mile-long assembly included 228 sailing ships, another 800 craft, and 53 naval units, along with aircraft carrier *Forrestal* with President Ford and Braynard aboard. Keeping ten thousand small sightseeing boats on the sidelines were 150 Coast Guard vessels. The tall ships, which had raced from Spain to Boston, later sailed to Baltimore and Norfolk, all the way promoting public waterfronts. The parade, unparalleled for its day, was watched by some six million viewers on shore. "Almost single-handedly," *Newsday* wrote, Braynard "saved the Bicentennial from banal commercialism and gave America the most meaningful observance of its independence by far."[27]

Braynard's Quaker education prompted his own contribution to détente. While lining up Op Sail participants, he and Slotnick went to Kiel, Germany, in 1972 to meet with the captain of the Polish tall ship *Dar Pomorza* and arrange an exchange, whereby USCG *Eagle* would visit Poland in 1974 and *Dar Pomorza* the United States in 1976. "We were pleased that, in a small way, we were helping to break down the division between East and West," Braynard thought. But Secretary of State Henry Kissinger vetoed *Eagle*'s visit. Instead, Braynard recruited the yacht *America*, and *Dar Pomorza* reciprocated in 1976. "Terribly worried about the arms race," Braynard rejected the ideological quarrels and suggested, "When people are at sea, you don't ask them what their politics are, you ask how they hoist their sail." He thought that the regatta's thirty thousand officers and cadets, who received a ticker-tape parade, were "a very special kind of people." After meeting so many, he knew, "In no time those we think of as 'foreigners' become friends. It follows, quite naturally, that we should all be like seamen. After all, we are all seamen on spaceship Earth." That last line became his mantra, but "sea*men*" should have been qualified because *Sir Winston Churchill* was "manned" by an all-female crew.[28]

Braynard's regatta was upended, however, as he was naïve to think that a disgraced nation such as Chile could be invited without controversy. The Organization of American States had reported that scores of political prisoners were tortured and hundreds held prisoner on *Esmeralda* after the US-backed military toppled a democratic government in 1973. Sailing *Pioneer* in the parade, Walter Rybka recognized, however, that the regatta's sailors were "a pretty apolitical lot." Said an Episcopal priest who organized the protest, *Esmeralda*'s presence undermined the "the very principles of democracy and human decency" that America was celebrating. While City Council President Paul O'Dwyer asked the mayor to ban the ship at any city-owned dock, as San Francisco had done in 1974, protestors occupied Op Sail's offices and demonstrated at Battery Park and Pier 86. Still, Slotnick, who handled the logistics, remembered that no one from City Hall ever got in their way. Not knowing that the ship would be used as a prison as late as 1980, Braynard told the *Times*, "We're trying to do something positive, not dwell on past horrors. . . . Operation Sail is nonpolitical."[29]

With the waning of détente and the waxing of concerns about human rights, the Soviets faced a different problem. According to Slotnick, Op Sail had to request "a special dispensation" from the State Department to allow Russian and Polish ships entry into US harbors. But the Jewish Defense League, which had been implicated in numerous attacks in metropolitan New York, made threats against the USSR's *Kruzenshtern* (ex-*Padua* of the Laeisz line). As Slotnick recalled, he and Walter Cronkite, who provided television commentary for the regatta, boated out to the ship and warned the captain, who consulted with KGB agents aboard and decided not to dock. After sailing in the parade, the Soviets closed their ships to visitors and canceled further port calls. That also hid from the public what Slotnick called their "starving crews." After he raised money to feed them, Russian officers later remembered the kindness. Op Sail thus created "a little bit of a crack in the Cold War," as did Warburton of the American Sail Training Association (ASTA), who was sailing "to preserve our planet by bringing people of the earth closer together." Hosting Op Sail and the Democratic National Convention also eased the city's malaise after its near bankruptcy and forced austerity. Op Sail's legacy was long discussed. It was, said analyst Mitchell Moss, "conceived and carried out by an ad hoc organization with virtually no assistance or input from the city government," but it succeeded because citizens had "the skills and time to overcome bureaucratic resistance and inertia." But, added Richard Fewtrell, it "caused all manner of trouble" for the museum.[30]

"In the End They Rose Up and Devoured Him": Peter Stanford Walks the Plank

Op Sail obscured the fiscal crisis that had been building for years with the Seaport's land and ship acquisitions. As pressures mounted and deep rifts developed with the museum's board, Stanford considered quitting, but he first asked Kortum to become director in charge of ship and building restoration. With Stanford as president and Kortum as director, the latter said, it would have been "the most powerful team" in the field, despite their decidedly different personalities. In a letter written to Kortum while alone at the Square Rigger, Stanford outlined his shortcomings. "The *only* thing that could happen here to make this project come through," he wrote, was "a strong director, one strong in life stuff not in rhetoric."

Stanford preferred to conceive ideas and wanted Kortum to implement them. If Kortum accepted, he cautioned, his trustees would be "no bed of roses." He drafted a one-year offer, which was narrowed to director of restoration for *Wavertree* beginning in May 1972. But, said Stanford, "Karl FRIGHTENED" them, and the board rejected the move. With the impasse, the Friends of South Street Seaport circulated a highly critical petition about the Seaport's leadership, but Cantalupo persuaded them to table it.[31]

While Pete Seeger's conservative board gradually forced him out because of politics, many Seaport trustees simply did not share Stanford's vision. In one revolt over land development in 1971, the board added Richard Buford, who had left the mayor's development office. The board revealed what Stanford's friend and trustee Joan Kaplan Davidson called his "tragic flaw": "his judgment about people." As such, his board became "heavy with yachtsmen and suburbanites" who shared little of Stanford's perspective. His battles made him "deathly tired," but he admitted that so many factors were "just not possible to predict." Yet the Seaport's public face was upbeat, as the *Times* praised its workers' "vision of love and joy and passion for life." There were one hundred steady volunteers. Among the salaried employees, who mostly "took large salary cuts" from the private sector, there was a readiness to work eighty-hour weeks because, said one, "We have a dream here, and you can't stop it from becoming a very part of you."[32]

Trustees, committed to corporate thinking, were increasingly led by James R. "Brass Knuckles" Shepley. Once a relentless right-wing reporter, he rose through the ranks to become president of Time Inc. in 1969 and served until 1980. "He never wasted his time going around an obstacle; he just plowed right through," said later Seaport president Christopher Lowery. He "spoke in a perpetual growl that perfectly complemented his persona." More bluntly, admitted trustee Peter Aron, he "was an arrogant son of a bitch" and "would have been proud of that description." Yet he had excellent connections to City Hall, Albany, and Washington. Introduced to the board in 1972 by chairman Isbrandtsen, who had raced with him to Bermuda, he muscled the appointment of friends, developed a bloc, and led a mutiny, first by displacing Stanford in 1974 with his own appointee and then pushing Isbrandtsen aside in 1976 in favor of a surrogate. While Davidson blamed Stanford for the board, and Stanford blamed Isbrandtsen for board policy, City Hall and the banks pushed Shepley's rise. Not only did the banks force drastic austerity measures on the near-bankrupt city, but they wanted their Seaport loans repaid and air rights sold. Lindsay aide Richard Weinstein insisted that strong business leaders take the Seaport helm because, he said, Stanford and Isbrandtsen "weren't up to the knock-down, drag-on fight to negotiate" the area's development. Known for action, Shepley had little patience for Stanford's vision or flat organization.[33]

To capitalize the district, Shepley decided to leverage the Bicentennial. Providing a design team from Time Inc., he produced what Stanford called "a forceful and moving" film promoting the Seaport as "a vital project" integral to Manhattan Landing and Battery Park City developments. Approaching Governor Rockefeller, he won "high-level support" for its leading role in the celebration. Yet the support was financially limited. A Nixon supporter, Shepley expected federal help with Bicentennial funding after Nixon's reelection in 1972, while Stanford preferred to focus on individual, corporate, and philanthropic donations. At the same time, the preservation movement was rethinking issues such as the pace of development, the source of funding, and the role of museums. The National Trust, for example, was promoting business-oriented initiatives, including entrepreneurship, adaptive reuse, tourism, and market-oriented solutions, which Stanford embraced. Meanwhile, as military spending squeezed money from urban programs, federal agencies moved to the sidelines, generating few "innovative ideas" and even fewer dollars for urban development. Stanford also wanted a gradual process, as he reflected more of the small-is-beautiful approach than corporate capitalism. Emphasizing the latter, however, trustees accelerated commercial development to get "money flowing into the Seaport's coffers." They believed that a bigger bang for the buck could be achieved "through the economics and efficiencies of scale."[34]

From 1974 to 1976, Shepley remade the Seaport. Though Isbrandtsen, who served as chairman until early 1976, characterized it as "a fight between the do-gooders and those who wanted to make a buck," Stanford wanted to do both, but emphasized the former. Instead, the board curtailed his authority and revised his organization. Introducing a corporate order, it had little tolerance for Stanford's flat organization of committees. Originating in the grassroots movement, the committees could include trustees, advisers, staff managers and workers, and even Friends, all of whom could discuss and vote. In so doing, a relative democracy existed. As Kent Barwick remembered, Stanford "empowered people" whether in a committee or the larger society. Shepley and his trustees instead introduced a corporate, stratified chain of command in which decisions were made "up and/or down the line through channels." As Norma Stanford explained, "They wanted a structure that fit their picture of a traditional organization."[35]

Largely through the Executive Committee, which, said Peter Aron, "ran things as it saw fit without too much exchange with the rest of the Board," Shepley went after the Stanfords. At an ExCom meeting held at his Time-Life suite in March 1974, Shepley proposed hiring Robert T. Bonham, who entered the room on cue, and, Barwick recalled, it was a done deal. Stripping Stanford of his authority as president, Bonham became executive director. Shepley's imperious hiring of Bonham was approved, the board explained, "to put the running of the Museum on a more businesslike basis." Formerly a Bronx land developer, Bonham listed David Rockefeller as a reference, leading some staff to call him "Rockefeller's man." Shepley reportedly ordered him "to get Stanford out." Though Peter remained as titular president and what he called "the shill, or barker at the tent door," the board went after Norma because she was his logistician. The museum had closed 1973 in the black, but the balance sheets worsened under Bonham. As Binger recalled, they were "so short of [operating] funds that more than once, we had to pay the staff out of petty cash, since the bank account was empty."[36]

Because Bonham had no museum experience, the board created a new position, director of museum programs. Philip Yenawine had served under Allon Schoener at NYSCA and had been employed in the Metropolitan Museum's education department, but he really "wanted to work in a place that was forging new definitions of museums and their capacities." He chose the right place but knew little of the Seaport's rifts. Though wary, Norma welcomed him and explained the operation. Staff was one of the Seaport's "most valuable assets," she said. While admitting that the unconventional structure confused the average businessman, she insisted that the flat organization was successful but warned that it would fail in an "atmosphere of expediency, deception, threat or abuse." Enforcing a corporate reordering, Bonham tried "to tighten up the operation," not only with the staff but with the volunteers. The outcome was not surprising.

"No one liked Bonham," said Yenawine, because most of the staff "were united behind Peter's vision but still loners" doing their own thing. Volunteers ran "much of the place," but they were "as idiosyncratic as the rest of us, and not easily managed." Still, "it was chaotic, often fun, often maddening, and a huge amount was accomplished," he said. Objecting to Norma's firing, the staff forced its reversal. As secretary of the Friends, Marie Lore bluntly told Bonham that everyone was "down and negative" about his management.[37]

In ExCom, Dick Rath saw "a sharp division" develop between the Stanford and Shepley forces. While Stanford reflected the belief that the Seaport "should be a place of serious and even sometimes radical relevance to contemporary New York City, with a wide variety of activities open to all citizens," Shepley reflected "the modern businesslike attitude" of success at any price. As a result, Bonham had "an expedient concept of honesty, a respect for historical values ranging from lip service to contempt, and a total absence of feeling for . . . Peter's 'people' concept." Complaining that ExCom had "stripped Peter of any real power to control basic issues," he warned, "If this trend continues, . . . I don't want to be part of a land speculation, or an amusement park. Even a nautical amusement park." As the Stanfords held on, tensions increased, partly because their work and thinking were so intertwined and familial. "With all couples who work together," said Yenawine, "there were frequent strains on everyone." Peter was the "spiritual leader," Jennifer Stanley added, but he had "little understanding of what they did," leading volunteers to scold him for not hearing them out.[38]

Bonham was failing miserably. Not only were the books poorly kept and finances in the red, but membership dropped. After only nine months, Shepley humiliated and fired him at a board meeting in January 1975. Impressed by Richard Buford's self-assurance, Shepley then hired him as CEO and managing trustee. Buford's close ties to bankers and developers raised eyebrows among the staff and volunteers. Ultimately Buford shared Bonham's faults. Both used restricted funds to meet the payroll, giving the appearance of being underhanded. Both, said Stanley, had very little concern for the staff, volunteers, and membership. In a stinging rebuke, the MAS judged that both men "estranged the very public whose loyal support had pulled the Museum through its roughest hours." As bottom-liners, they "lost sight of the one quality" necessary for success — "an ardent sense of mission." That was Stanford's strength: even Weinstein regarded him as "an effective, sophisticated advocate of the Seaport." Stanford's idealism was also infectious. It was what Yenawine loved about the place: the "spirit of doing something significant against great odds, a sense of mission and occasionally of SSSM-wide esprit de corps."[39]

Hoping to make an end-run around Shepley, Stanford pushed to open board elections to the membership, which could act as a counterweight to both the board and its director. To increase members' turnout, the Friends provided box lunches with free beer and soft drinks at the annual meeting in 1974. Such a change would be, Stanford told Isbrandtsen, "reminding us all where we came from, and reassuring us when difficult decisions must be made, that those decisions are in the ultimate reviewable by those we ask for support." While Isbrandtsen supported the voting proposal because he had had troubles with the board over *Wavertree*, Rath opposed the idea. "There are situations where democracy does not work," he told the chairman, and that was in running both a ship and the Seaport. After the board shelved the proposal, Stanford gave up his president's salary but, retaining his title and board seat, worked as a consultant. Isbrandtsen dejectedly watched the board shift further to Shepley's side.[40]

The museum itself split into competing factions. In February 1976, Stanford complained to departing board chairman Isbrandtsen, who was distracted by his legal difficulties, about the museum's "harsh realities" in which volunteers were accused "of setting fires, destroying property, stealing things" and Stanford accused "of everything under the sun." With *Mathilda* sunk in the river, Stanford was desperate and told Kortum that the ships were symptomatic of the Seaport's rot. Because it was more dependent "than any other maritime museum in America" on donations, he knew that change was necessary. At Buford's behest, ExCom met at the NYYC, which was closer to the offices of board members, some of whom, Stanford claimed, had never even been to the Seaport. Mindful that it owed over $10 million, Stanford called for "a small business approach" until the budget improved. Reflecting a developer's strategy of growth, Buford instead proposed "a course of expansion" and a substantially increased budget, despite the lack of revenue. What most irritated the board was not the wash of red ink but Stanford's "overt criticism" of its recent actions. Painting Stanford as a defeatist, Buford told the board to decide between the two. The Seaport fractured, said Yenawine.

"Everyone was expected to take sides, and most did. The content people, historians, designers, educators, writers, basically sided with Peter even if they had their own disagreements with him. Peter could galvanize people and he could also exacerbate conflict, and often did. The board, funders, and the city sided with Buford; the power came to reside there, and not with the content people." He added, "What most people thought was that the downfall of Peter was the death knell to the South Street vision, and because of the polarization forced by the personalities, it virtually came to be so."[41]

Then, in a resolution proposed by Shepley, ExCom voted to fire Stanford. As Stanford explained, Shepley had "introduced a rule that the executive committee cast a unitary vote when reporting to the board." With the unanimous vote, he had few options. Because his undated resignation letter had been submitted earlier, the board saved face by accepting the resignation. Differing interpretations arose. *Daily News* reporter Dick Sheridan wrote that developers more interested in land than ships forced Stanford "out of his own enterprise." To which, Stanford nodded, "Perhaps I was naïve, but I chose not to fight, because I thought it would hurt the museum." He later added, "I innocently welcomed the bigwigs, thinking that they would bring us support and corporate wisdom." Likewise, Seeger said he was sacked "for being more interested in boats than boutiques" by profit-minded businessmen.[42]

Rath explained the sea change in leadership styles. The first wave of preservationists, such as Stanford, were "analogous to conquering Vikings" because it took daring and determination against formidable odds, but the second wave brought managers with business-minded ways. Said Creamer, "Peter Stanford was our champion. He knew the value of the old ships and of dreaming large." Yet others perceived his weaknesses. There was "always a feeling on his part, if they'd do it my way," it would be better, said Peter Aron. While praising Stanford, Yenawine also recognized the so-called founder's syndrome. "I think what many of us wished," he wrote, "was that Peter's personality could have allowed others to help him create his vision," but "he couldn't." However, trustee Thomas Gochberg said it was a lack of fiscal restraint; for Stanford, "a budget was a wish list." Even Isbrandtsen admitted his frustration because Stanford began many projects but was impatient seeing them though. Stanford "drew the dots but assumed they'd be filled in" by someone else.[43]

Stanford told the *Times* that philosophical differences had prompted his resignation. Publicly he exuded hope, so much so that a *Times* reporter mistakenly referred to him as "Mr. Stanhope." He admitted to Kortum that he "should have retired with a thunderclap" but was tight-lipped even though a *Times* reporter said it "would be a page one story." Overly generous, Stanford told Kortum that Shepley was "a fair man, working out of the wrong culture, on the wrong side." That culture, based on corporate hierarchy, was reshaping the world of museums and learned societies and was hostile to the idea of a people's museum. Yenawine compared Stanford's firing to a funeral, and "a lot of air went out of the place." Removed from the board, Stanford ran for the presidency of the Friends, but Cantalupo won by a three-to-one margin. Adding insult to injury, Buford evicted the NMHS from its Seaport headquarters. Stanford knew it was coming and moved it across the river to Brooklyn. The NMHS and its president were barely solvent. Still, from the pier made famous by Walt Whitman's "Crossing Brooklyn Ferry," Stanford hoped to make his own crossing—back to South Street to retake his museum.[44]

"The Basic Question Is Simply Survival": Keeping the Museum Afloat

As the Seaport's crisis worsened, Jack Aron told trustees in August 1976, "The basic question is simply survival." Buford closed the museum and ships for two days a week. He shelved the fleet's scheduled maintenance and dropped creating pension and contingency funds. He also retrenched the staff. At a meeting of middle and upper managers, he proposed cutting Norman Brouwer. But, Rybka recalled, "Brink jumped up and shouted 'Wait a minute! This is supposed to be a god-damned museum. Norman's the only one who knows a fucking thing about the history. How the hell are you going to have a museum if you fire the only historian!?'" Brouwer kept his job, but Rybka became disillusioned and resigned. As layoffs were unfolding and middle staffers plotted to replace Buford, he jettisoned his critics. By September, he had eliminated twenty-one of sixty-eight full-time staff and was chopping fourteen of the twenty-five part-timers. Brink, Yenawine, and others quit, either in disgust or over a plan to charge admission to the piers, which City Hall ultimately rejected.[45]

The turmoil forced ExCom to meet in November. Slotnick interpreted the resignations "as an open revolt," while Eric Ridder chastised Buford with a "God bless the revolt." Shepley griped that, with the exception of managing Time Inc., he had spent "more time on the Seaport" than anything else. Besides forcing Buford to resign, ExCom asked Melvin Conant, former Exxon executive, for an assessment. As expected, he blasted Stanford's management, suggesting that the Seaport's mission statement was too "philosophical and theoretical in nature," leading to a myopic focus, overly ambitious acquisitions, and "a deep division" between the uplands and waterfront. Calling for a streamlined management and a three-year plan, he rejected governance by broad-based committees. He stressed, moreover, that the Seaport's goal—"To tell *the story of the rise of the Port of New York*"—must become more central to decision making. Every "program, asset, and opportunity" must pass "three *inseparable* tests, . . . *Tangibility, Fundability, Manageability*," meaning, is it materially related to the whole, is it financially doable, and is it workable? Measured against this yardstick, programs such as the Pioneer Marine School seemed extraneous. Implying that Stanford and Shepley had aggravated the divisions, Conant targeted Stanford directly, stating that "management direction and stability [have] been absent from the beginning of the Seaport; visions are not enough." As a result, he suggested, "A *manager-fund-raiser* with skills in *development* and *administration* must be the chief executive; another person of high excellence in museum fields must be at his right hand." He also stressed the hiring of "*professional* quality staff" to win accreditation. Without such changes, he warned, the museum was "in danger," even "in peril." Part of a broader campaign against the Sixties' personal, democratic, and experiential approach, his plan set a professional norm.[46]

In so doing, Conant rejected the Seaport experiment. Combating alienation, it had engaged hundreds of thousands of people; taking on the river's pollution, it made the waterfront cleaner and fun; opposing imperialism, prejudice, and corporate greed, it spoke for older traditions of decency, responsibility, and community; and seeing the toll taken by historical rootlessness, it built bridges between generations and diverse people. By 1976, its troubles resulted mostly from forces beyond its control. Huxtable thought, for example, that all were blindsided by "the extraordinary rise in Manhattan land prices," which led to the boom-and-bust cycle that pushed City Hall to near bankruptcy. Others pointed to Lindsay and Rockefeller, who, while using the Seaport as a pawn in their agendas, either offered too little help or set near-impossible terms for its development. Yenawine attributed its crisis to "timing as much as anything," whether associated with a ship nearing the wrecker, a landmark facing the bulldozer, a politician or banker seeing insolvency, or a developer wanting ever higher buildings. Conant was right, however, in that the Seaport needed better funding, planning, and administration, which was expected of John Hightower when he arrived in mid-1977.[47]

6

"Shopping Is the Chief Cultural Activity in the United States"

How the Seaport Sold Its Soul

Bonham's and Buford's tenures had been unmitigated disasters. Shepley blamed the crisis on the Seaport's original design and convinced the board to turn the gritty area into a slick shopping mall, euphemistically calling it a festival marketplace. When Phase I opened in 1983 with what *Newsweek* called "all the fanfare of a NASA space shot," the developer, James Rouse Company of Columbia, Maryland, featured the New Fulton Market, along with the restored lower floors of Schermerhorn Row and the Museum Block. Phase II's shopping pavilion on Pier 17 followed in 1985. Phase III was projected to rehabilitate the remaining urban renewal district, which had some two hundred buildings. It would be, said the Seaport's president, "one of the largest restoration and development projects ever undertaken." Many New Yorkers, such as Huxtable, were bewildered. Some saw deceit. In 1985, a Gotham preservationist told his peers that Rouse had "foisted" on the museum "perhaps the grossest atrocity to be passed off as a bonafide preservation project." A later Seaport president faulted City Hall. Yet Seaport trustees had instigated the idea. Setting a trend for other museums, the Seaport gave key assets to a smart-talking developer. In so doing, Shepley expected to fill the museum coffers, institute a business regimen, and undo the 1960s experiment.[1]

The Seaport was founded on a wing and a prayer. With few dollars, Stanford admitted in 1967, "I am profoundly tired and my hunch is we'll have to give the Seaport development away" to focus on "the ships, the soul of our enterprise." But, funded by Isbrandtsen, pushed by the Friends, and adopted by City Hall, the museum committed itself in 1969 to Blocks 74E and 96 E-W. Thanks to Brooke Astor's intercession, Laurance Rockefeller, a venture capitalist who aided conservation and culture, took interest. The younger brother of Nelson and David, he joined Stanford, Cantalupo, and architect Bronson Binger in January 1973 for a walk through the district.

After lunch "in the unheated upper floor of Sloppy Louie's Restaurant," where Astor kept "her mink coat over her knees to keep warm," Rockefeller offered a $200,000 planning grant to make the Seaport "economically viable" and spur public feedback. That led to the Seaport Plan of 1973, which would be implemented by restoration director Binger, a former chairman of the MAS Landmarks Committee and its Historic Districts Council. Paralleling the Manhattan Landing Plan, the Seaport Plan proposed expanding the restoration to Blocks 97 E-W and creating a floating restaurant to keep its piers clear for pedestrians. With a "capacity exceeding any shore" rival, Captain Lacey's *Robert Fulton* became a hot spot. There Mayor Lindsay held a retirement party, Rockefeller a luncheon, and Governor Hugh Carey a wedding dinner.[2]

Using Rockefeller's grant, the Seaport briefly hired architect Jonathan Barnett as its master planner. His recommendations appeared in his textbook *Urban Design as Public Policy* (1974), for which his former boss Mayor Lindsay wrote the foreword, and in the museum's *Reporter*. He proposed a $32 million expenditure for a mix of shops, museum facilities, and low-rent studios for artists. Of the total space, he suggested only 15 percent for the museum. With drawings by Edward L. Barnes, the neat streets, awninged shops, and a canopied esplanade set off a debate. Opposing the change, many critics deplored any new or trendy commerce: they wanted to exclude peddlers who sold everything from jewelry to hash pipes, while some even disdained crafts shops, fearing a possible strip mall. They liked the seaport authentic. A volunteer waxed affectionately about "the dreadful fish-glue stench" near Sweet's Restaurant, suggesting "preservation can —and should—be eclectic, for the sake of keeping vitality." The *Reporter* stoked the critical feedback. Facing complaints about the "'mod boutique' look," Binger, who was in charge of implementing Barnett's recommendations, wanted to keep "any slickness, even accidental," out, while showing the district's "traditional grunginess." Stressing that the redesigned seaport had to be financially self-supporting, Binger said that the work would be "historically appropriate, viable in the 20th century, and compatible with Museum and community needs." As such, he was walking a tightrope as precarious as Philippe Petit would do in 1974 between the twin towers. The Seaport Plan of 1973 unraveled, however, as the city postponed removing the FFM and balked at tearing down FDR Drive. Primed by a

Fig. 6.1. Looking east toward 207–11 Water Street (Block 96W, *foreground*), with the old Beekman Hospital being converted into condominiums (*left*); at center in background are the Fulton Fish Market's New Market Building (*left*) and the Tin Building (*right*) on the East River, 1981. (HABS NY-568-3; photo, Walter Smalling Jr.; American Memory Project, Library of Congress)

$1 million Astor grant, the Seaport focused on its Museum Block (96W), whose façade would be restored, fire escapes removed, and shell leased to shops and eateries.[3]

On the east side of Front Street in the Market Block, the Seaport rejected the mod-boutique look by introducing its Fulton Market in 1975. In its half of the 1950s garage on Block 96E, it staged a "modern-day Bazaar" and rented space to craftsmen, antiques sellers, and food vendors (see fig. 2.1). There Wall Street and Main Street mixed, said a visitor, as they lunched on health food and ethnic cuisine, but most lined "up for portions of fish and chips and the large, cheap paper containers of beer." The building's peeling paint, pockmarked floors, and "puddles of beer and water" recalled the district's history. The Seaport also sponsored an out-door flea market, but a marine executive complained about "a mess of push carts and rickety stands selling everything from sausages to second-hand clothing." All the while, pedestrians sought out the vistas offered by Pier 16, which Huxtable recommended enjoying "the same way one visits Florence and Rome" as it was "quintessential New York."[4]

City Hall, the D-LMA, and Seaport moguls were considering a dramatic change from the course set by Van Arkel, Barnett, and Binger. In Boston, Van Arkel won the right to develop Faneuil Hall Marketplace, but the city, which was dissatisfied with his incremental pace and funding, turned instead to Rouse as master developer. New York took note. Pressured by City Hall's Public Development Corporation, Buford fired Binger and looked to hire a master developer. That led staff to fear that a faster pace would privilege commerce, compromise the district's authenticity, and target the fish market. But City Hall, which was begging for a federal bailout, was being squeezed by Wall Street. While the *Daily News* defended the fishmongers and ridiculed the Seaport Plan of 1973 as a Disneyland, local capo Carmine Romano derided the idea of displaying a "half a dozen or so" fish stands as tokenism. Yet, as planner Ann Satterthwaite told the National Trust, fish markets were being displaced across the nation by cities remaking their waterfronts with "dramatic, one-fell-swoop plans."[5]

Whether in the 1860s or a century later, slumming brought sightseers to the Fulton Fish Market. Employing fifteen hundred workers by the 1960s and handling some two hundred million pounds of fresh and frozen seafood yearly, it operated in the early morning from two city-owned buildings on South Street and scores of privately owned shops nearby. "Everything was prehistoric, mysterious," said a fishmonger. Many FFM workers ate at Dirty Ernie's, which really was dirty, but the food was, said Sal Celona, "out of this world—the best." The mood was enhanced by "shots of whiskey to keep warm" on cold days. Like anthropologists in a foreign land, Margaret Mead sent her classes to the FFM. Observing with a camera was Barbara Mensch, who experienced "a side of life" that she had "never seen before." Recognizing a distinct subculture, she learned to respect those "tough, serious, and hardworking men, who lived in an internally policed world governed by their own philosophical and moral principles, and by their old-fashioned ideas of loyalty to one another." Becoming their voice, she sympathized with their resistance to corporations, government, and the museum. The mob also won her respect, and she showed them her interviews for *The Last Waterfront* (1985) for prepublication approval. Beginning in 1974, the museum's six a.m. tours tried to capture that culture. Sometimes led by Joseph Mitchell, they ended with a genteel breakfast of chowder and muffins, but not at Dirty Ernie's.[6]

Since the demolition in 1948 of the Fulton Market Building, which was designed by the architect George B. Post and built in 1883, the city planned to move the FFM to the Bronx, but fishmongers resisted. When the plan was resurrected in the late 1970s, the portion of the catch arriving by boat already had fallen below 1 percent. To push fishmongers out, the US government intensified its crackdown on the Mafia. District Attorney Mike Seymour and Mafia associate Joseph Cantalupo ironically sat together on the Seaport board. At a meeting on fundraising, Seymour suggested that while "every Board member should contribute to the Museum according to their capacity," he added, worrying about the money trail, "We would not expect the nice Italian gentleman to give more than a token amount." Extracting a service charge on every fish, the Genovese family extorted some $700,000 from 1975 to 1981, the Wall Street Journal reported, while the mob-linked, fish-unloading cartel stole thousands of pounds daily. The city conceded the widespread crime. So it was no surprise in 1975 that the chairman of the Committee to Save the Fulton Fish Market, which was called "a mob front group," was Romano. To block the move, he hired architects and engineers to study how the market could be rehabilitated and its congestion alleviated.[7]

When Romano was indicted, the government admitted that law-abiding businessmen would rather lie than testify against the mob. Fear intensified after a government witness was gunned down in front of Carmine's Restaurant. Romano, collecting his IOUs, received hundreds of testimonials, including one from Seaport president John Hightower. Calling Romano an "enormously positive force," Hightower appreciated that Romano ordered "members of the union not to break into the museum." He urged a dismissal of the charges. While he called his testimonial the "best insurance possible" for the Seaport, others assumed they would "be floating in the river" if they did not cooperate. Christopher Lowery, who headed the museum's real estate arm, admitted that Romano "was very helpful," crafting "a working relationship between the museum and fish market." According to Stanford, Romano knew that "messing with the museum" would mean more investigations. He was nonetheless convicted in 1981, and when he was sentenced to prison, his brother took over. A Seaport staffer who was asked about the museum's relationship with the Mafia admitted, "It's a very delicate subject."[8]

"Shopping Is the Chief Cultural Activity in the United States": How Commerce Overwhelmed a Museum

After Stanford was jettisoned in March 1976 and Van Arkel failed to develop an acceptable financial package, Shepley replaced Isbrandtsen as board chairman with a surrogate, Robert McCullough. Heading the Seaport's real estate committee, Shepley persuaded the board to opt for a master developer. In ways other than commercial leases, the Seaport was setting a trend. As the *Times* later reported, museum boards elsewhere were becoming "like a business board room," where businessmen "speak the same language. . . . So if it becomes an issue of program or money, money always wins." Shepley and Rouse, who were friends, worked out the deal "during a bird-shoot in Virginia at the Time Inc. retreat," said Peter Aron. The board then asked the Rouse Company to appraise the district's potential as a festival marketplace. Of all trustees, Howard Slotnick added, Shepley was "totally enamored of Rouse."[9]

That guaranteed a sea change. Rouse believed that Disneyland was America's "greatest piece of urban design," and his company, which was loaded with failing suburban malls, was trying to reinvent itself. As a model, he chose Ghirardelli Square, which had used Kortum's museum, ships, and Victorian Park as a platform. Situating his malls near popular or historic attractions, he wanted to draw an affluent clientele. That raised the hopes of countless mayors trying to restore their city's bond rating, increase their tax base, and revitalize urban life. In line with what historian Jon Teaford called "Messiah Mayors and the Gospel of Urban Hype," Rouse preached that gospel in the aftermath of urban riots and suburban surge. As was the case elsewhere, said Norman Brouwer, boosters "figure their waterfront needs a ship as a tourist attraction."[10]

The Seaport hired Benjamin Thompson Associates as its master planner in 1976. Two years earlier, Thompson had persuaded the Rouse Company to submit a proposal to transform the deteriorated Faneuil Hall and Quincy Market into its first festival marketplace. Also designing Rouse's Harborplace in Baltimore, he predicted that they would reverse white flight, although he once claimed that Gotham was so cold that it "strikes you dumb." Thompson was more designer than preservationist, and his dream of re-creating cities was difficult to explain to skeptical Boston bankers. But as the urban tide was turning, said the critic Robert Campbell, he changed "the face of America." While Rouse and the Seaport were quietly courting, Quincy Market opened to resounding success in the summer of 1976. As the Seaport Museum was laying off staff, Jim Rouse toured the seaport in November. He arrived without publicity, partly because his plans for Baltimore had just been vehemently opposed. In the following March, he told Buford he could make that corner of Manhattan "warm, intensely human, safe and beautiful." Whether he was capitalizing nostalgia, suburban ennui, or antimodernism, it became a trend. As Calvin Trillin grumbled in the *New Yorker*, old bricks were "being scrubbed up into boutiques" all over for "middle-class sophisticates." They represented "the new kitsch of advanced capitalism." That cash infusion converted a naysayer such as retired LPC chairman Harmon Goldstone. "Talk about dollars and cents is reaching ears that were deaf to arguments about the loss of cultural values," he told tradesmen. That spending jumped nationally from $1 billion to $10 billion from 1975 to 1976.[11]

Although Shepley was responsible for the Bonham and Buford disasters, the board gave him the task of replacing Buford. Shepley's real estate faction, which cared less for the museum, realized that the museum's lofty status made Wall Street bankers, especially Chase Manhattan Bank, more accommodating, said Peter Aron. That partly explained the choice of John B. Hightower as its president and CEO. Nelson Rockefeller had helped secure Hightower's move from NYSCA to the Museum of Modern Art in 1970. Arriving during a strike by the Art Workers Coalition, his sympathy led one artist to call him an "an Art Worker." Yet, at a time when few, if any, museum directors regarded themselves as businessmen, Hightower was; he even suggested that a museum director should be, as he unabashedly described himself, "a politically astute businessman, an excellent administrator, and a humanist." He was fired after eighteen months. While he irritated trustees with unconventional comments and his lack of museum experience, more damning, said the *Times*, was his ineffective fundraising. MoMA chairman David Rockefeller parachuted him to an arts advocacy group, which eventually landed him at the Seaport. Perhaps with Rouse funding in mind, Shepley and ExCom ignored his MoMA failure.[12]

After Hightower's arrival on July 1, 1977, the city comptroller charged the Seaport with fiscal mismanagement. It had passed yearly audits in the early 1970s, but after inspecting the books under Bonham and Buford, the comptroller faulted the inappropriate use of restricted funds. J. Aron & Company sent its accountants over pro bono, recalled Peter Aron, but they reported "that it was impossible to get a handle on the Museum's financial affairs." Forced by necessity, Hightower continued using restricted funds to pay his staff of fifty, but the city rents and bank loans remained in arrears. To begin restructuring, the Seaport hired two new administrators. Underwritten by the Rockefeller Brothers Fund, the Seaport's vice president for finance was told to put the books in order, while the director of museum shops was expected to downsize staff, control inventory, and introduce efficiencies. Hightower also needed corporate giving. On the heels of fifty industrial firms listed in the Fortune 500 leaving the city since 1969, ninety were still headquartered there by 1975. Seaport trustees were expected to make corporate donations. When a senior vice president at IBM, Robert Hubner Sr., joined in 1976, Shepley asked him for $200,000. Head of the Seaport's development committee, Hubner also granted a one-year public-service leave to an IBM systems analyst in 1977–78 to assist the Seaport's fundraising, though Op Sail more generously received two employees for two years.[13]

Hightower predicted that dramatic changes to the seaport were on the horizon. They began when Mayor Abraham D. Beame (1974–77), "no friend to historic preservation" after his inaction on Grand Central Terminal, staged a public-relations event to announce that Washington would be giving $2.8 million to develop the Museum Block and $2.5 million for Pier 16. But the area north of Beekman Street was generating controversy because city proposals still showed high-rises there, despite its inclusion in the National Register district (1977). Emerging from near bankruptcy and pressured by the banks, Beame wanted private development and tax dollars. Calling the Seaport "an exciting complement" to the World Trade Center, City Hall marked only Blocks 74E and 96W for restoration, while the rest, including the Ward house and Dover Street, could be demolished for high-rises using the banks' air rights. Peddling a neoliberal policy, City Hall planner Robin Burns, who wanted a return on investment in financial, not quality-of-life, terms, demanded that the Seaport give those blocks north of Beekman Street to a private developer. Seeing the Burns plan, Barnett wondered if City Hall had "panicked and sought to create development at any price."[14]

With Boston's success, Shepley said the Rouse deal was "the golden path" to finance the Seaport. He even told Isbrandtsen that it would be able to repay his loan, extracting him from default. Meanwhile, Rouse "was a good salesman" and hosted Seaport trustees for a personal tour of Boston. The negotiations had been guarded, but the *Village Voice* favorably scooped the story in early November. Focusing on city-owned properties in Blocks 74, 96, and 97, plus Piers 17 and 18, the Seaport signed an agreement with the Rouse Company on December 10, 1977, to complete a feasibility study, funded by Brooke Astor. In a statement that was repeated with derision, Hightower told the *Times*, "The fact is that shopping is the chief cultural activity in the United States," and it would occur within the museum. Expectations became exaggerated beyond recognition. "One way to advance a project," Chris Lowery admitted, "is to give the illusion that it is inevitable, and that's what I did." Inevitable meant doable, unstoppable, and profitable. While Bostonians had once been afraid to visit Quincy Market "at night or even in the day," said Robert McCullough, it now had "more people than Disney World." Orlando's forty-three-acre park attracted fourteen million yearly visitors, but Boston's six and a half acres drew about fifteen million. Rouse boasted that Boston's sixty thousand daily draw was nothing compared to the Seaport's projected one hundred thousand, though Hightower imagined a "constant bustle of 30,000 to 50,000 people a day, winter and summer." Still that was an eighteenfold increase over its then one million annual visitors. Hightower predicted it would "become the most exciting and perhaps the largest development project in the City of New York."[15]

Stanford cried foul, claiming that the board was betraying his concept of the museum *as people*. Gentrifying its audience, for example, it had scrapped his one-dollar membership plan, which he believed gave it "important [political] leverage with the city." He also charged that the board refused to consider development by smaller, diverse businesses. Hightower admitted as much, telling the *Times* that Rouse "would compress into 10 years what it would take 75 years to do with individual developers." Peter Aron saw efficiency and speed as crucial. With so many competing forces, the single developer would expedite the process and abbreviate the debate. Stanford asked Hightower for help, but Shepley was in charge. Meanwhile, the Seaport was challenged from all sides. With City Hall needing the most tax money and rents from its land, it, for one, wanted to rescind the Seaport's role as district developer and remove it from the Rouse negotiations. It urged the museum to focus on its ships, exhibits, and shops. Ridiculing the Seaport's inability to "run a nonprofit business in a profit-making world," a state official also wanted it to get "out of the museum business and [let] the state do it."[16]

"What You Have Here Is an Organization Gone Wild": Firing Fewtrell and His Crew

Critics decried the neglect of the ships, but that was mostly rooted in the funding conundrum and the nature of preservation. Stanford tried "to make one or two fit for public presentation—and keep the rest in safe storage, against the day that they could be funded and brought up." But storage required maintenance and money. *Lettie G. Howard* was "under the axe," Fewtrell warned because the Rouse Company wanted the piers. As it was rotting, the Seaport was willing in 1979 "to give it to anyone who would restore it." No one came forward. *Ambrose* was every bit as bad, as *WoodenBoat's* Peter Spectre discovered in 1980. It was "a discredit to the Coast Guard and an embarrassment to former and present servicemen," said the ex-Coastie. "I would indeed prefer to see her go to the shipbreakers" than stay at South Street.[17]

The square-riggers forced the issue. *Peking* dominated the waterfront, but there was a world of difference between its restoration and that of *Wavertree*. Jack Aron, with his deep pockets, maintained what Fewtrell called a "furious pace" of work, but Aron was "very impatient with the gobbledegook and fussy pace of marine restoration," said George Matteson. "To him [the ship] was a utilitarian object to be used as needed." While Aron controlled *Peking*, the ship committee managed *Wavertree* through Fewtrell. As *Peking* became ready for Bicentennial visitors, Fewtrell said, "our efforts appear[ed] laughably slow and ineffective." It even lost its berth to visiting Op Sail ships. A painstaking craftsman, Fewtrell wanted to "do a completely accurate job," but his regimen taxed the Seaport's funders. While the Arons, Ridder, Shepley, and Isbrandtsen provided "modest funding," said Peter Aron, "nobody wanted to commit large amounts" to the "brilliant but 'impossible'" Fewtrell. It was "a typical money pit."[18]

Few people realized how deep the *Wavertree* pit was. "Covered in construction materials," said young volunteer Philip Levy, "it was really a hulk." Deep below, "it was musty and very creepy. Older folks told us stories about dead bodies hidden in the ship." Meanwhile Stanford searched for a live body with deep pockets at an NYYC dinner. Advertising Fewtrell "as the 'authentic' English ship restoration expert," the artisan arrived, said Michael Creamer, "authentically ridiculous in his tar stained work shirt and boots." Yet "NO one is allowed in the NYYC dining room without a jacket and tie," and Fewtrell had not worn any since leaving the army. "Under great protest he made his entrance in a waiter's jacket and bow tie!" Later Shepley and Hightower met with Brooke Astor's board, which agreed to consider significant funding, but the outcome was disastrous, said Hightower, because Shepley only gave a hard sell for Rouse's plans.[19]

Hightower called Fewtrell "meticulous to a considerable fault." With their class and cultural differences, they seemed, said Stanford, "from opposite sides of the moon." Fewtrell mocked Hightower as "one of those boring stick and carrot guys." To quicken the pace of *Wavertree*'s restoration, for example, Hightower offered to buy Fewtrell a bottle of wine. A teetotaler, Fewtrell passed on his crew's very pricey recommendation, but "of course the poor sap couldn't deliver and provided something less which was jeeringly consumed next day on the poopdeck." There also was a clash of culture—the traditional craftsman versus the corporate board. Yet, said Rybka, who became the Erie Maritime Museum's director, Fewtrell "was always right about what you should do to a ship and how you should go about it," but he was "a poor fit with a management who knew nothing about ships but did think in timelines and budgets." Fewtrell was "a proud and stubborn craftsman [who] refused to recognize the hopelessness of the situation created by a nautically ignorant management."[20]

After Jack Aron complained to ExCom about Fewtrell, Hightower "set in motion a plan to force results" in mid-1978. Instead of paying Fewtrell an hourly wage, he used the contract system. As he told Shepley, "If specified work is not completed on a specific date, payment for work on the *Wavertree* will stop." Fewtrell went public, complaining to *Soundings*, "[The Seaport] has over the past three or four years, been less and less interested in any form of historic authenticity or honesty or anything I would call real values." While the board thought the project was moving too slowly, ironically, said crew member Charles Deroko, "they actually never moved faster." Hightower could have heeded the advice of Captain Kenneth Reynard, who inspected *Wavertree* in 1977 and presented his perspective at a Mystic conference. Restoring the iron-hulled *Star of India* (1863), Reynard became, he said, "'a one ball juggler' because as we would get into a job, many obstructions would arise, . . . so then we would go immediately to another project that we could work on. This procedure provoked criticism from some quarters as 'too much started, nothing finished' but this is indeed the nature of a restoration project." Within a year of Hightower's complaint and *Wavertree* being listed on the National Register, Fewtrell had replaced the "fore topmast, along with the main and mizzen topmasts." To begin the process, he said, his crew moved the three lower masts, which were between eighty and ninety feet in length, "one at a time through heavy downtown traffic with the aid of a home built trailer and two forklift trucks. This was an extremely tricky operation and was done without police escort, any kind of official permission, insurance or support."[21]

Prioritizing commercial development, Hightower and Shepley took a different route. They not only tried to sell *Lettie* but fired *Wavertree*'s seven-man restoration crew, including Fewtrell. As the *New York Post* charged, the museum was "seeking to trim sail before selling out to a real estate developer." Said a bitter Fewtrell, "What you have here is an organization gone wild"; museum administrators were trying "to dispose of vessels as they needed costly repairs." Isbrandtsen tried to defend the ships but, as Aron remembered, Shepley said at a meeting, "Jakob, God damn it, shut up." Stanford dismissed the museum's leaders as "corporate know-nothings." Management did know enough to offer to rehire *Wavertree*'s crew, minus its outspoken master, and three workers accepted for the ship's sake.[22]

"The Battle to Hold Back the Tide of Change Had Finally Run Its Course": Christopher Lowery and the Negotiation of a Rouse Deal

With the Rouse Company's study completed and a deal not yet struck, James Rouse proposed Phase I. In addition to a refurbished Museum Block (96W), a pedestrian plaza on Fulton Street, and the restoration of Schermerhorn Row's façade and lower two floors, it introduced a New

Fig. 6.2. *Wavertree* restoration crew; Charles Deroko (*front right*), Axel Ekstand (*back left*), Richard Fewtrell (*back center*), 1979. (Photo, Charles Deroko Collection)

Fulton Market. Replacing the 1950s garage, the three-story, full-block market would include fish stalls on its South Street side to accommodate part of the FFM's $3 billion annual sales. Phase II, a shopping mall on Pier 17, would open in 1985. In all, the Rouse Company would create over 250,000 square feet of retail space. However, with five parties involved (the Seaport, the state, fishmongers, Rouse's Seaport Marketplace, and the city), negotiations would be complex. Like most private developers who tapped into public treasuries, the Rouse Company demanded concessions such as new streets, walkways, and a pier. In the end, some $61 million came from the public purse.

Negotiating for the Seaport was Christopher J. Lowery. When a student at Notre Dame, he had landed summer jobs in Lindsay's planning department after his uncle, the first African American fire commissioner in a major US city, forwarded his name to Donald Elliott, chairman of the City Planning Commission. Lowery was lucky, he said, that Elliott "took a personal interest in me." Kent Barwick added that he was one of those "very bright, inevitably arrogant people" who wanted to remake the city. Lowery said he loved the district, but he thought "that the battle to hold back the tide of change had finally run its course." Rising to deputy director of the Mayor's Office of Development, he helped package the Rouse bid. Through the public-private revolving door, he was hired by Hightower for the newly created position of vice president for operations in March 1978. Hightower said "he talked a good game." Lowery regarded himself as "the only guy who seemed to have the trust of the Museum, the city, the state, the banks and Rouse." Restraining Shepley and City Hall from too quickly accepting Rouse's terms, Lowery bargained for contractual revisions. In addition to the Seaport having "final say over plans," it also achieved "a complicated rent formula" giving the Seaport a better deal. After that, Lowery said, Shepley "became my biggest supporter on the board," but Lowery's successor (Peter Neill) claimed that Shepley "created Chris, . . . and Chris did his bidding."[23]

Under Mayor Edward Koch (1978–89), City Hall was uncomfortable with the Seaport Museum as a stakeholder and wanted it to offload its real estate. Protecting its dowry, the Seaport board instead created an autonomous affiliate, the South Street Seaport Corporation (SSSC), which assumed its leases and debts. Insulating "the Museum from the obligations and liabilities arising out of the development process," the SSSC was incorporated in early 1981 with Lowery as president. His use of the revolving door prompted suspicion. Journalists Jack Newfield and Paul Du Brul had warned that the revolving door had led to "legal graft." Those insider connections were, said the *Times*, "the old dilemma" faced by "virtually all city officials who do not retire or die in office." Yet the city's Board of Ethics could "rule only when its opinion is asked." After someone did, however, it found no fault with Lowery's move.[24]

To meet Rouse's demands, the SSSM and the SSSC perpetrated unscrupulous actions against waterfront restaurateur Capt. William Lacey. After Lacey turned down a $100,000 buyout, Shepley and Buford turned up the heat by installing a gate to discourage his customers, encouraging banks to deny him loans, and pressuring City Hall to close his *Robert Fulton*, "the only floating restaurant [in the city] ever certified by the U.S. Coast Guard." After Lacey died, the New York Fire Department ordered it closed in 1977. Arguing that the ship's federal permit superseded city oversight, Capt. Jeremiah Driscoll volunteered to be its captain. If he had "six security guards with side arms and shotguns," he told Lacey's son, "when the Fire Department comes, I will call a Mayday. To the effect that pirates are upon us." That would "get the Coast Guard here to defend the certificate." Instead, Lacey's family filed a lawsuit. While negotiations ensued, Shepley and Lowery ordered his pier restaurant bulldozed and forced *Robert Fulton* out. After Shepley refused to settle out of court, the Society of Maritime Arbitration held a hearing. Stanford testified, as did Driscoll, who authored an unpublished book on the saga, "They Pissed in the Chowder." Lowery believed the law was on his side, but the panel ruled in 1984 that the Seaport broke its lease. Facing a $1.4 million settlement with the Laceys and three separate third-party decisions, which included a $130,000 payment to Driscoll, the Seaport used *Peking*'s $650,000 endowment and a $750,000 JACF loan to settle. The case symbolized Shepley's unethical move to land his big fish.[25]

"The Prospect of Serious Conflict": Absorbing the State Museum

The Rouse negotiations were further complicated by the New York State Maritime Museum. In 1966, Stanford pinned his hopes on the state, but NYSMM existed on paper only. Contracted in 1969 by the New York State Historic Trust to begin the planning process, architect John G. Waite appraised the Row's architectural merits and researched its history. Recommending that "no attempt should be made to retain any cutoff date or 'magic period'" for the Row's rehabilitation, he suggested hiring a staff of twenty-four and an operating budget of $372,900 for the state museum. He wanted, moreover, to leave "the feel of canvas, and the smell of the brine," to the Seaport. Precious little followed his report, however, and the state backed off by folding its board into the Seaport's in 1972. Trustee Walter Lord, whose book *Night to Remember* had become a blockbuster movie, joked that the Seaport "came up like the *Carpathia* to the *Titanic* and hauled aboard some board members." In 1974, Albany finally bought Schermerhorn Row, agreed to the Seaport's conditions on its restoration and rental, and pledged up to $11 million. It hired Giorgio Cavaglieri to design a new museum building on the "corner lot" at South and John Streets and to plan the Row's restoration. Cavaglieri warned that its nonfireproof, load-bearing walls "would make compliance with the [City Building] Code completely impossible" and added that the roofs, stairwells, and perhaps the deteriorated façade would have to be rebuilt and the floors would need realignment. His impressive plan, however, disturbed Seaport volunteers. "Our own identity will be lost in their spending aura," one warned, while Marie Lore thought the Row would become "a memorial to some administration's showy use of taxpayers' money."[26]

The Empire State wondered if that old block was imperial enough for its ambitions. It hired Leonard C. Rennie, an exhibit designer, as a consultant. Nixing the Row, he proposed in 1974 that NYSMM instead be developed in Brooklyn at the 341,000-square-foot Empire Stores (1870–85). Impressed by Disney's audio-animatronics, Rennie wanted to outdo the Smithsonian Institution, whose limited coverage of marine history was to be expanded in 1976 with its Hall of American Maritime Enterprise. The Brooklyn site, whose eight and a half acres were privately owned, was "infinitely superior." By acquiring Empire Stores, he said, New York could create "one of the world's great museums of maritime industry," and it could "serve all America as our national maritime museum." That proposal worried the Seaport. As the Bicentennial approached, the state appointed Clifford Lee Lord in 1975 to complete its plans. Former director of the Farmers' Museum in Cooperstown, Lord was suitably credentialed, but he ran aground in the state's red ink. Realizing that prospects were dim for Empire Stores, he promised to develop a dynamic, living museum at the Row with perhaps a ferry across to Empire Stores, for which Stanford asked the state to partner with his National Maritime Historical Society.[27]

Despite the state's promises, it only briefly opened a small Fulton Street exhibit in 1976 about the Row's past occupants. With Clifford Lord's departure, a cash-strapped Stanford applied for his position. Kortum endorsed his application, but Stanford knew that Shepley would balk. In October 1977, Governor Hugh Carey promised $10.75 million to jumpstart NYSMM if a bond measure passed. Voters overwhelmingly rejected the referendum. Fearing that NYSMM would raise private funds and compete with the Seaport, Hightower warned State Parks Commissioner Orin Lehman that the two museums "overlap in such a way as to offer the prospect of serious conflict." As Peter Aron joked, these "two institutions [were] trying to decide what they were, but neither had any money." Hightower proposed merging the two, whereby the new operation would contract with the state for all museum responsibilities, be governed by an independent board, and be free from direct public influence. That would free the Seaport Corporation to focus on land development. The state did not take his bait or want another annual appropriation. Meanwhile, it knew of Rouse's demand for 250,000 square feet of prime commercial space and that the Row's lower two floors were an absolute necessity for retail.[28]

Albany offered a deal. First, it gave the Row's title to the state's Urban Development Corporation, which had not only changed its urban renewal mission considerably since its 1968 creation but defaulted in 1975 after the governor refused to honor its debt. Heeding Mayor Koch's directives, it would pump tens of millions of dollars into the seaport and Manhattan's Jacob Javits Convention Center and luxury hotels. Second, as a "developer of last resort," it could override local zoning ordinances and building codes, thus sidestepping Cavaglieri's warnings about the Row's structure. Third, it would transfer the restored Row to the city, which would lease it to the Seaport Corporation so that it in turn could sublease space to Rouse and earn income. "I was surprised but not complaining about the State's plan," said Hightower. The Rouse Company signed a letter of intent on December 28, 1978. The Seaport was close to failing, but Aron said, "Rouse was seen as the last chance, and a good thing if it worked." The state then turned to Empire Stores, which it acquired in 1978.[29]

"We Have the Right to Stay Here": Neighborhood Residents Resist the Museum and Its Developers

The FFM district had been claimed since the 1950s by artists who, violating building codes, had lived in studio lofts. Near South Street, a thriving colony developed, which included painters Robert Indiana, Jasper Johns, Robert Rauschenberg, Agnes Martin, and the SFMM's Anita Ventura. Appreciating the district's working-class vitality and history, Rauschenberg wove its detritus into his work, becoming "the most influential painter since Jackson Pollock." His friend composer John Cage lived there, finding the FFM's ethereal spirit via Zen philosophy. "Even though we were poor, we lived with such a view," he recalled, "that life was enjoyable and not oppressive." It was primitive too, as was the loft above Creamer's Water Street shop. Living with Brink and Fewtrell, Creamer said, it "had no partitions which meant one could view the sleeping loft, the kitchen and the remaining space whilst seated on the john," the last of which was portable.

"You could tell when someone was changing lofts," he quipped, "when you saw a bloke walking down the street with a toilet on his shoulder."[30]

The demolitions, loft conversions, and gentrification forced most artists out. Still, the Row retained tenants such as sculptor Marco Polo "Mark" di Suvero, who worked for twenty years there. While his cavernous attic housed some of his large metal sculptures, most were exhibited at the nation's major museums. In 1968–69, recalled John Young, he helped Urban Deadline formulate "opposition to the predatory developers he had battled from day one." He was also, said Stanford, "a great hit" with kids from the projects, who rode his ersatz ponies—"two or three brilliantly painted 50-gallon oil drums hanging on long ropes from the overhead, with rope tails and mane to represent horses." He was generous to the museum, once giving a $1,000 check. His opposition to the Vietnam War drove him to France in 1971, but he returned to the Row, married future Department of Cultural Affairs commissioner Kate Levin, and resisted later developers.[31]

With the museum bailout in 1972–73, however, residential artists became suspicious as the Row's title switched from Atlas-McGrath to City Hall to the Seaport to the state and back to City Hall. Fearing eviction, the Artists and Residents Association pressed bureaucrats to protect their investments. As a result, the city and state stipulated that up to $300,000 of the payment to the Seaport be used as a relocation fund for the Row's residents. Instead, Buford "spent the money on general operating expenses." By 1977, as the State Parks Commission contemplated the restoration, its Orin Lehman warned Seaport chairman Robert McCullough that, unless the Seaport acted, the state would evict the tenants. Predicting bad publicity, Lehman knew it would be "a ticklish matter," so he met with and reassured wary tenants about their occupancy. But they most worried about the Seaport, whose every move was suspect. When it instituted a voluntary pier entrance fee in 1977, their fears led City Council member Miriam Friedlander to complain about the "atmosphere of coercion" and violation of the Seaport's lease. Tensions increased as the Seaport absorbed NYSMM, scrambled to meet Rouse's demands, and allegedly acted in an imperious manner. Rumors circulated that Seaport administrators had even threatened to use eminent domain and evict those who criticized its actions.[32]

In the spirit of Jane Jacobs, some residents were more committed to preservation than the Seaport was. Taking a cue from Sidewalk History, the artists placed posters around the district describing the history of each building, including their own improvements, while highlighting the district's economic mix and social vitality. Some squatted in the Row as it changed hands; others paid rents or bought nearby buildings. Brian O'Neill, a sculptor and sometime CETA manager on *Maj. Gen. Hart*, paid $75 a month for "three floors on the Front Street side" of the Row. With Creamer, he set up a business to convert lofts for occupancy. For a decade, he said, "We poured time and money into old, derelict buildings and saved them from ruin. We have the right to stay here." In fact, recalled Creamer, when O'Neill's son was born, Cantalupo "laboriously hoisted his 300lbs to Brian's 3rd flr. loft and made the announcement: 'This is the first baby born in the Fish market in 30 years and you tell anyone who wants to know that I am the godfather.'" Pressing $100 into the hands of O'Neill's wife, he added, "Any problems for my godchild, you tell 'em to come see me!"[33]

Artist-teacher Christopher "Kit" White warned that the Seaport had long had "designs on this neighborhood" but now had "the power to put them into operation.'" Having invested $100,000 to buy and repair an early nineteenth-century building at 226 Front Street, he pressed for action from Community Board 1. A planning body representing most of Manhattan south of Canal Street, CB1 was the first step in the review process and was designed to encourage grassroots participation. Ironically, the museum, which began as a people's coalition, was opposed by the people's delegated voice. CB1's vice chairman, for example, praised residents for "the kind of gradual 'organic' restoration and investment originally envisioned by the Seaport." O'Neill and White, who both served on CB1, blasted the Rouse deal as a "city giveaway." Tenants issued a broadside, warning that the Seaport planned to displace an entire community. While millions in public dollars would support a seaport Disneyland, they charged, the Rouse Company would take "80% of the profit" and leave the museum a mere 15 percent and the city 5 percent. Predicting increased traffic, sewage, and waterfront privatization, they demanded "a moratorium on all development" until the community had full disclosure, representation, and participation. They concluded, "*We demand* the maintenance of the original purpose and philosophy of the South Street Seaport Museum as an institution for historic preservation, education and recreation, and not a retail and real estate development." Because the Rouse project reportedly only had a fifty-fifty chance of approval by the review boards, Hightower and Lowery assured the Seaport board—in words that came back to haunt them—that "in its design, merchandising and operations the new Marketplace will be integrated with the operations of the Museum and will be compatible with the creation of an historic maritime neighborhood."[34]

With a cover sketch of Mickey Mouse, Goofy, and a pier, the *Washington Market Review* headlined in 1979, "Will the Seaport Become Another Amusement Park?" Instead, residents wanted an urban cultural park, a newly legislated device to enliven communities. Their proposed park would include low-retail businesses and free community spaces in the Row and would also preserve a community garden, the Square Rigger, and the Green Coffee Exchange. Anti-Rouse protestors in Boston had similarly endorsed a nonprofit developer's proposed community center that was "far more public-oriented" and "more sensitive to the traditions of the market and its delicate economics." CB1 hired planner-architect Barry Benepe, who had debuted the first of the city's Greenmarkets and locavore in 1976, to design an alternative to Rouse in 1980. Critics were also inspired by Seattle's Pike Place Market (1971), "a bustling arena of farmers, historically authentic, yet updated to meet current trends in taste and style." But Pike Place evolved into a decidedly different operation.[35]

In the summer of 1979, the *Times* carried news of another debate over a proposed super mall, a mere ninety miles east in Branford, Connecticut. The president of a local land trust denounced the proposed mall as "an exercise in neolithic thinking." In the scramble for revenue, he complained, public planners were abandoning "all principles of orderly growth to satisfy the mall's insatiable appetite." Antithetical to the conservation ethos, those malls symbolized much of what was wrong in America. Endorsing his frank assessment, an ally blasted "the tunnel vision of our local politicians, who insist blindly that short-term tax benefits are the sole objective of living." That conservationist, Peter Neill, was to head the Seaport in 1985.[36]

"What Is Really Going On Down at South Street?": The Rouse Deal Is Reached

On September 27, 1979, City Hall and the Seaport announced their deal. As Lowery described,

There were agreements between the SSSM and SSSC; leases from the city and the state to the SSSC; a four-party operating agreement among the city, state, SSSC and Rouse Company; separate leases with merchant coops for each of the major fish market facilities; license agreements for the streets; and leases with the residential tenants in the Schermerhorn Row block. This was among the most complicated public-private projects ever undertaken in the city, with the number of parties involved and the very complex distribution of rights and responsibilities among the parties.

Mayor Koch hosted the ceremony with Governor Carey representing the state's Urban Development Corporation (UDC). Prioritizing the white-collar economy and service industries, Koch cared little for the museum, said Peter Aron. "It was all economic development." His priority came at the expense of the city's past, present, and future. Though Koch had warned in 1980 that Times Square "cannot and should not become Disneyland," he allowed the demolition of the famed Helen Hayes and Morosco theaters for development by none other than Disney. He boasted that the seaport-district deal was a major economic investment and waterfront revitalization. Meeting Rouse earlier in Boston, Koch had accepted his complex proposal, which would be overseen by the city's Public Development Corporation. Accordingly, (1) the Seaport would complete the restoration of its Museum Block and erect a new building on Block 96W's southeastern corner; (2) the city would demolish Pier 17 and 18, construct an even larger Pier 17, and improve the infrastructure; (3) the Rouse Company would build the New Fulton Market and a Pier 17 shopping mall; (4) the UDC would restore the Row's façade and rehabilitate its lower two floors for retail; and (5) a private developer would erect a high-rise on Block 74W. The state assisted current Row artists with fifteen apartments at below-market rents, but other nearby tenants were excluded and protested. According to O'Neill, residents in some sixty lofts and small businesses would be forced out, leaving up to 150 artists and their families homeless. He took a contingent to Albany, where the Rouse Company, the UDC, and the state were scheduled to discuss the project's implementation, but they were illegally barred from entering. Meanwhile, CB1 voted 18–8 for its own proposed urban cultural park.[37]

Project delays are typical in Gotham. The Rouse Company complained that its estimated costs rose substantially before the review boards and city agencies approved New Fulton Market in December 1981 and Pier 17 in September 1982. The New York and Baltimore malls were proposed at the same time, but Gotham finished last. Yet Rouse's fate was worse in Chicago. There it had proposed a festival marketplace at Navy Pier in 1980, but Rouse demanded too much. The city then developed the pier, creating its own number-one tourist attraction. In Gotham a public-relations battle ensued. Siding with Rouse and Thompson, an editor of *Progressive Architecture* claimed that they had placed malls "only in abandoned areas, not displacing other commercial enterprises." That was hardly the case in either Boston or Baltimore, where older shops gave way. The seaport's development would be further complicated by a threefold jump in land values when news of the project was leaked. Long-established businesses, such as ship chandlers Baker, Carver & Morrell and the Meyer's Men's Hotel, were forced out. The hotel had included an office where Thomas Edison introduced the city's first electric lighting; more recently, while the Mafia operated at its Paris Bar, the SRO hotel housed pensioners like Mitchell's fictitious Mr. Flood. The hotel's new owner wanted to gentrify it, as did Hightower. Other developers were evicting tenants and converting undesirable buildings into pricey apartments, as was the case in the East Village. Rouse's architects pretended there was no "social displacement," but there was; and residents united against the Seaport by 1981. Moreover, the Rouse Company promised that its shops would mostly "be run by distinctive independent merchants," and pro-Rouse architects claimed that it did not "allow franchise operations into these projects." The *Village Voice* reported that Rouse charged such high rents in Boston that eateries turned to fast food, and lawsuits followed. If Rouse did the same in New York, it warned, "the museum will bear the brunt of the blame." Hightower rejected all comparisons.[38]

Critics of Rouse included professional preservationists. Before demolishing most of Block 107E, Con Ed had given the Jasper Ward house at 45 Peck Slip to the Seaport. After being assured a renewable, twenty-five-year lease, Columbia University's Center for Building Conservation invested $140,000 for a materials laboratory there. But after 30 percent of the CBC's work was completed, the Seaport only offered a five-year lease and threatened to deny an extension unless it passed its professional review. Preservationists were shocked. The MAS asked if the Seaport was "qualified to make such judgments." Betrayed, the CBC voted to sue, so Hightower evicted it. Thinking that the Rouse Company was behind the eviction, the MAS asked, "What is really going on down at South Street?" Facing bad press, the Seaport offered a short-term lease.[39]

While the Rouse plan went before the review boards, the Seaport claimed that it was "in the vanguard of an entirely new approach for financing arts institutions." Most importantly, Hightower told members in 1979, the plan would guarantee "financial stability for the future." At a time when inflation was over 12 percent, he said that the Seaport's earnings would be equivalent to an "endowment that increases faster than the rate of inflation and produces enough income to support the curatorial and education programs of the institution over the years to come." Its income would be "something like a $50 million endowment." A later administrator recalled that "enthusiasm was so great that fundraising letters to potential donors said that their donations would be needed for only a few more years." Hightower compared his plan with MoMA's use of air rights for a condominium and the Metropolitan Museum's direct-mail catalog. Asked later if he had harbored doubts about his lofty predictions, he simply replied, "Oh my, yes!"[40]

Believing the Rouse-Hightower predictions and ignoring O'Neill's claim that they were "absolute lies," WCBS-TV told its audience of 3.9 million, "We say full speed ahead." David Rockefeller also told businessmen that the plan would "stimulate significant ancillary activity." That was good news when the jobless rate hovered above 7 percent, and it would, the UDC predicted, "create 1,700 construction and 800 permanent jobs." Shepley's magazines laid it on thick. While *Fortune* called the Rouse Company in 1979 "one of the ten greatest business triumphs of the decade," *Time* placed not only Koch but Rouse on its cover two years later. Focusing on Harborplace, *Time* showed how the "urban visionary" was using his marketplace to help "restore a sense of community and vitality to a divided, decaying, once apathetic older city"; it predicted that Rouse "may bring a little Baltimore pizazz to a moribund area of Manhattan." Little did anyone know that Harborplace was to lose money for five years before realizing a profit. Significantly, Baltimore developers demolished much of the blue-collar, African American town. After that, Rouse capitalized "the romance of Baltimore's bygone seafaring tradition" with the privately owned, three-masted USS *Constellation*. It placed advertisements promoting Harborplace in the museum's newly retitled magazine, *Seaport*, and included impressive testimonials. John Chancellor of NBC News rejoiced that the Baltimore waterfront was "transformed into happy and productive space." Meanwhile, the *Village Voice* was calling the seaport "the most important retail project in America."[41]

The approval of Phase I meant the remaking of a historic corner of Manhattan. From a quirky, people-oriented enclave that had sold fish, sailed ships, and housed working people, the district was on its way to becoming a homogenized, me-generation-oriented, festival marketplace that promised profits to a city and museum chiefly interested in financial returns. The mall boosters flatly dismissed any and all critics who questioned the likelihood of those promises. Abandoned was the Seaport's earlier policies of encouraging public participation, retaining some gritty authenticity, and incrementally introducing diverse commerce. "This Museum *Is* People" became as passé as a Sixties Be-In. Undoubtedly the Seaport had needed to steer its ship better, but the coming sea change was felt and heard everywhere, whether aboard *Wavertree*, in the Row's lofts, at the Square Rigger, or in the hearts of Seaporters who wondered how, where, and when it would all end.

7

"They Tore Down Paradise, and Put Up a Shopping Mall"

How Speculators and Rouseketeers Created a Bubble

As the Rouse Company plans became public in 1979, Huxtable washed her hands of the Seaport. "What surely will be lost," she knew, "is the spirit and identity of the area as it has existed over centuries." She was even more dismayed that a shopping center was "at the end" of historic preservation's rainbow. An editor of *Progressive Architecture* dismissed such criticism as "sheer snobbery." *Time* magazine's critic Wolf Von Eckardt used a false dichotomy, claiming, as did Hightower, "The alternatives are Colonial Williamsburg or continued decay." Ironically Hightower had recently praised Huxtable as "distinguished and constantly incisive." But he told Stanford that her hope of preserving the "enduring charm of the place" was "too much of an opiate," and he confessed to "rather perversely enjoy[ing] the harsh anvil of New York's insistent, often angry, scolding criticism."[1]

Almost deafening, that anvil rang. While CB1 feared losing its own Les Halles, an open-air market that Paris demolished in 1971 to create a tourist trap, a Seaporter played off Joni Mitchell's popular tune, "They tore down paradise, and put up a *shopping mall*." Huxtable rejected any comparisons with Boston's Quincy Market because the seaport had "a more fragile, discontinuous group of small structures" than the three large buildings at Quincy Market. Fearing the worst, she predicted that the Rouse Company "would push the museum's facilities upstairs and around corners," which happened in Boston with a branch of the Museum of Fine Arts. Kent Barwick, whom Mayor Koch appointed LPC chairman, was as uncomfortable thinking that the Boston mall reflected his era's concept of preservation. Before the deal was approved, an unsigned *New York Times* editorial, likely penned by Huxtable, criticized the museum's misrepresentations of the project and its vague details. Regretting that "the Seaport has sold its birthright," she asked it to "leave something" behind of its "tough, plain, honest and genuinely evocative" waterfront. Critics were already citing Jane

Jacobs, who had warned that "all big plans are inevitably big mistakes." Harborplace was as problematic, said Paul Goldberger, who replaced Huxtable as the *Times*'s architecture critic. The Rouse Company promised to create spontaneity and diversity in Baltimore, but it introduced the sub-urb's order and conformity. Historian Nicholas Bloom dubbed Rouse "the Trojan horse of the suburban reentry into the center city."[2]

Hounded by critics, Hightower defensively touted the credentials of James Marston Fitch, who served on his restoration committee and super-vised the Museum Block's restoration. With Charles Peterson, Fitch had founded Columbia University's graduate historic-preservation program in 1964. Embracing history, technology, and craftsmanship, he was a maver-ick. While many colleagues scoffed at the idea of either teaching about or working in preservation, Fitch saw things differently and liked to turn his classes loose with such topics as "what made a clipper ship a thing of beauty." Retiring from Columbia in 1979, he became director of historic preservation at the architectural firm Beyer Blinder Belle (BBB). His work on the Museum Block became, said Richard Blinder, "our bridge" not only to Ellis Island's Immigration Hall but to Grand Central Terminal.[3]

Fearing public wrath, the Seaport expected that "the public approval process would be intense, demanding and highly critical," and trustee Robert Hubner urged his colleagues to "react strongly to adverse reports." Unlike the spirited debate in the *Reporter* about its 1973 plan, the museum kept *Seaport* free of disparaging comments and, despite its cash crunch, hired a public-information director to encourage "enlightened reporting." The National Trust followed suit. Regarding the Seaport as "a high prior-ity," it gave not only "continuing advisory and technical assistance" but friendly coverage in *Historic Preservation*. Riding a wave set off in 1976 by federal tax incentives for rehabilitating historic, income-producing prop-erties, the Trust was promoting private-sector leadership. In an upbeat cover story, Patricia Leigh Brown quoted Hightower, who argued that the Rouse plan would give the seaport "the critical mass of visitors that it needs to survive." Yet she did not ask if visitors paid an admission fee or simply shopped at the mall. Nor did she question Fitch's remark that Rouse was just a "bigger and more powerful" Peter Schermerhorn. But she did mention historian Thomas Bender's contention that the new seaport was destroying real history. While the public would be shortchanged by the 1980s public-private partnerships, Brown concluded that the Rouse project "has already given the museum the economic shot-in-the-arm necessary to ensure its survival."[4]

Regarding the Rouse scheme as a shot in the head, the Municipal Art Society undertook a study of the Seaport's recent past. With two years of research and interviews with over thirty-five participants, the authors of the *Livable City* discovered a "story in which few people are willing to be quoted, but many have an earful to tell." Recognizing the partnership as a pioneering step that others would imitate, they asked, "How does a museum join forces with a developer and still maintain its own independent vision?" Their answer was damning, as they concluded that Bonham, Buford, Hightower, and Lowery, as well as their boards, were more developers than preservationists and had thus allowed the Rouse Company (from which James Rouse retired in 1979) to set the agenda. The MAS reminded the Seaport that it was "a public trust" whose artifacts were "literally owned by the public," who had "every legal right to comment on" the decisions.[5]

Meanwhile, the five-party Seaport Development Plan (1980) had reached its last step in the approval process, the Board of Estimate, in November 1980. Considering Phase I and II, the board unanimously okayed a $209 million package with Rouse's $70 million, $93 million from Block 74W's developer, up to $10.6 million from the state, $20.5 million from Urban Development Action Grants (UDAG), and the remainder from City Hall. Under the agreement, which revised the 1973 lease, the Seaport Corporation (SSSC) leased the properties for ninety-nine years from the city or state and subleased them to various tenants, who included the Fulton Fish Market co-ops, smaller businesses, and Rouse (doing business as Seaport Marketplace Inc. in a fifty-year lease). Though the lease initially stipulated that the SSSC's rent payments to the city "would not exceed 30% of rental income," City Hall forced a revision in 1981, pushing rent as high as 60 percent. Rouse kept its rate for its 264,000 square feet set at "the greater of $3.50 per square foot or 15% of gross receipts less certain deductions." Little did the museum know that the 1981 revision would cause its doom. Fearing the Seaport would fail without Rouse, Stanford swallowed his objections and supported the plan, telling the Board of Estimate, "It is indeed a realization of our dream." As details leaked, many observers wondered, as did the *Village Voice*, why of all the negotiating parties the Seaport was the one to "recoup the smallest return on its investment." The agreement was sealed in December 1981, but its costs continued to grow. While Hightower pegged them at $268 million, a later analyst estimated $350 million.[6]

"A Wrongheaded Act of Corporate Hooliganism": Deep-Sixing the Pioneer Marine School

If the Rouse Company was supposed to save the ailing Seaport, the cure almost killed the patient. The Seaport's lingering problems only worsened when corporate and individual gifts plummeted, construction disrupted tourist and rental income, costs rose for relocating district tenants, and legal expenses mounted while the SSSC and City Hall renegotiated the leases, whose devilish details few people understood. As a result, in 1981 the Seaport incurred "its greatest annual operating deficit to date"; 80 percent of the $750,000 shortfall stemmed from legal fees. Because the SSSC had no capital, the museum took the cuts. In 1982, twenty-five of its seventy-five employees were furloughed and its budget slashed by 54 percent to $1.7 million. The staff was cut again, to about twenty-five, in 1983. The SSSC escaped the cuts, though its top salaries were double or quadruple those of the museum, and it continued to provide Lowery with a leased Lincoln Continental and his chief aide a Mercedes Benz. Meanwhile, Shepley was consolidating his hold, and his ExCom "was given almost unlimited decision making power."[7]

It was more than budget cuts, however, that sank the Pioneer Marine School in February 1982. Four years earlier, Hightower had known little of the school except that it added "a kind of lustre . . . that would be difficult to duplicate in any other way." Receiving over $3 million in federal support from 1975 to 1981, as well as grants from Brooke Astor, it was a moneymaker and publicity boon. While an English preservationist was complaining that young Britons were averse to hard work and little interested in the marine crafts, City Hall was ranking the Pioneer School as "the crème de la crème of the job training programs." It had already placed seven hundred graduates in jobs by 1981 and was adding new courses in shipyard welding and fiberglass repair. "Incredible! Astounding!" the *Daily News* editorialized on April 3, 1981. The school was so successful that "even the tight-fisted, budget-conscious Reagan administration has agreed to continue funding it."[8]

Yet, five days later, the *Post* headlined, "Scandal Makes Waves at South St. Seaport." The problem was CETA's requirement that 75 percent of all students be placed in jobs for a minimum of thirty days. State administrators had not forced the issue, but after a city-appointed bookkeeper "created a number of fictitious students and, in concert with a check cashing shop up the street, was embezzling . . . [and] shaking down students for kickbacks," the city ordered an audit and discovered the root problem. Subsequently, City Hall and the Seaport quarreled and missed a CETA grant deadline. With a budget shortfall, the Seaport forced the school's faculty and thirty-two students to walk the plank in February 1982. As at the School of Boatbuilding in Norfolk, Virginia, Hightower suggested privatization. Some supporters questioned if racism killed the school. Fearing that its minorities would deter affluent shoppers, the Rouse Company commanded, said the Pioneer School's head, David Brink, "Get rid of the niggers." Dick Rath also blamed Seaport trustees who did not want "black and hispanic faces around to discourage Rouse shoppers." As in the case of *Clearwater*, Pete Seeger's troubles increased when trustees objected to his hiring "an ambitious black organizer" who encouraged racially mixed audiences. And Rousification would remove "anybody scruffy or ragged-looking around" its mall. Rath was so outraged that he quit the Seaport. Rejecting the charge of racism, Stanford still called the school's closure "a wrongheaded and economically counterproductive act of corporate hooliganism."[9]

Hoping to divert the media from the scandal, the Seaport exploited the visit of Britain's Prince Charles in June 1981. Eight months earlier, his father, Prince Philip, the Duke of Edinburgh, had inspected *Wavertree* and *Peking*; stood for photos with Stanford, Kortum, and Hightower; and promoted a proposed ship trust. Dubbed by one child the "Prince of Whales," Charles boarded Malcolm Forbes's yacht *Highlander*, whose perimeter had been searched by police frogmen and bomb experts. Accompanied by First Lady Nancy Reagan, her friend Brooke Astor, and Mayor Koch on a Hudson River cruise, the security employed twelve hundred police and countless Secret Service personnel. The cost to the New York Police Department was $300,000, enough to keep the Pioneer School afloat. All in all, the Seaport basked in the limelight.[10]

Real estate unequivocally took center stage in 1982. After hiring Lowery at Shepley's urging, Hightower became, said Peter Aron, "extraneous

Fig. 7.1. Peter Stanford (*left*), Karl Kortum (*center*), and Prince Philip (*right*), aboard *Wavertree*, 1980. (Photo, Peter Stanford Collection)

during the Rouse construction." Pushed down the ladder, he was treated in what Capt. Jeremiah Driscoll called "a dishonorable, disrespectful manner." Given the perfunctory title of museum director and vice chairman, he was relegated to a side office and told to look elsewhere for a job. Lowery lacked any experience in museums or cultural institutions, but in October 1982 he became president and CEO of both the Seaport Museum and the Corporation, though trustees expected to separate the two presidencies once the real estate development was completed. Further displacing Hightower, Ellen Rosebrock became the museum's executive director under Lowery. Hightower's ouster reflected a national trend as similar institutions placed more emphasis on corporate connections. According to William Murtagh, the National Trust had chosen its new CEO in 1980 on the basis of "his fund-raising capabilities and experience in the corporate world." Was it any wonder that Hightower described Lowery as "the Iago of South Street. . . . He was young, promising, and treacherous." Before Hightower's demotion, he told members to prepare for the worst. With Phase I construction and a national recession, the Seaport's revenue stream dried up. It was an awful year, he admitted.[11]

Those major construction projects at the seaport excited the city's Real Estate Board but worried the fishmongers. They had long resented the encroachment of outsiders, whether it was the IRS, the district attorney, or weekday drivers on their congested streets; now the Seaport became the face of evil. Unable to distinguish between the SSSM, whose staff prized the fish market's authenticity, and the SSSC, which undercut the fishmongers at every step, they regarded them all as "their enemy." City Hall, on the other hand, could play its cards differently and gave the FFM a $3.1 million federal grant to update its facilities. Lowery scorned City Hall's "schizophrenia" because, while demanding that his SSSC maximize revenue and institute order, it refused to raise the fish market's rents. Since the fishmongers only paid a dollar and change per square foot in rent, the SSSC stonewalled their requests for renewed leases. It reportedly told one dealer, "Why should we give you guys a long lease when in a few years this property will be worth millions?" The fishmongers were outmaneuvered by City Hall and the Rouse Company, which led the negotiations. "We are getting screwed," a dealer said. Whenever "we get some verbal concessions from Rouse in our talks, they never appear on paper, and the company denies ever having said anything." With their parking restricted, handcarts unworkable on restored paving stones, and access hindered by construction, fishmongers asked for changes, but the Rouse Company allegedly told them, "Drop Dead."[12]

"This Is So Charming. It Reminds Me of San Francisco": Rouse Opens Its Festival Marketplace

Phase I's opening on July 28, 1983, was a lovefest. First, the Rouse Company held a three-tiered preview. While four thousand cabbies and tour-bus drivers savored hot dogs and lemonade, another ten thousand community members went to a Preview Party. That same night, a select group of 650 people, including Raquel Welch and Walter Cronkite, attended a gala dinner in honor of Brooke Astor. To separate them from the hoi polloi and provide access to the free bar, they were given a pin bearing the likeness of Astor, who humbly declined to wear it and was initially denied bar service. The next day opened with a ten-thousand-serving breakfast, followed by a parade starting at the new World Trade Center and ending at the old one, Schermerhorn Row. The parade attracted over one hundred thousand revelers, and the air was filled with daytime fireworks, thirty thousand American Express balloons, and the bombast of politicians, including Ed Koch and his rival Governor Mario Cuomo (1983–1995). Recently reelected, Koch walked the streets like it was his coronation, said Barwick. With City Hall a short walk away, Koch boasted to reporters, "I will eat here almost every day. You should join me—Dutch treat."[13]

Some New Yorkers concluded, however, that the Rouse development was only a poor caricature of their New York. Carved out of the Museum Block's core was Cannon's Walk, a small courtyard that connected the museum's Seaport Gallery, Model Shop, and Bowne Printing Shop plus an array of merchants. *Architectural Record* beamed that it was "a picturesque hodgepodge of materials, unmatched windows, and crazed wall surfaces." A well-off woman chirped, "This is so charming. . . . It reminds me of San Francisco." A couple from Long Island complimented the New Fulton Market, whose sixty thousand square feet of leasable space was devoted to food, saying, "It's about time suburbia moved to the city." Rouse Company workers, nicknamed Rouseketeers, monitored the market: "Nothing tacky, no fast foods, and a uniform, attractive look." A young doctor who lived a block away knew that his visiting parents would love "the cute outdoor cafés" and say to themselves, "It used to be such a dump." Yet that dump was the real New York for many people. Joseph Mitchell loved the old market, remarking, "In Victorian England they *built* ruins" to evoke history. Despite Stanford's earlier endorsement, he told the press that it accented "high-priced shops" instead of his living "monument to the blue-collar values that created New York's first port." Moreover, the Seaport's role had been reduced so much, the *Washington Market Review* noted, that "in all of the expensively printed Seaport promotional literature one can hardly find the museum mentioned."[14]

Much of the debate centered around Schermerhorn Row. Since its construction in 1811–12, the Row had shown the evolution of the district's history, but its future generated controversy. Early on, preservationists focused on its bricks. Huxtable thought that "there is no brick quite as handsome as that of the 18th and early 19th centuries." Terry Walton loved the patina. The "textures and grime of generations" showed, she thought, "how [those bricks] shaped men's lives and how their past still shapes our lives today." The architect Charles Evans Hughes advised in 1972, "We in turn must avoid prettifying the Seaport buildings." But Norman Brouwer

Fig. 7.2. Front Street, Museum Block (96W), with Cannon's Walk (*right*),
New Bogardus Building (*left*), and One Seaport Plaza (*background*),
2006. (Contrast with fig. 1.4; photo, author)

saw a paradox. Because patina was confused with dirt, he said, "the public
has to be educated to understand the value of seeing things in the raw
more." It also had to be educated on the differences between preservation and restoration, exemplified by the debate over the mansard added
in 1868 to part of the Row that later housed Fulton Ferry Hotel (2 Fulton
Street and 92–93 South Street). As early as 1966, the Stanfords had recommended that the old hotel "should be reconditioned in the style of 1870
to house visitors." In 1968, however, Tom Van Arkel's architectural model
showed the Row without the mansard. That ran counter to Leevi Kiil's first

model, Huxtable's advice, and Giorgio Cavaglieri's later plan. The debate led architect Bronson Binger to ask, should the Row "reflect the passage of time and its mansard roof thus be kept? Or since the Row was built as a unit and is the largest row of Federal style commercial buildings left in the city, should the lower, original gable be restored?"[15]

Chairing the preservation committee, Jim Fitch muddied the waters. While he thought that these buildings pictured "what life in our city was truly like," he did not like the Row he saw. In theory, he said, "restoration is less desirable than preservation" because "it represents a radical and irreversible intervention in the life of an old building." In the Row's case, however, he wanted it "restored to its original configuration" with ground-floor arched entrances, second-floor exterior stairs, shuttered windows, and gabled roof. In 1973, he urged the committee to remove the hotel's mansard. Believing that the hotel "was the life of the block," Mitchell, Cantalupo, Brouwer, and Stanford wanted the mansard kept. Binger agreed, saying that the museum was supposed to celebrate "a century of waterfront history." With a 10–5 vote, the mansard was retained, unlike at Quincy Market, whose roofs were restored and homogenized. The *Times* called Fitch "the outspoken antithesis of a freeze-it-in-amber sentimentalist," and he did reject preservation in this case. Yet the Seaport was inconsistent with the Row's preservation, as it removed a 1935 flat-roofed attic story at 12 Fulton Street and the façade's fire escapes. Moreover, the museum privileged the Row's Greek Revival storefronts over the original Federal, further prompting Fitch's laments.[16]

In 1976, Jan Hird Pokorny, who taught in Columbia's preservation program, was hired by Albany to begin the Row's planning. It was "once the most important block in the city," he said. It was also unique because "no two walls are parallel and there are no right angles anywhere," and it had a hotel room and laundry that had been sealed for fifty years. Still, the *Post* said it "looked as bad as any burned-out tenement in the South Bronx." Finally in 1978, Albany allocated $7.6 million—"the largest sum received by any historic neighborhood in the state"—to begin its first phase. In 1981, the state's Urban Development Corporation took charge of the building and Pokorny's work and reluctantly kept the mansard. In 1983, the UDC transferred the Row to the city's Public Development Corporation, which reimbursed Albany for its acquisition and restoration costs. Indicative of the museum's lack of oversight, it published a freelancer's lead story in *Seaport* on the near-completed Row. Glossed over was the museum's sixteen-year role in the project, the Row's human dimensions, and an acknowledgment that the mansard's removal would have destroyed the sealed rooms. Moreover, the bricks' patina was lumped together with the "half-gone paint and efflorescence," all of which would be removed and make the finished Row "almost unrecognizable," the author gleefully predicted.[17]

With the Row's opening in 1983, it was panned by leading architecture critics of US newspapers. "One of the city's real treasures," Paul Goldberger thought, became "flat and dull"; Philadelphia's Thomas Hine added, it lost "much of its character and dignity." One young boy asked his mother on opening day, "Is this new?" Some criticism was offset when the Albert S. Bard Award was bestowed on Pokorny's firm. What was not included in Phase I's opening but was proposed since the 1966 feasibility study by Fred Rath was a supplement to the Row on the block's corner lot. Included in the press releases on the merger of NYSMM and the Seaport Museum and in the Seaport Development Plan (1980) was a five-story orientation center, which was supposed to have been designed by Pokorny and funded and built by the state. Its turnstile was crucial for the Seaport's financial health, but the state jumped ship.[18]

Immediately to the west was Block 74W, which was inside the urban renewal zone but outside the historic district (1977). Some critics remembered that the Seaport had okayed the demolition of 74W, including its old row and Green Coffee Exchange. After the telephone company relinquished an option and dashed residents' hope for a low-end department store, the SSSC maximized its space with the bankers' air rights. Jack Resnick & Sons, whose $13 million purchase of the block enabled the city to retire its bonded debt from the 1972–73 bailout, wanted to build a million-square-foot, high-rent office block on speculation. In the midst of an office glut, the city refused Resnick's request for a grant and tax abatement. The resulting One Seaport Plaza, whose ground space was leased by Rouse, was "distressing on all counts," said Boston critic Jane Holtz Kay. Its thirty-five stories, complained American Institute of Architects award winner Donald Canty, were "heavy enough to sink Schermerhorn Row into the fill on which it is built." Joan Davidson called it another one of those "egregiously tall buildings at the Seaport's edge." As such, it blocked "the sun from noon to sunset in fall and winter." But the location was its selling point. With a photo of the East River, a *Seaport* advertisement declared, "Views like this can improve your company's entire business outlook."[19]

Another "uncompromisingly contemporary" building was erected at Front and Fulton Streets. The 96W corner lot was cleared in the 1950s to provide a subway air shaft. The Seaport had plans to place the Edgar Laing store (1849) on the site. Built by James Bogardus near Washington Market, the store was dismantled in 1971 when a massive tract of historic structures fell to urban renewal and the World Trade Center. The Bogardus cast-iron structure was "painstakingly removed piece by piece and stored." When the Seaport planned its reassembly, Binger heard, "Someone stole our building." Incredibly, the storage site's fence was not locked. Scavengers netted sixty-three dollars in scrap, noted critic Peter Blake, but "the real culprits, the city's screwer-uppers, will go scot-free, as they always do." The museum's backup plan was worse, as Huxtable called it "a kind of Disney historicism or scholarly sideshow." Funded by UDAG, BBB mimicked the purloined original, creating what Fitch called a "phantom abstraction of its former self."[20]

"The Sense of Funkiness Is Now Gone Completely": Longings for the Past, Welfare for the Affluent

The seaport was also an abstraction of its former self, as it lost what Goldberger called its "sense of funkiness." In *Time* magazine, Wolf von Eckardt used distorted imagery to mock those who liked the old district. "Would it have been more authentic to leave the special place to rats and rapists?" he asked. "Are the historic values better served if they are bulldozed for parking lots or office towers?" His counterpart at *Newsweek* correctly noted that the Rouse Company had ripped "apart the delicate fabric of downtown New York." But for those who had what Tom Wolfe called *nostalgie de la boue*, Blocks 97 E-W, 107W, and 106 still were, Brouwer joked, a "grungy neighborhood." Like *The Seven Lamps of Architecture*, in which John Ruskin admired a building's natural decay, antimodernism ran deep. Those unrestored blocks were "a perfect counterpoint," said Goldberger, to the Seaport's artificial restoration. An op-ed *Times* essayist lamented "the loss of the quiet and solitude of a few square blocks of forgotten harbor and its replacement by a carnival of ersatz charm . . . into which no

Fig. 7.3. Fulton Fish Market, South Street under FDR Drive: Block 97E (*right to center-left*), Block 96E and its one-story garage (*left*), Fulton Ferry Hotel (*far left*, with mansard), 1981. (HABS NY-6368-1; photo, Walter Smalling Jr.; American Memory Project, Library of Congress)

sailor worth his salt would set sail or foot." Because the waterfront was only a contrived backdrop, he appreciated yesteryear's "spiritual charm."[21]

These critics' last hope was the FFM, but to Lowery's dismay, City Hall granted it a fifty-year lease in 1984. Its original letter of intent was converted into a six-hundred-page lease. "The only two books that are longer than this are *War and Peace* and *Gone with the Wind*," griped a fishmonger. "We had to pay our lawyers $125 an hour to read this bullshit." But the fishmongers had more clout than expected as City Hall turned a deaf ear to Lowery's plea to raise their artificially low rents, which would be frozen for a dozen years. As bad, some stalls were illegally subleased to phantom operators who paid sky-high rents only to the mob. Differing with the SSSC, a museum staffer said, however, "We're okay" as long as the fishmongers stay. "I hope to hell it continues to smell."[22]

Rouse critics smelled worse things than fish. As debates intensified over Reaganomics, they called these projects "the playthings of the upper-middle class" and "welfare for the affluent." Noting that UDAG monies "were originally intended to spur construction in inner city areas where private investment alone could not be obtained," the *Washington Market Review*, like many who thought that Koch was selling city lands and services to the highest contributor, asked, why did the mayor "open wide the public purse to primarily benefit prosperous private developers?" In all, South Street Seaport was the most subsidized of any American festival marketplace, with UDAG providing $15 million for the new pier and some $5 million for Seaport Museum's facilities; the federal Economic Development Administration providing $4.3 million for the Museum Block and $3.3 million for Fish Market repairs; New York City providing $23 million for infrastructure; and the state providing some $10 million for the Row. This was all part of what Robert Fitch called "the debt-propelled, subsidy-driven" building boom of the 1980s. In addition, there were tax credits for the rehabilitation of historic, income-producing structures. The Rouse Company also borrowed $90 million, of which half was secured at a 17 percent annual interest rate and the remainder at usurious rates. Having none of its own equity in the project, it took advantage of shelters within the Economic Recovery and Tax Act of 1981. The private sector benefited at the expense of the public, or as Shepley spun it on opening day, "Never has the public and private sector meshed so well." With the boom, there was "a Renaissance for Manhattan," but "the Dark Ages" for the other boroughs and for the museum, which became a come-on for Rouse. As donations plummeted and criticism increased, a crisis flared in late 1983. Lowery implemented more cuts, while expanding the magazine to assure the public that the museum was alive.[23]

Yet the ships were dying of neglect. Stanford kindled fears that *Wavertree* would be jettisoned after seeing "a picture of the development with only one square rigger in it—the big bark *Peking*," the backdrop developers most wanted. Isbrandtsen "used to bitch so much" about the neglect that the board marooned him. "The yacht club crowd never liked Jakob," explained Peter Aron, because he was "too much of a wharf rat." At one meeting, Isbrandtsen yelled, "When the hell are you going to do something for the *Wavertree*?" Shepley replied, "Do it yourself." He did. Unable to work in business "lest his gain be attached by creditors," he focused on this hulk, whose work was more real, he said, than "reading about it in a book." At Hightower's request, the NMHS subsequently took over the project in 1981, aided by the Arons, the Mellon Fund, and Washington, D.C.[24]

Isbrandtsen put up a sign at Pier 15: "Long hours, dirty work, no pay!" and volunteers rolled in. As many as one hundred strong, a devoted cadre worked on Saturdays and Wednesday evenings. Investing "more than 1,500 hours" in 1981, their commitment was, the *Times* headlined, "A Restoration of Spirit." A real camaraderie formed. While some with "highly intellectual managerial jobs" enjoyed the physical labor, others felt spiritually restored or empowered. Many admired Isbrandtsen, who admitted, "I really don't understand why some of them came in." An old ship had "an individual meaning to individual people." Volunteers also worked in almost every Seaport department: a broker worked as a mechanic, a rock-and-roll musician as a carpenter, an aerospace engineer as a repairman, an insurance executive as a project manager, and an import/export manager as a woodworker.[25]

They saved *Wavertree*. As in Reagan-era mythology, they had, said a reporter, "that old-fashioned, free-market capitalist pride in starting with whatever you can lay your hands on and taking on the world—to literally sink or swim by your own wit, daring, and skill." Nearing the ship's centennial, they were "happy, loyal, and productive," but they were loyal to their ship, not the museum. As the Seaport meandered, the volunteers split off into the Friends of *Wavertree* and acquired, through Isbrandtsen's own New York Ship Trust, *Vernie S.* (1897), the nation's oldest certified cargo lighter, and *Black Pearl* (1948), ASTA's former flagship. Facing a power vacuum, John B. Ricker Jr., whom Shepley chose as board chairman, took charge. As the head of Continental Insurance Company, Ricker was not "afraid to take on the opposition," said Lowery. In late 1984, he kicked out the NMHS, despite its raising nearly $1 million for *Wavertree*. Volunteers kept working.[26]

"South Street Has Forgotten What It Is and Why It Started": Creating a New Demographic for the Museum

Stanford had built the Seaport with a people-oriented movement, "This Museum *Is* People." In 1978, he recommended "reorienting staff to volunteer-supported activities." As the Seaport was being redefined around the Rouse mall, however, Shepley, Hightower, and Lowery wanted a more affluent demographic. Yet who was the museum's audience, and how did it fit into the mall's potential base of customers? The museum had evolved since the early Friends. Though not clearly delineated, a shift had occurred not simply from the "we can change the world" of the 1960s to the "me decade" of the later 1970s but also in the meaning of those streets and ships. Cultural critics such as Robert Hewison and David Lowenthal have written about the shifting interpretation of heritage elsewhere, but it was readily apparent at the Seaport. For one, the museum and historic district began to emphasize a message that was less reform minded and personal. Whether one looks at the decisions to end the working-class Pioneer School, to introduce the multimedia show *Seaport Experience*, to reshape the *Reporter* into a glossy magazine, or to prioritize shopping over community, the Seaport was going upscale. Though staff still wanted to explore the port's legacy, the board emphasized entertainment and consumption.[27]

The introduction of *Seaport* magazine in fall 1978 ushered in the change. The *South Street Reporter* had come a long way from its inception in 1967 as a monthly broadside. Later running as many as two dozen pages, it focused on the Seaport's many activities, its face-to-face community, and its advocacy of maritime preservation. That led the Smithsonian Institution's Melvin Jackson to state, "I know of no other maritime museum that covers its activities in publications so well as South Street." At a time when the nation was racially polarized, the *Reporter* published timely feature stories, such as "The Black Man and the Sea" in the winter of 1973–74. A sensitive topic that few museums broached, the six-page story addressed the issue of racism. Dissenters were bashing other museums, as when black poet June Jordan told a Gotham conference, "If you cannot show and teach [me about black America], then why shouldn't I attack the temples of America and blow them up?" The *Reporter*'s Stephen Canright portrayed antebellum black sailors experiencing "unusual equality" and "upward mobility," but those conditions worsened after the Civil War. Noted leftist historian Herbert Aptheker called it a "most informative feature," and Seeger agreed, saying that the *Reporter* "set a model for other organizations—meaningful, beautiful, but not slick."[28]

Hoping to outgrow the financial crisis by increasing membership to one hundred thousand, Stanford suggested remaking the *Reporter* into "the organ of historic community interests throughout New York." Shepley wanted more, offering the services of Time Inc. to create a triannual magazine that would be "national in interest and local in focus." The remake was dramatic; gone was the spotlight on the Seaport itself, reduced considerably was the public feedback, and increased significantly was the visual array, particularly full-page ads for major corporations. *Seaport* became less a museum voice and more a glossy magazine about New York City history. Under editor Marshall B. Davidson, formerly at *Horizon* magazine, it was attractive and exciting, but it had its critics. Rosebrock said that "the Museum itself doesn't get through" after the regular coverage of the ships, buildings, and programs was deleted. "It is so slick it lost its substance," an angry member charged. "It almost seems that South Street has forgotten what it is and why it started." But *Seaport*, which Lowery increased to a quarterly, was targeting a more affluent base—either through memberships, advertising, or corporate links—and trying to fund the museum.[29]

The Seaport's theatrical program also shifted. Since 1970, it had sponsored an outdoor summer theater-on-the-pier under artistic directors Michael Fischetti and Jean Sullivan, both skilled actors. In 1974, it staged a superb rendition of *Moby Dick* in which a *Times* writer really felt Melville's presence on the waterfront. Wanting an indoor venue, the Seaport asked actress Helen Hayes and Mary Lindsay to establish South Street Theater. Using a space on Water Street, it was up and running in 1974—but only briefly, as the Seaport's fiscal crisis hit. In 1978, the troupe moved to midtown on its own. Once Hightower arrived in mid-1977, he wanted a more "sensory experience," à la Marshall McLuhan's media. Mayor Koch urged the Seaport to develop a show using new technology. But with a worse fiscal crisis looming in 1982, the Seaport and the Rouse Company partnered with the Trans-Lux Corporation, "a pioneer in the development of 'environmental theater.'" Rouse advanced "a $3 million vote of confidence" to produce the multimedia show and remake an old building as a theater. Once Rouse was repaid, the museum would receive "a sliding scale commission."[30]

Accruing no expense, the Seaport privatized its introduction to the district. *South Street Venture* was produced by Paul Heller and written, designed, and directed by Rusty Russell, both of whom had created *The New York Experience*, a popular attraction at Rockefeller Center. In what would now be called edutainment, the Trans-Lux theater lobby resembled a Hudson River Palace Steamer, its employees dressed in period costume, and its walls pictured the seaport's wharves, taverns, and brothels. "If you didn't lose your life on board," warned an ad, "you might lose your soul in port." Even more alluring, *South Street Venture* relied on state-of-the-art technology in which seventy-six motion-picture and slide projectors showed a collage of movies and photographs on a forty-five-foot-wide cyclorama screen, with Quintaphonic sound delivered via thirty-three speakers synchronized by a computer. "As one eats buttered popcorn," said *Gourmet*, "the film dazzles the eye and wraps one in the voices, sounds, and smells of the nineteenth century."[31]

Though *South Street Venture* premiered at $3 a head on July 27, 1983, it was ceremoniously debuted on November 16 when its $250, invitation-only tickets drew such celebrities as Charlton Heston, Dustin Hoffman, and Donald Sutherland for an American Film Institute benefit. As the 289 seats swiveled and tilted and as sea spray and fog filled the theater, the fifty-five-minute production, narrated by Tony-award winner Colleen Dewhurst, depicted a clipper ship rounding a stormy Cape Horn, the burning of the clipper *Great Republic* at its South Street wharf, and the festive openings of the Erie Canal and Brooklyn Bridge. "Much as I generally can't stand educational movies," said a *Daily News* columnist, *South Street Venture* was "a painless way to learn history." He unequivocally closed, "The South Street Seaport is one of the cleanest, safest places in New York. Do yourself a favor and plan a visit." However, a *Newsday* reviewer dismissed it as "a glorified slide show" in the " 'I Love New York' spirit." Puzzled by the show, the *Times* listed it in the newspaper's "Spectacles" section next to a laser rock show. It was later renamed *Seaport Experience* because, said Trans-Lux chairman Richard Brandt, "We did not want it to sound like an investment request to our patrons." Perhaps it should have.[32]

First showing daily on the hour, *Seaport Experience* ran only on weekends by 1990 and then disappeared. Trans-Lux faced difficulties because of its continuing losses. Brandt blamed the SSSC for higher rents. The SSSC's later head said that the show reflected the board's "poor understanding of the power of authenticity" and that it "died of its own weight." It also hurt the museum, said Seaport program director Sally Yerkovich, as many showgoers "seemed to feel that they had 'seen the museum' " and skipped the museum's own ticket booth. *Seaport Experience* was, unlike Colonial Williamsburg's film *Story of a Patriot*, also difficult to reformat and show elsewhere. Its absence left the Seaport with no orientation. It could have shown *The Street of Ships*, an independently produced film on the battle to save the district and its traditions, but because it praised Stanford,

Isbrandtsen, and their allies, who had fallen out of favor, the Seaport chose not to show it. Moreover, said a reviewer, it did not "gloss over the difficulties and conflicts that have dogged the Museum since its founding."[33]

"New York Is Being Americanized":
Pier 17 and the Suburbanization of Gotham

More upscale than Phase I's New Fulton Market's 60,000-square-foot space, Pier 17's Seaport Mall opened in 1985. When announced by Ed Koch in 1979, Phase II was billed as a two-story, 110,000-square-foot pier. Phases I and II's total 264,000 square feet exceeded Rouse's malls in Norfolk, whose Waterside opened in 1983 with 80,000 square feet, and Baltimore, where Harborplace rented some 150,000. They were all inspired by San Francisco's Ghiradelli Square, as was Liverpool's historic Albert Dock, which reopened in 1988 but was "a contrived space" devoid of history. Yet it was "one of the most popular 'free' attractions in the UK." Cut from the same cloth, Albert Dock, Quincy Market, and the Seaport Mall were the era's leisure suits.[34]

Ever since the unveiling of Pier 17's plans in 1979, it had generated controversy. As the Rouse Company wrung "as much income-producing space from the [Seaport] project as possible," the SSSC approved "a much larger, three-story retail pavilion," said Lowery. The heavily subsidized, gargantuan structure jutted four hundred feet into the river and obstructed views of the Brooklyn Bridge from the museum's piers. Moreover, Rouse's revised plans forced *Peking* initially to move upriver out of sight. While the National Park Service controlled its museum pier in San Francisco, Rouse was controlling this space. Complaints mounted when it charged tenants a hefty $600–$650 a square foot. Former Urban Deadline architect Michael Sorkin warned that it would exclude poor and working-class people. The MAS meanwhile thought it made the adjacent historic buildings and ships "look like doll-house accessories." Objecting that it lacked the promised open space, the Parks Council was dismayed that City Hall was accepting design changes without the required approvals. Still, Pier 17 won a design prize and Thompson the AIA Gold Medal, ostensibly placing him in the ranks of Frank Lloyd Wright. As its New Fulton Market sales were disappointing and tenants rebelled, Rouse admitted before Pier 17 opened that the Seaport Mall had been "a shot in the dark."[35]

Tensions flared in the district. As Lowery recalled, construction vehicles were vandalized, but "when we asked Carmine [Romano] for help in stopping it, it did stop." Similarly, as Rouse had rushed in 1983 to open Phase I, its contractors were forced by mob-influenced unions to sometimes pay quadruple the going wage. Even tenants faced shakedowns. "It's scary, it's threatening, and it's pervasive," said one. Reporting on the construction industry, the *Wall Street Journal* focused on the Row, where there were four separate labor strikes and "a daily cash payment" to buy peace. But the Row's wiring was cut a week before opening, and electricians worked overtime to repair the damage. With organized crime as the law of the land, said the district attorney, the Mafia controlled "every facet of the Fulton Fish Market with virtual impunity."[36]

Fireworks heralded the 1985 opening of Pier 17 on September 11, a date that was to be eclipsed sixteen years later by tragedy one mile to the west. With four days of events and fireworks by Grucci, who had staged Reagan's second inaugural, it included a speech by Mayor Koch, who claimed, "This is one of the most important developments to have taken place over the last eight years of this administration." Closing the ceremony, a one-thousand-member choir sang "I Love New York." Later that day, a Rouse spokesman admitted that the mall would not make a profit for three to five years but predicted it would become very profitable and attract more visitors, as tourism was forecast to become "the biggest business in New York State" by 2000. Critics undercut that optimism. The publisher of *Harper's*, John R. MacArthur, penned a *Wall Street Journal* essay regretting that once-authentic waterfronts such as South Street were being replaced by 1980s glitz. His preference for an "Old-Time America without the Gloss" was troubling to Rouse because it needed the business of *Journal* readers. His worry was shared in Maine. Portland's city managers hired Rouse in 1981, but that incensed locals who fought against the waterfront's remaking for upscale customers.[37]

Pushed by neoliberalism's public-to-private transfers of wealth, those waterfront developments represented an increasing class divide. As Jim Fitch said, "under capitalism, all real estate development tends toward gentrification," but he naïvely hoped it could be accomplished "without evicting the population." Koch was frank: "We're not catering to the poor anymore. . . . There are four other boroughs they can live in. They don't have to live in Manhattan." Kurt Andersen wrote in *Architectural Digest*

Fig. 7.4. Schermerhorn Row, with Fulton Ferry Hotel (*left*) and One Seaport Plaza (*right, background*), 2010. (Contrast with fig. 1.5; photo, author)

that developments such as the "cute 'n' corporate South Street Seaport" were erasing Gotham's "gritty, high-spirited, helter-skelter charm." Like a dozen cities elsewhere once known for their uniqueness, "New York is being Americanized" with "spic-and-span places for tourists." Fitch felt vindicated when Rouse drew millions of people to the district. His firm, BBB, rehabilitated the Museum Block, and Fitch, a former Communist, derided critics as "from the professional left."[38]

"Do Fish Oil and Perrier Mix?": Cultural Clashes on the Waterfront

Since the Seaport's first discussion with Rouse, it was recasting itself as more chic and elite. For a ball aboard *Peking* in 1978, it employed "Pat, the Bonwit Teller doorman," so that "when he opens the car doors, he can greet everyone by name." As it groped for funds but faded into the district, the Seaport shifted from respectable to pandering. Said *East Side Express, Peking* became "the sophisticate's fresh choice for benefit galas and business blasts," as well as debutante parties and fashion advertisements. For the launch of a $120-per-ounce perfume, Opium, designer Yves Saint Laurent installed a one-ton Buddha, four thousand white orchids, and red silk Chinese lanterns aboard *Peking* for the seven hundred celebrities attending its "coming-out party," which cost $250,000. Lowery had said he would avoid any "incident inimical to the dignity of the institution," but pushing Opium crossed those bounds. The ad included a beautiful blonde in a sensuous Oriental robe and a drug-induced haze. As the perfume's sales skyrocketed to the fifth-best seller worldwide, "the Opium War of 1979" started. A Chinese American antidrug group threatened a national boycott; the chairman of New York's civil-rights commission called the ad "cynical beyond imagination." Exploiting *Peking*'s cultural chic, however, the Seaport made $70,000 yearly from renting the ship. Sometimes designers reciprocated, as in 1981 when Lord & Taylor hosted an Oscar de la Renta dinner dance that raised $40,000 for the museum. Such galas were defining moments for polite society, but some critics questioned their frivolity. Investment banker Felix Rohatyn set off a storm when he criticized the opulent balls of Brooke Astor and Annette de la Renta. Although he had saved the city financially in the 1970s, he was blackballed by the socialites.[39]

When the MAS asked in 1981, "Do fish oil and Perrier mix?" the answer was no. Not only did the odor from 140 million pounds of fish yearly permeate the area; its working-class culture was a world apart. For one, Barbara Mensch demonstrated that in her photo essay *The Last Waterfront: The People of South Street*, and a Seaport Museum staffer praised the book. For another, the eccentric Edmund Francis Moran was a Seaport fixture. After spending three decades at sea, he became a museum factotum but had "pretty severe behavioral disabilities," said Matteson. "I suppose that South Street, like the fictional version of the cathedral of Notre Dame, had to have its very own hunchback; and, like the Opera, its very own phantom." Wall Street's lunchtime workers flocked to Pier 16 to see Moran work. He was "dear to us," said a staffer, as he represented "our vanishing American nautical heritage." In a feature article, Moran told the *Times*, "As a lifelong seafarer, I am a hedonist, an insatiate of sail." Eventually he was sent to a sailors' home because, as Joseph Conrad noted, "Too much time ashore rots ships and men."[40]

Perrier eventually won out. While the *New Yorker* selected a sketch of a crowded Fulton Street for its cover in 1984, a four-color, forty-eight-page *South Street Seaport Guide* was placed in the *New York Times Magazine*. The museum zeroed in on tristate-area suburbanites, Manhattan singles, and Wall Streeters who numbered half a million workers. With "the air of Upper East Side chic," exclusive chains such as Ann Taylor moved in. The Fulton Supply Company had sold nautical wares for three generations, but Rouse replaced it with a Neiman Marcus. Even individual entrepreneurs remade themselves. In 1892, David T. Abercrombie opened a South Street shop to sell expeditionary gear to explorers, but by the 1980s Abercrombie & Fitch sold trendy clothes to urban thrill seekers at the seaport. The district became, said *East Side Express*, the "emergency supplier of cashmere and caviar," not caulk or cable.[41]

In tandem, more affluent audiences attended Seaport concerts. Some featured top artists at modest costs. In 1981, the Seaport's summer-long "Save Our Ships Benefit Concerts" included not only the eclectic rocker Leon Russell but jazz greats Lionel Hampton, Dizzy Gillespie, and Dave Brubeck. Other concerts were free, including Mobil Oil Corporation's Summerpier series (1980–87). Music and gentrification went hand in hand. "Thirty years ago, if any corporation had underwritten free jazz on the waterfront," the Seaport explained, "people would have feared for their lives. . . . The waterfront was inhabited by black-jacketed youths personified by Marlon Brando." Unlike the modern yuppie, those 1950s characters were "ethnic, anti-Establishment, and of the streets."[42]

The FFM's streets had long drawn the curious. On one walk, for example, Helen Hayes and a friend came upon the Meyer's Hotel on Peck Slip. Its Paris Bar, they said in shock, "looked so lusty that it crossed [our] mind its patrons must be a far cry from those we meet in the cocktail lounges of mid-Manhattan." However, they felt "uplifted both physically and emotionally" by the sheer thought of entering, which they did not. But Mensch was curious about the fishmongers and did. After moving to the fish market in 1979, but not knowing that the Mafia operated at the bar, she entered at four a.m., the middle of the FFM's workday. She encountered "the toughest-looking men" she had ever seen. The area once included Sailortown, but when museum folklorist Tom Walker explored, he found "old sail lofts and signage" but nothing else. The FFM had long attracted other visitors—the slummers—whether high school kids such as Kent Barwick or "uptown revelers" who came "in stretch limos" for breakfast.

"Dawn is the only time to visit," said one. "Here you see a vital life—like some mad circus. Then, suddenly, at 10 a.m., it is quiet again."[43]

The pace picked up at noon in the Bridge Café at 279 Water Street, one of Manhattan's rare wooden buildings (1794) and its "oldest drinking establishment." Though historically worthwhile, it was initially slated for demolition, as it was, said Stanford in 1971, "outside our area." But it survived to tell its sordid history, one that the Seaport's walking guide omitted. Known by sailors as "the Hole in the Wall," the bar and brothel had been "the domain of drunks and degenerates." Sailors most feared its buxom bouncer, who would club an unruly sea dog, bite off an ear, and deposit it in a pickle jar atop the bar. Later, Ed Koch was a regular customer at the gentrified café and preferred instead "its nouvelle cuisine," while having the ear of "Wall Streeters in Brooks Brothers suits."[44]

The drinking tradition continued three blocks south at five p.m. "They call it Yuppie Square," reported the *Post*. While a Rouse manager watched "the swarming crowds," he claimed that "their shipboard predecessors would [have been] proud of them." The *Wall Street Journal* noted that the NYSE's young traders sought the seaport's "light beer, bouncy barmaids and throbbing David Bowie music." The "huge and unmanageable" crowds frightened Sally Yerkovich, however. Even Ed Moran complained that it was difficult to enjoy a beer. Up to five thousand people jammed Fulton Street, creating "the Disneyland of happy hours," said a banking executive. But as the museum floundered, the owner of Roebling's, a three-floor bar in the New Fulton Market, what he mistakenly called "our beautiful 19th century building," said, "I love the aesthetic value the museum brings, but if it closed, the people would keep coming down." Residents complained, as did Peter Neill living in the Low Building, that "the drunken yuppies . . . would find John St. a convenient place to piss, vomit, or copulate on the way to the subway." It worsened on weekends, reported the *Journal*, when suburban teens made "the seaport feel like Times Square on New Year's Eve." The bad PR compelled Rouse to create its own police force. Proper New Yorkers, once fearful of Jack Tars and the Mafia, remained "wary of the place."[45]

Though Huxtable said that the Seaport had "sold its soul," its heart was also in peril. In the mid-1970s, the museum had five landside galleries. Rouse promised "125,000 feet of new exhibition space," but it did not happen. Instead, Rouse maximized its sales, Trans-Lux took a building for

April 30, 1984   **THE**   Price $1.50

NEW YORKER

Fig. 7.5. *New Yorker*, April 30, 1984, cover. (© 2010 Condé Nast; all rights reserved; cover by Arthur Getz; reprinted by permission)

its theater, and the state reneged on its Visitors Center. The museum lost space again when the SSSC rented 75 percent of its exhibit area to commerce by 1983. Lowery and Shepley not only admitted that the SSSC had "drained the Museum," which "would take years to redress," but promised that 1983 would "be the last year" the SSSC would need an SSSM subsidy. Lowery projected that it could "make $17,000,000 yearly" for the museum. Trusting those predictions, observers concluded that the Seaport had "enormous potential in the years ahead."[46]

"It Is Better to Work These Things Out in a Positive Vein": The Board and Volunteers Plot against Lowery

Critics cried out that the SSSC emperor had no clothes. That led to a painful process of putting the museum first and reasserting its control. In 1984, the first step was to search for a new president who would build "the best maritime museum in the world." Focusing on the completion of Phases II and III, Lowery would remain as SSSC president, but as criticism swelled, Stanford could take no more. He and Lowery were scheduled to talk separately at the National Trust's 1984 annual meeting, but Lowery, anticipating Stanford's critique, did not attend. There Stanford denounced "the urban manipulators, profiteers and make-out artists" associated with the Rouse deal, but he was challenged by the Trust's new maritime director, Peter Neill. With "a plan to get rid" of Lowery, Stanford began what a trustee called "a waterfront brawl."[47]

While few institutions air their dirty laundry so publicly, intrigue and suspicion were in the air. Coincidentally, the Seaport served as the background for *Sabotage*, a Harlequin thriller written by the spouse of the waterfront director, who was having his own troubles with the board. Charles Deroko read the "potboiler" and said its villains and heroes were "easily identified to their real-life counterparts." Reality was as worrisome because Lowery saw the Seaport's factions uniting against him. In early 1985, dissident trustees formed an emergency committee, in which Peter Aron argued that Lowery had failed in handling museum programs, trustee relations, and public image. Privately Aron wondered if Shepley's ExCom had a "hidden agenda" to phase out the museum. Yet, thinking "it is better to work these things out in a positive vein," he wanted Lowery to gracefully step down. "Some kind of radical change must take place—and promptly," he said, "if the institution is to survive at all." That included forcing "a substantial portion of the Board" to resign and revising the bylaws to limit ExCom.[48]

At the same time, Stanford wanted to expose the SSSC's alleged fraud. It was no surprise that Gotham's high-stakes real estate industry was more concerned with profitable deals than with someone else's ethics. There, "manipulations of money, law, politics, and morality" were so routine, said Huxtable, they made "Machiavelli and the Medici seem like simple country folk." As the museum was financially imploding, Stanford charged that dishonesty permeated the operation, and he accused Lowery of "fraudulent" accounting. Meanwhile, *New York* magazine reported that the SSSC had "netted more than $9 million since its inception," but the museum had received nothing. Stanford also discovered that the SSSM had subsidized the SSSC in 1983 through an interest-free loan of $738,000, "plunging the debt-ridden Museum still further into the red." Lowery countered that these were "professional expenses" for the negotiating, planning, and approval process. Believing the scandal had reached stygian depths, Stanford readied an editorial for *Sea History* charging that the SSSC had also paid John Lindsay and his law partner Donald H. Elliott, who served as museum counsel, "over $1.7 million" in "what we used to call 'honest graft'" for simply "playing a standby role during the settlement of the Rouse deal."[49]

One part of that alleged payment was a "check for $200,000" reportedly passed by Lowery. As Hightower maintained, "The $200,000 that went to the law firm through Don Elliot . . . was indeed conveyed by Lowery without the approval of the Executive Committee and my knowledge of it." If that check represented legally contracted services, why was it done without ExCom's knowledge? Hightower admitted, "I doubt that any other trustee knew of the transfer except for Shepley," whose "unilateral decisions" were accepted by the board "as the chairman's prerogative." As such, Hightower regarded it as legitimate. Stanford differed. "In good old Tammany style," he said, the money was given to "compensate a former mayor for his past services as mayor in advancing the cause of the Seaport Museum." If that was the case, according to laws regulating charities, it was hardly "honest" graft.[50]

As an NMHS trustee and Seaport librarian, Brouwer nervously watched the episode unfold. As he explained, "Peter learned that large amounts had been paid to lawyers, he believed most of it for no actual services rendered. He was going to expose this with a full page editorial in *Sea History*. He apparently believed the State would then dismiss the South Street board and appoint a temporary replacement in which he would play a central role." Yet Brouwer balked, wondering if "his charges were adequately backed up with evidence." Fearing a lawsuit, he resigned from the NMHS board. His caution was warranted because Stanford's allegations were in a gray area, being difficult to prove or disprove. While Lowery denied Hightower's claim of a $200,000 transfer, Elliott would not discuss it years later.

Fearing legal fallout, NMHS trustees forced Stanford to pull the editorial. Regarding the charge of "honest graft," little can be said but that a fog of mistrust and desperation settled over the museum. That charge shaped its subsequent course.[51]

Meanwhile, Isbrandtsen was telling his volunteers that the board was "trying to get rid" of him and *Wavertree* to make room for developers. In fact, Donald Trump wanted to build the world's tallest building (1,940 feet) there. The *Chicago Tribune* called the hotel-office complex "one of the silliest things anyone could inflict on New York," prompting a $500 million libel suit by Trump. It was later deemed a "risky venture," and he was not able to secure the site. As Lowery was trying to sell the SSSC's leases to developers, volunteers told the press that if Lowery had his way, the Seaport would "sell the boats and go into real estate." Supporting the grassroots, the museum staff added that the corps of volunteers helped the Seaport "remain true to its original ideals and thereby ensures its future success." Prodded to action by the Trump plan, the plot to expel Isbrandtsen from the board, and the museum's layoffs and fiscal crisis, Volunteers in Support of South Street Seaport Museum (VISOSSSM) formed in March 1985. Encouraged by Stanford, volunteer Joseph Baiamonte hesitated because of the difficulties forming a "highly political organization" to defend the ships. With Capt. Driscoll paying the legal fees, the VISOSSSM launched its investigation of the museum and corporation and took it to the press.[52]

By February 1985, the museum's losses went from bad to dismal. Volunteer Gerald Boardman noted that, as it was "going into debt at the rate of $100,000 per month," this was the "worst it has ever been." Isbrandtsen, surviving Shepley's attempt to expel him, won a cautious board majority to force Lowery's resignation as museum (but not corporation) president. Shepley had finally lost control. One trustee told the *Post*, "There's too damn much emphasis on real estate." Lowery countered that he had been hired to develop "the district, by whatever means necessary, and within a very narrow scope that was imposed by the city and state." Still, Stanford asked Koch, whom he called "an old pal from Reform Democratic politics," to investigate this "first-class scandal," but the developer-friendly mayor did nothing. At the board's urging, the museum's executive director, Wentworth Durgin, slashed its budget. Because Lowery maintained his own accounts, the museum's Emergency Committee asked for, but was denied, access to his books. Lowery reportedly called them "trouble-makers." The resulting "Monday Morning Massacre" in early March jettisoned one-third of the staff; included among the twenty-two layoffs was the head of educational programs, the public affairs director, and *Seaport's* editor.[53]

Even then, the board could not make its next payroll. With trustees meeting on March 13, Shepley promised $200,000 from area developers if Isbrandtsen and Stanford "would stop making damaging remarks to the press and giving community." He also alleged that Stanford had urged Koch and Rouse not to bail out the museum, which Stanford denied. What Peter Aron did next became legendary. Shifting the focus, he said that "poor management" had caused the fundraising and operating failures. Without naming Shepley, he went after his lieutenants, chairman John Ricker, vice chairman Robert Hubner, and Lowery. He came to the meeting with a $300,000 challenge grant, but when no one volunteered to help, he told his colleagues, "The giving community doesn't have confidence in the present board and the present staff, and so I can't give you this check." He then tore it in half. Confirming Aron's fear, Ricker, who was also SSSC chairman, replied "on [Lowery's] recommendation" that "the Museum should close its doors," an even more lethal idea than his earlier suggestion "that the trustees turn the institution over to Rouse to manage." Some trustees were jolted to their senses, and "the motion never came to a vote." Megadeveloper Larry Silverstein "spoke enthusiastically in behalf of carrying out the museum's mission & was applauded." When the power brokers called a recess, Ricker, Hubner, and a handful of others resigned. After the catharsis, the mood changed, and the board "agreed to end the bickering." With the corporate–yacht club alliance holding on, Robert McCullough, a former chairman (1976–78), was elected interim chairman because, he explained, "I seemed to be the only one on the board they would back." Aron then rewrote his check.[54]

The press exposed the rift. Because the Seaport's managers had become "so obsessed with real estate," said the *Journal*, it had only one exhibit, which was borrowed, in late 1984. For the first time, moreover, NYSCA rejected a grant request in 1983 and for several years after. Ellen Fletcher quit as executive director in late 1984 because "there was nothing left to direct." From 1984 to 1985, paid admissions fell by 34 percent, foundation grants by 67 percent, and membership by 30 percent. Saddled with an $89.5 million mortgage, Rouse was only paying the minimum rent to the SSSC, or about $500,000 in 1985, of which 60 percent went to the city and the rest covered the SSSC's overhead. Isbrandtsen told the *Times*, the deal was supposed to give the museum "70 percent of its income," but this had evaporated. That was nothing new for Rouse, which experienced similar difficulties and made similar promises elsewhere. As a result, former boosters turned sour, including Hightower, who was axed in early 1984. Perhaps as acerbic as his dealings with Lowery, he later returned to Pier 16 vending homemade vinegar. As he told the *Journal*, the Seaport's board was at fault.[55]

By 1985, the Seaport was insolvent, demoralized, and ridiculed. Motivated by Shepley's plan to reverse the 1960s experiment, remake the district, and redefine the museum, its Seaport Development Plan (1980) had promised so much but ended up alienating the base of the city's largest historical society. Carrying out the agendas of City Hall and the D-LMA, the Seaport under Shepley's leadership privatized the waterfront, began to prettify the district, terminated the city's most successful job creator, and destroyed its own program. By 1985, it was a disaster. Yet the Seaport still had remarkable physical assets, including its ships and an impressive site. As is said in the real estate industry, "location, location, location" could perhaps save it.

8

"The Museum Was Intellectually and Financially Bankrupt"

How the Seaport Fared after the Bubble Burst

Upon arriving as president in 1985, Peter Neill realized that the Seaport "was intellectually and financially bankrupt." Museum reformers did rein in the SSSC, whose development-minded trustees, said Lowery, were "either gone or thoroughly dispirited." Still, Lowery pursued his Phase III plans for a hotel, a marina, and high-rises but was limited by Manhattan's real estate swings, the LPC, and the fish market. As part of a national shift away from hiring curators or historians to administer museums, Peter Aron, as chairman of the SSSM search, was looking for a person well versed in museum management who could develop educational and cultural programs. Aron asked Neill, head of the National Trust's Maritime Division, for suggestions, and Neill unabashedly suggested himself. After being selected, he asked to keep his Washington job, which Aron rejected as embarrassing to the Seaport. Neill made it clear that he would not be answerable to Lowery. Thus, he would set his own course, especially after Aron began a twelve-year stint as museum chairman in 1987 and Neill merged the presidencies of the SSSM and the SSSC in 1989. But his success depended on gaining the necessary income, philanthropy, endowment, and city subsidy.[1]

Sharp and creative, Robert "Peter" Neill III skippered the Seaport for nineteen years. Seymour liked him because he "looked so good on paper, and he talked so good." But he was not a curator, scholar, museum manager, or even an expert in large-ship preservation. Though occasionally an outspoken renegade in the crusty museum world, he could pour on the charm with the media, yachtsmen, preservationists, activists, and residents who were often hard to please. As a youth, he had watched the Mississippi River's traffic, read C. S. Forester's Horatio Hornblower series, and was enthralled by Irving Johnson's *National Geographic* travelogues. "I learned of another hemisphere beyond St. Louis," he recalled, "of native girls with bared breasts, and of tides and squalls and other natural phenomena." Johnson inspired his "teenage flight from the Midwest to subsequent roaming." That was typical. "Most seamen are dreamers," said Melvin Madison, a nautical shopkeeper in Gotham. "Most seemed to come from the Midwest, from farmland, where they'd never seen anything but a river—a lake. They never saw an ocean. And possibly reading, or from movies, the allure of the ships, the allure of foreign lands, brought them to the waterfront. Now once they were bitten it was hard to get away." Leaving St. Louis before its Gaslight Square failed, Neill was sent to a prep school in New Hampshire. He first saw the ocean when he visited Mystic Seaport and toured *Charles W. Morgan* before heading to Stanford University to study English. After completing a master's program at the University of Iowa's Writers' Workshop, he moved to Connecticut, lectured at Yale University during its tumultuous 1970s, and then headed the Branford Land Trust, which fought a proposed shopping mall. Criticizing developers who pushed unlimited growth, he wrote in the *Times*, those malls were "a flagrant violation of the conservation ethic."[2]

In 1979, Neill was hired as executive director of Schooner Inc., in New Haven. Inspired by *Clearwater*'s program, it had formed in 1975 and expanded by buying *J. N. Carter*, a bugeye ketch that had been restored by *Pioneer* owner Russell Grinnell. Schooner relied on school contacts for 70 percent of its operating revenue, and Neill used new business models to float his ship. He read about Lance Lee, who applied Kurt Hahn's Outward Bound philosophy to establish boat-building apprenticeships, and in 1981 offered his ship to an educator who was creating the Sound School. Funded by the city of New Haven, a federal grant, and a philanthropist, it began with one hundred students—60 percent male and 70 percent minority—and became a marine-centered, magnet public high school. Just as the Pioneer Marine School had been praised, the National Trust applauded the school's use of *J. N. Carter* for giving students "a sense of self worth and connectedness." To prorate the cost of the ketch and shipwright across multiple users, Neill also formed and headed the Connecticut Marine Science Consortium, in which he joined the Sound School, Schooner, and four campuses of Connecticut State University. It was, said the *Times*, one of the state's "most innovative marine science programs." To build a $1 million marine studies center, he struck a deal with the city of New Haven and a developer, thus boasting that he was "one of the few folks around" who had helped found a maritime high school and headed a private development corporation.[3]

Before that deal ran aground, Neill was hired by the National Trust in 1984 to direct its Office of Maritime Preservation. Initially funded by Op Sail 76, the Trust's maritime office had held conferences in 1977 and 1981, formed a task force that met periodically, and helped distribute moneys that Senator Edward Kennedy had first earmarked for Stanford's American Ship Trust. As a result, it assisted maritime projects in thirty-three states. While the National Trust focused on teaching and publishing and disseminating information, it had done little for ship preservation, other than start an inventory, which was finished by Norman Brouwer and documented the neglect. By 1984, for example, only 24 of 112 historic vessels had a comprehensive restoration plan, and only 37 had a comprehensive maintenance schedule. Neill learned that the ship-preservation movement was fractured and paralyzed and that most Americans regarded it as "alien and useless." Considering the setting of standards, he hired White Elephant Management (later, Tri-Coastal Marine) as a consultant. Its Donald E. Birkholz Jr. warned that, without any regulatory or licensing boards, standards were unrealistic. The ship community even questioned whether the Trust should "be a moving force in maritime preservation." Neill backed off, saying that the Trust's strength was "diversity and decentralization." He instead encouraged sail training, legislation for archaeology, waterfront revitalization, and better public relations.[4]

With conservatism running high in the ship community and Washington, Neill tossed familiar lines. Touting the Reagan era's self-help solutions, he lauded values "frequently mourned in our society," including the work ethic, individualism, and teamwork. When he saw inner-city teens at the Sound School "discover discipline and order as tools for survival," he said to himself, "that's what preservation is all about." As with his Connecticut consortium, he also emphasized the era's "joint private-public efforts," which were already a Trust policy with its Main Street program of the mid-1970s. Like "something in the window to attract a client into your store," he also thought businesses could benefit from maritime programs. "By being wrapped in the development," the museum could then "spend more time on programs and activities that generate financial stability for it *and* for the development." Still, Neill was unhappy with the Trust's traditional focus. Suggesting that what most mattered in history

Fig. 8.1. Peter (*left*) and Jack (*right*) Aron, aboard *Peking*, 1975. (Photo, Peter Aron Collection)

was not the artifact but rather its inspiring "way of life," he thought that too many places regarded their waterfront merely as a backdrop for commerce. He said that was wrong. *Historic Preservation* magazine featured him favorably, but he discounted his work, later telling a reporter that "the job was pleasant" with "a lot of canapés at cocktail events in D.C., [and] a lot of jetting around the country cheerleading for the program," but it was "not particularly challenging." Despite a real need, he realized that his position was more show than substance. One of his successors regarded him as "definitely the most dynamic and visible of the Trust's maritime people," but the organization "never really committed to maritime preservation."[5]

Then came the Seaport's job opening. Neill knew that South Street "was notorious for sinking ships, not saving them." Some colleagues warned it would be a bad career move. He said, "*what* career?" Walking Pier 16, he told himself, "This is the most exhilarating possibility you could ever have." Besides, he would be, according to Stanford, "the highest-paid maritime museum director in the world," with a salary of $150,000, compared to Lowery's reported $92,000. Driving the Seaport's remaking was Peter Aron, who hoped to create "a 'world class' museum"; he sensed that Neill had the necessary "ego and enthusiasm" for the task. Even if the crisis-prone museum failed, "it really wouldn't be [Neill's] fault." Reflecting years later, Aron added, "I was young and foolish, was lucky enough to have access to some meaningful financial resources, and just didn't believe that we should give up." Still, Neill fully understood "the dire realities," particularly of preserving large ships.[6]

"My Metabolism Is Absolutely Driven": Neill's Baptism by Fire

Neill's three-year contract began on June 1, 1985. "I am not sure I could even read a balance sheet," he said, "but I had plenty of ideas, energy, and no career to put at risk of failure." While Wentworth Durgin served another year as executive director over finance, operations, and community relations, Neill became acclimated. But, said Howard Slotnick, he was "naïve, like a rube," and he "didn't know how to do business" in Gotham. Still the media gave him favorable press and did so throughout his tenure. The *Wall Street Journal* called him "charismatic and energetic," while *Soundings* noted, "Like many goal-oriented people, he assumes that everybody else shares his vision. It makes him impatient with some, but it also makes him a hard man to refuse." Neill conceded, "My metabolism is absolutely driven." That would create friction with staff. Lowery agreed, saying, "he came in like a whirlwind, demanding to take control of everyone and everything."[7]

The board gave Neill a mandate to change course, so as an early step he redefined *Pioneer*. Rejecting the advocates of the drug-rehab program as "agents of nostalgia" distant "from funding realities," he committed *Pioneer* to money-making school programs and recreation. Endorsing the latter, *Crain's Business* urged its passengers, "open the wine and feel the sun on your shoulders and sea spray on your face." Those with sea legs could even help with the sails. For the harried sort, this was "a tonic from the noise, dirt and tensions of New York living." *Pioneer's* shift from social reform to the Me Decade's personal enrichment was, said George Matteson, "a necessary evil" because its "economic survival was in real jeopardy."[8] That survival also required dealing with volunteers. Calling them "an extraordinary resource," Neill needed their support but warned those in the VISOSSSM that it had a "bad reputation." As the VISOSSSM was cast in the mold of "This Museum *Is* People," however, its leaders feared that he wanted "to control all aspects of the Museum." To gain political strength and a "say in the day-to-day operations," the VISOSSSM invited the mayor, a congress-man, and a raft of neighborhood and business leaders to its South Street Revival in 1986, but only a smattering showed. Its feel-good spirit, said *Newsday*, was a polite fiction because of the bitter divisions over the mall. Pointing to the mere forty there, Stanford sneered, "What happened to the vision of a citizen center?" Taking such comments poorly, Neill would endure what he called the "endless bad-mouthing and second-guessing by Stanford and friends."[9]

Criticism of the seaport mall continued to swell. In 1985, Columbia University had held a conference honoring James M. Fitch and his found-ing of the historic preservation program. Conferees were taken aback by the remarks of Wayne De La Roche, a graduate who was presenting his "swan song to the preservation field." Referring to a large holiday advertis-ing supplement in the *New York Times* that promoted seaport vendors, De La Roche focused on the district's commercial takeover. Voicing a pres-ervation philosophy like that of William Morris, he took on his mentor. What "irked developers and city officials," he said, was "the real history of the Seaport," as shown in its "cumulative buildup of age and grime." Just as Neill had criticized the National Trust for privileging artifacts, De La Roche charged that Columbia's program and affluent Americans mistook "aesthetics for history," causing "old buildings, like makeup or fashion, to become marketable and therefore exploitable commodities." Calling the seaport mall "the grossest atrocity to be passed off as a bonafide preserva-tion project," he regarded himself as Daniel in the lions' den. The mod-erator "tried to usher [him] off stage," but when he closed, "a loud round of applause" followed because, he thought, he had "touched a chord they could not deny."[10]

Rejecting the commodification of history, De La Roche suggested that the seaport mall reflected the "economically and environmentally tenuous" trends of Reagan's America. The fusion of the museum and retail experiences, which was also occurring in Britain, meant, accord-ing to *Progressive Architecture* editor Suzanne Stephens, "that one kind of value system (commercial) can easily dominate the other (cultural) without the culture-seeker being aware." Hence, as the marketplace was pushing consumption and titillation, what developed at the seaport was "an amusement park ambiance" of self-absorption. New York State had already ramped up vacationing with its "I Love New York" campaign in 1977, and "messiah mayors" such as Ed Koch were stressing tourism to improve their city's image, to employ unskilled workers, and to push a service economy. The emphasis increased when the Alliance for Downtown New York, which succeeded the D-LMA, joined with the Kaplan Fund to develop a Heritage Trails project in the 1990s. While downtown became the city's second cultural hub, that commercialization of history, noted Thomas Bender, stifled creativity and threatened "to turn the metropolis into a museum of its own culture." Yet it capped what David Rockefeller started in the 1950s, the deindustrialization of Manhattan.[11]

"How Does a Museum Join Forces with a Developer?": Thinking of Phase III

De La Roche said the Seaport was selling "history by the pound," but by the square foot was equally accurate. Though Neill's board wanted him to focus on the museum, not real estate, the SSSC was still the unassisted developer of the urban renewal district, and he, like Lowery, wanted to sell its leases to raise money and stimulate growth. Calling this "a groundbreaking and complex issue," the Municipal Arts Society had asked in 1981, "How does a museum join forces with a developer and still maintain its own independent vision?" For Phases I and II, it recommended that the Seaport "lock friendly horns with Rouse." But Neill, still believing Rouse's grand predictions and facing the Seaport's deep debt, took a pro-development approach. Deriding critics, he pointed to Phase III, suggesting that the area north of Beekman Street be "developed as a retail-residential mix," like in SoHo or the East Village, "where the artists have money in their pockets." A former manufacturing district, SoHo was remade with bistros and chic shops. "That's the price of getting something saved," Margot Gayle conceded. "There's got to be money in it for someone." Yet SoHo was unlike the Seaport, said planner-turned-professor Richard Weinstein, as it drew "lots of small entrepreneurs." The bohemian East Village also gentrified as nostalgia became its fare. But there was a fine line, noted the *Times*, between hipification and crassification. After founding the Lower East Side Tenement Museum in 1988, its president realized, "We risk losing conscience about what it is to be a stranger in the land."[12]

Fig. 8.2. Seaport overview: Block 98's parking lot (*left*), Block 97W-E (*center*), Block 107 W-E (*rear, left center*), 1981. (HABS NY-5632-1; photo, Walter Smalling Jr.; American Memory Project, Library of Congress)

The museum's Seaport Plan complicated Phase III development. Pressured by the D-LMA, Stanford had earlier accepted the conversion of the blocks north of Beekman Street (97, 98, 106, and 107) to residential high-rises (see map, fig. 2.1). That commitment collapsed, however, after critics pushed for rehabilitating older buildings and constructing compatible newer ones. Still, larger trends—the overbuilding (1970–75), recession (1973–75), and high inflation and interest rates that lasted until the mid-1980s—dampened Lower Manhattan's market. While wooing Rouse in 1977, city planners tried to force the issue by only earmarking Blocks 74E and 96W for restoration. To give developers more land, they marked Blocks 97 and 107W as under "future consideration," despite their significant historical fabric. In 1983, Rouse publicized its interest in Phase III, which included the waterfront above Pier 17.[13]

Literally out of the blue, Edward Kennedy took interest in Phase III. Sailing in the Mayor's Cup, he docked at Pier 16, where Lowery introduced himself and made his pitch. Investigating a possible UDAG grant,

Kennedy's senate staff told Lowery that if City Hall would apply, it would help. Lowery calculated that an $18 million grant was needed. "In essence, together with Phases I and II," he said, "the plan called for developing a giant ring of restored historic streets and buildings, and a pedestrian esplanade and marina, around the fish market." Lowery had reportedly lined up operators for a hotel, marina, and a ferry to Brooklyn. While the Department of Housing and Urban Development promised to "look favorably on a grant proposal," Koch, who was beholden to his real estate allies, did not. Said Robert Fitch, that was because "the Rockefellers, with a consortia of foundations including Ford and J. M. Kaplan," had asked the city to "shut down real estate development on the east side" to uplift their West Side interests. Then came the Wall Street crash of 1987, when the Dow Jones lost 20 percent of its valuation. That led to a recession, a real estate slump, and the downsizing of perhaps one hundred thousand jobs in Manhattan's financial service sector over the next decade. Almost 30 percent of Wall Street offices stood empty. Gotham's 1988–94 recession was "much deeper and longer than in other cities in the US and Europe." While business leaders feared downtown was dying, Rouse blamed its problems on the museum, saying, "We're waltzing with a corpse." It knew the feeling because some of Rouse's tourist-based malls had fiscal rigor mortis, such as at AutoWorld in Flint, Michigan, which Michael Moore lampooned in *Roger & Me* (1989).[14]

The FFM's tenancy hurt the district's marketability. To the north of the Rouse mall, its waterfront near Peck Slip was "ragged, with dilapidated chain-link fences, rotting timbers, and strewn garbage." Many people complained about the fish stench, but Neill praised its authenticity, saying, "Breathe deeply." He also regarded the fishmongers as the last genuine tradesmen and recalled that his "kids played there among the fish-heads." However, that debris created problems, said resident Gary Fagin. "There were rats—big ones," but the feral cats "kept them somewhat under control." Once fascinating Ada Louise Huxtable and Sidewalk History, the cats were fed by Capt. Jeremiah Driscoll "by the hundreds" until anonymous complaints led the Humane Society to remove them. After the earlier run-ins between the two men, Driscoll blamed Neill.[15]

Though on the defensive, fishmongers held on. When Neill suggested closing John Street for museum programs and ship restoration, they

Fig. 8.3. Fulton Fish Market, Peck Slip, 1982; note the many boarded-up windows above the ground-floor fish stalls in Block 97E (*left*) and 97W (*right*). (Photo, Andrew Moore)

successfully resisted. The FFM was again threatened when the Port Author-ity opened its high-tech Fishport in Brooklyn in the late '80s, but Fishport instead failed. In 1986, US Attorney Rudolph Giuliani began investigat-ing the Mafia at the FFM. "I was interviewed several times by the special prosecutor and the FBI," Neill recalled, but "I never saw any evidence" of the mob, which operated in the stealth of night. While Mensch thought that the Mafia had "an honor among thieves," Neill called Giuliani's probe and attempt to revoke the SSSC's lease "sudden and uncompromising." Manhattan Borough President David Dinkins, who defeated both Koch and Giuliani in the 1989 mayoral elections, took the market's side, while the courts stymied federal attempts to take over the union in 1989. Still, a federal administrator warned that "physical coercion, not the laws of New York," prevailed there. Some neighbors feared the market's ouster. The Seaport Community Coalition (SCC), which replaced the VISOSSSM in 1986, called on City Hall to "forge 'a positive partnership' with fish market operators," with whom they had not had a problem.[16]

"New York Seemed a Pale Reflection of Boston": How a Mall Undercut a Museum

Both the mob-backed Local 359 and Rouse proclaimed their good intentions, but their not-so-public agendas were murky and their tactics underhanded. Yet Neill believed that an accommodation could be reached with Rouse. After convening a select group of museum directors, trustees, and foundation and business leaders, the American Association of Museums issued a report, *Museums for a New Century*, in 1984. The Seaport was "in the vanguard," said Neill, and the AAM praised its partnership with Rouse as "the kind of joint venture enterprise by which other museums can benefit." Presciently Neill said, "our success or failure will have implications for other museums as they become more and more entrepreneurial." Only later did he concede, "I was naïve and had bought into the Rouse mystique." The report reflected more of Reagan-era market ideology and less of Fulton Street's reality. *Museums for a New Century* pictured a unique, cooperative partnership in which the developer and Seaport had "the right to review and approve the other's plans" because "collaboration with museums is good business." Whether "good business" meant Rouse could undercut museum programs, cancel the leases of popular vendors, or push unsympathetic development was not mentioned. The AAM repeated Rouse's claim that "everyone wins" with the museum "in the midst of the market." Still, the Seaport's turnstile did not turn. "A lot more people came to the Seaport," said Joe Doyle, "but they tended not to set foot on the ships, in the theater, or in the museum buildings. As a result, the promised pot of gold for SSSM programming never materialized."[17]

Moreover, while Rouse's Seaport Marketplace began with a bang with the company reporting in 1985 that it "led all urban and suburban Rouse Company retail centers in sales per square foot," business flattened as newer or revamped shopping plazas opened at the World Trade Center and its offshoot, the World Financial Center. But the SSSC was in far worse shape, reporting a $2 million deficit in 1985. After museum trustee Slotnick demanded cuts, James Shepley, who sat on both boards, curtly said it was not the museum's business. Suspecting fraudulent bookkeeping, Slotnick told his board in 1987 that "Rouse was realizing a substantial profit margin." As Peter Aron conceded, "there were always accounting ways" to dissemble the moneys so that "the museum never got a nickel." Oddly, *Crain's Business* concluded in 1987 that the seaport was "a great place . . . to make a buck." But not for the museum, whose membership fell from a high of 25,000 in 1973 to 6,800 in 1982 and bottomed out at 4,447 in 1985. Worse yet, the Seaport lacked a visitors' center to capture revenue. When it placed a small Pilot House from a 1923 tug on Pier 16 to sell tickets, the Seaport Community Coalition objected and fought (unsuccessfully) the loss of public space.[18]

Few people understood the differences between the SSSM, the SSSC, and Rouse's Seaport Marketplace. First using the name "South Street Seaport" in 1967, the museum trademarked it in 1991, as it had the term "Seaport" for its magazine in 1979. But the public and press used the two trademarked terms for the entire district. *WoodenBoat*'s Peter Spectre, for example, conflated the museum, corporation, and mall in 1989. "South Street isn't much of a museum," he wrote. It was a hodgepodge of "boutiques and restaurants and gifte shoppes decorated in a crypto-nautical motif." Some scholars followed suit. Failing to consider that the lease left the museum penurious, one historian asserted that the museum "must produce consumers in the mood to purchase the particular commodities the Seaport sells." Confusing the hordes on the street with the handful at the turnstile, this historian contended that consumers were drawn in through the "museum's interpretative programming . . . into a special network of associated meanings" that energized consumption. That critique fit Colonial Williamsburg's tightly controlled space and marketing but not Fulton Street's chaos.[19]

The Seaport Museum's grapes had turned to vinegar, but the seaport district seemed to bubble like champagne. In 1987, when the district became "the city's third most popular tourist attraction" (after the Statue of Liberty and the twin towers), Rouse achieved a "record-breaking sales figure of $560 per square foot." But with high rents, shop owners pleaded for help, especially after Wall Street crashed in late 1987 and a recession set in. Sponsored by the mall and museum, a 1988 ad blitz placed posters in all Metropolitan Transportation Authority trains and major commuter railroads, copies of *Seaport* in the Pan Am shuttle and airports, and an exhibit in a WTC hotel. The blitz succeeded but confused the public about the difference between the mall and museum. That year, a Gallup poll proclaimed the district the city's number-one destination. "You go to the Statue of Liberty only once," Neill said, but the seaport was "always changing." The numbers game was illusory, however, as figures included lunching Wall Streeters and short-term pedestrians. Rouse also exaggerated its success, failing to separate the then-booming Pier 17 from the failing New Fulton Market. City Hall was "the biggest winner," with $1.2 million in annual rents and "$5 million to $7 million in sales tax." That did not count parking fees, income taxes, or One Seaport Plaza's contribution of over $11 million annually to the city. City Hall called the $375 million development "an astronomical success."[20]

Despite the seaport district's being number one, there were too few customers. Twelve million annually visited the district in the late 1980s, but that was "just one-third of what Rouse originally predicted and not nearly enough to support the stores." As Downtown Express concluded, "Either those early figures were inflated enormously for the benefit of legislators, or the planners did a staggeringly bad job." Regarding the district as slick and touristy, locals stayed away or just cruised. That tourist identity was exactly what Benjamin Thompson had wanted to avoid at Quincy Market, and the National Trust made an about-face, regretting "the 'Faneuilization' of waterfronts." Rouse blamed the fall in tourism on the sky-high number of homicides in 1990, the Persian Gulf War, and a fear of urban terrorism in 1991. Then came the 1993 bombing of the World Trade Center and more fear. While Seaport founders had pictured the gritty district as the *real* city, Rouse increasingly marketed its image as a suburban-like refuge, especially after *Time* pictured a "rotting big apple" in a cover story. One of a half-dozen television spots Rouse paid for in the summer of 1991 pictured an egg frying on a city sidewalk, a cooler waterfront, and the tagline, "The South Street Seaport, where New Yorkers go to get away from New York." As the recession-wracked city cut its public services, the seaport not only was, said the Rouse ads, "interesting, safe, clean, [and] well-kept" but offered "a lot of things to do for free." But free was not the case for the museum, which desperately needed admission fees. Initiating a 10 percent budget cut in 1994, Neill laid off his public relations director, whose last act was to angrily notify the press. Neill griped that "the next day there was 18 inches in the NY Times about [the museum's] lay offs and financial collapse."[21]

"Turning Over More Times than a Restless Insomniac":
Failing Tenants and Shifting Identities at the Mall

As the developer and museum quarreled, the 120 Rouse tenants felt, said one, "like we're the children of a bad marriage." That bond had begun with lofty promises. Assuring historical accuracy, Rouse had pledged that it would "authentically reflect the best that the Seaport was and can again become, while maintaining its heritage and unique New York atmosphere." Moreover, it had promised to feature a "reasonable number" of stores specializing in "maritime and sea-related activities and products." Wanting to maximize its return, however, Rouse reneged on its promises. Neill warned Rouse, "I will not allow this place to be turned into a strip mall." With all the infighting, *Downtown Express* caustically defined the seaport "as a vicious circle housed in a 12-block rectangular historic district." After Rouse planners proposed a superentertainment store for the empty New Fulton Market, Neill retorted that "a Disney-like experience [there] would be a travesty." The mall's manager rebutted, "[It's] what we are." Disney-esque spectacles were on the rise elsewhere, whether at Colonial Williamsburg's nightly closing ceremony or at battlefield reenactments. Pressured by residents to restrain the glitz, Neill ended up in shouting matches with mall executives at CB1 meetings. City Hall further deferred to Rouse, giving its security officers first-call policing in the district. Said a museum lawyer, Rouse's officers ignored museum properties. As a result, *Pioneer* was sabotaged, a gangway pitched in the river, and museum buildings repeatedly urinated on.[22]

Meanwhile, merchants "turned over more times than a restless insomniac." New Fulton Market was almost empty on its tenth anniversary. Even Roebling's bar, which predicted it would prosper if the museum failed, was jumping ship. In late winter and early spring, the place was a ghost town. The mall blamed Neill, but Peter Aron suggested that Rouse had changed, and he asked, "Is it only the economic times in which we live? Is it a lack of vision and imagination, or is it simply worship of the 'bottom line?'" Rouse was desperate and had cleared the New Fulton Market of "its small, locally based tenants hoping to lure big, national retailers." Its architect, Benjamin Thompson, had hoped that it would be part of the community, but those big retailers, said sociologist Sharon Zukin, unified investment, production, and consumption within international capitalism.

As historian Nicholas Bloom concluded, Rouse's focus on maximizing returns created "chain-dominated selling environments." Typical was its lease to the Nature Company. Pete Seeger had asked New Yorkers to appreciate the East River, but the company's boss called it "the least ideal" location because it did not "have the space and feeling to be contemplative about nature."[23]

Rouse also forced out Sweet's, the district's oldest restaurant, which had served seafood since 1842. Whether Lucille Ball or John Doe, customers came for the fresh fish. Since the FFM was closed on Saturdays, Sundays, and holidays, Sweet's was too, prompting Rouse's displeasure. With the restaurant unable to pay its rent, which had risen from $2,000 to $12,000 per month, saddled with back taxes, and damaged by a nor'easter, Scrooge evicted it shortly before Christmas in 1992. Rouse replaced it with Ann Taylor, an upscale retailer more appropriate for Rouse's desired demographic in Gotham, whose average income in 1995 was $59,500, some $25,400 higher than the nation's median household income. By then, the district's foot traffic was 60 percent tourists, 25 percent Wall Streeters, and 15 percent other New Yorkers. In 1998, Rouse also forced out Sloppy Louie's, which was immortalized in Joseph Mitchell's *Up in the Old Hotel*. Like Sweet's, it had "amazing name recognition worldwide," but it was old-fashioned with cafeteria seating. Rouse emphasized, said Jakob Isbrandtsen, "the buck before the character."[24]

With more glitz and pizzazz, the $2.2 million Ocean Reef Grille opened in 1987 on the top floor of New Fulton Market, but it set off a different kind of controversy. The interior setting was stunning because above its multitiered, simulated ship deck were suspended thirteen historic boats. The array caused a legal and ethical storm. After "a $24,000 donation [was] made to the museum by the restaurant for the purpose of purchasing the boats" and giving them to the museum, Neill leased the fleet back to the restaurant. Museum staff and volunteers questioned the deal, location, and neglect. In addition, Isbrandtsen loaned *Sun Dance II*, a lapstrake ketch entrusted to his safe keeping, but it was ruined by the installation. A museum volunteer and Seaport Community Coalition president, Joseph Baiamonte, contended that "the small craft collection of the museum is being intentionally damaged." He demanded that the boats be "brought back into the control of the museum for . . . real public viewing and education." The boats stayed put, as a new restaurant, Bridgewaters, competed for clientele with the New York Public Library, the Museum of Modern Art, and others with artifact-rich reception areas. As more galleries rented out their space, critic Michael Kimmelman warned, "museums, having devalued their principles for short term gains, may earn the public's contempt in the long run."[25]

Rouse torpedoed the seaport's oldest retailer. Captain Hook's Marine Antiques & Seashells had rented a Row store since 1973. "As motley an assemblage as has ever been gathered crams the shop and pushes on onto the street," observed the *Times*. Customers readily paid the twenty-five cents to enter the re-created pirate's cave store. Said an investment banker, "It's very New York." When Rouse raised the monthly rent from $2,000 to $20,000, owner Joe Hill protested, "There's a man-eating shark in our midst." Collecting donations in an empty toilet bowl for a court battle, he sued, saying, "They're bringing suburban stores to the Seaport, which is against the lease requirement. . . . And the city is sleeping behind the wheel." Hill was evicted in 1998, and City Hall was to blame. After rescinding the SSSC's leases in 1995, the Economic Development Corporation (EDC), which succeeded the city's Public Development Corporation in 1991, maximized its return. In a feature article on the district, the *Times* gave the last word to Stanford, who fumed, "The commercial development is all trash." What was not mentioned was that the mall had finally become profitable in the mid-'90s boom.[26]

Dealing with Rouse was so difficult that the Seaport hired Stephen Kloepfer in 1998 as executive vice president and general counsel. He was asked specifically "to improve the Museum's relations with the City of New York, and curb Rouse's worst excesses." In 1999, for example, the museum scheduled a Summer Sea Chantey Concert series aboard *Peking*. Rouse deliberately scheduled its own simultaneous program, whose "eardrum-blasting" music "drowned-out" the chanties. When approached, the mall manager refused to lower the volume. The Seaport complained to its landlord, the EDC, that the Rouse concerts attracted unruly crowds, enraged district visitors and residents, and disrupted other businesses. But after its complaint, the situation got worse, not better. While Neill objected to a strip mall, Rouse allowed events—including male strippers—that were out of place, especially in a historic district surrounding a state-chartered educational institution. Writing the EDC, Kloepfer complained that Rouse allowed everything from distributing condoms to exhibiting photographs of nude women to displaying inflatable beer cans. But, he said, EDC's intervention "was underwhelming," and "Rouse's level of taste or conduct," which resembled old Sailortown, did not improve. He blamed the city's deaf ear on the Seaport's lack of "influence or patronage in City circles."[27]

A "Very Rough and Tumble" Neighborhood:
Residents and Developers Eye the Seaport

Manhattan trends were also shaping the seaport's fate as land values soared. In 1982, a run-down, four-story walk-up sold for $350,000 but by 1986 was going for $1.5 million. Land speculation and upscale housing were spurred in 1981 by federal tax advantages promoting restoration and adaptive reuse. The problem was aggravated by the spillover population from Greenwich Village, the high cost of Manhattan housing in general, and the transference of wealth into fewer hands. These changes, said critic Jim Sleeper, would "make the New York of 1995 unrecognizable to keepers of the civic flame ignited by Al Smith and Fiorello H. LaGuardia." After zoning changes took effect in Lower Manhattan, affluent residents also moved into the upper floors of older, nearly empty skyscrapers to enjoy their world-class views. But the Lower East Side, whose northernmost section was dubbed the East Village by realtors, showed the worst gentrification. Since the 1950s, bohemians and artists had been drawn there, but they were challenged by Wall Streeters and professionals in the early 1980s. The older residents, warned a developer, would "all be forced out. They'll be pushed east to the river and given life preservers." Protests followed at Tompkins Square Park, where dissidents distributed leaflets that read, "GENTRIFICATION = CLASS WAR!" In the mid-1990s the gentry surged in, so that the East Village was "downright Victorian" by 2004.[28]

Two miles away, the SSSC slowly started Phase III in the late 1980s. North of Beekman Street, many buildings owned by the EDC, fishmongers, or speculators were vacant above the first floor. In 1986, when musician Gary Fagin moved to Water Street in Block 106, it "was very rough and tumble" and still looked like "that famous, evocative extended scene in the 1970s film *The French Connection*." It was policed by the Mafia, who set their own parking fees. "If someone mistakenly parked in a fish market area," a forklift "would just pick up the car and move it, and not very delicately. Repeat offenders found their windows broken and a pile of dead fish inside their cars." There also were squatters and transients. A legend in the making was Fish Market Annie, a peddler and reputed prostitute; once "a raven-haired knockout," she became coarse, ribald, and gray. Another peddler hawked "folk art ships" he made from scraps. Owners complained to CB1 about the homeless squatting in gutted buildings whose bare-brick walls, plank floors, and exposed timbers were ironically becoming chic in gentrified homes. Though residents lacked amenities such as a grocery store, they established "an incredible sense of community," said Fagin, as with Water Street's annual neighborhood street fair, where, thanks to Driscoll, they grilled trays of lobster and shellfish. Some gentrified buildings rooted the upwardly mobile—just like the instant ancestors one acquired by buying old portraits or the quick erudition that the Strand bookstore sold for five dollars a foot.[29]

What affected seaport developers, however, were the countervailing interests of the LPC and the SSSC. In 1977, ten blocks and three piers of the Brooklyn Bridge Southeast Urban Renewal District were listed on the National Register. The Board of Estimate excluded Block 106, however, as its post office considered expansion and the banks wanted to sell their air rights there. Thus, a conflict developed between the SSSC, which needed developers of its own leased lands to pay its debts and spur further development, and the LPC, which protected the historic district. An impasse followed, leaving many buildings in Block 97E-W and 107W, as well as 106, deteriorating. By law, said former landmarks commissioner Anthony Tung, any transfer of air rights required the LPC "to certify that tall new buildings . . . achieve a 'harmonious' or 'appropriate' design relationship with the historic structures from which the air rights originated." Yet Block 106's projection for a skyscraper, variously set as between twenty-six and fifty floors, was overwhelming. When the LPC suggested including Block 106 in the historic district, a *Times* editor cried foul. Picturing it as a battle between NIMBYs and the banks, he declared that it "would betray the banks" and "cripple use of 500,000 square feet of air rights" reportedly worth $15–20 million. While high-rise tenants to the west lobbied to protect their vista, the district's residents, said Fagin, wanted to preserve their views of "the majesty and uniqueness of the Bridge" and its nearby low-rise buildings. The Seaport Community Coalition, CB1, and the MAS supported the LPC's proposal for Block 106 and raised suspicions about the developer who was maneuvering to buy enough parcels to erect a high-rise. Adding to the intrigue, the developer, rumored to be "a Rockefeller cousin," hired an associate, who was allegedly an adjunct ethics professor, to pester residents to sell. With the help of borough president David Dinkins, who was to serve as mayor (1990–93), the Coalition won Block 106's inclusion in the Seaport Historic District in 1989. One developer's gripe reflected the national attack on land-use restrictions that protected historic, scenic, and public sites. "Landmarking the block deprives us and other owners of a reasonable use of our land without any compensation," he said. "I believe it's nothing short of a naked taking and I think it's unconstitutional."[30]

To the south, the fate of Block 98 was up in the air. In 1972, it had architecturally worthwhile buildings that the museum let fall for a parking lot. Billionaire brothers Paul and Seymour Milstein, "two of the shrewdest, hard-playing developers in Manhattan," entered the picture. It became, said Fagin, a "classic David versus Goliath" contest. For a reported ten dollars, the Milsteins acquired the block in 1979, but the deed stipulated its inclusion in the historic district. With "the inside track at City Hall," however, the Milsteins pushed for a showcase project to jumpstart Phase III. With Lowery's nod, they repeatedly proposed a high-rise at 250 Water Street. Kent Barwick and the MAS coalesced opponents, and the LPC rejected the Milstein proposal, despite City Hall's opposition. The principal issue was the floor area ratio, which determined building size. Nearby buildings had a FAR 4 or 5, but the Milstein proposal in 1983 called for a whopping FAR 18. Other proposals in 1986 and 1989 were also nixed by CB1 and the LPC. City Council member Miriam Friedlander called the proposed fourteen-story building in 1989 "a front for gentrification." Neill testified that it was "a complete violation of the spirit and understanding with which the district was created." Yet the Seaport itself had once proposed a high-rise there but backed out after the Friends and preservationists protested. In 1991, the LPC approved a plan for a ten-story structure, but it fizzled as a recession again hit the city.[31]

During a debate over a Milstein plan for Block 98, the MAS issued a 1990 report, *Zoning and Historic Districts*, which highlighted the seaport's dilemma. Advocating contextual zoning within and around such districts, the report proposed height controls so that newer buildings reflected existing FAR patterns. Rejecting the charge that the MAS was antidevelopment, Barwick emphasized tourism, which was "the second biggest industry in the state." With Giuliani as mayor, the Milsteins inaugurated "round eight of one of the longest landmarks battles in the city's history" by proposing a shocking thirty-two-story complex in 1996. Finally, as contextual zoning became accepted, the block was rezoned. The Milsteins' lawyers threatened that if they were blocked, "nothing would ever be built on 250 Water Street." The Seaport Community Coalition proposed a six-story townhouse development that could win "a handsome profit." The Milsteins refused, but their opponents had legitimate concerns that in the end were validated, said Lowery years later. Financiers then turned their attention to the East Village. Block 98 remained vacant.[32]

Blocks 95E, 97, and 107W illustrated variances in funding. On 95E, private developers had converted the seven-story, former Beekman Downtown Hospital into condominiums, most of which were sold to Wall Streeters. A building on Block 107W had been rehabilitated as a seventy-room Best Western hotel on Peck Slip. The SSSC, which was deep in arrears to its city landlord, controlled much of Block 97 but was unable to find a developer because of its own poor record, the Milstein flap, and the air-rights debate. Since it lacked an ability to borrow or issue bonds, it transferred development rights to companies vetted by the EDC. But the recessed economy, tight financing, and unrealistic schemes killed proposal after proposal. Block 97W's major success was the Seamen's Church Institute. Moving there, it redeveloped a landmark building and empty lot on Water Street into a $12 million structure with a chapel, sailors' respite, and exhibit space. Most of Blocks 97E-W remained, however, in a "sad meltdown condition."[33]

Pressures increased on the SSSC. While the *Times* noted in 1990 that the area was "at the mercy" of the Seaport's "real-estate empire," City Council member Kathryn Freed demanded that the Seaport "just be a museum." The SSSC also pointed to unprofitable leases that the PDC and the EDC had refused to revise since 1981. With annual rents pegged at "$1.65 per square foot," the FFM paid only $27,000 a year, but the SSSC spent $120,000 annually on the facilities. In effect, it was subsidizing the city, and it wanted better terms or an exit. In 1992, the Dinkins administration offered a deal, but, beset by the city's fiscal crisis, it took a year to finalize. Though the SSSC had $17 million in liabilities to third-party creditors, besides what it owed the EDC, the city signed a memorandum of understanding on the last day of Dinkins's tenure, December 31, 1993. In return for a limited-term subsidy and a capital contribution for the Row, it agreed to assume the SSSC.[34]

The next mayor, Rudolph Giuliani, shelved the deal, left the SSSC hanging, and directly confronted the FFM's mob and union. His enemies retaliated. On March 29, 1995, two days after City Hall announced its plan to take over FFM operations, the Tin Building was torched. After its sprinkler system was turned off and gasoline poured in the hallways, one third of the structure was destroyed, causing $4 million in damage. The *Journal of Commerce* called it sabotage. Then the mayor's Commissioner of Business Services led an early morning raid, but an angry crowd prevented any arrests. A former federal prosecutor called the FFM "the most intractable organized crime problem in the Northeast." Still, a truce was brokered, leading to "the beginning of the end of Cosa Nostra control over the market." Unwilling to let the ruin deter tourists, and despite plans to move the market, Giuliani rebuilt the structure to what Phillip Lopate called "a frontless, functional, breathtakingly unadorned state."[35]

Giuliani refused to proceed with the Dinkins-SSSC agreement for another reason besides his determination to wrest control of the FFM, and that was "the debt to third parties" that went back to the 1972–73 bailout and amounted to some $17 million. Chase Manhattan Bank was willing to discuss forgiving its loan, but Isbrandtsen's Seaport Holdings balked. Deeming the Dinkins memorandum of understanding "null and void," the city demanded that the SSSC pay $1.4 million in back rents. Knowing it could not, the city declared it in default. Terminating its lease on August 17, 1995, the city seized the property and raised FFM rents ninefold in 1996. The city also acted on the SSSC's leases in Blocks 97E-W, as residents warned of "irreparable damage" if matters lingered. After lengthy court battles, the EDC reclaimed those properties in 1998 and resolved to develop them individually. Meanwhile, the Seaport retained its leases for Piers 15 and 16 and its museum spaces on Water, John, and Fulton Streets. Finding plenty of poor business decisions but nothing sinister, board chairman Aron told trustees that the SSSC had "failed as a business, but there was no impropriety." He did blame Rouse, however, for dragging the museum down. Stanford faulted Neill for thinking that "no one would ever foreclose on a museum." Neill, who had announced a decade earlier the board's intention of discharging the Phase III leases, countered that larger issues—the city's agenda, the SSSC's failure, and the museum's own needs —set the framework.[36]

Giuliani forced the FFM out to remake the waterfront and to boost rents and revenues. In 2001, he agreed to locate the planned Guggenheim museum, which *Newsday* called "a modern pretzel-like edifice," just south of Pier 15. Had the Guggenheim plan succeeded, the district might have been perceived better because the seaport was the place New Yorkers loved to hate. A local urban dictionary defined South Street Seaport as "a tourist trap mall." Was it any surprise when Hollywood remade a sci-fi classic in 1998 that Godzilla, smelling something fishy, emerged from the river to crush South Street one big foot at a time?[37]

When Peter Neill was hired to put the museum first, Rouse was the eight-hundred-pound gorilla in the district. Inheriting an operation shaped by Mayor Lindsay's urban renewal plan, the Shepley-Koch-Rouse deal, and the fact that the museum occupied choice real estate, he was hamstrung by the era's market ideology and the city's fluctuating economy. He struggled to regain the Seaport's identity, but it became evident that, trademarked or not, New Yorkers regarded it as a mall. His attempt to capitalize the seaport district's number-one tourist ranking showed little return, as Rouse, which was plagued by debt and poor management, squeezed every commercial cent it could out of what was supposed to represent an authentic, old-time scene. It thus became Neill's task to attract the throngs who visited the mall, loved its ship ambience, or read about its seaport. But first he had to create what Peter Aron had mandated: a world-class maritime museum and busy turnstile.

9

"It's Tough When You Have a Museum in a Mall"

How the Seaport (Almost) Succeeded

As conceived, the Seaport was pure Sixties. Its district—a "museum without walls"—offered an open-ended, personal experience; its decentralized exhibit spaces accorded with the era's notion of self-discovery and disdain for conventional institutions. Small was beautiful. Personal was political. The museum, said the founders, "lives best if it is broken into manageable bits that can be encountered and entered into casually. Thus, we avoid putting the past away in a separate room, and we also avoid the sense of overwhelming collections that generate awe but little relevance to life today." Whitney North Seymour Jr. had wanted a building with conventional exhibits, but Philip Yenawine, its program director in the mid-1970s, was "100% in favor" of a museum without walls and what critic Paul Goldberger called "a joyous jumble of exhibitions." But by 1984 the Seaport had been whittled down to one gallery and a borrowed exhibit. Visitors asked, Where's the museum? Not seeing one, they retreated to Rouse's shops.[1]

In hiring Peter Neill, the board redefined the Seaport. Peter Aron faulted Stanford's loosely structured organization and presentation. His concepts "did not build confidence in the donor community." Since the Seaport had lost its identity and needed revenue, its new leaders decided to create an "all weather, all season facility" that was "behind a single turnstile." On par with movie-ticket prices (then four dollars), the fee was expected to cover about 55 percent of the operating budget of $3.5 million. In *A Museum like No Other: A Master Plan, 1985–1990*, Neill reassured ship-minded supporters such as Jack Aron. "While this plan places heavy emphasis on exhibits and upland activity," he stressed, "it does so *only* to create an institution with the credibility and financial stability that will allow it to provide necessary resources to sustain the ships. Above all, South Street Seaport is a *maritime* museum and the ships are both symbol and reality of the demands of our commitment."[2]

Where to locate the museum was the first question. Despite a consultant's warning about the Row's inadequacy, Neill proposed using its vacant top three floors to create a twenty-five-thousand-square-foot exhibition space, whose main feature would be a permanent exhibit on the Port of New York. Peter Aron, whose family wealth was built on global trade, urged that it be "international in scope." Based on a volunteer's proposal, Neill also suggested restoring the Seamen's (Fulton Ferry) Hotel, above Sloppy Louie's, made famous by Joseph Mitchell. Because the upper floors of the Row had not been rehabilitated, his plan would be slow in coming. Neill created waves at the FFM by proposing to take over John Street for a children's museum. In the spirit of Barnum's American Museum, which operated from 1841 to 1865 a half mile away, the P. T. Barnum Children's Center would, he said, "create a unique ambiance for participation, performance, games, and childhood fancy." But he most wanted to match Barnum's twentyfold increase in gate receipts over two decades. Addressing the need for a visitors' center, he also proposed building on Block 74E's corner lot an International Maritime Heritage Center that would include temporary exhibits.[3]

The *Times* jumped in with "Not Yet a Nautical Museum," an editorial cautioning that the Seaport's success depended "on making South Street the thrilling, partly open-air nautical museum it should be." At a time when transatlantic cooperation was a diplomatic priority, it politicized the Seaport's focus on the port exhibit, suggesting that "the story of New York and the sea can be made sharply relevant to current problems." The *Times* added, the Seaport needed "generous support." Applauding Neill's bold plan, *Newsday* went further. Calling the city shortsighted for contributing nothing to the Seaport's budget, it said, "The city's Department of Cultural Affairs should lead the way in funding the five-year expansion plan," as that "would encourage foundations and the business community to follow suit." This funding was a "must if these vessels — coveted in ports such as Boston, Philadelphia and Baltimore — are to remain in New York."[4]

"The Biggest Street Fair in Its History": The Statue of Liberty Centennial

Neill's timing was right in 1986 as New York staged the mother of all commemorations, Lady Liberty's centennial. Yet the unprecedented,

Fig. 9.1. Jacques Cousteau visits Pier 16, 1985. (Photo, Joel Greenberg)

corporate-funded extravaganza was criticized as "a gala of garish proportions and elitist principles." Standing on Governor's Island before forty-
five hundred invited guests, who paid $5,000 a ticket, President Reagan
opened the festivities on July 3 by unveiling the restored statue. While
forty thousand pleasure craft reflected the harbor's revival, the 450 Tri-
athlon swimmers did not, as they faced "sewage-filled, jellyfish-infested
and beer-can-strewn waters." On July Fourth, there were two million sightseers in Lower Manhattan; the *Washington Post* featured a photograph of
350,000 at the seaport. The piers' nine ships were open free of charge,
thanks to Nabisco and Stroh Brewery, the purveyors of modern hardtack
and grog. Recalling the nineteenth-century waterfront, but without its
drunken mayhem, the Seaport was, said Neill, "lined with bowsprits." The
PR boost was not able, however, to spin his turnstile. Nor was July Fourth's
closing ceremony, which Mayor Koch described as "the best fireworks
since Nero set Rome on fire."[5]

The celebration featured Op Sail 86 with a July Fourth Tall Ships Parade
and an International Naval Review. Watched by Reagan from the battleship
Iowa, the review included a British aircraft carrier, a Japanese destroyer,

and other craft. Tall ships were invited from around the world by Op Sail chairman Emil Mosbacher, but tragically, *Pride of Baltimore*, a re-created Baltimore clipper topsail schooner expected to colead the parade, sank in an Atlantic squall in mid-May. Op Sail 86 attracted more spectators than in 1976, roughly fourteen million to six million, and more tall ships. Capitalizing the moment, the Seaport drew the glitterati with a $600-a-ticket evening cruise. Lacking USCG certification to sail, *Peking* and *Wavertree* sat at the dock but were noticeably larger than USCG *Eagle*, which led the parade and joined half a dozen tall ships at the Seaport. Still, only three of the ships in Op Sail's parade were US owned: *Elissa* (Galveston), *Ernestina* (New Bedford), and *Gazela of Philadelphia*.[6]

Out of the limelight was *Esmeralda*, a four-masted barkentine of the Chilean navy that, as in 1976, caused controversy. Asserting that "the Statue of Liberty would weep" at the sight of the torture ship, Sen. Edward Kennedy succeeded in passing a nonbinding vote against its invitation, while Rep. Bill Green (D-NY) circulated similar objections unsuccessfully in the House. Kennedy also pressed Op Sail vice president and Seaport trustee Howard Slotnick, who retorted that "these are cadets and we're not dealing with the country." While a human rights activist argued that America was "condoning a regime it ought to condemn," few people spoke up, and Norma Stanford was "relieved that there was just a small protest outside the pier gate." As *Elissa*'s chief mate, Walter Rybka could not "recall a single discussion about politics or human rights with sailors of any ship." Meanwhile, newscasters escaped to the romance of windjammers. Sailing devotee Hugh Downs of ABC's *20/20* took his crew aboard *Pioneer*. Americans are "fascinated with the maritime past even more than with other aspects of history," he said, while praising the sailors' "independence and teamwork." He called their crews titans.[7]

Thanks partly to Op Sail and the Seaport, enthusiasm for Ellis Island's preservation was spiraling upward. After 1820, most of the port's twenty-five million immigrants entered through South Street or the Battery's Castle Garden, but Ellis Island, which opened in 1892, came to symbolize the nation's gateway to opportunity. Yet its fate was uncertain after closing in 1954. With an approaching centennial and a restoration of the Great Hall pegged at $64 million, the Reagan administration proposed its privatization. Rouse saw "exciting possibilities," but after the seaport debacle, critics imagined not huddled masses yearning to breathe free but corporate types yearning to line their pockets. Preservationists said that showed "a lack of sensitivity for one of the most historic monuments of the nation." Stoking the debate, *Seaport* magazine's special issue on immigration included writers who not only contrasted Reagan's exclusionary policies with the city's historic diversity but said that "short-sighted, narrow, and racist groups" were undermining "the heart of America's strength and growth." As such, Ellis Island should be revered as "a priceless blueprint of the nature of this country." Governor Mario Cuomo, remembering his own immigrant roots, praised the Seaport for reminding Americans of "the responsibility we have for one another's welfare."[8]

Neill leveraged his capital and space to create an immigration exhibit. To install it in the Low Building, the board sold and leased back its headquarters at 207 Front Street. Neill heard through a third party that a Norwegian visitor wanted to make a gift; that visitor had a fat wallet, a not-too-hidden agenda, and a prepackaged exhibit. As director of the private Norsk Forum, which distributed public cultural funds abroad, Erik Rudeng was taken to the John Street building, where Neill "invented there and then the idea of two floors of renovated galleries with storage above." Neill guesstimated its price tag at $500,000. After a month's interlude, Rudeng phoned Neill, "Peter, I've done it!" That funded the construction of the Norway Galleries. While that work was being done, Brooke Astor visited the district, this time to inspect the Low Building. There, Neill added, she "scraped her shin and was bleeding profusely." While "the burly construction workers made a circle around us, backs in, faces out," he "assisted Mrs. Astor out of her torn panty hose and washed her bloody leg." Upon departing, she said she enjoyed her visit and later gave $250,000 to the general fund.[9]

With Norway's boom in oil revenues and hopes for increased tourism, it staged an exhibit at the Seaport on Norse immigration, with later exhibits on exploration and fishing. Norsemen had first visited South Street in 1980, when *Odin's Raven*, a fifty-six-foot longship replica, arrived at Pier 16 to inaugurate a Viking exhibit at the Metropolitan Museum. In 1986, "The Promise of America" was a two-floor exhibit that traced the journey of a brother and sister from Norway to Brooklyn and then to the Midwest. The title played into plans of the Reagan administration for Ellis Island, which highlighted immigrants who pulled up their bootstraps and served the nation. Yet the Norse identity in New York was waning; their locally

Fig. 9.2. Peter Neill (*left*), Mayor Ed Koch (*center*), and King Carl XVI of Sweden (*right*) at the Seaport, 1988. (Photo, Joel Greenberg)

published *Norway Times* was, by then, mostly printed in English. Hoping to boost Norse pride, the Norsk Forum paid handsomely because, as it told the *Times*, "there are 4 million Norwegians living in Norway and 4 million Norwegian-Americans living in the United States." New York State, however, had no county with more than 1.5 percent Norwegian ancestry. Surprisingly, the exhibit's benefactor received only 1.5 percent coverage in *Seaport*'s immigration issue: one page, in which a Norse seaman began his interview with, "It was the dream of my life to come to this country. Anything was better than over there."[10]

The galleries gave a better impression of Norway, as did Ed Koch, who, as he cut the ribbon, praised the Norse: "No nation but Ireland gave America a higher percent of her sons and daughters as immigrants." Joining him at a Norwegian Traditional Arts Celebration were Norse American musicians and craftspeople. Onstage, former vice president (and Norse descendant) Walter F. Mondale noted that Norway's 241-foot, full-rigged *Christian Radich* (1937) was the first to arrive for Op Sail. With a city fireboat spraying Norse colors, it docked at Pier 16 to a cheering crowd of two thousand, band music, and a half-hour barrage of fireworks. At summer's end, other Scandinavian sailors braved the stormy Atlantic. Sailing

Norseman—which the *Times* called "a dainty copy of a Viking ship"—to Pier 16, they staged a PR event guaranteed to irk the Sons of Italy by marking the one thousandth anniversary of their claimed discovery of North America that occurred, they said, five hundred years before Christopher Columbus. The forty-eight-foot fembøring was a gift to the American people, but the Norse had a bigger mackerel to fry. Strapped to a flatbed truck, *Norseman* soon left the Seaport for the Norwegian pavilion at Walt Disney's EPCOT, where it was later joined by the exhibit. Though the line between bonafide exhibit and commercial spectacle was blurred, what mattered to the Seaport was cash flow as it relied on "a more entrepreneurial approach to revenue generation." After the Norse left, their former overlords arrived when the Seaport hosted a New Sweden Festival in 1988. There the nation's king and queen bestowed a knighthood on Neill, despite his assurances that "the staff and volunteers must know that [he] come[s] from their ranks." All the while, he was expected to institute a sea change at the museum.[11]

"As Energetically as Our Resources Will Allow": Mounting Exhibits and Building a Collection

Neill's exhibits and collections increasingly became the test of the Seaport's quality. Unlike the Mariners' Museum or Mystic Seaport, South Street was a latecomer and woefully short of a critical mass of artifacts. Karl Kortum, who knew that everyday materials were fast disappearing, gave Neill one piece of advice in 1985: "Peter, only collect!" South Street had a more challenging mission than either Mystic Seaport, which told the story of an ocean-minded village, or Salem's Peabody Museum, which collected art, trade goods, and Pacific crafts. That was because South Street's stated mission was to "preserve and interpret the artifacts and skills which document the maritime contribution to the history of culture and commerce of the City of New York, the State, and the Nation." In the meantime, it borrowed exhibits, such as in 1985 the Peabody's "Dogwatch and Liberty Days, Seafaring Life in the 19th Century." What Salem did not send was an artifact familiar to most New Yorkers. As the exhibit label read, cockroaches were "as large as mice" aboard ships. Sailors admitted that they had "some value on shipboard—they ate bedbugs." Curators put out an APB to the public to send the museum their "VERY DEAD and large" cockroaches. In 1986, it

Fig. 9.3. The Seaport's early morning Fulton Fish Market tour, 1988. (Photo, Joel Greenberg)

showed another Salem exhibit, "A Treasure Greater than Gold—The New England Fisheries." Both attracted little press, even though "Treasure" had been a prize-winning display. As a teaser, the Seaport offered "a full range" of educational activities, public programs, documentary films, and food relating to the Fulton Fish Market. But, like the era's large factory trawlers, the seafood buffet at Roebling's in the New Fulton Market was better at hauling in those who, it said, wanted to "fall in love" over cod.[12]

More in line with the Seaport's own waterfront, it acquired the John A. Noble Collection. Poignantly capturing the city's maritime decline, Noble had built his own floating artist's studio, which *National Geographic* featured in 1954. Moored near a Bayonne refinery, everything reeked of oil. After Stanford championed Noble's cause, the Seaport opened its first art gallery in 1973 with Noble in attendance and a borrowed medley of his oils, charcoals, and lithographs. While a gallery in Norway devoted an entire room to him, he was ignored by traditional New York museums, which typically displayed romanticized paintings of ships. The Seaport quipped that "there is more to marine art than hulls and swells." Because Noble identified with workingmen, he showed his gritty art not at salons but in the port's saloons. The city exhibited his work posthumously aboard its miniferry *John A. Noble* (1986), while the Seaport produced a show and book with three dozen lithographs, arranged by Erin Urban. Aboard his canoe or rowboat, Noble had sketched wooden sailing vessels in the East Coast's largest boneyard at Port Johnson, New Jersey. They were doomed by neglect, nature, and the oil terminals. He preserved their memory because, like those seven hundred schooners, they were "the greatest wooden artifacts of man's stay upon this Earth." A contrarian equated him with Victorian "poets obsessed over ruined abbeys." Such differing points of view were common. While Norman Brouwer called a Staten Island salvage yard "the most significant collection of harbor craft anywhere," gentrifying neighbors called it an eyesore.[13]

The Seaport needed similarly successful exhibits because, by the late 1980s, more than six hundred million people annually visited US museums, and that number increased in the next decade. Neill told the board that a mere 1 percent of those who walked the district visited the museum; it was actually much less. Affirming Melvin Conant's report (1977), he declared that the Seaport should be accredited by the American Association of Museums, despite Aron's cautionary note that only 1 percent of the nation's museums were accredited. Ellsworth Brown, who was remaking the Chicago Historical Society, reported in the AAM's initial review of the Seaport that it was "sadly delinquent" in its collection development, waterfront maintenance, and financial regimen. Moreover, the AAM demanded computerized record-keeping, which Neill called "an insatiable generator of work."[14]

Neill recognized, as he did in New Haven, the need for institutional collaboration. Hoping to fill his gallery, he proposed a partnership with the city's fledgling Ocean Liner Museum, which was squatting at the Seamen's Church Institute. "Nearly as extinct as the clipper ship," those liners had docked at Luxury Liner Row, a series of piers on the Hudson that had since decayed and dwindled to six berths for cruise ships. Allowing the "pro-rating of overhead and personnel costs," the joint venture's first exhibit—"The Great Liner: Trans-Atlantic Passage between the Wars" —opened in 1987. After the Ocean Liner Museum failed to find its own home, it merged with the Seaport, which had also bought the holdings of architect Der Scutt. A prodigious collector, Scutt confessed, "Some people do drugs, I do ship models," but he was overwhelmed as prices reached higher than the Trump Tower he designed. With his collection, the Seaport owned "the world's largest collection of ocean liner models and memorabilia." So credentialed, it even hosted a private auction of *Titanic* artifacts in 2005. But, while a folding deck chair was expected to fetch $60,000 and a life jacket $40,000, the auction hit an iceberg—the deck chair only brought $8,500 and the jacket $7,500.[15]

"History Is a Tremendous Social Narrative": Struggling to Develop a Professional Museum

In step with the national economy, the Seaport seemed to be improving in 1986. With increased revenues from admissions, *Seaport* advertising, *Pioneer* cruises, and excursion boats, as well as corporate and philanthropic gifts, it reported a "significant surplus." In addition, City Hall began to help financially with the NYC-owned Low Building. That financial success led Neill to predict that the museum's membership, which had sunk to 4,447 in 1985, could reach 20,000. Others blasted his optimism as unwarranted. Even the *Wall Street Journal* reported that it had difficulty finding his museum amid the shops. In rebuttal, Neill distributed buttons with the inscription, "I FOUND the museum at the South Street Seaport," but his buttons only danced around the fact that, as one staffer conceded, "It's tough when you have a museum in a mall." To energize the Seaport, he hired Sally Yerkovich as director of museum programs in 1986. With a Ph.D. in anthropology and folklore, she had risen to deputy director of public programs at the NEH. Arriving at the seaport, she recalled, its streets were packed, but "the museum seemed hidden." Believing that the Seaport had "enormous untapped potential," she recognized the necessity of professionalizing its operations, developing an interpretive plan, and establishing more substantive programs. With NEH support, the museum conducted a self-study in 1987–88; its impressive panel included historians Jesse Lemisch and Virginia Yans-McLaughlin and Plimoth Plantation's assistant director, Richard Ehrlich. Besides endorsing Neill's five-year plan, they recommended that the Seaport incorporate "a thematic approach" and "up-to-date perspectives" into the interpretation. As such, they crafted a tighter mission statement:

> The South Street Seaport Museum preserves and interprets the history of New York City as a world port—a place where goods and labor are

exchanged and where cultures interact through work, through commerce, and through the interaction of diverse communities. From trans-Atlantic shipping to immigration to New York's rise to economic pre-eminence, the waterfront world has played a critical role in developments that have transformed the entire city. The Museum interprets those changes to explore and explain the city's roots in its maritime heritage.

Reflecting the era's new social history, they identified three main themes: (1) "the *work* of laborers, artisans, and merchants who built the city, what it was and how it changed," (2) "the *commerce* that made New York a city of wealth and renown, the destination of countless ships, and the focal point of an international trade network," and (3) "the many and varied *communities* of people who gathered around the port and contributed to the vitality of the city."[16]

To develop the permanent exhibit, "World Port New York" (WPNY), Yerkovich hired Charles L. Sachs as senior curator in 1987. Formerly chief curator at the Staten Island Historical Society, he was concerned that the exhibit would be time-consuming and expensive but was reassured by Yerkovich, who was able to attract idealistic and energetic staff. Those included Steven Jaffe, a recently minted Ph.D. from Harvard University who was to inherit WPNY after Sachs's departure. Committed to the new social history, Jaffe intertwined its approach with the traditional "stories of wealthy merchants and ship captains." Yet WPNY was on the far horizon, and the Seaport immediately needed to fill its galleries. Neill mostly chose the exhibits, some of which challenged federal policies that misused history, or what historian Mike Wallace called "historicide." "History is a tremendous social narrative," Neill wrote. "To ignore it, or to deny its value as a window to the future, is perilous." As such, the museum would address the politics of immigration, the collapse of the Atlantic fisheries, and the legacy of the slave trade, but other issues such as the decline in US shipbuilding or unionized shipping went untouched. Through a mix of exhibits on traditional art, pop culture, and hot-button topics, the museum developed a respectable program. By 1989, there were six changing exhibits in five galleries. Neill reported 425,000 visitors, but as the Brooklyn Museum admitted, "The whole attendance figure game is just that—a game."[17]

Increasing attendance was worth fighting for. In 1990–91, the Seaport staged "Men's Lives." A David-versus-Goliath story, it was based on Peter

Matthiessen's *Men's Lives: The Surfmen and Baymen of the South Fork* (1986). The author of the acclaimed *In the Spirit of Crazy Horse* (1983), Matthiessen empathetically portrayed Long Island's fishermen he knew so well. With his title based on Sir Walter Scott—"It's no fish ye're buying, it's men's lives"—he depicted their struggle against nature and less obvious (but ultimately successful) forces: (1) environmentalists who protected a dwindling striped bass population by outlawing seine fishing, (2) bureaucrats catering to wealthy sport fishermen, and (3) residents and vacationers gentrifying the area's harbors. The exhibit included photographs by noted artist Adelaide de Menil, artifacts, and recorded accounts by the fishing community. Their defeat meant "the end of a surfboat tradition that began when the Atlantic coast was still the frontier." A unique example of an exhibit's power, "Men's Lives" defied convention by linking past and present and by showing the nuances of environmentalism.[18]

The Seaport also showcased forgotten waterfront lives. In 1992, it celebrated its anniversary with "Of Sailing Ships and Sealing Wax, 25 Years of Collecting." Displaying its own collection, it tied together person, place, and memory, as exemplified by Charles F. Sayle's model of the Gloucester schooner *Avalon*. Reflecting on his work aboard that seine boat, which sold mackerel at the FFM, the octogenarian said, "It was a good life. I wouldn't trade that for anything." His finely crafted model was a memorial because he was aboard its sister schooner in 1927 when *Avalon* was sliced in half by a liner off Cape Cod, killing most of the crew. Yet that model could "never testify as eloquently as the people who made and used them," said museum folklorist Kathleen Condon, who did not question if memories were similarly crafted. A portrait of the clipper *Hornet* evoked faraway travels. Upon returning to South Street in 1853, its captain brought "souvenirs now in the Museum's collection," including "tiny shoes worn by a Chinese woman with bound feet." Retold by a young Mark Twain, the ship's sinking in 1886 took the lives of most of its crew and passengers.[19]

The Seaport struck gold in 1991 when the Seamen's Bank for Savings, a Lower Manhattan institution since 1829, was seized by the Federal Deposit Insurance Corporation (FDIC), which then inherited "one of the nation's most impressive collections of marine art." Numbering two thousand pieces, its ship models, paintings, scrimshaw, clocks, barometers, spyglasses, and logs were, said a Cape Cod auctioneer, worth $10–15 million. Some models, carved from bone and rigged with human hair by prisoners during the Napoleonic Wars, were worth as much as $50,000. At a time when investors were privatizing the public's heritage, the FDIC was required to recover the maximum return. Once the default hit the newsstands, collectors and museums scrambled. Neill told a reporter, "If the FDIC 'tries to squeeze the maximum money from the collection,' it will be showing 'the same pathetic motivation' that caused the banking crisis. That is 'unrestrained greed.'" The Seaport needed to bolster its fine-arts collection, so Neill tried to pull some strings, but New York's US Senate delegation failed to deliver, and the FDIC refused to talk. Then Seaport trustee David Olsen, CEO of Johnson & Higgins, wrote Prescott S. Bush Jr., the brother of President George H. W. Bush. Olsen's request went to White House counsel C. Boyden Gray, who "passed a note to the administrator of the FDIC/savings bank bail-out." The FDIC quietly gave the museum "the exclusive right to bid on the collection by the September 27th deadline."[20]

The Seaport offered $2 million, but after its rejection, it raised the bid to $3,412,500—the FDIC's conservative appraisal value. A bidding war would have sent "the prices sky high." The Seaport was short of funds, so Peter Aron loaned it $230,000, of which $212,000 went for the FDIC's deposit. The news hit the fan once the FDIC accepted the bid on November 9, 1990. "Why didn't they let anyone else bid? It's so blatantly unfair to the American taxpayer," complained an auctioneer. Mystic Seaport and the Mariners' Museum remained silent, but collector Thomas H. Gosnell, who had offered a higher bid of $3.5 million, blasted the "closed backroom deals" and sued. US courts upheld the sale, ruling that it served the public good and the FDIC's responsibilities. "Rendered speechless," Neill finally had a real collection and "a state-of-the-art conservation and storage house" for it after the Low Building reopened in 1990.[21]

In the meantime, the Seaport mounted its own very traditional exhibit, "Ship, Sea and Sky: The Marine Art of James Edward Buttersworth," which was accompanied by a symposium and an attractive catalog. "This was (and still is) what lovers of marine art" want, noted a reviewer in *Lloyd's List*. Connoisseurs valued aesthetics, but others emphasized that Buttersworth was part of an aggressive nineteenth-century America that regarded sea power as the means "to achieve its place among the world's leading nations." Emigrating from England in the mid-1840s, Buttersworth recorded the end of what *Newsday* called "one of the most romantic eras

Fig. 9.4. Burling Slip: Low Building, 167–71 John Street (*right*); 165 John Street (*center*); and 159–63 John Street (a.k.a. 181–89 Front Street; *left*), with One Seaport Plaza (*background*); 189–91 Front Street was once occupied by the shipping and commission house of Josiah Macy & Sons, 2006. (Photo, author)

in our nation's history." Neill was delighted that the show made money, traveled to Salem and Chicago, and "enjoyed national coverage" in the *Magazine Antiques*.[22]

While "Men's Lives" invited viewers to think about contemporary issues, one traveling exhibit that could have inspired comparable debate, but did not, was "Nantucket and the China Trade." Organized by the Nantucket Historical Association in 1994, it was featured in *Antiques*. Supplemented with Seaport objects related to Burling Slip's A. A. Low & Brothers, the exhibit illustrated, said *Antiques*, how Nantucket's China trade "helped undermine the provincial Quaker culture" and began to "transform the island." Modern China trade was also transforming (some critics said undermining) the United States in 1994 into a consumer of cheap goods, financed by a debt-burdened public and available at that palace of consumption, Pier 17.[23]

"Most Important Is the 'Message' the City Must Send— That It Wants the Museum": Rolling Snake Eyes with Funders

Neill's plans for "World Port New York" were formidable, but his shortage of funds was even more so. Approaching potential funders in 1988, Aron, Neill, and *Newsday* publisher Robert Johnson visited the Port Authority's executive director, Stephen Berger. But the Port Authority offered nothing, explaining that it was "meeting its responsibilities to the community through its activities relating to the city's homeless." After a museum consultant suggested relying more on the board, Peter Aron asked for "100% Board participation" but conceded that there was "no 'price tag' for being a Trustee." Slotnick then asked each trustee to contribute at least $1,000. (By 1994, Neill upped the ante to "give or get" $25,000.) The board also approved its first ever capital campaign in 1989, but consultants warned that the philanthropic community was "confused about the nature and mission of the Museum." With the recession, moreover, two likely contributors—finance and real estate—were giving less. When Larry Silverstein suggested in 1990 that the Seaport needed a more "emotional and thoughtful rationale," Neill replied that it was improving the quality of life for downtown workers, families, and schoolchildren. Stanford had proposed just that in the Seaport's early days, but its public-service message had been lost in the Rouse shuffle. Such a role was a major shift for museums. By the 1990s, said analyst Stephen Weill, public service was a particularly critical function of newer museums.[24]

The museum wanted its fair share of funds from the city. In 1969, City Hall had expected that the Seaport would support itself by redeveloping the district. But after the stringent terms of its 1972–73 bailout and the

1981 Rouse deal, City Hall milked the marketplace and left the museum an empty pail. When the museum asked City Hall for a regular subsidy, or what was called "operating support," it responded by only investing money into its city-owned buildings. That prompted the Seaport to ask for higher rents or a revised lease, but it was rebuffed. Arguing in 1989 that City Hall gave "some $16 million" to the Metropolitan Museum "for general operating support," the Seaport noted that City Hall received the same sum from the seaport district in "rent, sales tax, and employment tax." In effect, it was underwriting the Met. Mayor Koch only agreed to postpone his rents if interest was paid and the museum slashed its budget.[25]

The museum requested a subsidy from Koch's successor as mayor, David Dinkins. After the Seaport saw "a marked shift in the City's attitude" in 1992, it received a tentative offer for an operating subsidy of $450,000 per year for fiscal years 1992 through 1997 through the Department of Cultural Affairs (DCA). When the city demanded the museum cut its budget, Finance Committee chairman Lawrence Huntington said, "The fat is gone, . . . and we are well into bone." Negotiations followed on eighteen key points, but the Seaport's lead negotiator, Robert Johnson, emphasized that it wanted a solution that was not "susceptible to changing administrations," whereby it would be permanently placed (as were other museums on city-owned property) on the DCA list for annual operating support. Once the SSSM was listed in the DCA's Cultural Institutions Group (CIG), the SSSC would relinquish its leases. Hurt by a lingering recession and polarized politics, City Hall delayed and only gave its "verbal confirmation" of acceptance in mid-October 1993. Assuming "de facto responsibility" for the leases, it agreed to legally take them once the deal was signed. When the plan was announced, the board applauded.[26]

The memorandum of understanding was signed on December 31, 1993. The next day, the new mayor, Rudolph Giuliani, shelved Dinkins's pledges. City department heads included the Seaport subsidy in their budgets, as well as a $3.9 million capital grant for Schermerhorn Row, but Giuliani, who held a grudge against the SSSC for its alleged inaction on the Mafia, removed them for fiscal years 1995–98. DCA head Schulyer Chapin oversaw the thirty-two-member CIG, which absorbed 85 percent of his funding; he acknowledged, "Politics are at their worst in the arts world." The *Times* did not report on Giuliani's animosity against the SSSC, but it noted that the mayor had proposed ending all support for the DCA list. It was "a kind of cultural Darwinism," said Paul Goldberger, in which "the economically strongest" would survive. Yet Giuliani's radical plan went nowhere.[27]

As Johnson negotiated with City Hall for aid, its DCA and EDC "threw the ball back and forth," claiming that the Seaport was the other's charge. Fearing Giuliani's widely known temper, the museum board said, "We do not want a public confrontation at this time." City Hall held the cards for rehabilitating Pier 15 and the Row, and the board knew "adverse repercussions" could follow. But after the DCA included a subsidy for fiscal year 1999, City Hall "reneged at the 11th hour." The usually upbeat Aron told trustees, "Historically we have looked to the City as part of the solution, but it is part of the problem. Every other major cultural institution gets reliable city funding, and we get none." Aron covered the final payroll of 1998 himself but told the board, "Most important is the 'message' the City must send—*that it wants the Museum*." In June 1999, City Hall did offer a four-year aid plan. By then, Giuliani had forced the SSSC's default, and the EDC had taken the income-earning leases. The mayor required the Seaport to agree not to seek further operating funds, which was unprecedented. In effect, fiscal year 2000 included a $450,000 operating subsidy, plus $75,000 for utilities, but the aid dropped incrementally to zero by the end of the fourth year. The mayor then backed out of the deal, leaving the Seaport, said Neill, as "the only major cultural institution" on city-owned property that was excluded.[28]

The Seaport turned to the private sector and its well-heeled friends. In 1987, for example, it staged a twentieth-anniversary gala, underwritten by Shearson Lehman, organized by Larry Silverstein, and honoring distinguished trustees Walter Cronkite and Jack Aron. At another gala in 1988, a corporate table went for $10,000. The Monday-night dance on Pier 16's apron juxtaposed the departing tuxedos, ball gowns, and chauffeurs with the arriving fishmongers and truckers. In 1995, a 375-guest dinner dance, which raised $355,000, included "a moving tableau" as *Lettie* and *Pioneer* sailed to and fro, demonstrating the changed meaning of those work boats. At the museum's "Evening under the Stars" in 1998, which coincided with a capital campaign for the buildings, ships, and Pier 15, a Seaport brochure dispelled the myth of a Rouse goldmine, reminding friends that the museum had "never received any income from the commercial development."[29]

Times were tough all over. Even the 188-year-old New-York Histori-cal Society, the nation's second oldest, was forced to temporarily close its doors in 1992. Thinking that America could face historical amnesia, Neill told members, "I can think of no event more destructive to our col-lective psyche than the loss of memory implicit in the Society's failure." Unlike the biblical story, in this case Jonah wanted to swallow the whale because the Seaport toyed with the idea of acquiring the N-YHS. While one trustee feared it could be "a millstone around our neck," chairman Peter Aron asserted, "We are not vultures." With similar financial difficul-ties at the Museum of the City of New York (MCNY), Neill said, "This is South Street's moment to come out as the City's pre-eminent history museum." But, while City Hall, the Carnegie Endowment, and financier Lewis Lehrman rescued the N-YHS, the Seaport's difficulties were taking an increasing toll. Without funds for the Row and WPNY, Yerkovich left in 1992 partly because, she said, Neill was "not always realistic about what it might take to move the museum forward." With her departure also went Sachs and what he called the "imaginative and collegial group" that had formed around her. Thus, the Seaport was, said the *Times*, "experiencing more leadership trouble than the *Bounty*." Neill "had huge responsibilities to juggle," Yerkovich conceded, "and I'm not sure that the various aspects of his job were always reconcilable."[30]

"Preservation Has Earned Public Indifference": Restoring Identities through Folklife Programs and Social History

Others saw a problem with historic preservation in general. William J. Murtagh, former head of Columbia University's program, thought its small membership reflected its narrow appeal. The Seaport tried Madison Avenue to expand its membership, using the pro bono services of Scali, McCabe, Sloves, which made Frank Perdue's chickens fly off the shelf. The problem went deeper, and Neill told a national audience of preser-vationists that they had "*earned* public indifference" by being compla-cent, exclusive, and unimaginative. As he had once warned the National Trust, too many focused on material things and buildings instead of seeing them, as social historians did, as "contexts for history, places for people." Moreover, too many gauged preservation's success only on business stan-dards: "dollars invested, main streets renewed, inner cities rehabilitated, tourism promoted, tax dollars derived." Seymour told the board that Neill launched "a bombshell at 'self-satisfied' preservationists."[31]

The Seaport's waterfront provided those "contexts for history." Unlike "the Absolute Fake" that Umberto Eco found across America's restored landscapes, the Seaport was "linking the stories of the past with the traditions and practices of the present." An increasing number of preservationists were advocating eco-museums, recognizing that "the conservation of activities" was "the biggest single element missing." After anthropologist Thomas Walker inventoried the city's maritime folklife, the Seaport held a professional conference and a two-day outdoor festival in 1988. Drawing a big crowd, "Maritime New York: Holding Fast to Tradition" featured demonstrations of rope work, sail and net making, wood carving, and tattooing. Two years later, it mounted a two-day "Festival of Shad Traditions" and separate, free shows on marine skills, while half a dozen children's programs ran a similar gamut. Those skills were being lost as the port's waterfront jobs had declined by 75 percent since the 1950s.[32]

Crafts programs also pleased waterfront crowds. Besides a steady flow at the Seaport's Maritime Crafts Center on the pier, the museum developed a show that traveled—"Twelve Ties to Tradition: Model Making in New York City." While two World War II submariners were honoring lost comrades as they made models, another modeler built boats to identify with the struggles of the Irish, American Indians, and Québécois. Meanwhile, Murray Cukier crafted a model of SS *Arabic*, on which he emigrated in 1928. In 1998, the Seaport featured a show on Cukier. "I can do anything" with pizza boxes, he beamed, including a seven-foot model of *Titanic*. Passing skills to the next generation, the craftsmen embodied, said Neill, the Seaport's goal "to preserve the stories not just of the powerful and wealthy, but also of the laborers, seamen, and poor immigrants who contributed to the creation of this great port city." As a result, he created a new position for Kathleen Condon as curator of folklife. The *Times* noted, however, that "Twelve Ties" was "a male affair," as "very few women create boat models." Starting in 1990, the Seaport sponsored a waterfront role play of Herman Melville, who lived in Manhattan for most of his seventy-two years. Yet Melville wrote little about it, perhaps because he had, said a scholar, "the same sort of love-hate relationship with New York that most people, natives and pilgrims," shared. That gave an artistic license to actor John B. Putnam, who performed a one-man walking show.[33]

"We Ignore Newer Audiences at Our Peril":
A Mix of Edgy, Kitschy, and Social History Exhibits

Though the Seaport accepted an eclectic range of temporary exhibits to fill its galleries and appeal to a broader swath, its mission statement emphasized work, commerce, and community. As such, its exhibits on cod, tattoos, immigration, and piracy filled the galleries and addressed timely concerns. While the Norse were defying the international ban on hunting whales, their policy on cod became instructive to North Americans. By the 1950s, a curator said, "the cod was humankind's most caught, most eaten fish, a symbol of the sea's seemingly endless bounty," but by the 1990s, the Atlantic stock was dangerously depleted. In 1995, the Seaport staged "When Cod Was King" at two of its galleries; one used Norse materials, and the other artifacts came from Newfoundland. Interweaving work, commerce, and community in a cross-disciplinary approach, the exhibit emphasized the threats to folklife and the need for environmental sustainability. Because the Norse instituted "cooperative fishing and managed catches," said Neill, its cod industry and culture survived. But the fishery's collapse in Newfoundland and a Canadian ban that came too late in 1994 left "the cultural life of cod-fishing communities 'alive' only in memory." Combining past and present, said an admiring reviewer, the exhibit challenged its audience to assess the root problems. The Seaport ironically added programs to savor the humble fish. Just as Mark Kurlansky did in his best-selling *Cod*, it held three food tastings, including one aboard *Wavertree*, whose victuals were presumably a cut above its galley of 1885.[34]

Causing a stir was the 1995 exhibit "The Devil's Blue: American Tattoo Art and Practice through the Port of New York (1840–1961)." The title phrase came from Melville's description of Queequeg's tattooed face. Popular with sailors, the city's second tattoo parlor had opened in 1875 about a mile from the Row on the Bowery. After tattooing had been outlawed in the city in 1961, it was an edgy topic, said guest curator Amy Krakow, though two SoHo galleries had concurrent displays and the ban was shelved in 1997. Still, Neill saw a chance to differentiate the Seaport from other maritime museums, which largely showed "ships at the dock, in frames, bottles, and boxes." He warned, "We ignore [newer audiences] at our peril." "The Devil's Blue" showed 140 eclectic pieces, but their interpretation varied. While they "spoke" to sailor-turned-professor

Steve Gilbert "of things dangerous and desirable," Michael Kimmelman thought they raised issues about "social marginality, fetishism and anti-establishmentarianism." As such, they were "still startling. Which is the bottom line." In the aftermath of another fiscal crisis in 1994, the Seaport watched its own bottom line, hoping to attract revenue. Krakow thought it was "well ahead of its time" exhibiting "a nasty topic that had been in the closet." As tattoos became fashionable, the exhibit also won praise from the *Daily News*, which said it was "learned and very entertaining." Its debut was more sensational after Neill "invited a chapter of the Hells Angels." Accompanied by 150 members, "the head Angel rode his bike up the stairs to the second floor of the Low building." While a photographer snapped shots of elderly Seaport members with heavily tattooed Angels, *Vogue* covered the exhibit. Neill said, "We were momentarily hip," but there was "a large element of bourgeois slumming," added Kimmelman, who loved the show. Besides a workshop by Lyle Tuttle, the "reigning king of tattoo," the Seaport made it more wholesome through its "For Children & Families: Tattoo Arts—make your own!" The turnstile vroomed, but, said Neill, "I doubt if we added members."[35]

After the reopening of Ellis Island in 1990, immigration became a timely topic. In response, the Seaport mounted three exhibits in 1996. "Across the Western Ocean: American Ships by Liverpool Painters" catered to art patrons, while two other shows tied past and present. At a time when the Smithsonian's Air and Space Museum and other cultural institutions were facing right-wing attacks, Neill warned that if museums succumbed to such "politically manipulated" assaults, it would lead to lies, censorship, and an inability to understand recent events such as the attempt to smuggle into New York a boatload of Chinese immigrants "seeking refuge from tyranny." Curated by Jaffe, "Immigration in the Age of Sail" showed the miserable, exploited passage of 3.7 million émigrés from 1820 to 1860 through the use of ship models, artifacts, and texts of parliamentary hearings, Melville's writings, and distortion-filled broadsides from emigrant brokers. Those emigrants suffered, he said, "all for the shipowners' and brokers' almighty dollar." However, more people read the magazine than visited the display. As the nation debated border fences and acculturation, readers found a message of tolerance in another exhibit, "Flesh and Blood: New Yorkers Search for Their Immigrant Roots." While a Chinese American museum director remarked that the national xenophobia made him identify more with New York than with America, another admitted that his genealogical search had become an obsession. "It's almost like a disease."[36]

If the Seaport ever staged a blockbuster, it was in 1996–97. "Under the Black Flag: Life among the Pirates" was guest curated by David Cordingly, who had mounted a similar show at England's National Maritime Museum. There was a receptive market for his pop history, which was aided by news that Disney was going to redesign its thirty-year-old "Pirates of the Caribbean" ride to make its drunken pirates lurch for plates of grub, not buxom wenches. Though Neill predicted, "It should be a blockbuster!" the *Times* and *Daily News* ignored it. Oddly enough, even *Seaport* missed the exhibit, but its front cover pictured the personalized "CAPNHOOK" license plate of merchant Joe Hill, who regarded Rouse as his piratical nemesis. For the exhibit's ten-month run, it included the captain's costume from Stephen Spielberg's *Hook* (1991), but the real crowd-pleaser was the questionably authentic silver-plated skull of Blackbeard. Some youngsters felt squeamish seeing the sixteenth-century engravings of Incas torturing Spanish sailors. "Only older kids should be allowed to glimpse this stuff," *Newsday* warned. "It includes a barbecue. Don't ask what's on the menu."[37]

"Under the Black Flag" was frivolous when compared with another simultaneous exhibit, "Blood upon the Waters: Contemporary Piracy in the South China Sea." These modern-day Filipino brigands who used high-speed boats and automatic weapons, said the *Times*, were not the type to "chant 'Yo-ho-ho and a bottle of rum.'" As later in Somalia, piracy supplemented these men's meager fishing income, which was depleted by foreign trawlers that swept the oceans. Trapped in peonage and manipulated by crime bosses, they were more desperate cutthroats than Captain Hook. Rarely in a museum is the romanticized past so juxtaposed with grizzly reality. "Blood upon the Waters" encouraged its audience to consider a pressing issue.[38]

An Unprecedented Partnership in the United States: America's National Maritime Museum

Ignored by Gotham's big dailies, "Under the Black Flag" was a difficult beginning for a marriage between the Seaport and the Mariners' Museum. This was the Seaport's second bid for a partner. In 1986, Neill explored a deal with Liverpool's Merseyside Maritime Museum to help with

Wavertree's restoration and share admissions, publications, and exhibits. Yet the deal went nowhere because neither could fill the other's requests, whether for a visiting square-rigger or restoration funds. The courtship between the Seaport and Mariners' was rough, as the two had earlier clashed over the display of the Brooklyn-built USS *Monitor*. Yet, after the Seaport sent its pirate exhibits, Newport News reciprocated in 1997 with "The Bard Brothers: Painting America under Steam and Sail," a traditional show on nineteenth-century ship scenes in New York Harbor that boosted amity and attendance. Both pledged "to organize a joint show on the transatlantic slave trade" for installation "at each museum."[39]

An eight-year collaboration, the so-called National Maritime Museum Initiative gave each institution the chance to capitalize the other's strengths. While the Mariners' was facing the end of a major endowment, the Seaport was stalled at the 30 percent mark of its capital campaign. It would be "a 'stature bump,'" said a trustee, and "attract new donors" to fund the long-proposed Maritime Heritage Center. Despite the improving economy, Manhattan museums were "under severe financial pressure" because of reduced government and corporate support. Moreover, Neill needed high-quality exhibits because a study revealed that, contrary to previous assumptions, "Museum ticket buyers come to the Seaport expressly to visit the Museum—they're not walking in off the streets." While the alliance had no assets, it would uniquely "employ joint programs, shared collections, exhibits, educational services, publications and other related activities." Some staff worried that *Seaport* magazine would lose its New York identity, but the AAM called the deal unprecedented, though the Smithsonian had already affiliated with smaller museums to share exhibits and programs. Only drawing one hundred thousand visitors in 1996, the Mariners', which was headed by none other than John Hightower, had, said Neill, "the largest and most distinguished collection of local, regional, national and international maritime artifacts in the nation." The Seaport's marketing would then reach into Virginia. AAM executive director Edward H. Able said, "This is truly one of the most positive and creative endeavors that I've ever seen in the museum community." He knew that "other museums nationwide will be watching."[40]

They were. Thomas Wilcox, president of the Council of American Maritime Museums (CAMM), thought the alliance "sounded like a good idea." But, at Hightower's urging, senators John Warner (R-VA) and Daniel P.

Moynihan (D-NY) went a step further by inserting an amendment in a fiscal year 1999 defense authorization bill that designated the two "America's National Maritime Museum." Hightower conceded that his "legislative sleight of hand" infuriated many in CAMM who feared that federal funding for the alliance would follow. When the bill went to conference, Mystic Seaport and CAMM failed to overturn it. The name itself was disputed because in 1978 Congress had designated San Francisco's collection as the National Maritime Museum, but South Street, Mariners', and Mystic protested, said Michael Naab, former head of the National Trust's maritime office. (Congress later renamed it the San Francisco Maritime National Historical Park.) President Clinton signed the bill in October 1998. Reactions within CAMM "ranged from being annoyed to laughing at the effrontery." Being an easy target because of the Rouse debacle, South Street particularly took the heat, and its ploy was deemed absurd and pretentious. Aron was shocked by "the amount of jealousy, backbiting and ill-will [the Seaport] found in the other parts of the maritime museum community," but Neill joked, "What is CAMM going to do, rip my epaulettes off and drum me out of the ranks?" The maritime community's dysfunction was evident, as the National Trust closed its maritime office and CAMM looked suspiciously on the NMHS. Mystic pressed CAMM to lobby to broaden the designated list of museums. Edward Kennedy, Dianne Feinstein, and others tried to expand the list, but their bill never sailed out of committee. "Warner's standing," said Hightower, "could beat back all other maritime museums." Neill grinned, "It was a glorious moment."[41]

"The Focus of Our Museum's Mission": World Port New York

There was nothing glorious about the long-delayed permanent exhibit, "World Port New York." It had been Neill's plan to boost attendance, fund the fleet, and separate his regime from his predecessors. But WPNY hinged on rehabilitating the Row and developing display space. As conceived, it was structured on historian Robert G. Albion's *The Rise of New York Port, 1815–1860* (1939) and Norman Brouwer's nineteen essays on the Port of New York, 1860–1985, which were serialized in *Seaport* from 1986 to 1991. Working with academic advisers, Sachs developed a script but could not move forward until the Row was funded. Finally, an EDC promise of $3.9

million in 1993 "completed the matching requirements" for $1.4 million from two other grants, but Giuliani nixed the deal.[42]

WPNY also needed artifacts. The Seamen's Bank collection had a rich array, but the Seaport's debt for its purchase was only resolved after Aron, who had seen crisis after crisis, helped establish a foundation to assure donors "that their gifts would continue to be protected and serve the maritime/historical community even if the Museum failed to operate." In 1998, he donated $3.25 million, the Seaport's largest charitable contribution to date, to entrust the collection to the SSSM Foundation. Receiving a standing ovation at a board meeting, Aron hoped that "there would be more people joining the parade." But no bandwagon developed. Curators needed more artifacts for their social history, because, Neill said, WPNY would tell the stories of "the rich merchants *and* the street-corner peddlers; the ship captains *and* the deckhands; the occupants of the fine mansions *and* the workers who crowded the area's boarding houses and tenements." So he issued an APB to the public: "Search Your Closets, Barns & Basements," but he came up empty-handed, as did Sachs when searching for "well-documented, authentic materials" from Burling Slip's Josiah Macy & Sons, the department store forerunner.[43]

Archaeology offered a new cache. For years, work crews had ignored the detritus of the old port, but when a ship was partially unearthed at 175 Water Street in 1982, Kent Barwick and the LPC ordered a dig. They found an eighty-six-foot, 250-year-old merchant frigate that had been junked between 1746 and 1755 to create a pier. "It was the first time in this country that an 18th century merchantman was found," exclaimed an archaeologist. British developer Howard Ronson delayed construction of his thirty-one-story tower for five months while funding a forty-three-member team that worked six-day weeks on the so-called Ronson ship. At Mayor Koch's request, he even built a walkway for public viewing. While Seaport president Hightower showed no interest, Slotnick pressed the board, which unanimously agreed to pursue the ship's acquisition. Meanwhile, the public was pushing the Seaport to keep the hulk in New York. After Hightower told the board that the ship's timbers were "deteriorating rapidly," it abandoned the effort. However, John Sands, director of collections at the Mariners' Museum, made a different assessment. "I was staggered by the extraordinary state of preservation that was evident," he wrote. After costs skyrocketed, Ronson only underwrote the preservation of the ship's

bow "to keep this unique relic in New York." In the end, the ship was documented, an eighteen-foot section was saved, and the rest was crushed
by the pile driver. For two years, the bow soaked in a preservative, but
the Rouse-obsessed Seaport did nothing. This was Hightower's "lowest
moment," said Barwick. Wanting the bow displayed in New York, Koch
offered $50,000 to any interested city museum in 1984, but Mariners',
which had struck a private deal with Hightower, pledged $400,000 to dis-
play it. In May 1985, it was shipped to Virginia, where a temporary exhibit
was staged, but, said archaeologist Warren Riess, the Mariners' never put it
on permanent display. Neill saw its pieces piled indiscriminately in a base-
ment storage room, and Mariners' was "eager to get rid of it."[44]

Using federal and private grants, the Seaport created an archaeological
arm under curator Diana diZerega Wall. By 1989, it owned nearly a million
objects, which it earmarked for WPNY, and was, said Neill, "the single
largest repository in the nation for urban archaeology materials to be used
for public exhibition and programs." As such, the *Times* praised the Seaport for "aggressively seeking archeological finds that will expand its range
beyond the 19th century." It then opened New York Unearthed in 1990 at
17 State Street, which was three-quarters of a mile away at Battery Park. Its
origins were unique. Breaking ground for a forty-two-story office tower
in 1986, developer Melvyn Kaufman began bulldozing without an LPC
site analysis. "The city made all kinds of terrible threats," he said. "I can't
put it back. You want to shoot me? Shoot me." Instead, the LPC ordered
him to fund an archaeology museum. Since the Seaport was best suited
to run the museum, Kaufman paid for a full-time curator, promised up to
$100,000 annually for five years, and gave 18 percent more for overhead.
But his high-rise was a dud, so he sold it to TIAA-CREF, which covered
the rent and paid a subsidy to the Seaport. Open five days a week with free
admission, New York Unearthed included exhibits and public viewing of
its "state-of-the-art conservation laboratory." That deal generated debate,
as some board members claimed the Seaport was "veering away from its
primary mission of maritime history." Seymour retorted that "everything
came to New York over, under or on the water." After another trustee
added that Unearthed had substantial support and provided good exposure and public relations, the dissenters were outvoted. Jakob Isbrandtsen
moaned that while the "waterfront shrinks," the Seaport was "claiming

every bottle and its stopper." By 1999, the museum was called the "unofficial repository" of Gotham archaeology.[45]

The city's most significant dig, the African Burial Ground, was outside the Seaport's bailiwick, though only half a mile away. The African Burial Ground was discovered in 1991 at a federal construction site, and uproar ensued when human remains were uncovered. Most New Yorkers did not realize that their port once had the North's largest slave trade or that the graveyard was filled with as many as twenty thousand souls. Mayor Dinkins compared it with Plymouth Rock and Ellis Island. After much debate, the government left two hundred burials undisturbed and funded a memorial. Picking up the story, a special issue of *Seaport* focused on the city's early black population, while the Seaport's Children's Center created a mix of programs. "If These Bones Could Speak" respectfully gave a "proper burial" to those Africans.[46]

"Transcending the Dry Enumeration of Facts": Schools, Magazines, and Cash Flow

By the 1990s, US museums were facing a fork in the financial road. While some eyed blockbuster exhibits, prompting accusations of pandering to the public, more were developing educational programs, which the AAM declared were a primary purpose. The Seaport launched its first Adopt-a-School partnership in 1988 with PS 119 in Brooklyn, and Neill was thrilled to hear the "recitation of John Masefield poems and Gilbert and Sullivan lyrics by 800 newly adopted sailors." In so doing, the ships became learning centers that were yearly reaching "over 40,000 New York City schoolchildren." Most city kids, like *Pioneer*'s captain Kevin Jones, "grew up totally ignorant of maritime history." Neill's second five-year plan in 1990 shifted more focus to school and service programs, which eventually raised the museum's "revenues from about 15% in 1988 to 75% in 1998." Neill thought it was "the only way for museums to survive." Thinking that the city's schools were "overwhelmed by bureaucracy, drugs, and the violence of modern times," he brought thirty superintendents to the Seaport and pitched sailing's traditional values as a remedy. That was "a brilliant act," said Seymour, who worried about the widening "gap between the well-to-do and the poor in our City."[47]

Fig. 9.5. PS 119 students perform songs by Gilbert and Sullivan as part of the Seaport's Adopt-a-School program, 1988. (Photo, Betsy Jordan Hand)

Sail training became a worldwide program. Believing that modern ways had undermined experiential learning, Outward Bound founder Kurt Hahn suggested that it was "less a training for the sea, than through the sea" to "benefit all walks of life." Its American advocates included Seaport stalwarts such as Dick Rath, *Boating*'s associate editor, and Barclay Warburton, founder of the American Sail Training Association; they held that its lessons were necessary "in these days of an overprotective society." At South Street, sail training began with school visits and progressed to sailing aboard *Lettie* and *Pioneer*. Kevin Jones said that sailing taught him "responsibility, teamwork, how to deal with stress, how to plan ahead, [and] respect for the environment." CBS anchorman Walter Cronkite, "the most trusted man in America," shared those sentiments. An avid friend of South Street, Mystic Seaport, and the NMHS, he said, "You know we can't succeed as a nation without recovering our sense of our selves, our self-esteem, our essential Americanism."[48]

Subsequently in 1995, Neill hired former *Pioneer* captain Eric Rice as the Seaport's first director of marine education. He also proposed an experimental School of the Sea, but the city declined funding. As in New Haven, he found partners who introduced a much-revised concept. Replacing one of Brooklyn's educational "factories of failure," the New York Harbor School opened to 125 ninth-graders in 2003. Funded by the Gates, Soros, and Carnegie foundations, the school used the Seaport as a satellite classroom one day a week; students there learned traditional subjects through sailing, boat building, and exploring the harbor. After the city received title to Governor's Island, it relocated the Harbor School there in 2010. Meanwhile, "The Penny Project" blended a core of science, history, archaeology, and the arts, with work and a sail aboard *Pioneer*. It gave at-risk youth, said a Police Athletic League chaperon, a "more positive adventure" than they would find on the street. By 2002, it had served over two thousand youth.[49]

The museum's magazine represented an even larger audience. As in the cases of the Rouse mall, *South Street Venture*, and the membership fee, James Shepley and his board revamped the museum to attract a more affluent clientele by creating *Seaport* magazine in late 1978. Initially subtitled *The Magazine of South Street Seaport Museum*, it evolved into *Seaport: New York's History Magazine* in 1986. That prompted a volunteer to complain that it was trying to be "all things to all people." Yet the Seaport saw an opportunity after almost all other city museums "dropped their interpretive publications." Despite a budget crisis, Seymour noted in 1989 that the four-color magazine "should be maintained at all costs" because it attracted members and was their "most important" benefit. While the *Reporter* had included ads for local and ship-oriented businesses, *Seaport* appealed to people with deeper pockets through larger, more general, and often upscale advertisements. With a photograph of yachts and midtown Manhattan, for example, the full-page ad for a New Jersey yacht club bragged, "Country club–like setting, with mini workout center, heads, conference room, lockers, and business services," all of which had convenient Manhattan access. Yet "the various schemes to generate advertising were never as successful as Peter hoped," admitted Yerkovich, who noted the conflict "between the sale of ads to 'maritime-y' businesses and the stronger history focus that the magazine developed."[50]

With the new subtitle, *Seaport* hoped to fill a niche because it was "the *only* New York history magazine remaining." Defining maritime broadly, Neill wanted to cover "all aspects" of the city's history. Pledging to "transcend the dry enumeration of facts" and the "narrow confines" of ship societies, antiquarians, and local museums, he sought a wider audience by exploring the new social history. One critic, who loved the Seaport of 1974, thought that was the job of the MCNY. As the museum was less visible, if not lost, within the Rouse development, it was coincidentally becoming less visible within its own magazine. The *Reporter* had been loaded with museum news, but all that remained by the early 1990s was a few pages. Whether this was mission creep or mission impossible was hard to say, but the new *Seaport* won a wider readership with its well-illustrated, popular history. In 1988, for instance, the Pan Am Shuttle placed issues in its airplane seat pockets for the more than two hundred thousand annual passengers. *Seaport* included a full-page ad for the Pan Am water shuttle between Wall Street's Pier 11 and La Guardia Airport. Demographically, the shuttle's riders were an important audience. Wall Street's young professionals were generally indifferent to the study of history. Though they frequented history-motif bars such as Roebling's, their education in history was superficial. As was increasingly to be the case in the 1990s, they graduated from college, even the nation's top universities, without having taken a single history course.[51]

The *Reporter* had appealed to people with a personal interest in things maritime, including its unions. But *Seaport* tacked a different course with its potential audience of moneyed landlubbers, thus missing, said labor historian Joe Doyle, the veterans of the working port. *Seaport* not only gave academic historians a popular (and profitable) outlet for their work but entertained the city's gentry with often top-notch essays based on state-of-the-art history. *Seaport* was, said Doyle, "an interesting read, chock-full of history." In fact, historians such as Kenneth Jackson took notice of the museum through *Seaport*. But what made *Seaport* most engaging was the museum's multilayered pitch. Daniel Czitrom's "The Wickedest Ward in New York," for example, focused on Sailortown. The museum offered a tandem "Vice on South Street" tour. In tune with Lou Reed's 1972 song "Walk on the Wild Side," storyteller Lisa Lipkin recounted the nineteenth-century district with thousands of gambling dens and saloons. Whether this tour exposed Sailortown's sensationalism, the audience's voyeurism, or New York's distance from Jack Tar could be debated, but little of the architectural fabric remained to visually tell the story after Robert Moses demolished the reputed Sodom. In a later issue, *Seaport* sympathetically portrayed the era's seamen when Steven Jaffe examined the Sailors' Strike of 1869. Their "voices are silent or, at best, muted in the historical record," he said, but the strike "allows us to hear at firsthand the anger and self-assertion" of workers controlled by exploitative shipowners and boardinghouse keepers. Yet the voices of the modern port were infrequently heard in *Seaport*. An article about *Obo Buzzard* revealed that the Swedish-flagged tramp with an all-Filipino crew and an Algerian cargo typified the vast majority of ships entering the port, but the voices of the crew and captain were like that of "the ship agent, unknown to most New Yorkers."[52]

The magazine's most unique contribution was the occasional back-page feature "Seaport People." In developing the series, Doyle was "most interested in workers' lives." Continuing the populist streak of the 1960s museum, it debuted with "John Singleton, 'The Lonely Life.'" Crippled by infantile paralysis, the teenager was sent to work "on a bloody hell ship" by his father, who wanted him to "come back macho macho." Sixteen months later, he was an old man with wrinkled skin, quit, and went to work as a steward aboard steamships. Later giving Seaport tours, he was, said Doyle, "a one-man committee to dispel illusions that life aboard a sailing ship was 'romantic.'" Interviewing other "Seaport People," Doyle wrote of Mike Bull, who taught boat building at the Seaport, and Rose Chevell, who recounted a seldom-heard tale as a Grace Line waitress. Radicalized by the works of Lincoln Steffens, John Reed, and Jack London, which she read in the ship's Glory Hole, where waitresses bunked, she discovered that the National Maritime Union "was no different from the company in discriminating against women." Doyle told stories of landlubbers too: "George the Waiter," who worked at Sloppy Louie's for two decades; Brooklyn store owner Sal Celona, who bought fish on Fulton Street for over three; customs broker Ernest Chambré, who collected discarded port records for four; and Melvin Madison, who sold provisions to the longshoremen and seamen of the Hudson River for five. As Madison told Doyle, "We built this building in 1936. Basically it's the same as it was then." He was the last outfitter along the West Side docks. Doyle thought that his shop looked "like a shrine to the steamship age." Doyle's interviews were refreshing and current, but *Seaport* editors jettisoned his feature and shifted the focus to "19th century waterfront characters." Perhaps the column's effect was too melancholic. That shift resembled architectural restoration by scrubbing the cultural environment of its blue-collar past and creating a more nostalgic present.[53]

By 2000, Neill, his board, and their staff had re-created the Seaport as a "museum with walls." However, their funds never matched the agenda, and rehabilitating the Row, re-creating Fulton Ferry Hotel, and crafting WPNY were left hanging. After consultants recommended hiring a professional staff versed in the new social history, the Seaport staged provocative, timely exhibits, prompting the *Daily News* to praise "the energetic little" museum. Lacking the rich collections of older museums or their flush coffers, Neill needed more and developed a trailblazing partnership with the Mariners' Museum. That won AAM kudos and congressional recognition but CAMM scorn. When that partnership failed, Neill pinned his hopes on educational services, which would cover the lion's share of his income by century's end. The Seaport had become one of the key institutions exploring the city's history, whether it occurred at New York Unearthed, in the Penny Project, within the pages of *Seaport*, or aboard *Pioneer*. Every ambitious step was intended to ensure the survival of the museum's fleet at the Street of Ships.[54]

"A Ship Is a Hole in the Water into Which You Pour Money"

How Maritime Preservation (Almost) Won

In 1983, Jakob Isbrandtsen and the two Arons voiced their frustrations at a board meeting about the fast-deteriorating ships. Not only had John Hightower joked to the *Times*, "You know the saying—'a ship is a hole in the water into which you pour money,'" but Chris Lowery had put what little money the Seaport had into landside programs to improve "the Museum's image," which had been damaged by the Rouse deal. As a result, Peter Aron successfully presented a resolution that stated, "Before any other uplands projects are funded the priority . . . should be given [to] the ships." Arriving in 1985, Neill accordingly called them the Seaport's "single greatest asset and obligation." He knew that its record was disappointing; it lost not only the steamer *Alexander Hamilton* and the lighter *Aqua* to neglect but the square-rigged *Moshulu* and the tugboat *Mathilda* to other ports. With eleven major ships, the Seaport boasted that it had "the largest historic fleet ever assembled by any museum anywhere at any time," but it failed to maintain them. *Lettie* was rotten, *Wavertree* a rusty box, *Hart* abandoned, and *Ambrose* kept afloat with its pumps. After Neill's stint at the National Trust, he knew that other museums had also acquired problematic vessels, failed to finance them, and lacked qualitative standards. Promising better stewardship, he directed that the Seaport "accept no additional vessels without the necessary funding and a clear historical justification."[1]

Neill derided the Seaport's "compulsion for collecting ships," but he recounted ship preservation's history more sympathetically at a San Francisco conference. In its first phase, "a very small number" of pioneers such as Karl Kortum and Peter Stanford had acquired ships "at any price" because they realized that the nation was "about to lose an extremely valuable part of our heritage and patrimony." He said, "We owe these people a great debt of gratitude. Without their passion and their commitment, we would have simply lost it all." The second phase was one of " 'trial and error' [but] mostly error." While Mystic made "every mistake in the book," South Street had "some very public failures." The third phase consolidated working wisdom, as exemplified by Walter Rybka and David Brink's restoration of *Elissa* in Galveston. Neill hoped to advance the fourth phase, "the institutionalization of success," at South Street. *WoodenBoat*'s Peter Spectre emphasized the movement's underlying problems—the lack of standards, funding, and priorities. With similar concerns, the US Senate directed the National Park Service (NPS) in 1984 to develop those standards, which were published in 1990. As Neill did at the National Trust, he hired Rybka's consulting firm to assess his fleet. In late 1985, Neill also hired Charles Deroko as his waterfront manager. Deroko was raised in Manhattan's "Hell's Kitchen," where he played along the Hudson River. After serving in the navy, he discovered *Wavertree* in 1972. He worked for the Seaport, Capt. Lacey, and *Peking*'s rigging crew prior to the Bicentennial. As waterfront manager for over a decade, his recurring problem was a shortage of funds.[2]

A *New York Times* editor, who privileged land exhibits, warned that Deroko's ships required costly work. As in the case of the Mariners' and Salem's Peabody Museum, most museums had resolved, said Neill, "never to accept a vessel into their collection." He dismissed them as upholding "the 19th-century concept of vast storehouses of bric-a-brac of all cultures." Focusing on the nation's historic vessels, whose merchant sailing fleet once numbered in the tens of thousands, he noted that only two hundred ships still existed of those that were fifty feet or larger and fifty years or older. Many were badly deteriorated. Even worse, there were only seven survivors "of the more than 3,000 iron-hulled vessels" such as *Wavertree* that Great Britain built between 1838 and 1907. New York, Mystic, and San Francisco were the only US museums to have "three or more" large vessels, and they faced intimidating costs. The necessary restoration moneys for San Francisco's and New York's fleets were conservatively "estimated at $25 million." A philanthropist had funded a drydock for Mystic's 113-foot *Charles W. Morgan*, but New York and San Francisco had much larger ships, little space, and no drydock. Coordinating a national campaign to protect large ships was difficult because most CAMM members did not have any in the water. Chiding them, Neill said that "to exclude the objects that are at the center of the tradition we celebrate is to build a museum round an empty hole."[3]

Neill's plan to increase ticket sales to fund the ships was a gamble, but he had little choice. Certainly USS *Intrepid* was on many minds. Decommissioned in 1974 and consigned to the scrap heap, the rusting World War II carrier was saved by developer Zachary Fisher, who in 1982 made it the nucleus of what became the Intrepid Sea-Air-Space Museum at Pier 86 on the Hudson. Three years later, it filed for bankruptcy. The city had already lost its stationary school ship *John W. Brown* in 1982. While government aid and Fisher's philanthropy refloated *Intrepid*, its presentation of history was troubling. Sociologist James Loewen called it "a feel-good museum that would rather exhibit anything but the realities of war." Still, it captured donors who eluded Neill. Although the nation annually spent hundreds of millions of public dollars preserving its artistic, architectural, and natural heritage, he wrote, "the total Congressional investment in the preservation of maritime resources" was $5 million in 1977, divided among 135 projects in thirty-three states. He also knew that millions of private dollars were being spent building replicas of old vessels instead of preserving authentic ones. Frustrated by it all, he warned, "Lose the ships and we lose our heart." San Francisco fleet manager Michael Naab bluntly told the *Daily News* that the ship-preservation movement was treading water.[4]

Yet diverging forces were also at work. Even the Seaport's self-study in 1987, whose panel lacked a ship specialist, set no priority for the fleet, suggesting instead "equal attention and care" for its diverse collections. As curator Steven Jaffe recalled, it was "a Balkanized place" where the uplands and waterfront were separate. He said the ships were "the most successful component . . . from a public relations and public service standpoint," but their neglect instead garnered bad PR. Incited by angry volunteers, a former colleague wrote the *Times* in 1988 that the rotting *Lettie* was "a scandal and a disgrace." Instigated by Stanford, the *Daily News* fired a volley in 1989 with a Sunday magazine cover story, "Port of Missing Ships: Whatever Happened to the South Street Dream?" It was the Seaport's most weighty and damning news coverage ever. With a cover photo of a cocooned *Lettie* and abandoned *Hart*, reporter Dick Sheridan opened, "Ships are rotting at the South Street Seaport." Blaming the "high-salaried, high-profile" SSSC managers who had pushed the Rouse development,

Fig. 10.1. Steam ferry *Maj. Gen. Wm. H. Hart* (*left*) and schooner *Lettie G. Howard* (*right*), 1989. (Historic American Engineering Record NY 206-3; photo, Jet Lowe; American Memory Project, Library of Congress)

the *Daily News* included a photograph of rivals Stanford and Neill, as the latter conceded that his Seaport had "zero assets and a lot of debt." After seeing the story, Spectre commented in *WoodenBoat*, "South Street isn't much of a museum." Stung, Neill fired off a letter. "I was shocked, then offended, then angered by your gratuitous comment." He rejoined in Sailortown's tradition, "I ought to punch you in the nose," but instead asked for Spectre's help. No help was forthcoming. In 1991, a *Downtown Express* headline read, "Lost at Seaport: Is It a Museum? Is It a Mall? Do Enough People Care?" That final question was the heart of the matter as Neill scrambled to fund his fleet.[5]

"The Museum's Greatest Artifact Is the Port Itself":
Capitalizing the Waterfront as the Port Changes

Characteristic of the era's free-market enthusiasm, Neill believed that "nonprofits need to be run like businesses." As waterfronts across the nation were turning to water-based tourism, Spectre observed that Mystic Seaport nicely mixed promotion and preservation with its restored steamer *Sabino*. Neill took action after New York State passed enabling legislation in 1982 for the Urban Cultural Parks System; Harbor Park, a collection of six water-accessible sites, including the Seaport, opened in 1985. Unlike Mystic, he sought a partner to own and operate the excursions. Rouse tried "to stop it," but McAllister Towing won the bid, as it hoped to reinvent its 122-year-old, declining business. In 1985, operating from Pier 16 as the Seaport Line, McAllister built, owned, and operated both the three-hundred-passenger diesel sidewheeler *Andrew Fletcher* and the twice-as-large, propeller-driven *DeWitt Clinton*. The latter was christened in 1986 by Matilda Cuomo, with her husband the governor at her side. Both vessels, said Norman Brouwer, re-created the "excursion boats that might have been seen in the Harbor around the turn of the century." Despite the diesels' soot and smell, the daily cruises offered "a release from crowded city neighborhoods, crowded suburbs, and crowded highways." In 1986, Mayor Koch boasted that 350,000 people rode the excursion vessels, from which the Seaport received 15 percent of the gross ticket sales. Sailor Ed Moran wisecracked about their "trip to no place." Yet they sailed in red ink after 1986, and the McAllisters sold both ships to Mississippi River gambling companies. The ships closed in 1992, and they departed "the Seaport literally in the dead of night." After McAllister offered to substitute what Neill derided as plastic yachts, Neill terminated the contract and signed the Circle Line.[6]

Pier 15 was more troubled. Given a ninety-nine-year lease in 1973, the Seaport agreed to restore it to its 1968 condition by 1998, thus privatizing a public responsibility. While Manhattan Landing planners and Christopher Lowery eyed the area for development, the Seaport was just too broke to consider its refurbishment. The city agreed in 1985 to fund "substantial improvements" but backed out with the 1988 recession. Then, in 1992, a freak nor'easter, whose damage was to be repeated with Superstorm Sandy two decades later, walloped the pier and brought "water up to [the] cash registers" on Fulton Street. Neill then discovered a possible funder, the quasi-independent state Dormitory Authority. As was verbally agreed in 1993, it would "issue bonds on South Street's behalf" so the Seaport could borrow funds to rebuild the pier and construct its International Maritime Heritage Center. But the novel scheme failed to attain the necessary permits and approval. The pier's fate was sealed after the Seaport Community Coalition complained to the EDC, which closed the pier in 1996 and the NYFD condemned it.[7]

Then opportunity knocked. The Mashantucket Pequots were promoting their Foxwoods Resort Casino in Connecticut and requested a docking lease in 1997, said Neill, "for commuter service between lower Manhattan and New London." The Pequots sought temporary dockage at Pier 16 for their high-speed catamarans; for three years, they would pay the museum an annual lease of $250,000 and "a percentage on every ticket." In an "80–20 split," moreover, they would provide most of the financing for Pier 15's reconstruction, which at minimum would have run $5–6 million, and then use its south side for their ferry. Trustees debated the offer; the advocates of *Wavertree*, which once used the pier's north side, were excited. The board approved the proposal and submitted the plan to the city in mid-1997. Doing an about-face on the issue of gambling, Mayor Giuliani vetoed it because he wanted to build a city-run casino on Governor's Island, despite Washington's warning that it would not transfer the property for such a use. Still holding the pier's lease, the Seaport added its $5.5 million cost to a capital campaign, but the money was elusive.[8]

In 1998, the planning process for Pier 15 included an unusual computer-aided design (CAD) drafting contest, though unaffiliated with the Seaport. As contestants watched a slide show of breath-taking images of Manhattan, "a fenced-up, rotting" Pier 15 appeared. The teams had three hours to complete "a conceptual design of an entertainment complex on the pier, complete with an 800-seat amphitheater, a dance club, a four-star restaurant, shops, a microbrewery and a marina." Like the fabled working waterfront, however, that CAD proposal was lost at sea. Then, Neill excitedly announced a federal grant to rebuild the pier, but Giuliani again balked because he wanted to use the area for the district's air rights. Meanwhile, the Seaport placed a permanent barge between the piers for its maintenance operations. By 2003, Pier 15 was reduced to four stumps, which contrasted with the new Pier 11 at Wall Street built for water taxis.[9]

Like Pier 15, the seaport's working-class economy was collapsing. "Within ten years of the first container ships starting to come out," said Seaport rigger Lars Hansen, "all those ships with the booms and the winches and the wires" began to disappear. Longshoremen and stevedores were also decimated. In 1969, they numbered twenty-seven thousand, but by 2000 their numbers had dropped 90 percent. The D-LMA and Port Authority had long pushed to replace finger piers, break-bulk cargoes, and longshoremen with containerized ships. Facing stiff competition in 1985, New York lost its title of "the world's busiest container port" and dropped to third in the nation by 2000, despite its volume doubling between 1991 and 2008. Stanford compared the uptick to the Erie Canal's "defining moment," but Hansen knew better. Also troubling was the downsizing of the US-flagged fleet to a minuscule 2 percent of commercial traffic by 2001 and the demolition of port facilities, as with the legendary Todd Shipyard in Brooklyn. Within eyesight of Pier 15, the 140-year-old yard, formerly the East Coast's largest drydock, gave way to a gigantic IKEA store.[10]

The decline was noticeable as the Seaport hosted its annual Mayor's Cup, which was, said the *Boston Globe*, the nation's "longest running regatta for historic boats." The race was only made possible because of "a spectacular decline in the commercial traffic in New York's Upper Bay." Edward Kennedy skippered the winning schooner, his fifty-foot *Mya*, in the thirty-first race in 1997, and for the first time the Seaport allowed the winner to take the Tiffany trophy out of the city to display in the US Senate cloak room. In 1998, the thirty-second race showcased more than forty classic schooners and yachts, including *Pioneer* and *Lettie*, but they contrasted with the container ships steaming under the Verrazano Narrows Bridge. While *Pioneer* weighed in at forty-seven gross tons, the newest container ship in 1998 was two thousand times that weight.[11]

"When the Hell Are You Going to Do Something for the *Wavertree*?": The Fits-and-Starts Restoration of a Square-Rigger

Sailing through those same Narrows in 1895, the 279-foot *Wavertree* was but one-fifth the length of later behemoths. Mayor Lindsay still called it "the largest museum artifact ever brought to New York in one piece." *Wavertree* symbolized the Seaport's plight under captains Buford, Hightower, and Lowery, obsessed as they were with the great white whale named Rouse. It was pushed to the back burner until Isbrandtsen began recruiting volunteers in 1981, without whom, Hightower admitted, the Seaport "could not have functioned at all." Dissatisfied with the independence of Isbrandtsen's crew, chairman John Ricker threatened to send it to a shipyard which, Rybka said, would have been a bad choice for a real restoration. Neill had difficulty, however, "working out an amiable relationship" with Isbrandtsen. Neill, to prove his commitment to *Wavertree*, pledged that it would participate in Op Sail 92 during the Columbus Quincentennial. But that intensified the debate about whether a rare ship should sail risky waters, whether its restoration should use historical or modern materials and methods, and whether its own authenticity required such stunts to attract the fickle public. Before the NPS set standards in 1990, those issues were hotly debated, but Spectre admitted that they were "about as exciting as hog farming" to city slickers.[12]

As architectural preservation had recently evolved, the substantial differences among ship preservation, restoration, reconstruction, and reproduction were still being defined. The disciples of William Morris condemned restoration and much of what passed as preservation in the United States. As Liverpool's Fab Four once sang, "Let it be," the British magazine *Sea Breezes* included a rant about this Liverpool-based ship. "If such a ship is to be preserved," wrote J. J. Thompson,

> then she would be preserved in the condition in which she is taken over for preservation, whatever that condition might be, and that instead of restoration work being carried out, her exhibition to the public should be supported by photographs, drawings, descriptions and models to show what she was like in her hey-day, what alterations were subsequently made to her and why they were made, and how, generally, she came to be in the condition in which she was found and preserved. Such would be truly an exhibition of the ship and her life; it would be of far more interest and value to those who were genuinely interested in the ship herself, and no less interesting or attractive than a restored fake, I think, to the nautically ignorant visiting masses on whom such projects have to depend for financial support. Let me put this more strongly: I put it to these perpetrators of restorational vandalism that they are intent primarily on building for themselves a public attraction, and that in carrying out such work they are [more]

concerned with creating something that will draw people and money than with their ships as the ships they were.

But no US or British museum practiced preservation pure and simple for a ship such as *Wavertree*. Thompson's diatribe rankled Lowery, who scribbled on it, "What an asshole!"[13]

Since 1967, the Seaport had pledged to restore and sail *Wavertree*, but other goals complicated the effort. On one hand, they included retaining yesteryear's realia, perpetuating traditional craftsmanship, and illustrating old-time seafaring. Those goals embodied the "authenticity" that preservationists desired but was difficult to attain. On the other hand, an emerging professionalism considered cost, modern materials, and newer standards. Conflicts were inevitable and frequent. After three decades working on ships, Rybka said, "the value of preserving anything lies in what it has to teach," and that was "best learned by sailing them." What remained was the question of retaining realia or "original fabric" (the latter term being common and less subjective than "authentic"). There was a danger in subjecting a rare ship to the sea's rigors, and it would have been more suitable to build a replica for sail training. But realia was precious because reproductions have become so common and convincing that if anything "authentic" is to be found, it is often in a museum.[14]

Yet that was Thompson's point. Remembering that *Wavertree* had lost its rig and been gutted in Argentina, he claimed, "The *Wavertree* as a sand barge was, honestly and honourably, the hulk of the *Wavertree*," but it would "inevitably be fake" if restored. "Worse still," he added, the process of restoration "destroys all that is left of the original; it becomes so covered up with new material made to pass for original that the very fact that it is original begins to lack any relevance at all." As in the much-lauded, $4 million work on *Elissa*, Rybka admitted, "We kept feeling that our research was inadequate," but because of time and budgetary constraints, "it became a question of our best guess." *Wavertree* was even more compromised. Lacking restoration know-how, Capt. Bill Lacey's work in 1970–71 involved so much slapdash that it shocked Richard Fewtrell. Coming on board in 1972, Fewtrell upheld the craftsman tradition, but lacking original drawings and detailed photographs, he relied on Brouwer's research, his own conjecture, and archaeology. After Fewtrell was sacked in 1979 and

Isbrandtsen's volunteers took over in 1981, said Deroko, "the quality of the work . . . went down considerably." Isbrandtsen called his critics purists and left decision-making to his volunteers' "ingenuity and inventiveness," as he was most concerned with getting the job done within his budget. Rejecting that pragmatism, Fewtrell complained to Spectre, "In true *archaeology*, when they find a ruin, they call in the boys with the camel's-hair brushes. In ship restoration, they call in anybody and start mucking around indiscriminately. . . . But they don't have the training or the skills for the job." Some *Wavertree* volunteers, moreover, took an antiestablishment, proprietary hold, and there was "little cooperation with waterfront staff." In Texas, however, skilled tradesmen supervised *Elissa*'s volunteers.[15]

Contrary to Thompson's stance, the replacement of deteriorated materials was inevitable and necessary. "No ship lasts forever," said Rybka. "Usually the best that can be done is to slow the ageing process down to the point where it is no longer perceptible to the present generation." But introducing new materials became more contentious when restorers removed unwanted alterations, which some critics regarded as part of a ship's natural growth. USS *Constitution*, the nation's most venerable ship, was "rebuilt three times over," Neill wrote, so that the 1797 frigate had "little, if any of what preservationists call 'original fabric' remaining." But "that is how ships are meant to be. What is important is that she exists at all, and that she is visited by thousands who have not given up that ship to memory." Over the years, Fewtrell "witnessed a cascade of cheap and cheerful ship restorations," but "Old Ironsides" reflected, he said, "The Golden Age of Restoration."[16]

A parallel question concerned substituting modern compositions, such as aluminum and plastic. National Trust consultant William Avery Baker criticized those who used anything but traditional materials on historic wooden vessels, but old-time ship captains had used what they had on hand to maintain their vessels. Mystic Seaport's Donald Robinson recognized the constraints. "All too often the hard realities of little money, lack of appropriate materials, and lack of skilled personnel force the answer upon us," he said. There was "no universal answer," other than the requirement that the compromises that are made "are reversible." South Street staff knew of the work on HMS *Victory* (1765), where English restorers were using synthetics in the rigging, instead of the original hemp, and teak, not the original English oak, for wood substitutions. In so doing, said Rybka, "the process of renewal is more one of maintaining the knowledge and the skills than it is maintaining the material." A similar suggestion for *Wavertree* set off a storm. After three new topmasts were sent aloft by Fewtrell, he was fired before the rig was completed. In 1980, Prince Philip suggested using an aluminum alloy for the yards to reduce maintenance. "We did it with the *Cutty Sark* and we had no trouble," he said. "That ship is not going to sail again. The idea is to make it look right. With the old material you'll just be committing the next generation to endless work all over again."[17]

Stanford viewed the issue more philosophically. "Ships do not need merely to be 'restored' and then 'maintained,'" he said. "They need to be kept in life by a continuous rebuilding process," which would support craft training, enchant viewers, and generate funds. He and Neill rejected aluminum, as a result, and endorsed the renewal of the original Douglas fir for the spars. Brouwer also knew that modern materials created a different finish, performance, texture, and weathering. "The most difficult thing to re-create," he added, was the "original workmanship," as "subtleties of the craft, passed from master to apprentice" would be missing. Yet he most objected to Thompson's demand that *Wavertree* be shown as acquired, saying,

> I believe exhibiting an ugly barge and telling people it was once a sailing ship, and only showing photos to convey what it once was, would be pointless. And, I don't think many people would find it very interesting. How many New Yorkers want to see Argentine sand bins dating from 1947? If there had been changes during a vessel's working career that reflected chapters in its life as a seagoing vessel it would be another matter. The *Wavertree* was saved in part to pay tribute to the people who built, owned and sailed her. It was always the intent to do a restoration that accurately represented their lives and work on a scale people could actually experience. We will always have historic photos and ship models, but they hardly offer the same experience.

With scant archival evidence, Brouwer was pressed to document the ship's appearances over time. Fortunately, he discovered a glass plate negative in the Falklands from 1896 that showed the deckhouse amidships, and he extrapolated evidence from similar ships to devise a restoration plan. But it was altered by Isbrandtsen's volunteers.[18]

Like the Seaport, *Wavertree* was a mix of the authentic and contrived, as was its figurehead of Penelope. "Only a vague picture" of Penny existed, but a new figurehead was created by Seaport carver Sal Polisi, who after being laid off from manufacturing in 1983 became a full-time volunteer and learned the trade under a craftsman. Stanford had suggested that the model be "Victorian, sexy, womanly, [and with an] old fashioned face." Polisi's carving, which resembled *la poitrine* of Brouwer's girlfriend, was restrained, however, when compared with "Saucy Sally," a nineteenth-century Dutch model with partially exposed breasts that Mystic Seaport exhibited and Polisi replicated for a private customer. According to tradition, that flash of skin was powerful enough to stem nature's tempests.[19]

Another tempest—the debate over standards—was settled in 1990. After the NPS brought in the maritime community, other federal agencies, and the National Trust, it hired Michael Naab, who was directing the Trust's maritime office. In consultation with an expert panel, which included Brouwer, Rybka, and Don Birkholz, Naab wrote *The Secretary of the Interior's Standards for Historic Vessel Preservation Projects* (1990). Of the four customary options—preservation, rehabilitation, restoration, and reconstruction—the so-called Green Book recommended guidelines for the first three and acknowledged that some vessels would blend tracks. Applying the National Register's standards, Naab's primary concern was a ship's historical integrity. Interested in "retaining and preserving" authentic materials, the NPS frowned on "replacing historic elements with, or introducing, elements that are historically inappropriate to the vessel." Finding a balance between purists and pragmatists was central, but a wider gulf separated tourists and craftsmen because few sightseers could recognize an authentic restoration when they saw one. As it was, *Wavertree* did not sail in 1992 because its restoration was still unfunded.[20]

"It Was Never Meant to Be Historically Accurate": The Faux Reality of *Peking*

Splicing *Peking*'s wires, Lars Hansen said he took "a little more time so it looks good," but looks could be deceiving. The authenticity of the four-masted barque, which at 377 feet was "the world's second largest surviving sailing ship," was murky. For one, it had no pertinent link to US history, making it ineligible for the historic registers. "*Peking* never sailed to New

York," Aron joked. "It was built to haul guano, not Mrs. Vanderbilt." For another, its welded rudder and "flagpole" rig raised eyebrows. As Slotnick confessed, it was "never meant to be historically accurate." That led the National Trust's Harry Allendorfer to jeer that it was good enough for "the little kid and his mother" who wanted "a feel for a square-rigger." Perhaps a feel for danger too. "After 73 years," said Deroko, its "standing rigging was weak" and corroded, and falling pieces almost hit a visiting school group. In 1984, the board authorized its replacement, which took twelve years to complete without a full-time crew and was "the largest of its type attempted by a maritime museum in the United States." While the "flagpole" spars remained, the new wire rope resembled the cabling that John A. Roebling had specified for the Brooklyn Bridge. Over time, Deroko would revisit the issue of authentic materials, concluding that "it makes great sense to go with new materials if they look the part." Said Naab, the Green Book was not the king's law and only set the ideal practice.[21]

Still, *Peking* offered a world of amazement to less discriminating eyes. Joe Doyle recalled, for example, "lots of soulful exhibits" and its claustrophobic fo'c'sle, which was "extremely evocative of the harsh living conditions." Like many visitors, he loved its continuously running movie of Irving Johnson rounding Cape Horn "and real charts in the chartroom." Authenticity was approximate, however, as the chartroom had instruments from a later era and the fo'c'sle was representative. The retired sailors-turned-interpreters also impressed him. It was "engaging and authentic." Entertaining too. A "novel new program" offered an overnight stay for parents and children. Signing on as ordinary seamen and eating hard tack and cod stew, "the novice sailors swab decks, peel potatoes and stand watch in the night." Perhaps parents hoped that youngsters, once home, would do the same. Such overnighters became profitable. As a Halloween ghost ship, *Peking* staged scenes from Shakespeare's plays "with songs, eerie sounds and flashing lights." Later, a troupe performed a three-month run of an updated Gilbert and Sullivan *Pirates of Penzance* with jocular references to Madonna, Viagra, and Dick Cheney. Yet the real show occurred when darkness fell and Manhattan's skyline lit up.[22]

But nothing was more authentic than Lars Henning Hansen. "I got my lust for the sea" in Denmark, he said, where sailing "was like a big family." Commercial rigging jobs were "going the way of the dodo," however. Hired full-time by Deroko in 1985, he was featured in an admiring *Times* article,

Fig. 10.2. Overnight Life-at-Sea program aboard *Peking*, 1987. (Photo, Thomas Walker)

which called him "a sailors' sailor," a "Paul Bunyan of the sea," and "king of the still-gritty side of the seaport." A jazz enthusiast, Hansen even brought musicians to his master cabin aboard *Peking*, which was called "the finest private jazz venue south of Canal." As master rigger, said Deroko, "he was unstoppable. He'd be up at first light, work 12 hours, bathe with the fire hose, go out until 3, and be right back up the rigging the next morning." It reminded Hansen of his earlier life when, he joked, he "had to go ashore every night and see the girls and drink. It was pretty exhausting doing that every night!" He added with a big guffaw, "You never had money, of course." His Seaport was in the same boat.[23]

"Saving Ships Does Not Mean Merely Jerking Them Out of a Backwater": What to Do with *Charles Cooper, Lettie G. Howard, Pioneer,* and *W. O. Decker*?

The 165-foot *Charles Cooper* (1856) was called "the best-preserved, wooden-hulled square-rigger built in this country left in the world." But it was sixty-five hundred miles away in the Falklands, the graveyard of many great sailing ships. While a seventeen-foot hole had been cut in its side for a warehouse, its magnificent tweendeck had changed little. Brouwer could see its splendid workmanship, which he thought "people who build replicas today don't understand." As Maine museums were snatching up other ships, the Seaport toyed with the idea of bringing *Cooper* to New York, but Spectre warned that such ships "should remain in the Falklands until they turn to dust or for eternity, whichever comes first." He added, "Saving ships does not mean merely jerking them out of a backwater and putting them on display, hoping somehow that everything will come out OK in the end." Though *Cooper* was unharmed in the Falklands War, Neill later asked if it could be saved at all. Fearing a liability lawsuit, he gave the hulk to the Falklands. Moreover, Rybka rejected Spectre's opinion, as it would "write off just about any historic preservation efforts, and there have been some great saves."[24]

Fig. 10.3. Jakob Isbrandtsen (*left*) and Lars Henning Hansen (*right*), 1984. (Photo, Jeff Perkell)

The 102-foot *Pioneer*, for example, had been abandoned on a Cape Cod beach. It was like other work boats, Neill told the *Times*, which "were cheap to build, and when they were worn out, they were thrown away." With *Pioneer* having worked for sixteen different owners and undergone four major changes of rig and two rebuilds since its 1885 launch, only 20 percent of its original fabric remained. It was also excluded from the historic registers because the Seaport could not prove the authenticity of its appearance. In a novel move, Dianne Glennon, who had been a student in the Pioneer program, became its first female captain in 1983; for over a decade, she operated in a man's world. In the harbor, another ship radioed, not knowing her sex, "Where are you taking that old hooker, Captain?" Holding her tongue, she "realized it was a term of great endearment," as British sailors had referred to older, but still working, ships as hookers. USCG certified and the Seaport's best maintained vessel, *Pioneer* became a moneymaker, with each trip carrying up to thirty-five passengers, whether tourists during the summer or students during the school year. The school program, said Doyle, "was phenomenally good outreach—teaching the vagaries of the wind, seasickness, seamanship, navigation and a wealth of nautical lore."[25]

After being rescued in 1968, the 125-foot *Lettie G. Howard* deteriorated to the point where Hightower tried, but failed, to give it away in 1979. It was rotting at its dock, but the Waterfront Committee resolved that its restoration "must be done with little or no cost borne by the Museum." Volunteers finally acted in 1984. Gathering at Carmine's, they bemoaned the "lack of vision, planning and leadership," said Nora McAuley-Gitin, and after several beers concluded that if they started the restoration, they could win either museum or outside funding. Weekend volunteers were first led by Bill Goscener, a college history professor, and Joe Baiamonte, an ATT office worker. Besides nearby high-rise residents, volunteers included an engineer, a marine biologist, and a lawyer. They were close to those on *Wavertree* who organized the VISOSSSM in March 1985 to fight Shepley and Lowery. Left out of the hiring process, the VISOSSSM was suspicious of Neill and feared that he and the trustees were trying to get the volunteer group "under their thumb." Despite Neill's hope of saving *Lettie*, Jack Aron bluntly told him, "We are not committed to reconstructing her." Moreover, some trustees felt, as did Peter Aron, that a power vacuum had placed them "at the mercy of the volunteers." Yet the museum staff noted in *Seaport* that South Street had been developed by volunteers and still relied on their "spiritual lift" and talents.[26]

This rift illustrated changes in the preservation and museum movements. Within CAMM, for example, administrators were trying "to professionalize the group." In fields from archaeology to libraries to preservation, volunteers were being pushed aside by professionals. Relying on their college training, setting disciplinary standards, and arguing for efficiencies, these new professionals met noticeable resistance from amateurs. Because ship preservation was rooted in the unique world of sailing, it was slower than most disciplines in adopting new approaches, though curators felt the pressure from accrediting associations. The question "Who owns history?" had been raised when Stanford alleged that a narrow clique controlled history, art, and museums. In conjunction with the Association for Preservation Technology, a group of maritime professionals met in 1985 to discuss large museum ships. Many of them believed that "maritime preservation was twenty years behind the times" because it lacked standards, accreditation, and certifiable training. Criticizing the volunteers' restoration of *Lettie*, Neill knew it would not meet the proposed standards that outside funders would require. He said it was reprehensible spending "a single dollar" until those standards were considered. *Lettie* had been placed on the National Register in September 1984, but it required a complete reconstruction. There were few options. If left unrestored, said waterfront director Birkholz, its bones could have been exhibited, like *Australia*, whose restoration Mystic Seaport had botched, but visitors would have been confused because *Lettie* hardly resembled an 1893 Gloucester fishing schooner.[27]

With few options, Neill worked with the volunteers. Upon his arrival, VISOSSSM chairwoman Susan Fowler sent a detailed thirteen-page memo recommending projects and listing the various people and their responsibilities, skills, and years of service. Even so, he thought the Seaport "was an uncoordinated mess, each group with an agenda of its own, not always in sync with the Museum." A volunteer cautioned him that *Wavertree*'s restoration was "outside of the authority or control of the museum." Like a cooperative, the volunteers had organized "a model of 'economic de-centralization,'" but their democratic process ran counter to Neill's notion of professionalism. Brouwer also heard their "almost universal" belief that they "should have more say in running the organization" and that they "could run the Museum better than the paid staff." By then, said Neill, they "had taken *Lettie* as their personal project and club-house."[28]

The Seaport had no success finding donors for *Lettie's* $1 million restoration. Taking direct responsibility for the waterfront, Neill put the entire crew on notice. Six weeks later, he appointed Deroko waterfront director for the entire fleet. But Neill underestimated the volunteers' clout. He dismissed Baiamonte as "a gadfly" who "fancied himself [as] some kind of labor organizer." With other disgruntled volunteers, Baiamonte formed the Seaport Community Coalition in 1987, which succeeded VISOSSSM and won supporters by publicizing the sad state of the fleet and small-craft collection. Seeing it narrowly as a bout between professionals and amateurs, Neill rejected Baiamonte's plan to supervise *Lettie's* restoration, saying that "he had no experience, no skill," and "no real understanding of the standards, regulations, and other requirements for her new sailing mission." According to Neill, Baiamonte then led "an up-rising" and "ginned up the other volunteers." He met with them several times "to discuss their issues and demands." Removing the ringleaders was complicated because the volunteers aboard *Lettie* and *Wavertree* were close; the dedication of the latter's crew, said Sally Yerkovich, "was unquestionable in my mind." But they were loyal to *Wavertree* and its crew, not Neill and his museum. Deroko discovered that even Isbrandtsen could not control them, so Neill fired Baiamonte and Goscener in mid-1989. One compatriot was relieved, thinking that they "were basically all noise and offered very little in the way of concrete solutions." Baiamonte, like his mentor Jeremiah Driscoll, "had a tentative grip on reality from time to time."[29]

Neill then struck gold—*Lettie* was given National Historic Landmark status and initial funding. After the Seaport trimmed its estimate to $750,000, Albany awarded a $250,000 matching grant in 1989, and Rouse pledged $150,000. A panel of experts approved the plan, whereby *Lettie* would be measured by the Historic American Engineering Record, placed in a Lexan shelter, and reconstructed on Burling Slip, "much in the fashion of similar projects in Boston and Baltimore." Approved by the LPC, *Lettie's* three-story shelter still needed the approval of Community Board 1, the NYFD, and the Department of Buildings. But Neill had neglected to ask the fish market, which used Burling Slip, or its neighbors for their permission.[30]

Rallying the opposition was the SCC, which Neill told his board was "three people," two of whom were fired volunteers. At a stormy CB1 meeting, Baiamonte claimed that hauling *Lettie* would endanger it, although Mystic had earlier hauled the schooner *L. A. Dunton* for rebuilding. Driscoll added that the shelter would turn the restoration into a carnival. Baiamonte played his NIMBY card in what *Battery News* called the "Seaport Civil War." His focus on the proposed restoration's disruption of the fish market, its safety hazards, and its environmental threat to the neighborhood won over a majority of CB1 attendees. The SCC told the press, said Matteson, "that the hull was toxic from sitting in the East River and thus—if hauled out would present a public menace." Even the *Times* reported the spurious claim that the ship had been "soaking up impurities that may spread disease." The Seaport was framed as arrogant and threatening. Museum administrators "seem to feel they're a world unto their own and they can do what they want," said a resident. Baiamonte had the last word because his complaints to the city killed the plan. That gave Neill the idea of placing *Lettie* on a barge, he said, "where the city and no one else had any jurisdiction and the public got the same opportunity to engage with the work first hand."[31]

As Neill told a National Trust audience, he learned that volunteerism and professionalism were often at odds. "Individualistic and eccentric," volunteers could be "motivated by psychological forces that bureaucrats will never understand." They were still the movement's heart, but professionalization "over the last decade threatens to disenfranchise them." He paradoxically added, "We allow this to happen at our peril," suggesting that "every effort should be made to broaden" their contributions. That love-hate relationship was embedded in the movement. The SCC had won the *Lettie* debate, but other volunteers were hardly malcontents, including those aboard *Pioneer* and *Ambrose*. *Pioneer*'s were "extremely devoted people," said its Richard Dorfman, but Matteson cautioned, "Volunteers are very tricky to work with. They can very easily blow up in your face."[32]

After a fifteen-month delay, *Lettie* was hauled onto a barge in December 1990 between *Wavertree* and *Peking*. The Seaport hired a full-time crew of eight tradesmen. Supervised at first by shipwright David Short, Birkholz then stepped in but ran out of money, in part, because Rouse reneged on half of its $150,000 pledge. Aron wrote the company chairman that the Seaport considered the grant "an act of corporate responsibility and goodwill, and not as some kind of marketing deal or strategy." But Rouse did

Fig. 10.4. *Pioneer* crew, with Capt. Dianne Glennon (*fifth from left*), relief captain Kevin Jones (*fourth from left*), and Skeeter Harris (*right*). (Photo, Skeeter Harris)

not budge. As the $1.2 million restoration was the "first test application" of the Green Book, it was $250,000 in the red. With the hull completed, the festive rechristening in May 1992 "was a great moment," said Baiamonte, who had returned from exile. In the following March, the two seventy-five-foot masts were then placed, with the "ceremonial 1893 and 1993 silver coins" in the wells. There was "some original keel left," but *Lettie* had been "99% renewed."[33]

Lettie was expected to pay its own way. After minor changes for USCG certification, it became a sailing-school vessel with an environmental education program supported partly by NYSCA and the Department of Cultural Affairs. Its programs for disadvantaged youth emphasized "leadership, cooperation, responsibility, and self-esteem." In 1996, it also targeted affluent clients when the Seaport introduced a cruise for executive team-building. In line with corporate retention programs, it was premised on the belief that those who sailed together profited together. Through such programs, *Lettie* covered most of its operating costs. Meanwhile, the wooden-hulled, New York–built tug *W. O. Decker* (1930), which Matteson had given to the museum in 1986 and helped maintain, supplemented the school program by accessing hard-to-reach estuaries. Because the USCG annually allowed "up to six passenger charters on un-inspected vessels," *Decker* was booked for "six-pack charters" to the backwaters.[34]

That kind of self-financing was Neill's goal for *Hart*, which had become a rusting hulk since the Pioneer school closed in 1982. In late 1982, Isbrandt-sen sarcastically suggested that it be "modestly fitted to accommodate Museum administration" because Lowery would then fund the fleet. The Waterfront Committee was not committed to its restoration, so in 1988 Neill submitted a $2.4 million proposal to City Hall, supported by some council members, to restore *Hart* as a waterborne visitor center for Harbor Park. Swayed by a commercial developer, Mayor Koch instead promoted Pier A at the Battery for a multiuse facility. Subsequently, in 1992, the Seaport gave the unfunded *Hart* to the HMS *Rose* Foundation in Bridgeport, Connecticut, which promised to restore it as a school. Chairing CB1's Waterfront Committee, Baiamonte deplored the move. But when the *Rose* foundation failed to create its floating school, the unrestored ferry was towed "with pumps going to keep it afloat" to New Jersey, but it sank before finding a home in the Arthur Kill graveyard. With its upper decks above water, *Hart* joined the living dead by 2005, and kayakers used the hulk as a nighttime layover.[35]

"A Tall Ship for New York and the Nation": Operation Sail and *Wavertree*

Four years before the Columbus Quincentennial, the Seaport had declared that *Wavertree* would be restored at a cost of $5 million to its "original sail-ing condition" and participate in Op Sail 92. Its ability to sail was in ques-tion as it lacked USCG-mandated watertight bulkheads. Rybka advised that adding bulkheads "would so alter the character of the vessel that perhaps it's not worth doing." Nor did he propose sailing such a fragile, rare vessel with so much original fabric. Those concerns were academic because, with the recession, the Rouse imbroglio, *Lettie*'s delays, and an unrealistic sense of *Wavertree*'s issues, its preparations went nowhere. Bigger than in 1986 or 1976, Op Sail 92 attracted thirty-one tall ships and 250 other vessels, which made it, said director John E. Richard, "the larg-est grouping of tall ships since the age of sail began." As seventeen hun-dred cadets from three dozen countries paraded on Broadway, the *Times* editorial page praised sail training, while its boosters boasted that 90 percent of the world's general cargo still moved by sea. Despite *Wavertree's* setback, the Seaport was center stage for Columbus Quincentennial festivities. With five days of ship parades and tours, concerts, and street festivals, the July Fourth weekend was an extravaganza whose organizers ignored the debate about honoring a conqueror. Pier 16 was in the spotlight when pops great Skitch Henderson conducted its headline concert, which was telecast live and accompanied by "a dazzling Laser Spectacular" on a seventy-foot screen.[36]

Rouse undercut the Seaport's future role in Op Sail. After McAllister's Seaport Line failed, causing a financial nightmare for the museum, Rouse exerted control over Pier 17's south side, where *Ambrose* docked and visiting ships temporarily put in. In 1996, Rouse leased it to a commuter operation and told visiting ships to use an out-of-the-way pier north of the mall. "The word is out that the seaport is no longer a hospitable place," Neill complained in the *Times*. In one instance, he said, Rouse's "security guys actually began to untie a ship's line, a criminal offense, and only when the captain threatened to have the security officers arrested themselves did they back off and seek instructions." The dispute intensified so much that Neill and the mall's manager got into another "shouting match" at a CB1 meeting. Yet the EDC, which was Rouse's landlord, did nothing. City Hall also undercut the Seaport in announcing that Pier A would be the "headquarters for Op Sail 2000."[37]

When Neill asked Birkholz to ready *Wavertree* for Op Sail 2000, he did not tell him that it had been controlled since 1981 by volunteers. Birkholz tried to take charge, said Deroko, but Isbrandtsen "and his gang pretty much chased him off." Calling Isbrandtsen cantankerous, Birkholz griped that he "objected to everything." Neill shrugged, as he was unable to force change. Isbrandtsen had reason to be testy because his Seaport Holdings wanted its $2.9 million repaid from 1973. He complained that his requests for repayment were "relegated to the dead letter file," *Wavertree* was ignored, and his ketch *Sun Dance II* had been damaged when the Seaport allowed it to be improperly installed in a restaurant. After one too many "indignant outbursts," said Stanford, Aron asked Isbrandtsen to resign from the board.[38]

With Op Sail 2000 on the horizon, Neill boldly announced "the largest sailing ship restoration ever attempted in the United States." Halving his estimate to a questionable $2.5 million, he started the $1.5 million first phase with Deroko hauling the vessel at Caddell Dry Dock on Staten Island and preparing its hull. For the standing rigging alone, the Seaport used ten full-time riggers and forty-five weekend volunteers. With the first phase completed, the *Daily News* reported, *Wavertree* "should be fit to represent New York in the July 4 Parade of Ships." The second phase was scheduled after Op Sail and would include a full suit of sails and a deck replacement. With that, the *News* added, *Wavertree* would "conform to Coast Guard standards so that she can sail the seven seas again." Just who provided that incorrect information about USCG standards was not revealed. With eight months to go, however, the first phase was only half funded. In the *Journal of Commerce*, Neill described his "long and frustrating" search. Without naming such notables as Cutty Sark Whisky, media mogul and billionaire yachtsman Ted Turner, or the giant Maersk Shipping Line, he asked,

Why? Why, for example, has the marine industry failed to respond to what may be the most evocative expression of its long and lucrative history?

Why have companies that expropriate the image of sailing ships and their associated values failed to respond to what may be the most visible expression of that tradition?

Why have so many individuals who get such great personal satisfaction from sea experience declined to extend that opportunity to others?

What is most ironic is that the preservation of landside cultural resources—collections of fine art and architecture—flourishes today, frequently through foundations and endowments that were created historically by maritime enterprise.

America is a nation built by water transportation. The nation was capitalized by immigration and international trade, culture and commerce founded on maritime endeavor. The placement of our cities, our systems of distribution and transportation, our sustenance, our recreation—all were and remain an undeniable function of our connection to the sea.

That fact merits more than indifference. That fact demands public information and public celebration. My challenge to the marine industry is this: Let's sail *Wavertree* as an affirmation of our maritime history and as an investment in its future.

Instead, City Hall turned a deaf ear, Albany gave a modest $70,000, and the doldrums set in. New York was famous for its philanthropy, said Paul Goldberger, but its largest foundations paid little attention to their own city. The Seaport went ahead without their help.[39]

After Dorfman assembled a crew, Neill planned for *Wavertree* to make a shakedown cruise off Sandy Hook on the eve of the July Fourth parade. That was doable, said Deroko, "under tow on a flat day." *Wavertree* was then supposed to join the fleet at the Verrazano Narrows Bridge to begin the parade. Because it never had an engine, two tugs would push it up the Hudson in what was called "the largest peacetime maritime gathering in U.S. history." Captained by Stephen Cobb of Maine, *Wavertree* would have a fifty-five-person crew and forty-five guests. "We'll be the last in the line of the A-class ships," said waterfront director James Clements. "It's a position of respect." Meanwhile, Pier 16 would host seven visiting tall ships, including the behemoth 361-foot *Kaiwo Maru* (1989) of the Japanese Merchant Navy. Just the sight of that fleet, Neill predicted, would "evoke the history of South Street as the Street of Ships."[40]

Yet *Wavertree* hit a USCG snag on July Fourth when the Coastie in charge ruled that it was structurally deficient for lacking "bulkheads and watertight doors" and having a thin hull with damaged rivets. Shocked by the timing of the decision, Neill said, "I went nuts." On a technicality, he told the press that the USCG "believed that with the harbor so crowded today, it might be too congested for the *Wavertree*'s crew to sail the 2,400 ton ship." The USCG commander admitted that his task was like "directing traffic in Times Square on New Year's Eve." Unlike *Wavertree*, other vessels had auxiliary engines, and the captain of the port was most "concerned that if holed, she'd sink like a stone." The USCG gave Neill the choice of "the 'front row' adjacent to the aircraft carrier *John F. Kennedy* . . . or to remain in the Kill van Kull invisible." He chose the former. The *New York Post* creatively suggested that *Wavertree* had "passed a last-minute sailing test with flying colors," but Neill conceded, "there was no sailing test." Spinning the story, the *Post* added, "the grand dame . . . pulled off a maritime miracle . . . by successfully taking to the sea again after a 100-year vacation." There were no miracles, but *Wavertree* raised some of its sails while being towed. During the parade, it moored off the Statue of Liberty next to *JFK*, from which President Bill Clinton viewed the International Naval Review and the Parade of Sail. Their one hundred naval vessels, twenty-seven tall

Fig. 10.5. *Wavertree* at the new, double-deck Pier 15, 2013. (Photo, author)

ships, and sixty thousand pleasure boats constituted "the largest collection of ships ever since the Spanish Armada invaded England." Few were as historic as *Wavertree*. Led by *Eagle*, the fleet included replicas of the slaver *Amistad* and the immigrant transport *Jeanie Johnston* and the reconstructed Lake Erie brig *Niagara*, captained by Rybka.[41]

Wavertree's rig of sixteen yardarms was the most complete it had been in ninety years, but the hull's deficiencies had been recognized earlier. The USCG ruling "came as no surprise," admitted Deroko, because old-time "windjammers with bulkheads were exceedingly rare." While its locally thin hull was taken "into consideration when the stress calculations were done," he concluded that *Wavertree* was not "structurally sound to sail, period. Her missing 'tween deck structure and lack of vertical stiffness restricts the angle of heel to about 10 degrees with a sea height to about 3–4'." Thinking that "they put on the icing before baking the cake," he was "happily relieved that *Wavertree* stayed put during the parade." The Seaport accentuated the positive. On July 5, Neill said with much hyperbole,

"We slipped the mooring and headed for the [Verrazano] bridge. . . . If we had the nerve and a few more supplies we could have just kept on going to Australia." Trustee Tom Gochberg also saw hope, believing that the second phase's deck replacement and full suit of sails "should be the principal focus of the museum." After that, they wanted to sail "on a regular basis," as was then the case with San Diego's *Star of India* and Galveston's *Elissa*. That would, said Neill, keep "the spirit and vision of the great Age of Sail alive in a world that is too often run by bean counters. We may have computers to keep us on track and in touch, but we still need dreams to keep us moving forward."[42]

Thus, the Seaport met the millennium with faith in the future, as *Wavertree* was finally close to sailing, *Lettie* had been restored according to the Green Book, *Pioneer*'s sailing program was flush, and *Peking* had a new standing rigging. With the EDC in charge of the commercial leases, the Seaport could focus on maintaining its fleet, preparing its "World Port New York" display, and developing its revenue-earning programs, after which it was expected that the three would be mutually supportive. Yet its goals were always limited by the shortage of funds in this, the nation's richest city. That was evident with Pier 15's decay, Giuliani's grudge, and *Wavertree*'s shortfall in Op Sail 2000. Still, the 21st century seemed to open full of promise and with expectations for success.

"Sometimes You Just Can't Get a Break"

How 9/11 Torpedoed the Seaport

In 2001, the Seaport hoped to put wind in its sails with its biggest gift ever. The agenda for the Port Authority board meeting on September 12 at the World Trade Center included an initial $5 million for rehabilitating Schermerhorn Row and exhibiting "World Port New York" (WPNY). The Port Authority had a modest display on the harbor in the North Tower's observatory, which drew two million visitors annually, but the Row offered better logistics. Expected to open in 2003, WPNY would add "tens of thousands" to the ten million people annually visiting Lower Manhattan. "Tourism is the lifeblood of New York City and its economy," declared Governor George Pataki. Tourism would buttress the Port Authority, whose harbor supported 226,000 regional jobs and $25 billion in activity. After the port's traffic dropped to third in the nation, its executive director, Joseph Seymour, admitted that the Seaport was a proxy, as it was earlier with the D-LMA, to regain momentum. "By increasing public awareness of the importance of the maritime industry to the region," said Seymour, the Seaport "will help build support for harbor improvements that are needed to ensure that the Port of New York and New Jersey continues to grow and to generate jobs." Because the Row's work would cost over $20 million, the insurance giant AIG, which contributed $2 million through its foundation, promised to assign a staff member to find funding. But the terrorist attacks of 9/11 changed everything. Just as Lower Manhattan's rebirth originated with the WTC and Seaport in 1966, the horrific devastation and deep trauma crippled it for years.[1]

"Nine-Eleven Put Us in a Financial Tailspin":
Coping with Nightmares, and Retelling the Story

Thrust onto center stage on Tuesday, September 11, 2001, the workers and residents of Lower Manhattan were witnessing an event of untold proportions. Richard Dorfman, director of museum volunteers, remembered sitting in his office on that sunny morning and hearing a boom like "a truck slamming into something on FDR Drive," but he kept working. When vice president Stephen Kloepfer emerged from the subway to the blare of sirens, he looked up to see the North Tower in flames. As Peter Neill and his staff assembled on Fulton Street, they saw a plane hit the South Tower and "the tremendous fuel column that descended the outside of the building." Senior managers quickly met, said Kloepfer, "to figure out how to get our employees and Museum patrons out of there." When the first tower plummeted to the ground, it "shook like an earthquake," recalled Neill, who had to address his own crisis. "Every museum has an emergency plan," he said, "but most never execute it. We did. We evacuated the various buildings, shut down the HVAC and air control system in Schermerhorn Row and the storage areas." When the burning towers collapsed, "an immense wave of dust and debris" hit the district. That "dust" was all that remained of building materials, office equipment, and many of the more than twenty-seven hundred souls who perished. A "stream of dust-coated, gasping refugees" moved in. While the Row's hard-hat workers gave them particle masks, *Wavertree's* crew, who watched the tragedy on a television, gave water and wet paper towels to the escapees moving like zombies to the Brooklyn Bridge's pedestrian ramp. The piers were soon engulfed in black smoke. After senior managers accounted for their staff, they escaped too; Kloepfer was "in a kind of catatonic trance" trying to reach suburbia.[2]

Lower Manhattan shut down for a week except for essential services, which included *Wavertree's* pumps. Neill vacated his apartment on John Street, as the police insisted that everyone leave. Six miles to the north, "the atmosphere uptown was surreal," he said. With the wind blowing south, "it was a beautiful evening," and the diners at outdoor cafes "seemed stunningly unaware of the disaster that had occurred." Vendors were selling price-gouged glass snow domes encasing the towers and an airplane overhead. In the seaport, residents and FFM workers moved out temporarily. Downplaying the recurring environmental dangers, Mayor Giuliani pushed businesses to open on Monday, September 17, and their employees passed through armed checkpoints. The museum was "ready to open for business" on the ninth day, but, said Neill, "no one came, not that week or for weeks to come, not really for a year," large school groups for almost two years. An October study revealed that 40 percent of area residents had posttraumatic stress disorder, while half reported physical ailments from the smoke and dust. "Everybody was depressed for months," said vice president Yvonne Simons. Exiting the subway by Ground Zero, she said, "the wet heat and smell of death caused me to throw up many times." In those weeks, recalled curator Steven Jaffe, Neill "tried to pull everyone together in a way that was dignified and respectful of the fact that we were a professional community that had to look forward, while also grieving."[3]

By early October, the Seaport restarted its Elderhostel program, which had been the largest in New York and "the third largest in the United States." Its success in 1999 had prompted an expansion, drawing one thousand seniors annually for the next three years. But it was never the same after 9/11. A tour leader admitted, "It's like when someone dies." But, thinking of the city's earlier travails, his resolve stiffened. Simons did the same. Though "shell shocked for about a year and a half," she took strength by nurturing her staff, especially those who "needed serious psychological help." Three weeks after 9/11, Neill attended a hastily convened meeting titled "The Role of the History Museum in a Time of Crisis," which the MCNY and National Museum of American History cosponsored. Drawing thirty local institutions, it centered on "collecting and preserving the raw materials" to retell the story. While "the up-town guys" talked about collecting, which Neill regarded as a "fervent something to do" to avert helplessness, it was too esoteric for Neill, who realized that the Seaport would face "an impossible time" with no earned income.[4]

Of the many pressing concerns after 9/11's devastation, heritage preservation was in the museum's bailiwick. WTC offices had lost works by Rodin, Picasso, and others valued at $100 million. Six World Trade Center had housed a federal depository with almost a million artifacts from the Five Points, which were bound for the Seaport. A mere eighteen pieces survived because they had been borrowed by the city's archdiocese. Including a tea cup, they offered, said the *New York Times*, "proof of a gentler side of that tumultuous place." With that loss, New York Unearthed was "the only such collection available in Lower Manhattan." The Seaport staff, channeling their depression, wanted to create an exhibit about the tragic day, but some larger issues were, Neill conceded, "so political that it will take a generation to look back with any meaningful perspective." They chose the waterborne evacuation that moved at least three hundred thousand people and was "far larger than the fabled ten-day Dunkirk evacuation." Neill lamented that the rescue boats had limited access because of the removal of so many working piers. He warned, "If we turn the waterfront completely into parks, promenades and restaurants, then we lose a vital component of New York's past, present and future." *Seaport* observed that, like blue-collar New York, the working waterfront ironically had been "gradually marginalized by a host of forces, not the least of which was the postwar dominance of global capitalism represented by the very World Trade Center that now lay in ruins."[5]

The staff agreed to create an oral history archive, collect a pictorial record, and mount an exhibit. Though modest in scale and budget, "All Available Boats: Harbor Voices & Images 9/11/01" was curated by Jaffe, researched by audio-documentarian David Tarnow, funded by an NEH emergency grant, and opened in March 2002. Relying on photographs and memories, it focused on the previously invisible waterfront crews whose selfless dedication saved many people. Traveling elsewhere, edited for radio, and inspiring a book, "All Available Boats" showed the city's "palpable spirit of humanity, collaboration, and resolve" after the attacks. Tom Sullivan of NYFD's Marine 1, for example, described the panicked people leaping onto boats or into the water. Years later, Neill recalled his worst memory: "the sight of what I later realized were individuals falling or jumping from the [WTC's] upper floors." Because marine rescuers probably only heard of those troubling scenes through secondhand accounts, Jaffe conceded, "We may have edited out a few graphic moments" of the exhibit's oral testimony. Neill questioned the exactness of his own memory, even wondering "whether or not [he] saw that at all," but he admitted that the sight of falling people was "a recurring visual" in his mind.[6]

Though Rouse's mall reopened on the eighth day after the attacks, its foot traffic fell by 80 percent. It only slightly improved by the holiday shopping season, even though its major downtown competitor, the WTC shops, had been obliterated. With sightseeing buses down about 75 percent, a Rouse manager said, "We're not seeing any tourists at all." One customer at an empty pub noted awkwardly, "There doesn't seem to be anyone enjoying happy hour." Others did come, besides the National Guard and many well-meaning volunteers from all over the nation. They included, said Neill, organizations of "self-righteous camp followers . . . in search of conversions." After many complaints about their squatting and damaging property, "they were invited to leave." All the while, the Seamen's Church Institute served hot meals to over six hundred emergency workers.[7]

The Seaport's financial emergency was acute. When the Port Authority's $5 million gift was in doubt, the EDC and the DCA failed to throw a life preserver. Enhancing city life and tourism, the DCA gave more than $200 million in fiscal year 2000 to three dozen museums through its Cultural Institutions Group by annually paying a subsidy and operating support, which included expenses such as electricity and heat. But, said Kloepfer, the Seaport had "the dubious distinction of being the only longstanding NYC cultural institution, operating on NYC-owned property," that did not receive annual DCA support. "As the saying goes, 'sometimes you just can't get a break.'" The Seaport needed four legs to stand on: an endowment, philanthropy, earned income, and government support. The proportion and strength of each became an issue. While the Metropolitan Museum held an endowment of $2–3 billion, the Seaport had built a very modest $2–3 million endowment by 2001. Its shift to an earned-income strategy was working before 9/11, as the Seaport had $9.9 million in revenue and support and only $6.1 million in expenses. But 9/11 destroyed its income "for almost two years." Not only was its Mayor's Cup canceled, its planned gala and Circle Line lease evaporated when Pier 16 was seized. Moreover, Giuliani had withdrawn his offer of an operating subsidy for fiscal year 2000–2004 partly because of what Peter Aron called "the deeply entrenched negative position taken by the staff of the EDC." Thinking that the defunct Seaport Corporation "left a bad taste in the City's (and EDC's) mouth," Kloepfer heard from longstanding EDC managers between 1998 and 2004 that "as long as Peter Neill was the Museum's President, every Museum request would be closely scrutinized and presumptively disfavored."[8]

Nearly insolvent, the Seaport considered closing. The American Association of Museums did help downtown institutions with pollution and security concerns but not with financial duress. The Seaport began calling itself "the city's first world trade center" to bolster its profile, and the *Times* followed suit. Helping hard-hit organizations, the Andrew W. Mellon Foundation granted $6.6 million to twenty-nine cultural institutions in early 2002. The Seaport's share of $350,000 was modest but, said Neill, "astonishingly welcome." More significantly, the J. Aron Charitable Foundation gave $5 million over three years, which partly covered *Seaport* magazine, daily operations, and the Row's rehabilitation. The Port Authority made good on its promised $5 million but gave no more. After what Neill called "some serious politicking," the previously resistant Giuliani and the EDC kicked in $5.3 million, but only for the city-owned Row. Operating support was most needed, and when newspapers began to report DCA's neglect of the Seaport, it contributed $200,000 in 2003 but gave a paltry $60,000 in 2004 for the Seaport's $5 million budget.[9]

Unexpectedly, tourism began to boom. After long lines developed near Ground Zero and a viewing platform opened in late December 2001, CB1 pushed the city for a more orderly process and, to lure pedestrians, proposed a ticket booth at the seaport. The museum received a modest fee to distribute free, timed tickets. Walking the "six blocks from the ticket office to the site," said a twosome, "we were struck by the subdued feeling on the street." As Simons recalled, "It looked like a major funeral procession." Some residents and families disdained this "ghoulish form of tourism," and tasteless described the hawkers who sold T-shirts that read "I Can't Believe I Got Out." By March, "a full complement of 6,300 tickets per day" was being issued. During the sometimes long wait for tickets, visitors shopped or looked at the ships, but few—maybe 10 percent—took advantage of the museum's free programs. As Simons lamented, they only came "to see the scar." The *Times* encouraged them to stay for dinner, but few had the stomach for it. After Ground Zero's cleanup ended, tickets dropped to two thousand per day by June. Once the ticket stand closed for the winter, the district's foot traffic collapsed. That was aggravated by Homeland Security's armed patrols. Israelis were perhaps used to it, said Dorfman, but the sight of armored personnel carriers generated "the odd feeling that we were being occupied by foreign troops." Despite the worldwide drop in tourism, Ground Zero brought record numbers to the city, including more than a million to the platform and some 3.5 million to the site by the end of 2002. Exceeding the 1.8 million who had yearly visited the WTC's observatory, the scar was Gotham's top draw in 2002.[10]

Hoping to increase numbers for "All Available Boats," the Seaport opened its store in late 2002 to *Atlantic Monthly*'s correspondent William Langewiesche for a book-signing. His look at the post-9/11 cleanup, *American Ground: Unbuilding the World Trade Center*, was far from sentimental, having claimed that some firefighters had been looting as their comrades were trying to save the dying. While Manhattan curators were asking, "Can we do good history in this climate?" his claim outraged the NYFD, which had become iconic. Its union sent letters to twenty-five hundred rank-and-file members urging a seaport protest. The city's press had ignored the Seaport's tribute, "All Available Boats," but the *Daily News* led in publicizing the protest. More than 150 uniformed firefighters, "accompanied by widows of comrades who died in the terror attacks," protested at the museum's door. They angrily shouted, "Liar! Liar! Liar!" It "took us by surprise," admitted Neill, because his staffer had not read the book. Though the author's claim was debated and revised, this was a public-relations gaffe that, Neill sighed, "came and went."[11]

Because it was so difficult to separate grief, history, and politics after 9/11, historians experienced what two critics called "an epidemic of professional squeamishness," while museums only exhibited what the *Times* dismissed as "gooey sentimentality." That undercurrent deepened as the Bush administration launched two wars. Acknowledging that objectivity was impossible, author Russell Shorto told New Yorkers that Gotham's three major history museums (the N-YHS, the MCNY, and the Seaport) were bound to anger somebody. By that yardstick, they were "doing a terrific job." His accolade was tested in 2005. Museums had supposedly learned how to handle controversy after the culture wars of the 1990s, but their critics had equally adapted, as when the Seaport, allied with Cooper Union, mounted a packaged art exhibit, "A Knock on the Door," on the fourth anniversary of 9/11. Demonstrating that the Patriot Act and Iraq War were undermining civil liberties, the show tried to "raise public awareness of the current retreat of our most basic rights," said its organizer, the Lower Manhattan Cultural Council. Yet the city's tabloids and 9/11 family organizations derided the Seaport in unison. Some of the artwork pushed the lines of taste, but the artists regarded it as creative, political, and protected speech. Seeing the controversy as part of the "ongoing battle between art and remembrance," *Downtown Express* noted that censors were extending their hold over "a much wider swath of Downtown." The *Times* called it "a thoughtful, legitimate exploration" and concluded, "the anger directed against the show reveals some chilling cultural trends," including "the persistent, wrongheaded idea that to question the government is to dishonor the memory of those who died."[12]

"A New Model Maritime Museum":
Outgunned, Peter Neill Takes to His Lifeboat

Since Neill's hiring in 1985, he had put the Seaport on a more contemporary footing and expanded its operations. He pushed educational service to raise "nearly 75%" of his total budget, which, in hindsight, exposed the museum's vulnerability because the attacks of 9/11 stymied those earnings and, said trustee Thomas Gochberg, "emotionally killed" him. Trying to juggle the Row's rehabilitation, the creation of WPNY, the loss of revenue, and so many other balls in the air, he became another casualty. The work on the Row set the crisis in motion. Though the stock market had begun to drop before 9/11, the board authorized a $16 million contract in mid-2000 to begin a thirty-thousand-foot refurbishment. In 1998, Neill had promised CB1 that the Row would "be the education and programmatic heart of the museum." Heading the project, John H. Beyer was completing a circle, as his firm of Beyer Binder Belle (BBB) had started its work with the Museum Block. To give the Row a sixfold increase in space, he reconfigured the old block's store rooms, lofts, and backyards. Because Rouse controlled the first two floors in all but 12 Fulton Street, the museum entrances on Fulton and John Streets led to an escalator and the upper-floor exhibits. The most novel element was the building itself, where visitors could see the interior brick and framing, including what the *Times* called its "Lascaux cave" with "130-year-old graffiti written in Gaelic." Its galleries would be downtown's first new ones since 9/11, but all museums there faced a bleak situation. As a result, the Lower Manhattan Development Corporation (LMDC, 2001) stepped in with a $4.6 million advertising campaign to rebrand them as "History and Heritage in Downtown NYC."[13]

Long promised, the Row's first exhibit, which was on the generally ignored topic of the slave trade, added to Neill's headaches. He was inspired by Liverpool's museum, whose port had handled 60 percent of the British slave trade in 1790. After soft-pedaling the atrocity, Merseyside was pressed to develop "Trans-Atlantic Slavery: Against Human Dignity," an acclaimed permanent exhibit in 1994. With the Smithsonian's Lonnie Bunch, Neill toured it in 1996, saying, "This was a big deal in the history museum business." After Neill negotiated the rights, Jaffe began script development but ran out of money. Neill brought in the Seaport's partner, the Mariners' Museum, and John Hightower took Jaffe's work and "committed the funds to design and produce the exhibit." Titled "Captive Passage: The Transatlantic Slave Trade and the Making of the Americas," it was, said Hightower, one of his "most powerful and compelling exhibitions ever." Neill attended its Mariners' opening. As he hoped for South Street, it attracted "more people of color in that place than had been there maybe ever. All love-fest." Besides publishing an attractive volume in conjunction with the Smithsonian, the Mariners' toured "Captive Passage." The *Times* favorably reviewed it at the Smithsonian's Anacostia Museum in Washington, D.C., in 2003 but only credited Hightower.[14]

Yet the love boat ran aground when Hightower started negotiating with the N-YHS "as the prospective NYC venue for the exhibit." As Jaffe recalled, "Peter was furious." In one telephone exchange, said Neill, "I went, politely put, BATSHIT and told him in no uncertain terms that he was violating our agreement, that he was abandoning the concept of our partnership, and that the script was ours and he [should] go start all over again, no deal. I also told him that I would not hesitate to explain the situation to our funders, Merseyside, and the press." Hightower blamed what he called Neill's testosterone for the outburst and said, "Peter had first dibs [only] if he could afford it." The storm eventually calmed, and the exhibit reverted to its only Gotham showing—in the Row. Then Hightower pulled the rug out from under him. Whether this was revenge or adherence to AAM specs, the artifacts were pulled. Shortly before the exhibit was scheduled to ship in mid-September 2003, said Neill, Hightower "called to say that his collections manager would not approve our facilities report because we did not have a ONE YEAR RECORD of climate conditions in galleries that were just being built." Hightower refused to compromise, and the exhibit panels arrived without their artifacts. Yet, while Kloepfer thought that the HVAC system was sufficient, it could only handle one floor at a time. Even though the exhibit was scheduled for a single floor, Hightower said, "I was not going to jeopardize the exhibition by shaving standards." Kloepfer felt that the Mariners' was kicking the Seaport "when it was down, post-9/11." As Hightower's collections manager Jeanne Willoz-Egnor admitted, "We were really tough on them about getting their environmental conditions up to museum standards" because of the lenders' requirements.[15]

Delayed, embarrassed, and unsure of what to do or say, the Seaport scrambled to borrow Janina Rubinowitz's collection of an African culture in Suriname. With the Mariners' empty cases in full view, Neill installed those artifacts in a separate gallery, calling the show, "Portrait of America: Africans in the New World—from Captive Passage to Cultural Transcendence." At the Row's dedication in October, that one gallery was open only to the press. Yet it was "a joke, and should not have been installed," Kloepfer confessed, but "litigation was not a serious option—there was neither the time, nor the money, to file a lawsuit, and the reputations of both institutions would likely have been damaged by a public airing of these issues in court." Still, the museum went ahead with ancillary shows, including the freedom schooner *Amistad* and a walking tour of African Americans in colonial New York.[16]

Finally, after lenders accepted "just two weeks of stable data," the Mariners' artifacts arrived on December 10 and were immediately installed. The first visitors to the expanded, seven-gallery exhibit, which returned to the original name "Captive Passage," arrived two days later. Unlike Merseyside, which initially included a re-created slave-ship hold, the exhibit was, according to Hightower, artifact lean because of their scarcity. Also missing were visitors. "Without significant advertising or publicity," said Jaffe, "it was a blip on the NYC cultural radar screen that quickly disappeared." "Captive Passage" paled in comparison to the $5 million, highly publicized "Slavery in New York" show at N-YHS, which was inspired by the Seaport's show. The Seaport spun its embarrassment, saying that it had planned a "soft opening." Soft indeed, as *Downtown Express* added, "few people realized there was an impressive gallery space" hidden above the Row's shops. With the delays and failure to deliver, said staff historian Sharon Holt, the city's "culture reporters literally laughed in our face." Major papers ignored "Captive Passage," but the *Times*'s one-liner labeled it "a display of African art and artifacts." Yet a year earlier, its reporter in Washington, D.C., praised it in an eight-hundred-word essay as "a story of critical importance."[17]

The New York exhibit was distinct from the Mariners' in significant ways. Presented in five parts (departure, Middle Passage, arrival, abolition, and legacy), its last section blended the Suriname material "to showcase the cultural creativity and survival that followed the experience of enslavement." In Newport News, Neill also added, "their evocation of the Middle Passage was this ridiculous gallery with flashing lights on paintings of tortured slaves with tape recordings of waves, groans, and rattling chains. I was appalled by the stereotypical presentation. . . . It was ghastly, and I refused it." Reflecting the sensitivities of 9/11 survivors, the Seaport depicted instead "an empty gallery, dimly lit with one panel that described the passage and the numbers estimated to have passed from one continent to the other. . . . It was respectful, reverential, silent, and evocative." Indeed, a reviewer of the Mariners' show noted that its Middle Passage's graphic violence would trouble many visitors, especially children. The exhibit left New York in April, but Merseyside's was so popular that it developed a separate and permanent International Slavery Museum on its top floor. Not surprisingly, another casualty of 9/11 was the museum partnership. After the divorce, each institution still boasted that it was "America's National Maritime Museum."[18]

Neill knew he had to earn more income. He then completed the Seaport's own circle by repackaging, unknowingly, a short-lived concept from the late 1960s to establish an Oceanographic Research Institute. City Hall had included it in the Manhattan Landing plan, but it never floated. Almost thirty-five years later, Neill wanted to create the World Ocean Observatory as the heart of his fifth five-year plan. With the world focusing on the ocean and climate change, he hoped to place it in his long-planned International Maritime Heritage Center. The building was conceptually designed by BBB for the corner of South Street and Burling Slip, approved by CB1, but omitted in BBB's submission to the city in 1999 because of objections to its modernist design. Pegged at $20 million, it would include a visitors' center and exhibits that, Neill told the *Times*, would show "the interrelationships between the world's oceans and the social, economic, political and cultural life of the city." Yet his "new model maritime museum" kicked up a Category 4 storm with Lawrence S. Huntington, former head of Fiduciary Trust, who became SSSM chairman in mid-1999. In 2003, he gave Neill three months to raise $250,000 and prove the plan's viability; when that failed, he declared it dead. Huntington, who served on the Woods Hole Research Center board, did not accept the merging of environment and history, reportedly stating, "This is not what maritime museums do." Others also questioned the plan's impact on WPNY, *Wavertree*, and funding. As a result, Neill retired in 2004. His retirement package included a year as emeritus president developing the concept, after which he took it with him to Maine.[19]

With Neill's bold and assertive style, some people were happy to see him go. He had been an outsider in the tight circle of what Aron called the financial decision-makers who shaped New York culture. Moreover, Neill knew he was hated by Rouse, the EDC, and the DCA, he said, "because I would not shut up." He regarded many of them as bureaucrats who were unable or unwilling to recognize the Seaport's worth. Said Aron, it was "time for Peter to step down; his major accomplishments were in place: the ships were all in good condition, the money he brought in was very substantial," and lastly WPNY was on its way. Even his spurned partner Hightower admitted that he had pulled off so much, saying, "I thought his magic wand and black cape maneuvers were astonishing." The museum, stanching its red ink, was finally breaking even. But with Neill's departure, the Seaport was about to sail into the Bermuda Triangle.[20]

Terminating "Sleepy, Underutilized" Programs: The Revenge of the Bean Counters

Huntington had agreed to a national search for Neill's replacement but then unilaterally appointed Paula M. Mayo as executive director. Aron resigned from the board. "Completely shocked," Simons and Kloepfer knew their days were numbered. In 1990, when the museum was building its school programs in the racially polarized city, Mayo, an African American, had been hired to manage the Seaport's box office, but she rose quickly through Neill's mentoring to become vice president for programs and development. Only later did he ask himself if his good favor was shaped "by race? by gender?" She represented what Dorfman called "the museum's blessing and curse," the ability "to come in with little experience and work up" the ladder. Others found her personal ambition and professional skills the curse. An unmitigated disaster followed. Like shipwrecked sailors in a lifeboat short on provisions, the strongest devoured the weak. Pointing to a $700,000 deficit in 2003, Huntington blamed Neill, but the shortfall mostly resulted from Huntington and board decisions on the Row's renovation. Huntington and Mayo quickly slashed $1 million, terminating the archaeology program, closing the library, scuttling WPNY, and cutting waterfront funding. Besides firing their department heads and staff, they fired two in the development office whose task was to raise the needed money. Kloepfer, who later quit, accepted the firings, thinking that "the budget math at that time was unforgiving." One question shaped their decision: Did programs pay their own way? Using corporate doublespeak, Huntington said, "We're not really eliminating programs; we're rationalizing the work force. . . . We're going to get the job done with fewer people." Yet the question was remarkably narrow-minded and revealed the pitfalls in a museum movement defined by corporate thinking.[21]

Simons, whose education program had become a cash cow, asked the question when making her cuts. Calling the library a "'sleepy' and under-utilized" component, she thought that supporting research, even for the ships or interpretation, "was too much of a luxury when no revenue was being produced." Library director Brouwer had written over one hundred articles for the membership-generating *Seaport* and *Reporter*, but the magazine had mostly shifted to freelancers and Gotham social history. Even Met curator Christine Lilyquist, who was researching for the SCC, was "amazed at the collections" he built. Mayo closed the library and fired the thirty-two-year veteran. He was "brilliant" in his field, but he was "not enough of a shark for this world," conceded former volunteer Nora McAuley-Gitin. Closing the library was unprecedented and weakened a critical link because, said Peter Spectre, "we will eventually reach the point where we will be surrounded by historical debris and nobody will have a notion of what it all means." Gotham archivists denounced the closing, but Huntington told the *Times* that the museum's mission "was explaining history through New York's port," which ironically Brouwer had done for years. Calling it the Seaport's death knell, Joe Doyle said it was "better to turn all the administrators into volunteers than to let go the cornerstone of the museum." Huntington assured Neill that the library would move from Water Street to the Row and reopen; but no plans were made for the library in the Row's 2009 redesign, and it remained closed.[22]

The archaeology program was deep-sixed because, said Simons, the Seaport "never much understood what to do with it." In making her decision, Simons looked at New York Unearthed, whose new landlord, while providing free rent, did not cover the $130,000 yearly operating expenses. She blamed archaeologist Diane Dallal for not helping to "find those funds." Revising the museum's stated commitment, Huntington said, "It's not necessarily related to the seaport's mission." The evidence proved him wrong, whether the Seaport's first dig at the WTC in 1967 or its own current exhibit on Nieuw Amsterdam, which was curated by Dallal, based on its collection, and highlighted in *Seaport*. The two-million-piece collection was, according to the magazine, "the stuff of meaningful history, easily transformed into local pride, a sense of place, and even legend, all of which are important in today's rootless and restless world." Moreover, as Huntington spoke, Sharon Holt was using the collection for WPNY. With Unearthed in limbo, city archaeologists begged, but "letters and phone calls to Paula Mayo" went unanswered. They also challenged the museum's compliance with its Board of Regents charter, which required it to maintain professional standards of care for the artifacts. Eventually, Mayo told the State Museum in Albany to take the artifacts or else. As the collection went to Albany, an editor of *Archaeology* blamed politicians, media, and "citizens of New York City, who didn't fight to keep their past."[23]

WPNY was also tossed overboard. When Holt was hired as senior historian and curator in late 2002 to complete the script, she was jokingly told that it "was old enough to drive." It was. Conceived in 1985, WPNY was developed by Charles Sachs and Jaffe. While funds were raised for the Row, "nothing was left over to pay for the design, finalization, and installation of the exhibition." That gestation allowed the concept to evolve into a multidisciplinary, innovative examination of the port. Said Holt, the Seaport then committed "$4 million in the budget for a 28,000 sq. ft. exhibit on all three floors." Unlike Rouse, which catered to out-of-towners, WPNY would appeal to residents "flooding into the neighborhoods in lower Manhattan, and Brooklyn, as a way to develop a firm sense of place and identity for their communities." They would then "contribute as citizens to contemporary issues about the port, the city, the ocean, water supply, and living space that they had come to understand as part of the region's maritime legacy."[24]

But the space was not prepared, and red ink was spilling. When the exhibit "was almost ready in the curatorial notebooks to be taken to design," it was pulled. Instead, the Seaport mounted "Soundings: Treasures from the Collection of South Street Seaport Museum." Contributing $200,000 in 2004 and then loaning $3 million, Aron regarded "Soundings" as a quick way to "send a loud, clear and positive message to the City's cultural and cultural-funding sources." After the slave-trade fiasco, the Seaport conceded, "We have a better chance of acquiring the 'mega-funds' we need for [WPNY] . . . if we can demonstrate our ability to mount first-class, public-friendly exhibitions in our new spaces." With Aron funding, *Seaport* included an exhibit catalog "as a PR/fundraising piece." Initially running in six galleries from mid-June to December 2004, "Soundings" was ignored by the press. Its debut was as disturbing. "On the literal eve of opening," Holt said, Huntington told "us that we HAD to display all 47 ship paintings by one artist that he admired. Since it was clear by then that we were all going to be fired as soon as the exhibit opened anyway, we just ignored that demand. But we could not believe either the ignorance or the administrative incompetence . . . to have a board member behaving like that." "Soundings" was, she said, "a sad shadow" of WPNY.[25]

WPNY was central to the Seaport's strategy of increasing revenue, but Simons admitted "that all the areas that were cut, were heavily research related. . . . When one looks at the bottom line of a revenue generating operation, those were the luxurious component of the museum." Yet her expectation that historians, archaeologists, and curators would raise their own funds was, said American Association for State and Local History president Dennis O'Toole, "way out of step with standard (history) museum practice." Instead, researchers "create the intellectual capital" for revenue-generating programs. In fact, laying off "research staff when it's crunch time is, in effect, a declaration that your museum has no future and hence won't be long for this world." Gochberg regarded WPNY as "the raison d'être of the museum," but he, Aron, and Matteson could not convince the administration to resuscitate it.[26]

Like inexperienced ship captains, Huntington and Mayo worsened the situation by opening the bilges. Lacking an appreciation of the Seaport's complexities, making decisions autocratically, ignorant of prevailing museum practices, and failing to communicate with and assure their audiences, they alienated friends, chilled potential donors, demoralized the remaining staff, and destroyed the Seaport's image that had been rebuilt by Neill in the 1990s. If, as Ford Museum president Harold Skramstad suggested, the requisites for success are authority, connectedness, and trustworthiness, Huntington and Mayo violated all three. "Trustworthiness and authority in a museum," said Skramstad, "grow directly out of skill and expertise well exercised as well as out of continual connection to the audiences served." But "once eroded," that "trust is very difficult, if not impossible, to rebuild."[27]

"Maintenance Is the Essential Art of Civilization":
9/11, Neglect, and the Once-Great Fleet

In the bloodletting of 2004, Huntington and Mayo fired waterfront director James Clements. Responsible for what the Seaport boasted was "the
largest privately owned fleet of historic 19th century vessels by tonnage in
the United States," he faced a triple whammy after 9/11: the steady deterioration of, inadequate support for, and invisibility of his nine ships as
landside issues took center stage. But, as Pete Seeger said, "maintenance
is the essential art of civilization." When asked about the neglected ships,
Huntington barked, "Nobody wants to support them, . . . and if they're
not cared for, they sink." Going further, Mayo once called the fleet "an
albatross." In 2005, Huntington proposed discarding *Helen McAllister*, the
harbor's sole surviving early twentieth-century tug, and *Marion M*, its last
wooden-hulled chandlery lighter, though he had okayed their acquisition
in 2000. Like the Intrepid Museum, whose *Brunswick, LV-84* was jettisoned
and sank in Brooklyn, he also targeted *Ambrose, LV-87*. That outraged Stanford, but others pointed out that the 1908 lightship did not fit the district's
"age of sail." Neither did *W. O. Decker* (1930), a wooden, steam-powered
tug that Matteson had donated in 1986 but had since deteriorated. With
the Seaport at an all-time low in 2005, Matteson said, "it was do or die" for
the tug, so he paid $840,000 for its rebuilding.[28]

Meanwhile, the Seaport mismanaged *Wavertree*, was pressed to sell
Peking, and allowed *Lettie* to languish. *Wavertree*'s rigging was complete,
but work on the decks and hull was postponed by 9/11. When Charles
Deroko returned as part-time waterfront director in 2008, he estimated
those repairs at $6 million; an additional $2.5 million was needed for
exhibits and sails. He also knew that *Wavertree*'s thirty-year-old masts
were at risk, with at least one having "rot that looked like coffee grounds."
Just what *Wavertree* would become was another matter. While Neill and
Gochberg had favored sail training, despite the issues raised in Op Sail
2000, their successors decided instead in 2010 to build a planetarium in the
tweendeck. Rumors flew about possible modifications, such as an elevator.
While Brouwer dismissed the idea as "errant stupidity," Terry Walton and
Peter Stanford, who had joined the board as nonvoting emeriti, endorsed
it as a moneymaker. Plans for the planetarium and Deroko's structural
repairs vied for the city's promised $5 million grant, which could not

cover both. Though considerable moneys were spent on the planetarium's design, it was, in the end, pitched.[29]

Peking's towering presence had long defined the Seaport, but realizing that the museum could not fund two square-riggers, Aron won board approval for its sale in 2001. Asking $11 million, Neill went public in 2003, saying that "having two tall ships doesn't bring a single extra person to the gate." Hoping to reallocate *Peking's* $750,000 yearly expense to the rest of the fleet, he lowballed the repairs needed for it to become a USCG-certified sailing ship to $1.3–2 million. He thought that the planned Hamburg International Maritime Museum would be a perfect buyer, as it was the ship's home port and "perfectly qualified to repair and show her." Rejecting Hamburg's $5 million bid, Huntington sought a better deal in 2004 from Lionel Amos, a self-made English millionaire who "credited his personal success to his experience as a trainee on *Peking* during the war." Incredibly, Huntington asked him for $100 million to reconstruct it as a modern dockside "learning facility that complies with all New York City Building Codes." Amos instead offered to create and fund a trust to "purchase and operate *Peking* as a seagoing training ship" under the Seaport's auspices. When Huntington nixed the offer, Aron was dismayed and asked Gochberg in 2006 to resurrect the Hamburg talks, leading to a $2.8 million agreement. But both boards hesitated: the Seaport because of the low price and Hamburg because it needed time to raise the money. Huntington also feared that a public backlash could hurt his request for city funding. For one, neighbors resented the sale. While one mother declared it was wrong, her second-grade daughter wrote in *Downtown Express*, "If you want my ideas on how to save the *Peking*, call me." Still waiting for that call four years later, she predicted that its loss would "make the whole [Seaport] fall apart." Despite its neglect, Stanford "deeply deplore[d] *Peking* being sold down the river."[30]

Frank J. Sciame Jr., a preservation-minded developer who became chairman of the Seaport in 2007, voiced no qualms about selling *Peking*, nor did his handpicked president and CEO, Mary Ellen Pelzer. Hired fresh out of law school as the Seaport's counsel at age twenty-eight, she was another example of Dorfman's "blessing and curse," being quickly promoted to its top slot in 2007. Her lack of experience in museums, management, and ships, as well as her obeisance to a developer-chairman, led many people to fear the worst. While Hamburg was delayed by the global recession, it had agreed to pay \$250,000 initially and the remaining \$2.55 million incrementally. When eventually restored, *Peking* would, like its sister ship *Passat* in Lübeck, symbolize Germany's once-great fleet. In 2012, the Seaport and City Hall announced that *Peking* would simply be given to Hamburg, but the details of its transfer were slow in being resolved.[31]

In 2008, the community was told that *Lettie* was "definitely safe." On Christmas Eve in 2010, however, Scrooge divulged that the 117-year-old schooner was up for sale. It had been working in the city school program, but Pelzer failed to secure its contracts. With its loss of income and maintenance, *Lettie* quickly deteriorated at its pier between 2009 and 2011. With so many ships in need and targeted for disposal, the Seaport was a faint shadow of its former self and by late 2010 had "descended into a kind of volatile misery." Fearing the complete loss of public confidence and philanthropic support, Aron thought the media would blame the sour economy and fickle public, but he faulted the chairman and his "unqualified CEO."[32]

"As Long as the Fulton Fish Market Stays, We're Okay": Whose Waterfront Is It?

By the 1990s, the tide was receding for fishmongers. Even before the Seaport's conception, City Hall and Wall Street had wanted to redevelop the waterfront, and the museum accepted the market's removal as a fait accompli. Still, Stanford told colleagues, "If the Fish Market ever leaves, I will throw dead fish on the roofs to keep the smell and seagulls around." After Congress tightened seafood standards in the early 1990s, the USDA succeeded where David Rockefeller and John Lindsay had not. The city's estimated relocation cost of \$75 million, which exceeded the land's resale price, and 9/11 pushed the date back to November 2005. But the new \$85 million warehouse in the Bronx had the personality, said painter Naima Rauam, of a "Costco with fish." Many people cheered the move. "On hot days, the smell of fish was nauseating," said a resident half a mile away. Rejecting romantics, a seafood seller snapped, "It's great for writers to be nostalgic about this place, but this is an industry, not a museum." Others feared what sociologist Sharon Zukin called the "crisis of authenticity" in Gotham. While resident Gary Fagin compared the loss of FFM to Paris losing Les Halles, Neill thought it was "too gritty, too connected to labor, too suggestive of a world opposite to the dreams of the planners and real estate moguls." Before its departure, the Seaport tried to capture that grit in its six a.m. tours, an exhibit by Barbara Mensch, and an illustrated talk by Rauam, who quipped that she had been there since "Tyrannosaurus Herring roamed." While stating that Mensch's photographs posed "critical questions about our changing urban landscape," the Seaport offered no answers, unlike a *Times* blogger who said they "captured the story of a way of life being squeezed. Squeezed by modernization, by corporate and real estate greed and by federal prosecutors." About FFM's loss, Mensch said, "It's like death to me."[33]

Calling the derelict space "a beautiful property," EDC head Michael Carey set a goal of "maximizing opportunities." Speculators bought nearby sites. Though Rouse faced its own empty stores, it went after the city-owned Tin Building and New Market Building. In the area south of Pier 15's stubs, plans ranged from the Guggenheim's $700 million, Frank Gehry–designed museum to a floating theater and hotel. Yet developers and residents clashed after the LMDC began to distribute almost $10 billion in federal post-9/11 funds. "I've lived in the area for over 20 years, and 90 percent of the change has happened in the last two years," said Fagin in 2007. City Council member Alan J. Gerson added, "This is really New York's last opportunity to preserve our historic, nautical, seafaring roots." Yet, how long do roots last in Gotham? An early gentrifier, Fagin watched the neighborhood's conversion with a chain hotel, upscale residences, and stores. "Ironically, it was when 'things got better,'" he said, "that the sense of community dissipated." Though New Yorkers have been long reinventing their communities, much of the character of the Seaport's former "museum without walls" left with the fishmongers. A thirty-three-thousand-square-foot complex, called Historic Front Street, was engineered by Sciame and his partners, who succeeded where the Seaport Corporation had failed. After buying 80 percent of the site from the city for $5 million in mid-2003, they were funded by the EDC with $46.3 million in tax-exempt Post-9/11 Liberty Bonds. Taking eleven abandoned buildings on Front Street, they renovated them, added some modern ones, and created "a vibrant residential community . . . similar to TriBeCa or Williamsburg." Gentrification and homogenization would follow, the National Trust warned.[34]

What did a seafaring heritage mean, if anything, to young newcomers wanting a home? Many old downtown high-rises were being converted to

Fig. 11.1. Becoming a pricey residential neighborhood, Front Street (Block 97E-W) is still being gentrified. The development, Historic Front Street, includes buildings on both sides of the street. Schermerhorn Row is in the distance, 2006. (Photo, author)

apartments for family-minded professionals; fifty-five thousand residents lived in the Financial District by 2010, with an average household income of $242,000. One of the John Street buildings, whose apartments accommodated additional bedrooms for growing families, was located next door to Local 359's Welfare & Pension Fund, setting a class and cultural contrast. As the finance industry migrated across the Hudson or uptown, the number of residential units in Lower Manhattan more than doubled between 2001 and 2007. The new 24/7 community was more interested in playgrounds than ships. While the museum begged for help, the city built a playground on Burling Slip for $7.5 million, which Mayor Michael Bloomberg (2002–13) dedicated in 2010, and rebuilt another no more than five hundred feet away. Meanwhile, the old FFM was "a vacant hulk of steel columns, dented corrugated metal and rust-stained cement block."[35]

Over four million tourists annually visited the seaport, which outpaced the Statue of Liberty, and Bloomberg claimed that New York City would be the nation's number-one destination in 2011. However, "among actual New Yorkers thinking about fun things to do," the seaport ranked "pretty close to zero," said a trendy columnist in 2008. Ridiculing the luxury development and failed festival marketplace and seeing little museum presence there, she wondered "how much of a draw maritime history would ever be." Even when raconteur Phillip Lopate visited, there was, he said, "something ghostly about it," perhaps because it included corpses. In a macabre venture that would cause P. T. Barnum to pause, in November 2005 the New Fulton Market was turned over to "Bodies, the Exhibition," a display depicting dissected and preserved Chinese cadavers in various poses. The Seaport Museum disassociated itself from this Midway. Launched by a for-profit entertainment company, and with an adult admission price of $24.50 that outdid MoMA and the Met and by a factor of three the Seaport Museum, "Bodies" displayed twenty-two whole cadavers, along with 260 organs, in what was purportedly an educational experience. Yet it raised ethical concerns after allegations circulated that the cadavers had been prisoners and medical guinea pigs. While the Seaport Museum across Fulton Street was as quiet as a morgue, "Bodies" was the liveliest exhibit in the district until Superstorm Sandy closed it in 2012.[36]

Fig. 11.2. New Fulton Market (*right*), New Bogardus Building (*center*), Titanic Memorial Lighthouse (*left*); note the "Bodies" exhibit posters in the market's second floor windows, 2006. (Photo, author)

City planners conjured other ghosts on Peck Slip. To fill new residents' need for open space, the Parks Department announced plans in 2007 for a maritime-themed area between South and Water Streets that was intended to evoke a ship. Using rib-shaped vertical steel posts, the landscape architects thought it would "represent the ghosts of ships that might have docked there in the past." But after a resident griped, "This is going to look like a memorial to the *Arizona* or Hiroshima," the stunned planners returned to the drawing board. Among CB1's complaints was that City Hall was catering to preservationists, "some of whom think that trees and greenery are out of context in the famously gritty historic district." The fate of Pier 15 was a big part of the fray. After it was condemned, CB1 successfully pushed Albany to okay its rebuilding, but it became "the lightning rod" issue in developing the East River Waterfront Esplanade. Like Pete Seeger's rumination about the unintended consequences of environmental victories, the Seaport had revived the waterfront, only to face a hostile City Hall and 24/7 community. While Lopate wrote that the city was controlled by "a fractious civic culture," Bloomberg catered to all seaport factions but the museum. After proposing a two-mile-long esplanade in 2002, the city revised its plan in 2005. The LMDC announced $150 million in post-9/11 federal funds for waterfront redevelopment. Expecting to retain control, the Seaport Museum wanted a one-story, ship-friendly pier, but the design competition yielded startling results. One sketched a grassy knoll, while another rendered a two-story facility for museum exhibits, public space, and excursion boats. CB1's manager complained that there was too much room for tall ships and not enough for the area's most pressing need, play space for children. An impasse followed in 2006, during which an ad hoc gathering of stakeholders, SeaportSpeaks, brainstormed.[37]

In 2007, the debate turned prickly over the schematic designs. Trying to please competing interests, the architects proposed a two-level recreational pier. A blogger joked that the top level's green space looked "like a great spot for yoga," but Lee Gruzen of SeaportSpeaks derided it as "a couch potato area." Agreeing with the Historic Districts Council, she suggested, "Every inch of the pier should function for boat use." A district entrepreneur was most excited by "the thrill of a foreign ship coming to port" and wanted space for "ships of all shapes, sizes, and functions." In addition to *Wavertree*, PortSide NewYork's tanker *Mary A. Whalen* and the Tug *Pegasus* Preservation Project wanted space. So what used to be the museum's pier was up for grabs. Bloomberg, with Governor David Paterson at his side, launched the pier project in August 2009, but details regarding the ships and the Seaport's role were still contested. Included in its first-level space would be commercial and maritime pavilions; the Seaport regarded the latter as vital to attract newcomers. The EDC had told a CB1 meeting in 2008 that it would open the bid to others besides the museum. An angry debate ensued. When Sciame claimed, "We still have the rights to Pier 15" for its pavilion and docking, the EDC countered that it had severed the lease in 2007. The EDC announced that it would award leases based on the plans and their economic feasibility, because each winner would cover its own operating costs. That left out the destitute museum. Though Pier 15 partly opened as a two-story, multiuse facility in late 2011, the lease for the maritime pavilion was later given to the Harbor School. By the summer of 2014, the EDC would be leasing the pier's south side (and a small part of the north) to a cruise operator, thus leaving *Wavertree* without a long-term berth if *Peking* remained in New York.[38]

Equally contested, Pier 17's feasibility was in doubt, as angry tenants hit Rouse with a lawsuit in 2004 alleging that it had engaged in "fraud, breach of contract, breach of fiduciary duty, bad faith and unfair dealing." Taking local merchants by surprise, Rouse then agreed in August 2004 to a $12.6 billion buyout of its fleet of malls by General Growth Properties (GGP) of Chicago. Rouse had been "on the verge of a deal," according to the *Times*, "to knock down Pier 17 and replace it with a theater for Cirque du Soleil." GGP killed the show, while still planning to demolish what some critics referred to as "that dreaded mall." Just what would replace it became a point of contention. Many people wanted to enhance the 24/7 neighborhood, as did CB1, which had moved successfully to downsize building heights in nine blocks of the historic district in 2003 to a 120-foot restriction. As Fagin told the press, CB1 was "the last line of defense" protecting the view of the bridge. Astonishingly, GGP proposed moving the landmarked Tin Building and replacing it with a view-obstructing, 495-foot-tall hotel and apartment tower. That illustrated, said Jaffe, "the utter failure of the powerful in New York and Chicago to grasp that architectural scale is part of Manhattan's jeopardized historical heritage." With a tall hotel, Stanford warned that the fleet below would "look like toy ships." Unlike the LPC, City Hall strongly favored the project. Stanford wanted Seaport president Pelzer to fight GGP, but she reportedly said "it would doom the museum." At the same time, her boss, Sciame, was promoting his own project, an 835-foot-tall building designed by Santiago Calatrava, at 80 South Street, which was opposite Pier 15 but outside the downsized area. It was luxury all the way, as its top condo would be offered at $55 million. Even the mayor was interested, but the financial plan failed. Highrises would nonetheless crowd the district's south flank.[39]

As the Pier 17 project deeply divided CB1, a blogger posted, "Prepare the battleships!" But a fiscal storm nearly sank the proposal. Caught in the faltering economy, GGP faced $27 billion in debt. In addition to the Tin Building, its hotel project hinged on a site it did not lease, the 1930s New Market Building, which was outside the historic district and not under LPC purview. The MAS quickly pushed for its inclusion in the state and national historic districts. In a largely symbolic move, the state agreed in 2009 to include the New Market Building in its district, but City Hall was free to decide the site's development. With the national recession, GGP declared bankruptcy and put its Seaport Marketplace and sister malls in Boston and Baltimore on the sale block in early 2009. As expected, no buyers emerged. It then spun off the malls and their leases to the Texas-based Howard Hughes Corporation (HHC), which owned properties in Las Vegas, Houston, and Hawaii. Because HHC's three principal investors could not sell their stakes until 2016, as Forbes's reporter Daniel Fisher noted, their incentive was to maximize their holdings. HHC's CEO David Weinreb said, "We know there's a handful of assets that will create a lot of money for us," and the seaport mall was a potential goldmine.[40]

"Trying to Be Too Many Things to Too Many People": Differing Visions of the Museum's Future

The Seaport's meaning had dramatically changed over the years. In the '60s and '70s, Stanford's museum, though shaped by City Hall's plans, defined the district, pushed the bounds of preservation, and largely spoke for the people. With the takeover by Rouse in 1981, the Seaport hit the doldrums. After 1985, it began to regain vitality as Neill gradually remade the museum. Both Stanford and Neill put the ships and port history first, defended the maritime tradition, and positioned the Seaport as one of the city's major history museums. After Huntington slashed its programs and staff, observers wondered if it could survive.

Four contestants—an ad hoc group, Stanford, Aron, and the museum itself—fought to shape its future. The first group, SeaportSpeaks, met at a two-day charrette in March 2006. It was moved to action by the FFM's departure, the city's waterfront plan, the entry of GGP, the area's changing population, the museum's crisis, and, as some critics said, dissatisfaction with its leadership. SeaportSpeaks wanted to ensure that the district's "roughhewn charm and maritime roots will be respected, not only because they are worthwhile in themselves, but because they draw new residents, visitors, and area workers to its piers and streets." Yet the charrette yielded little. With moneys provided by GGP, Milstein Properties, and Sciame Development, the developers drowned out other voices. Moreover, attendees failed to sway museum managers with their calls for protecting the archaeology, preserving the library, and making the maritime more visible. Asking the city for more docks and amenities, the meeting highlighted waterfront and district issues. It predictably called for building "a Seaport for Residents, Workers, and New Yorkers, rather than for tourists, so that it thrives as 'a New York experience' and finds its footing again." Charrette cochairs Gruzen and Fagin invited a handful of speakers including Sciame, Stanford, DCA commissioner Kate Levin, and LMDC president Stefan Pryor, but the few citizen-based organizations, such as CB1 and the Seaport Community Coalition, were no match for the retailers or private and public developers. While Huntington and Mayo attended, emeritus president Neill was not invited, saying there was "not an unconventional thinker, risk-taker in the bunch." In the end, the charrette cast the museum as a means to an end—to preserve the area's roots, guarantee its economic vitality, and enrich its residents and workers.[41]

Realizing that the museum was a sideshow, Peter and Norma Stanford offered their own plan, published by the NMHS. Committed to a ship-oriented museum and working waterfront, Peter privately said in 2006, "The track record of the present board" was so dismal that he could imagine nothing short of either a rebirth of the State Museum as the district sponsor or the creation of a City Control Board to revive the Seaport. He was also suspicious and felt uncomfortable "giving a pep talk to the Charrette," but some participants "were caring people" who were "truly seeking a way forward." He hoped it would be "a seedbed for ideas" but later concluded it was a fruitless act that put no life into the Seaport.[42]

The museum's longtime but now disillusioned benefactor Peter Aron, who resigned from the board in 2004, kept the charrette at arm's length. Its participants were, he thought, "mostly bureaucratic types," that is, planners, developers, and professionals trying to shape the city's agenda. "They were very happy to tell people what to do, but had no plan to raise the money." While still aiding the museum foundation, for which he served as president, he convened an ad hoc group with Gochberg and Matteson. Believing that the museum was "trying to be too many things to too many people" and that the chairman had set the tone, he blamed Huntington, whose tunnel vision and mindless cost-cutting kept him from realizing that the Seaport was "collapsing around his ears, financially, programmatically, and in terms of morale of staff and the Board." Matteson bluntly called it "a rat hole." Aron cautioned incoming chairman Sciame in late 2006 that "the Museum may have just one more shot at long-term survival." Sciame had to "either *drastically* down-size the Museum and the fleet— or merge South Street's assets into another New York history museum." Submitting a five-page proposal, he suggested a merger with the privately run MCNY "with the goal of MCNY being the surviving institution." He called the ships the "elephant in the room" and suggested forming a new separate ship museum whose static, display ships would be supported by ship aficionados and earned income from working vessels. Aron met with MCNY's board chairman and director, who liked the idea of a merger to gain a downtown venue but were preoccupied with their own capital campaign. Aron also warned Sciame, "To go in with [the EDC and propose] another pie-in-the-sky program would just be foolish."[43]

Huntington had done just that by again requesting an annual DCA subsidy and a change in the EDC lease. Warning that the museum's "very survival [was] in jeopardy," he also asked for an annual pledge of $250,000 from GGP, a percentage of its gross sales, and revisions to allow the museum to sublease its library building, parts of the Row, and berths at the docks. The museum's future depended heavily on support from the city and GGP. But the EDC refused, stating that any change required revisiting the entire lease and a Uniform Land Use Review Procedure (ULURP), which the city mandated since 1989 for major developments. After Huntington's failed bid, the Seaport was, said Gochberg, "functionally bankrupt" by early 2007. It fell deeper in debt for its utilities and rent and begged City Hall to buy its lease on Block 74E's corner lot for $7 million.[44]

Many observers looked hopefully on the New Amsterdam Market (NAM), which was inspired by the city's earlier markets and CB1's Greenmarket plan of 1980. Designed for locavores, it started as a demonstration project in 2005 and moved to the New Market Building's apron in 2007, but it was only open for the summer and fall seasons. Calling it an "economic development organization," founder Robert LaValva hoped it would "reinvigorate a neighborhood battling to retain its authenticity." Etched in his mind was a youthful visit to the quaint fish market in the early 1970s, when he found it "vividly alive, with creaking ships, mysterious old shops, and lingering memories." He thought "the 'Friends of South Street' were trying to preserve" that "untouched, uncontrolled, and therefore very public" feeling. His NAM, moreover, dovetailed with widely voiced hopes that the seaport would serve city residents. But GGP not only tried to undercut the NAM in 2008 by hosting its own market; it wanted to demolish the New Market Building. Drawing many patrons who had previously avoided the district, the NAM won the initial support of City Council speaker Christine Quinn and local member Margaret Chin, who both said they wanted the NAM to occupy the New Market Building permanently. Their attention and that of the EDC was piqued, however, by comparison with Seattle's Pike Place, which attracted "8–10 million visitors a year." Yet, after CB1 and the Historic Districts Council asked the LPC to landmark the New Market Building, the LPC denied the request in its first review in 2013. At the same time, the City Council decided, with the endorsement of Quinn and Chin, to hand the Tin Building over to the Hughes Corporation. While the HHC promised to open two food markets there, LaValva felt spurned, noting that the NAM's assigned part of the Tin Building was much too small. Outraged, NAM supporters claimed that politicians had sold out to HHC lobbyists. With that, said a NAM spokesperson, the New Market Building and Tin Building were "one step closer towards being lost or engulfed within a mixed-use development whose details have never been revealed to the public." That sentiment was reminiscent of criticisms made thirty-five years earlier when Rouse maneuvered to win City Council approval of its takeover of the fish market by making numerous promises it failed to keep.[45]

After Op Sail 2000, the Seaport's future looked promising, as it ambitiously inaugurated the Row's refurbishment, readied its centerpiece WPNY exhibit, and reaped the bounty of its educational and public services. Then came the attacks of 9/11. As the nation mourned the tragic loss, Lower Manhattan ground to a halt. With a complete collapse of the Seaport's income, it experienced an unequivocal disaster. Once again Neill tried to reinvent the institution, this time as a "new model maritime museum," but his board chairman refused any change and forced his removal. Facing a financial shortfall in 2004, the museum's new leaders, who seemed ignorant of widely held practices of professional museum management, rashly terminated essential programs. That, in turn, alienated friends, residents, and philanthropists alike. While the museum focused on its own crisis, City Hall, eyeing almost $10 billion in LMDC funds, accelerated its redevelopment plans. With its East River Waterfront Esplanade, whose most contentious element was Pier 15, the city's decision to sever the Seaport's lease revealed its poor regard for the institution that had, since 1966, fought to preserve the district and its maritime past.

Conclusion

"Nobody Knows That We're Here":
What Happened to That Promised Salvation on the East River?

From the Seaport's inception, it has been shaped by diverse New Yorkers who dreamed of saving an urban renewal district, returning tall ships to South Street, preserving Gotham's fabled history, and anchoring what they regarded as a rootless city. Their ad hoc, poorly funded, idealistic campaign confronted the city's power brokers. Those politicians, bureaucrats, developers, and corporate barons were driven by other dreams—modernizing the city, introducing business efficiencies, wielding power, and winning fame and fortune. The clash between these two goals defined the Seaport's development. But, whether in the 1960s or half a century later, this was hardly a contest of equals, though both maneuvered to take advantage of the other's strengths. While the ranks of Seaporters mushroomed thanks to their raw energy, grassroots idealism, and popular message, as well as a national preservationist tide, the power brokers had financial and legislative might, using the Seaport when needed as a proxy to pursue their agendas.

The meaning of that struggle has been debated. Richard Fewtrell, with his salty fo'c'sle philosophy, suggested that City Hall's support of Peter Stanford's movement was nothing "more than the opening gambit in the great game of snatching the real estate for private profit. In short, it was all a vast swindle." Ada Louise Huxtable similarly concluded that city and state urban development corporations were "in charge of these things. . . . It's pure business." Yet Seaport leaders and friends thought that if they made concessions, they could accomplish their goals. Think back on the legislation leaving NYSMM unfunded, or the Seaport Museum's designation as the unassisted urban renewal sponsor, or the inclusion of high-rises in the city's plans for the district, or the bailout that left Jakob Isbrandtsen and the Seaport with high hopes but empty pockets. Because its decision makers were inexperienced, the economic context was so daunting, and preservationists were sailing uncharted waters, those concessions put the Seaport in a hole out of which it was difficult to climb.[1]

Incredibly, the Seaport was the first museum in the nation designated to undertake a major urban renewal project. Required to use its own financing, it moved to acquire land that was among the most valuable on earth. It relied on an untried broad coalition fired by 1960s idealism. It also experimented with novel mechanisms such as selling air rights and dollar memberships. Later critics have contended that those mechanisms did not work when, in fact, they did, at least until Manhattan's notorious land boom busted and pushed City Hall and the Seaport close to bankruptcy. Lacking a meaningful endowment, fueled by volunteers, and creatively combining architectural and ship preservation, the Seaport was not simply unique, it was living on the edge. It was also on the cutting edge when Joe Cantalupo pronounced, "This Museum *Is* People." Museum experts now repeatedly emphasize community empowerment, citizen stakeholders, and volunteer contributions. As Harold Skramstad said, museums should focus on "inreach," whereby "people, young and old, alike, can 'reach in' to museums through experiences that will help give value and meaning to their own lives and at the same time stretch and enlarge their perceptions of the world." Whether it was due to 1960s community building, the era's distrust of the establishment, or the practical need to build an institution, the early museum did it. With a dynamo of people power, it became the city's largest historical society.[2]

City Hall, Wall Street, and the American Association of Museums pushed in an opposite direction by stressing business-minded partnerships and corporate-ordered museums. Christopher Lowery defended his corporatist reordering, saying that when he was hired in 1978, the Seaport was a "funky little club of well-intentioned bohemians." Certainly, professional management is necessary in preserving a collection, mounting exhibits, balancing the books, and running an organization. Peter Neill noted, "As ambitions, expectations, and programs evolve the need for organization and management must follow." A cultural entrepreneur himself, he believed in such partnerships and in the 1990s redefined the museum through revenue-earning community service programs, especially in education. They provided most of the income, which was augmented by memberships, grants, and philanthropy. But 9/11 disabled his ship. The museum's distress was magnified by other factors. For one, as the waterfront opened up with the fish market's departure, the EDC, which regarded the museum as a failed pump primer, pushed the museum aside to accelerate the plans of developers, City Hall, and sometimes residents. The EDC could do this more easily because Lawrence Huntington alienated friends, donors, and the public through mismanagement. A slow death spiral followed, prolonged by millions in loans from trustees and cuts in programs that camouflaged financial and administrative bankruptcy.[3]

So how do we make sense of the ups and downs of this maritime museum? Some of South Street's downs could be attributed to its relatively late start, limited resources, ambitious agenda, contested role, and inexperienced leadership, all of which was magnified by bouts of mismanagement and bad luck. While its distress was far worse than that of any other major maritime museum, it was not unique. Today Mystic Seaport faces the same financial shortfalls, staff layoffs, and organizational friction that chronically plagued South Street, while San Francisco Maritime National Historical Park copes with Washington, D.C.'s mercurial politics, which fail to fund its fleet and develop the museum collection. Even though the Mariners' Museum lacked expensive ships in the water, tough finances led it to reinvent itself with a new wing devoted to USS *Monitor* in 2007. For those museums with a substantial commitment to waterfront and landside exhibitry, South Street's difficulties were, therefore, sadly typical, but they were tragically worsened by Gotham's commercialism, present mindedness, and real estate mania.

It is a wonder that the Seaport Museum advanced as far as it did. Undoubtedly, Peter Stanford, encouraged and bolstered by Norma, was a visionary and, said Thomas Gochberg, "a brilliant pied piper" who led waves of New Yorkers to their neglected waterfront. Later watching the thousands of recreational boaters and everyday people, Robert Ferraro suggested, "the opening of the harbor to its citizens is their enduring gift" to all New Yorkers. While Stanford could speak "the most poetic truth," Walter Rybka added, he had "the practical wherewithal of Don Quixote." Still he won Lindsay's endorsement to develop the district, and it was, said Joe Doyle, "wonderfully non-commercial in a city obsessed with squeezing every dime out of tourists." Plans changed dramatically after the real estate bust in 1972. Bailing out the museum, City Hall and Wall Street wanted a more effective proxy to pursue their development agendas.

As earlier defined by David Rockefeller, their goals included revitalizing the financial district and establishing a 24/7 community. By purchasing Isbrandtsen's holdings and leasing them back to the museum, City Hall revised Stanford's plan, leveraged the district's cultural resources, and sped up the pace of development.[4]

After ousting Stanford, who retreated to his more manageable NMHS, corporate interests remade the museum, as best represented by the leadership of Time COO James Shepley; the museum board obligingly ushered in the next phase. Shaped by the era's free-market frenzy and fooled by the developer's promises, it selected the James Rouse Company to create a festival marketplace. That deal, said Whitney North Seymour Jr., "doomed the museum." Only in retrospect did planner Richard Weinstein admit, "We in the city made a mistake" in choosing Rouse. With the die cast, the 150-year-old fish-market district forever changed. Seeing the swindle before the contracts were signed, Huxtable later sighed, "I am so weary of these stupid alliances between developers and cultural institutions in which the cultural institution is given a block of space and the developers overbuild the rest and make an enormous profit." Weinstein called Huxtable "our civic conscience in those days," but instead of following his conscience, he followed the commands of City Hall and Wall Street. Perhaps street philosopher Eric Hoffer was right when he suggested, "What starts out here as a mass movement ends up as a racket, a cult, or a corporation." It would have taken an equally adept racketeer to save the museum. Huxtable said, it takes "uncommon leadership and connections and city smarts" to succeed in New York.[5]

In 1978, John Hightower declared there was something lasting about the district. "Not only does the Seaport reach the primal nerve of New Yorkers to let us know who we are and where we all came from," he told Stanford, "but we sense in the time capsule of these buildings our past as well as what we have gained and what we have lost." If historic sites are places to tell such stories, what happens when "commerce overwhelms culture," asked Hightower's former colleague Allon Schoener, who admitted his own naïveté in underestimating the power of commerce. In the role of developer, the Seaport laundered those time capsules. Once-gritty buildings were prettified, a fishmonger culture was exiled, an old mixed-use area was replaced by chain stores, and, despite Gotham's claim of being diverse, homogenization set in. "The Rouse mall was," said Steven Jaffe, "a catastrophe for the Museum, robbing the Museum of its central role in the district. . . . It's the blunder that continues to plague and haunt the Museum today." As Phillip Lopate claimed, "No native New Yorker would be caught dead going to Pier 17."[6]

Ironically, it was the museum—undercapitalized and facing mounting expenses—that had initiated the Rouse deal. Though Seymour rightly faulted Shepley and the real-estate-minded board, the deal revealed how preservation had changed by the late 1970s. Think back to Stanford's Riverboat Ball in 1970—rich and poor, white and black, professional and blue collar together on the same boat. Remember Neill's characterization of the movement as "an equation between self and history so powerful that it makes us lie down in front of bulldozers, raise toppled statues, salvage old boats." Think also of those *Wavertree* volunteers who so loved their ship, distrusted the new corporate order, and believed in "This Museum Is People" that they undermined the Seaport itself. Contrast them with the SSSC and its real estate business, where Lowery and his lieutenant were given lavish corporate cars and expense accounts like the bankers and developers they dealt with daily. Touted as the wave of the future, that business-museum model was lauded by the National Trust and the AAM. They were *all* preservationists battling for the soul of the seaport, but their agendas were remarkably different.[7]

Whether the Rouse deal stemmed from naïve optimism, individual profit, or pragmatic decisions, what was thrown away, said Neill, was the authenticity of "the fish market, the working piers, the operational vessels coming and going, and the exchange of ideas that lie at the core of every port as purpose and meaning." After that sea change, many people agreed with critic Luc Sante, who called the Seaport the tombstone of the old harbor. Its once useful objects expressed "a state of inarticulate contempt for the present and fear of the future, in concert with a yearning for order, constancy, safety, and community." If a history museum's coin of the realm is authenticity, the Seaport was accused of trading in counterfeit currency. Moreover, while Lopate called South Street "a quasi-maritime historic district theme park," the port itself had changed. With its jobs decimated, its facilities placed on the region's fringe, its shippers loyal to global corporations, its Port Authority distracted by land deals, and its still-vital importance ignored by most New Yorkers, the maritime identity of New York, like the museum, was lost in the fog.[8]

In New York, critics talk, but money walks. The museum's main problem was financing its landside and waterfront programs. The board believed the promises that the festival marketplace would bankroll its operations. It scoffed at Rouse's opponents and hyped its own expectations. Unfortunately, as the city maximized its take from the mall, it let Rouse set the agenda. Neill increasingly resisted the marketplace's historicidal policies, but his inability to handle the leasehold gave City Hall an excuse to begin its long-desired takeover. Neill established significant revenue-earning programs, but 9/11 laid bare the Seaport's weaknesses: insufficient fundraising, an overreliance on educational programs, a subordinate role to commerce, poor relations with City Hall, and public confusion about its identity. As a result, said Stephen Kloepfer, "the incredible generosity of Peter Aron and the J. Aron Charitable Foundation, year after year, was the only reason the Museum was able to keep its doors open." Yet Aron, who had also forgiven past loans, lost confidence in the post-Neill administration, whose presidents were chosen not by professional job searches but by a powerful, flawed chairman. With the financial hemorrhage worsening, the Seaport reeked of failure.[9]

Besides financing, the museum lacked memory. As is often the case, managers and professional staff know more about the nitty-gritty of their work than about the museum's own history. That particularly characterized the Seaport when acrimony prevailed in the passing of the baton. Countless observers, from ship surveyor Don Birkholz to board member Tom Gochberg, said that it did not "have any institutional memory." Institutions must tell their own story better and, as Anthony Wood recommended to them, "be good stewards of your own history and your own records." Discontinuity instead defined the Seaport's administration. In its brief history, every president and chairman looked back suspiciously on their predecessors' work. It got to the point where Frank Sciame and Mary Ellen Pelzer changed the name to Seaport Museum New York to distance themselves from their predecessors.[10]

The museum's dysfunction became obvious after Huntington announced in 2005 his intention to deaccession much of the fleet. Stanford made ships his priority in 1966, but, as in the case of the independently owned *Alexander Hamilton* and *Moshulu*, he discovered that city bureaucrats were only paying lip service, not dollars and cents, to his waterfront. Neill faced the same problem with *Maj. Gen. Hart*. In a 1997 appeal, the museum conceded, "In almost any city but New York, the South Street Seaport Museum would be regarded as the leading cultural institution. As it is, surveys have shown that the vast majority of visitors come to the Seaport district precisely for its vivid sense of place," one that was defined by its ships. But ships are expensive, and few institutions have them. Their neglect, Neill said, was "a symptom of national indifference to our maritime patrimony." Eric Darton resultantly quipped, "The great harbor described in *King's Views* has now given way to a virtual port, supplied with a thriving nostalgia industry: tall-ships festivals, a seaport shopping mall and theme park, and an aircraft aerospace museum."[11]

If anything is certain about New York, it is that its landscape will change. "Many times I've wished," Joe Cantalupo said before his death in 1979, "that God would take 10 years of my life now, so that I could come back one year in every five to see how history will be in the future." He hoped that "this place will look then like it does now." He surely did not antici- pate the whirlwind ushered in by Rouse. Though deploring the Rouse fiasco, Huxtable admitted, "I am exceptionally grateful for every inch that got saved." True to her philosophy, "Change it but don't destroy it," the seaport's Brooklyn Bridge Southeast Urban Renewal District, unlike the clear-cut Southwest, is a blend of the old and new. Manhattan has long been an unsettling mix of creative destruction and destructive creativity. If the role of preservation is to moderate the mix, the museum's success in doing that was undercut by its trustees' commercial priorities, its 1981 lease, and its resulting financial insecurity. Pushed aside by the market- place and City Hall, its trademarked name corrupted, and its identity submerged under the glitter, it was almost invisible. "Nobody knows that we're here," Neil lamented—to which, Kloepfer added, "If the Museum dies, that could be its epitaph."[12]

Postscript

In 2011, the Seaport Museum reached death's door. Critics began to tem- per their voices. Lopate had ridiculed the museum but admitted later, "Once I took that potshot, my malice was expended." In early January, rumors spread about its mounting cash-flow problems, typical in winter, but its insolvency became apparent. "It's a barely functioning organiza- tion," one staffer told the press. Only surviving because of $4 million in loans from trustees, its distress prompted Stanford to accuse the museum of concealment. The truth came out in February 2011 when Pelzer laid off thirty-two staff in what Richard Dorfman called the "Ground Hog Day Massacre." Immediately after two smiling vice presidents shared his birthday song and cake, they gave him a present—a pink slip. A third of the trustees resigned in embarrassment. Besides closing long-running programs, such as the Bowne Printing Shop, it "eliminated its curatorial and development departments." In shock, Stanford, who had refrained from publicly criticizing its administration for years, called for the resignations of Pelzer and Sciame. Pelzer refused to talk, and most critics blamed Frank Sciame.[13]

With no immediate recourse, the Stanfords helped form a new grassroots group, Save Our Seaport (SOS), to lobby City Hall, which reportedly said that "the Seaport must succeed." To cut maintenance costs, the museum looked for out-of-town berths for *Decker*, *Pioneer*, and *Lettie*; the latter two went up for sale. Friends asked, Who was taking care of the ships? The answer was, No one. Beginning in May, word leaked out that City Hall was negotiating a bailout, or what former N-YHS president Kenneth Jackson called "a shotgun marriage." Supported by $2 million from the LMDC, the MCNY agreed to step in. But the EDC was calling the shots. The deal was premised on a clean financial and administrative slate, whereby the EDC got what it had long wanted—the lease on Block 74E's corner lot—in return for paying off the Seaport's debts to its trustees and vendors. The agreement, however, only had an initial term of twelve months, plus a six-month renewal. While the Seaport remained a separate entity, the MCNY took charge in November 2011. At first, the big question was the fleet. MCNY director Susan Henshaw Jones, who had worked in banking and preservation, had turned around the MCNY, and now also captained the Seaport, priced *Wavertree's* requirements at $20 million. The fleet itself "might cost close to $100 million." After Mayor Bloomberg warned, "It's really the private sector that has to come through," many people wondered if the city would financially support the Seaport like others on city-owned property and give it a freer hand by revising the thirty-year-old lease. First signs seemed hopeful. The galleries reopened in January 2012, even showing a juried exhibit on Occupy Wall Street with a photo of a young woman with a sign: "Look, Mom, No Future." For now, the Seaport had one.[14]

Fig. C.1. Embodied in the museum's volunteers and staff, the spirit of "This Museum *Is* People" came alive with Save Our Seaport, 2011; *Peking* (*right*) and Pier 17 mall (*background*). (Photo, Nelson Michael Chin)

Then in late October 2012, Superstorm Sandy devastated the coast, including the seaport, and it changed everything. With an eight-foot surge, it swamped the shops and galleries, but the stationary fleet rode out the storm. Attention focused on the area's needs, not the museum's distress. Repairs to the museum's infrastructure in the Row were pegged as high as $20 million. After MCNY's contract expired in April 2013, it received a three-month extension. Laying out the Seaport's dire realities, MCNY's Jerry Gallagher told a CB1 meeting on April 16 that it needed the storm damage repaired, revisions in the 1981 lease, ground-floor space from the Hughes Corporation to attract pedestrians, ample dockage at Pier 17, and the ability to earn its almost $4 million annual operating costs. Calling the historic ships the district's "heart and soul," CB1 said it was "so important . . . to keep [the museum] alive." Ominously, the EDC skipped the meeting. Many critics feared that City Hall and the EDC were bowing to every HHC wish, including its request to redevelop South Street and the pier for a high-priced hotel, apartments, and retail.[15]

Fig. C.2. At 12 Fulton Street, the Seaport's banner: "Yes! Post-Sandy. We Are Open." After Superstorm Sandy hit on October 29, 2012, the museum reopened in mid-December, while neighboring shops remained shuttered. (Photo, Brian Lindgren)

Shortly after the April CB1 meeting, Sheldon Silver, the state assembly's Democratic majority leader, joined City Council member Margaret Chin and state senator Daniel Squadron in calling on the HHC and the EDC to act on the museum's behalf. But political talk is often ephemeral, especially before an election. Action was necessary not simply because the Seaport was almost out of cash but mostly because the lease was a noose around its neck. The EDC was clearly the problem. It refused to cover the museum's HVAC and electrical redesign and repairs in its own Row. That forced the Seaport to close the Row in April and keep alive a diminished presence at the reopened Bowne Printing Shop on Water Street. Then the EDC announced that, according to the 1981 lease, if the museum's buildings went unused for six months, it could be evicted. The Seaport accused the HHC of trying to put it out of business to grab over eighty thousand square feet on Water, John, and Fulton Streets. At the same time, a city audit of the EDC prompted charges of HHC-EDC intrigue. Such charges were nothing new, as the Rouse relationship with the PDC (and then the EDC) had been similarly marked by duplicity, favoritism, and conflicts of interest.[16]

Refusing to revise the 1981 lease without a ULURP, the EDC seemed to be handing the Seaport over to the HHC. In early July, as a result, the MCNY severed its ties with the Seaport, which was placed, in an unprecedented act, under a DCA-administered oversight board. While the DCA was trying to find a long-term patron for the Seaport, an SOS spokesperson complained that "people don't know what's going on" inside the EDC. Then on August 31, as required by an earlier agreement, the HHC submitted its development plan to the EDC, but without any explanation or publicity. The reasons were quickly apparent. In addition to the HHC's new building on Pier 17, whose opening was scheduled for 2016, and its previously proposed high-end hotel, condos, and marina on South Street, it wanted to lease most of the Tin Building. But as the Seaport had most feared, the HHC also brazenly asked for properties leased by the museum, including Pier 16, its space in the Row, and the Water Street buildings housing its print shop, gallery, and former library.[17]

In secret negotiations, the HHC and City Hall had allegedly reached a deal over the transfer of museum leases, and, reported *Downtown Express*, it was "signed without public discussion and without public notification." All the while, the DCA was left in the dark. With the HHC anticipating that its commercial empire and profits would swell, it asked to be relieved of any possible payments to the museum stemming from the 1981 lease. All the while, the city's major daily newspapers ignored the story, and Seaport supporters worried that City Hall and the EDC would allow the HHC to have its way. Deflecting criticism, the Hughes Corporation then reached "an agreement in principle" in late October with City Hall, whereby the HHC would "take a larger role in running" the museum. The prospect of commerce controlling culture revived the specter of Rouse and its carnival atmosphere. But a glimmer of hope was raised that the DCA might be able to persuade a bona fide institution, such as the N-YHS, to step in. Save Our Seaport rallied its friends—it had already submitted a petition to City Hall with ten thousand signatures—and hoped that the newly elected mayor, Bill de Blasio, who had blasted the Bloomberg administration's overly generous giveaways to developers, would save the museum from this commercial juggernaut. The SOS declared that the Seaport's waterfront and landside holdings were "inextricably linked," but the Seaport's Jonathan Boulware differed. First hired in late 2011 as the Seaport's waterfront director, Boulware was appointed interim president by the city's three-person oversight board after the MCNY and its trustees departed. He privately admitted that, in this David-versus-Goliath contest, the museum could lose its buildings and be left simply with, as at the San Diego Maritime Museum, a pier crowded with ships. Thinking that the "loss of a shoreside presence was not necessarily a bad thing," he regarded those buildings as a "liability after Sandy." Boulware instead wanted to focus on select ships (such as *Wavertree, Pioneer,* and *Decker*), the waterfront, maritime issues, and educational programs. As such, his vision of the Seaport's future was more accommodating to landside developers and more limited than that of his predecessors. Thus the question in 2014 was, whose vision would prevail?[18]

Looking back over the decades, the Seaport had been founded to save not only a deteriorated waterfront and its heritage but a city wracked by social and economic tensions. While millions of people thronged the district's streets, the museum encouraged them to see New York's past, present, and future through its maritime culture and environment. By saving the city's first world trade center at Schermerhorn Row and its neighborhood, which were "the only cohesive survival of early New York City's commercial district," the Seaport also redefined the preservation movement. Almost fifty years later and despite the district's sometimes air-brushed look, the Row and its neighborhood still have a real sense of history. As such, the museum was an indispensable catalyst in the rebirth of Lower Manhattan. Too few New Yorkers, however, know about its decades-long travails. In 2014, as a result, the Seaport's friends were asking if its fate would be salvation—or damnation—on the East River.[19]

As a Lower Manhattan editor concluded, the MCNY intervention that saved the Seaport in 2011 "would never have happened without the grassroots effort" undertaken by Save Our Seaport, CB1, and a legion of volunteers and friends who believed in "This Museum *Is* People." Whether those community-minded supporters can again save the Seaport from being closed, absorbed by the HHC, or so dramatically redefined as to be unrecognizable is still being decided. Dismissive of those grassroots efforts, the EDC and its boosters were instead dancing to the drum beat of economic growth and individual profit. In purely physical terms, the seaport district has been significantly preserved, but in today's world, there is much more to preservation than creating a backdrop for commercial interests to make big bucks. Preservation is, as the National Trust now recognizes, "people saving places," and those people are activists for the community, environment, arts, and historical awareness. As such, the story within *Preserving South Street Seaport* is, if anything, a cautionary tale about allowing commerce to dominate all other matters, as Joe Cantalupo will surely conclude the next time he returns.[20]

NOTES

ABBREVIATIONS

CSM	*Christian Science Monitor*
DE	*Downtown Express* (NYC)
JACF	Seaport Museum files at the J. Aron Charitable Foundation, New York
JBP	Joseph Baiamonte Papers (given permanently to the author)
JoC	*Journal of Commerce*
NMHS	National Maritime Historical Society
NTHP	National Trust for Historic Preservation
NYDN	*New York Daily News*
NYP	*New York Post*
NYPL	New York Public Library
NYSN	*New York Sunday News*
NYT	*New York Times*
PSP	Peter Stanford Papers (selected papers in author's possession)
SFMNHP	San Francisco Maritime National Historical Park
SIA	*Staten Island Advance*
SSSM	South Street Seaport Museum, Institutional Archives
SSSMN	*South Street Seaport Museum News*
SSR	*South Street Reporter*
VISOSSSM	Volunteers in Support of South Street Seaport Museum (in JPB)
WB	*WoodenBoat*
WMR	*Washington Market Review* (NYC)
WP	*Washington Post*
WSJ	*Wall Street Journal*

NOTES TO THE PREFACE AND ACKNOWLEDGMENTS

1. James M. Lindgren, *Preserving the Old Dominion: Historic Preservation and Virginia Traditionalism* (Charlottesville: University Press of Virginia, 1993); Lindgren, *Preserving Historic New England: Preservation, Progressivism, and the Remaking of Memory* (New York: Oxford University Press, 1995); Clifford Geertz, "Thick Description: Toward an Interpretive Theory of Culture," in *Interpretation of Cultures* (New York: Basic Books, 1973); Michel Foucault, *Power/Knowledge* (New York: Pantheon, 1980).

2. Anonymous to author, Aug. 16, 2006, Mar. 13, 2009, email; Victoria Cain, "Exhibitionary Complexity: Reconsidering Museums' Cultural Authority," *American Quarterly* 60 (Dec. 2008): 1143.

NOTES TO THE INTRODUCTION

1. Editorial: "Salvation on the East River," *NYT*, July 17, 1971, 22.

2. Ada Louise Huxtable, "City of Hope, Despair," *NYT*, June 26, 1966, 98; Huxtable to author, Mar. 25, 2009, email; "Proposal for an East River Seaport," in Norma Stanford to Anita Ventura, Aug. 16, 1966, Kortum Collection, HDC 1084, Series 2:8, File 4, SFMNHP; Robert A. Caro, *The Power Broker: Robert Moses and the Fall of New York* (New York: Knopf, 1974), 734; Editorial: "A World Trade Center," *NYT*, Mar. 14, 1961, 34. The streets of Lower Manhattan are on a northwest-by-southeast axis, but the terms "east" and "west" are customarily used to describe river-to-river traffic.

3. Fred Kaplan, "Righting a Wrecking Ball Wrong in New York City," *Boston Globe*, Mar. 8, 1998, A30; [Ada Louise Huxtable], Editorial: "Farewell to Penn Station," *NYT*, Oct. 30, 1963, 38; Anthony C. Wood, *Preserving New York: Winning the Right to Protect a City's Landmarks* (New York: Routledge, 2008), 20n18. In 1962, Mayor Robert Wagner created the Committee for the Preservation of Structures of Historic and Esthetic Importance to prepare a survey, but this first-of-its-kind commission was advisory and played a limited role (Roberta B. Gratz, "Landmarks: A Rating after Ten Years," *NYP*, Jan. 12, 1973, 2). The story of the Seaport Museum has been mostly missed by historians, but its context is set by Wood, *Preserving New York*; Max Page, *The Creative Destruction of Manhattan, 1900–1940* (Chicago: University of Chicago Press, 1999); Randall Mason, *The Once and Future New York: Historic Preservation and the Modern City* (Minneapolis: University of Minnesota Press, 2009); Robert A. M. Stern, Thomas Mellins, and David Fishman, *New York 1960: Architecture and Urbanism between the Second World War and the Bicentennial* (New York: Monacelli, 1995), chap. 16, 1090–1154.

4. Ada Louise Huxtable, "A Vision of Rome Dies," *NYT*, July 14, 1966, 37; SSSM, *A Proposal to Recreate the Historic "Street of Ships" as a Major Recreational and Cultural Resource in the Heart of New York City* (New York: SSSM, 1967), 8; Peter Stanford to author, May 31, 2007, email.

5. John Hightower to author, Oct. 23, 2010, email.

6. Ada Louise Huxtable, "Down Town Blues," *NYT*, Apr. 16, 1967, X29; Norma Stanford to Philip Yenawine, Sept. 30, 1974, PSP.

7. William J. Murtagh, "Janus Never Sleeps," in *Past Meets Future: Saving America's Historic Environments*, ed. Antoinette J. Lee (Washington, DC: Preservation Press, 1992), 52; "3 Blocks for 99 Years," *SSR* 7 (Fall 1973): 6; Ada Louise Huxtable, "New Bedford Waterfront a Model Renewal Project," *NYT*, Nov. 21, 1966, 47; Barry Lewis and Virginia Dajani, "The South Street Seaport Museum," *Livable City* (Municipal Art Society) 8 (June 1981): 3; Stern, Mellins, and Fishman, *New York 1960*, 1091; Peter Neill, "Reflections on 20 Years —and Then Some," *Seaport* 21 (Summer 1987): 11–12.

8. Karen Rothmeyer, "Seaport the Focus of Push for Development," *NYT*, Feb. 12, 1978, R4; Peter Stanford, "Background Paper on the Development of Schermerhorn Row," Apr. 16, 1968, in SSSM History, 1968–69, SSSM; Peter Stanford, "Ambitious Plan to Renew NY Ship Era," *JoC*, May 20, 1968; Kent Barwick, interview, June 24, 2008.

9. Peter Stanford to Karl Kortum, May 20, 1970, Kortum Correspondence, SSSM; Peter Stanford, "South Street: The Street of Dreams," *Cue*, Sept. 20, 1969, 9; Peter Neill, "More

than Beautification," *Seaport* 27 (Fall 1993): 7. The trademark for "South Street Seaport" was filed by the museum's Seaport Corporation on Mar. 5, 1990, for everything from mugs to museum services to art galleries. The trademark for "Seaport," which was filed on Mar. 2, 1979, referred to its magazine (Trademark Search, http://www.trademarks411 .com). The term "South Street Seaport" was first used in 1967.

10. Patricia Leigh Brown, "Is South Street Seaport on the Right Tack?," *Historic Preservation* 33 (July–Aug. 1981): 12.

NOTES TO CHAPTER 1

1. Edward Robb Ellis, *The Epic of New York City: A Narrative History* (New York: Carroll & Graf, 2005), 273; Edwin G. Burrows and Mike Wallace, *Gotham: A History of New York City to 1898* (New York: Oxford University Press, 1999); Ann Buttenwieser, "Order from Chaos," *Seaport* 25 (Fall 1991): 34.

2. Colin J. Davis, "Warfare on the Docks: The Longshoremen's Strike of 1948," *Seaport* 35 (Fall 2000): 25. The term "Port of New York" now refers to the combined transportation facilities in New York City, New York State, and New Jersey, whether by sea, land, or air, operated by the Port Authority of New York and New Jersey.

3. Stuart E. Jones, "Here's New York Harbor," *National Geographic*, Dec. 1954, 778; Alex Roland, W. Jeffrey Bolster, and Alexander Keyssar, *The Way of the Ship: America's Maritime History Reenvisioned, 1600–2000* (Hoboken, NJ: Wiley, 2008), 345–55; Mitchell L. Moss, "Staging a Renaissance on the Waterfront," *New York Affairs* 6 (Nov. 2, 1980): 3–19.

4. R. E. Cropley to Carl Kortin [*sic*], Sept. 29, 1956, SFMNHP; James Morris, *The Great Port: A Passage through New York* (New York: Harcourt, Brace, 1969), 49.

5. Peter Stanford, "South Street: The Street of Dreams," *Cue*, Sept. 20, 1969, 8–9; Peter and Norma Stanford, "The Road to South Street," in "A Venture in South Street," ms. of book, 2007 (more than one draft of this manuscript has circulated; after the completion of my manuscript, the Stanfords published their memoir: Peter and Norma Stanford, *A Dream of Tall Ships: How New Yorkers Came Together to Save the City's Sailing-Ship Waterfront* [Peekskill, NY: Sea History Press, 2013]).

6. Ada Louise Huxtable, "The Man Who Remade New York," *WSJ*, Mar. 14, 2007; Robert A. Caro, *The Power Broker: Robert Moses and the Fall of New York* (New York: Knopf, 1974), 639–78, and illus. in section 2; *South Street Seaport: A Plan for a Vital New Historic Center in Lower Manhattan* (New York: SSSM, 1969), 25; Alice Sparberg Alexiou, *Jane Jacobs: Urban Visionary* (New Brunswick: Rutgers University Press, 2006), 108–9; Benjamin Schwarz, "Gentrification and Its Discontents," *Atlantic Monthly* 305 (June 2010): 85–89; Lewis Mumford, "Mother Jacobs' Home Remedies," *New Yorker* (Dec. 1, 1962): 148–79; Jane Jacobs, *The Death and Life of Great American Cities* (New York: Modern Library, 1961), 187, chap. 10 (187–99).

7. Robert Fitch, *The Assassination of New York* (New York: Verso, 1993), 100; Robert Battaly, *Records of the Downtown-Lower Manhattan Association*, January 2008, 2–3, http://www.rockarch.org/collections/rockorgs/dlma.pdf; Charles Grutzner, "Plan to Rebuild Downtown Area Outlined to City," *NYT*, Oct. 15, 1958, 1; Editorial: "A New Downtown Manhattan," *NYT*, Oct. 15, 1958, 38; Editorial: "Downtown's Big Future," *NYT*, Jan. 27,

1960, 32; Meyer Berger, "The Sagging Houses of the City-That-Was May Finally Yield to Progress," *NYT*, Oct. 15, 1958, 43.

8. Charles Grutzner, "A World Center of Trade Mapped off Wall Street," *NYT*, Jan. 27, 1960, 1; Anthony M. Tung, *Preserving the World's Great Cities: The Destruction and Renewal of the Historic Metropolis* (New York: Clarkson Potter, 2001), 360.

9. Samuel Zipp, *Manhattan Projects: The Rise and Fall of Urban Renewal in Cold War New York* (New York: Oxford University Press, 2010), 6; Charles H. Brown, " 'Downtown' Enters a New Era," *NYT*, Jan. 31, 1960, SM14; Richard Weinstein, telephone interview, Oct. 16, 2009. Since 1961, the area was zoned C6-4, which allowed a floor area ratio of ten to fifteen and encouraged the construction of commercial towers.

10. "Jennifer and Ted Stanley," *Seaport* 26 (Winter 1992): 18; Jacobs, *Death and Life*, 156–59; Manny Fernandez, "Caro Speaks to the Spirit of Jane Jacobs," *NYT*, Sept. 9, 2008.

11. "Marine Museum for New York," *American Bureau of Shipping Bulletin*, July–Aug. 1931, 15; Jacobs, *Death and Life*, 156–59.

12. Ada Louise Huxtable, "Architecture: How to Kill a City," *NYT*, May 5, 1963, 147; Huxtable to author, Mar. 25, 2009, email; "Eyes on the Environment," *Newsweek*, Aug. 23, 1965, 70; David W. Dunlap, "Ada Louise Huxtable, Champion of Livable Architecture, Dies at 91," *NYT*, Jan. 8, 2013, B15.

13. John G. Waite in "A Tribute to James Marston Fitch (1909–2000)," *APT Bulletin* 31, nos. 2–3 (2000): 4; John Young to author, July 28, 2008, email. For the shifting focus, see Randall Mason and Max Page, eds., *Giving Preservation a History: Histories of Historic Preservation in the United States* (New York: Routledge, 2004).

14. Ada Louise Huxtable, "The City on TV," *NYT*, Nov. 20, 1960, X25; Huxtable, "To Keep the Best of New York," *NYT*, Sept. 10, 1961, SM44–SM45; Huxtable, "Must Urban Renewal Be Urban Devastation?," *NYT*, Dec. 24, 1961, X14.

15. Ada Louise Huxtable, "The Attainment of Quality," *AIA Journal* 40 (July 1963): 91; Huxtable, *Classic New York: Georgian Gentility to Greek Elegance* (Garden City, NY: Doubleday, 1964), 34, 110; Russell Lynes, "Where the Wrecker's Ball Hovers," *NYT*, Nov. 15, 1964, BR6. Part of Huxtable's favorite row, including 41 and 43 Peck Slip, was destroyed in 1962. Besides the full block on Fulton Street (nos. 2, 4, 6, 8, 10, 12, 14, 16, 18), Schermerhorn Row also occupied 91, 92, and 93 South Street and 195 and 197 Front Street.

16. Anthony C. Wood, *Preserving New York: Winning the Right to Protect a City's Landmarks* (New York: Routledge, 2008), 153–55; Harmon Goldstone, "The Future of the Past," *Village Views* 4 (Summer 1987): 12; Gregory F. Gilmartin, *Shaping the City: New York and the Municipal Art Society* (New York: Clarkson Potter, 1995), 395.

17. Joe Doyle, "George the Waiter: Twenty Years at Sloppy Louie's," *Seaport* 20 (Spring 1986): 48; Whitney North Seymour Jr., telephone interview, Apr. 10, 2009; Seymour, "Plea to Curb the Bulldozer," *NYT Magazine*, Oct. 13, 1963, 80, 83; Gilmartin, *Shaping the City*, 395; Ada Louise Huxtable, "You Win Some, You Lose Some," *NYT*, Oct. 8, 1972, D29; Huxtable to author, Mar. 25, 2009, email.

18. Seymour, telephone interview, Apr. 10, 2009; US Conference of Mayors, *With Heritage So Rich* (New York: Random House, 1966); Ada Louise Huxtable, "Program to Save Historic Sites Urged in Report to White House," *NYT*, Jan. 30, 1966, 1, 68.

19. Seymour, telephone interview, Apr. 10, 2009; Seymour, *Making a Difference* (New York: William Morrow, 1984), 86; Whitney North Seymour Jr., oral history interview conducted by Anthony C. Wood, July 29, 2006, New York Preservation Archive Project, http://www.nypap.org/content/whitney-north-seymour-jr-oral-history-interview; Ada Louise Huxtable, "Landmark Plans Stir Wall St. Controversy," *NYT*, Dec. 17, 1966, 35.

20. Norma Stanford to Anita Ventura, Aug. 16, 1966, Kortum Collection, HDC 1084, Series 2:8, File 4, SFMNHP. The governor signed the bill on Aug. 2. Chapter 844 of the Laws of 1966 erased an earlier provision in Chapter 843 that allowed the acquisition "by purchase or condemnation" of "the area formerly occupied by the Fulton fish market, and adjacent piers, lands, waterfront and structure" and substituted "the power to lease or purchase any other real property as it deems appropriate and consistent with its said powers" (John G. Waite, Paul R. Huey, and Geoffrey M. Stein, "Chapter 843 of the Laws of 1966," in *New York State Maritime Museum* [1969; repr., New York: NYS Historic Trust, 1972]: 3–4.).

21. Huxtable to author, Mar. 25, 2009, email; Peter Stanford to Seaport & Museum Trustees, July 16, 1968, SSSM History file, 1968–69. For earlier Americans on William Morris, see James M. Lindgren, " 'The Survival of Truly Mediaeval Mannerisms in Construction and Detail': Cultural Politics and New England Antiquities in the Early Twentieth Century," in *From William Morris: Building Conservation and the Arts and Crafts Cult of Authenticity, 1877–1939*, ed. Chris Miele, Studies in British Art 14 (New Haven: Yale University Press, 2005), 213–35.

22. Ada Louise Huxtable, "Fraunces Tavern Controversy," *NYT*, June 6, 1965, X15; Huxtable, "Lively Original versus Dead Copy," *NYT*, May 9, 1965, X19; Huxtable, "Landmark Plans Stir Wall St. Controversy," 35, 68; Peter Stanford to Karl Kortum, Mar. 13, 1967, Kortum Collection, HDC 1084, Series 2:8, File 2, SFMNHP.

23. Alfred Stanford, *The Pleasures of Sailing* (New York: Simon & Schuster, 1943), 26–42, 170; Peter Stanford to author, Oct. 27, 2006, email; "Joan Davidson," *Seaport* 26 (Winter 1992): 20; "Boy, 15 Details Invasion Plans in Navy Journal," *New York Herald Tribune*, n.d. (1942), PSP; "Tactically Logical Cruiser," *Time*, Jan. 11, 1943, 52.

24. Alfred Stanford, *Men, Fish & Boats: The Pictorial Story of the North Atlantic Fishermen* (New York: William Morrow, 1934); Peter Stanford to author, Apr. 24, 2007, email; Richard P. Hunt, "Campaign on East Side Marked by Contrasts of the Old vs. New," *NYT*, Sept. 3, 1963, 22.

25. Peter Stanford, "The Scandal of New York," *New York Herald Tribune*, n.d. (1965), PSP; Peter Stanford, "Goals for New York," *New York Herald Tribune*, Oct. 16, 1964 (originally presented in *City Club Comments*); Robert Gallagher, "South Street Seaport," *American Heritage* 20 (Oct. 1969): 36–43; Peter and Norma Stanford, "The Road to South Street"; Alfred Stanford, *Pleasures of Sailing*, 13–14.

26. Howard Slotnick, telephone interview, Sept. 9, 2008; James M. Lindgren, " 'A Sailing Ship Stirs the Public Like Nothing Else': Remaking Identity and Landscape at the San Francisco Maritime Museum," in "Preserving Maritime America: Public Culture and Memory in the Making of the Nation's Great Marine Museums" (forthcoming).

27. Peter Stanford, "The Ships of San Francisco," *Sea History* 38 (Winter 1985–86): 10;

Peter Stanford, *The Ships That Brought Us So Far* (New York: NMHS, 1971), 39; Peter Stanford to Karl Kortum, Nov. 4, 1971, Kortum Collection, HDC 1084, Series 2:8, File 1, SFMNHP; William Grimes, "Celebrating Columbus and the Age of Sail," *NYT*, July 3, 1992, C1, C21.

28. Norma Stanford to Director, SFMM, Jan. 20, 1966, Kortum Collection, HDC 1084, Series 2:8, File 2, SFMNHP, and to Anita Ventura, Mar. 8, 1966, ibid.; "Proposed Maritime Museum in New York," *Mariner's Mirror* 52 (Aug. 1966): 250; Peter Stanford to author, July 12, 2007, email; Peter and Norma Stanford, "Schooner Sailing and Saving Old Brick," in "A Venture in South Street."

29. "Proposal for an East River Seaport," in Norma Stanford to Anita Ventura, Aug. 16, 1966, Kortum Collection, HDC 1084, Series 2:8, File 4, SFMNHP. The southwest zone was bounded by Beekman, Fulton, Frankfort, Pearl, and Nassau Streets.

30. *South Street Seaport: A Plan*, 3.

31. John Hightower to author, Oct. 23, 2010, email; Jeremiah Driscoll, interview transcript, Dec. 15, 1987, JBP; Joseph Mitchell, *Old Mr. Flood* (New York: Duell, Sloan and Pierce, 1948), viii; Robert Ferraro to author, June 6, 2007, email; Peter and Norma Stanford, "Racing the Clock," in "A Venture in South Street."

32. Peter Stanford to author, Feb. 12, 2007, Nov. 1, 2010, email; John S. Martin Jr., Sentencing Memorandum, *United States v. Carmine Romano, et al.*, United States District Court, Southern District of New York, Jan. 4, 1981 (SS 81 Cr. 514 LPG).

33. Elizabeth Barlow, "On New York's Aged Waterfront, a Pinch of Salt," *Smithsonian* 2 (Aug. 1971): 58; Tom Kaib, "Street of Ships," *Cleveland Plain Dealer*, Aug. 13, 1972, Magazine sec.; Peter Stanford to author, Dec. 20, 2007, email; Patricia Leigh Brown, "Joe Cantalupo, 1906–1979," *SoHo Weekly News*, Aug. 23, 1979, 5; Peter Stanford, *This Museum Is People* (New York: SSSM, 1973), 1 (this essay was originally published in *Curator* 13, no. 4 [1970]).

34. Peter Stanford to Karl Kortum, June 29, 1973, Kortum Correspondence, SSSM; Peter Stanford, interview, May 11, 2006; "The Founders of South Street," *Seaport* 26 (Winter 1992): 12; Anita Ventura to Norma Stanford, Sept. 15, 1966, Kortum Collection, HDC 1084, Series 2:8, File 4, SFMNHP; Frederick L. Rath Jr., "The South Street Maritime Museum Proposal and the Preservation of Schermerhorn Row in New York City," SSSM; Mel Greene, "Ship Museum Would Recreate 1811," *NYSN*, Jan. 29, 1967.

35. Paul Goldberger, "In Honor of the Fund That Loves New York," *NYT*, June 9, 1997, C12; Peter and Norma Stanford, "Racing the Bulldozer," in "A Venture in South Street"; Emory Lewis, "S.O.S. for New Yorkers: Save Our Landmarks," *Cue*, Mar. 13, 1965, 12, 26.

36. Peter Stanford to Anita Ventura, Jan. 22, 1967, Kortum Collection, HDC 1084, Series 2:8, File 2, SFMNHP; Anthony Flint, *Wrestling with Moses: How Jane Jacobs Took on New York's Master Builder and Transformed the American City* (New York: Random House, 2009), 165; Peter Stanford to author, Oct. 1, 2008, email; Peter and Norma Stanford, "Launching Friends of South Street," in "A Venture in South Street."

37. Jakob Isbrandtsen, telephone interview, Mar. 7, 2008; Lindgren, " 'Stout Hearts Make a Safe Ship' ": Individual and Community at Mystic Seaport," in "Preserving Maritime America."

38. Stanford, *This Museum Is People*, 8; Bill Miller, "Frank O. Braynard: An Appreciation," *Ocean Times* 2 (Winter–Spring 2003): 2; Marcelle S. Fischler, "Celebrating the Man Who Celebrates Ships," *NYT*, June 25, 2000, LI14; Dennis Hevesi, "Frank O. Braynard, Ship Maven, Dies at 91," *NYT*, Dec. 14, 2007, A39.

39. Peter and Norma Stanford, "Flags in the Wind," in "A Venture in South Street"; *The Street of Ships*, prod. Charles Richards, 1983, 16 mm film, NYPL.

40. "The Fall of Jakob Isbrandtsen," *Forbes*, Mar. 15, 1972: 23; Isbrandtsen, telephone interview, Mar. 7, 2008.

41. Peter Stanford to Karl Kortum, Mar. 14, 1967, Kortum Collection, HDC 1084, Series 2:8, File 2, SFMNHP; Ada Louise Huxtable, "New Bedford Waterfront a Model Renewal Project," *NYT*, Nov. 21, 1966, 47, 50; Bill Richards, "Making Waves on Old South Street," *Newsday*, May 10, 1969; Stanford, *This Museum Is People*, 4; James M. Lindgren, " 'Let Us Idealize Old Types of Manhood': The New Bedford Whaling Museum," in "Preserving Maritime America."

42. McCandlish Phillips, "Seaport Museum Urged Downtown," *NYT*, May 15, 1967, 85; Fitch, *Assassination of New York*, 141.

43. Peter Stanford to Friends of the SSMM, Jan. 10, 1967, SSSM; Terry Walton, "People," *Seaport* 15 (Summer 1981): 45.

44. "Our Edifice Complex," *Villager*, Mar. 31, 1960; Barlow, "On New York's Aged Waterfront," 60.

45. Richard Fewtrell to author, May 24, 2009, email; Helen Hayes and Anita Loos, *Twice Over Lightly: New York Then and Now* (New York: Harcourt Brace Jovanovich, 1972), 27, 29; Joe Doyle, "Seaport People: Edna Fitzpatrick's Waterfront World," *Seaport* 21 (Summer 1987): 64; Jennifer Stanley to author, May 4, 2009, email; Phillips, "Seaport Museum Urged Downtown," 45; "Founders of South Street," 12.

46. Peter and Norma Stanford, "Square Riggers '68," in "A Venture in South Street"; Ferraro to author, June 6, 2007, email.

47. Kent Barwick, interview, June 24, 2008.

48. Peter and Norma Stanford, "Flags in the Wind"; Terry Walton to author, Nov. 2, 12, 2006, email; Peter Stanford to author, Dec. 21, 2007, email.

49. Ferraro to author, June 6, 2007, email; Alan D. Frazer to author, Nov. 19, 2009, email; Hayes and Loos, *Twice Over Lightly*, 27; "Founders of South Street," 12; Michael E. Levine, telephone interview, Jan. 14, 2011. For an overview of history museums, see Michael Kammen, *Mystic Chords of Memory: The Transformation of Tradition in American Culture* (New York: Knopf, 1991); Warren Leon and Roy Rosenzweig, eds., *History Museums in the United States* (Urbana: University of Illinois Press, 1989).

50. Peter Aron, telephone interview, Oct. 7, 2009; Peter Stanford to Karl Kortum, Dec. 30, 1967, Kortum Collection, HDC 1084, Series 2:8, File 2, SFMNHP.

51. "Admiral Will Head State Museum Board of Trustees," *SSR* 2 (Jan. 1968): 4; Peter Stanford, "We Could Do No Less than Respond with Loyalty," *Sea History* (Summer 1981): 7.

52. Peter Stanford to author, Dec. 21, 2007, email; Patricia Leigh Brown, "Is South Street Seaport on the Right Tack?," *Historic Preservation* 33 (July–Aug. 1981): 16–17; "The South Street Plan," in "Report on the South Street Plan," *SSR* 7 (Oct. 1973): 4; Richards,

"Making Waves"; Bob Ferraro, "Some Quick Memories, a Gathering of Friends, Honoring Peter and Norma Stanford," Oct. 17, 2006, SSSM (a packet of submitted materials); *South Street Seepage*, n.d., in Printings file, 1967, SSSM; Peter and Norma Stanford, "Flags in the Wind"; Barbara Johnson, "Return of a Wanderer," *Nantucket Times Inquirer & Mirror*, Aug. 1970; Barwick, interview, June 24, 2008. See also Jürgen Habermas, *The Structural Transformation of the Public Sphere: An Inquiry into a Category of Bourgeois Society*, trans. Thomas Burger (Cambridge: MIT Press, 1989).

53. Edward I. Koch, "Message from the Mayor," *Seaport* 21 (Summer 1987): 9; Jason Hackworth, *The Neoliberal City: Governance, Ideology, and Development in American Urbanism* (Ithaca: Cornell University Press, 2007), 120.

NOTES TO CHAPTER 2

1. Peter Stanford to Trustees, Jan. 26, 1972, Kortum Collection, HDC 1084, Series 2:8, File 1, SFMNHP; Robert Fitch, *The Assassination of New York* (New York: Verso, 1993), 227.

2. John Hightower, "Report from the President," *Seaport* 15 (Spring 1981): 5; Glenn Collins, "New Body for a Seaport's Soul; at Maritime Museum's Remade Home, Old Walls Talk," *NYT*, July 3, 2003; Holland Cotter, "Remembrance of Downtown Past," *NYT*, Sept. 1, 2006.

3. Ellen Fletcher, "Saved from the Wrecker's Ball," *Seaport* 17 (Summer 1983): 32–33.

4. Ada Louise Huxtable, "Preservation in New York," *Architectural Review* 132 (Aug. 1962): 83; Huxtable, "Downtown New York Begins to Undergo Radical Transformation," *NYT*, Mar. 27, 1967, 35, 37; Anita Ventura, notes from Karl Kortum dictation, Apr. 13, 1967, Kortum Collection, HDC 1084, Series 2:8, File 2, SFMNHP; Karl Kortum, notes on a telephone conversation with Peter Stanford, Apr. 18, 1967, ibid. Huxtable limited her direct intercession because, she said, "For the critic, arm's length association is best" (Ada Louise Huxtable to author, Mar. 26, 2009, email).

5. Gregory F. Gilmartin, *Shaping the City: New York and the Municipal Art Society* (New York: Clarkson Potter, 1995), 385; Charles G. Bennett, "First Paid Head of Landmarks Group Is Sworn In," *NYT*, Oct. 22, 1968, 43; US Conference of Mayors, *With Heritage So Rich* (New York: Random House, 1966); Martin Anderson, *The Federal Bulldozer: A Critical Analysis of Urban Renewal, 1949–1962* (Cambridge: MIT Press, 1964), 367–68; Anthony Flint, *Wrestling with Moses: How Jane Jacobs Took on New York's Master Builder and Transformed the American City* (New York: Random House, 2009), 127; Richard Weinstein, telephone interview, Oct. 16, 2009.

6. "Why Save the Waterfront?" *SSR* 7 (Summer 1973): 3–4; *The Lower Manhattan Plan: The 1966 Vision for Downtown New York*, ed. Carol Willis (Princeton: Princeton Architectural Press, 2002), chap. 6, p. 85; SSSM, *A Proposal to Recreate the Historic "Street of Ships" as a Major Recreational and Cultural Resource in the Heart of New York City* (New York: SSSM, 1967), 7, 9, 11, 13, 17; Karl Kortum to Peter Stanford, Apr. 7, 1967, Kortum Correspondence, SSSM. Of the thirty-eight acres, approximately seventeen were off shore, leaving only twenty for land development, minus the roadbeds.

7. Charles G. Bennett, "City Plans—'Old New York' in Fulton Fish Market Area," *NYT*, Mar. 28, 1968; Peter Stanford, "Background Paper" and Minutes of Advisory Committee,

SSS & MM, May 21, 1968, SSSM; "Fulton Market Site for Restoration as Seaport Village Draws Support," *SIA*, Apr. 18, 1968; Jonathan Barnett, *Urban Design as Public Policy: Practical Methods for Improving Cities* (New York: Architectural Record Books, 1974), 77; Ada Louise Huxtable, "Where Ghosts Can Be at Home," *NYT*, Apr. 7, 1968, D25. In 1968, the LPC designated as landmarks 189, 191, 193, and 195 Front Street; 2, 4, 6, 8, 10, 12, 14, 16, and 18 Fulton Street; 159–63, 165, and 167–71 John Street; and 91 and 92 South Street ("Landmark Designation in Chronological Order, 1965–1986," *Village Views* 4 [Winter 1987]: 51).

8. Peter Stanford to author, May 3, 2013, email; "New Seaport Model," *SSR* 2 (July 1968): 4; Helen Hayes and Anita Loos, *Twice Over Lightly: New York Then and Now* (New York: Harcourt Brace Jovanovich, 1972), 22, 27–28.

9. Ada Louise Huxtable, "Where Did We Go Wrong?," *NYT*, July 14, 1968, D24; Karl Kortum to the editor of the *NYT*, July 25, 1968, Kortum Collection, HDC 1084, Series 2:8, File 2, SFMNHP.

10. Peter Stanford, Minutes of Advisory Committee, May 21, 1968 (a copy of which was sent to Huxtable); Gray Read, *The Miniature and the Gigantic in Philadelphia Architecture* (Lewiston, NY: Edwin Mellen, 2007), 69–70; "New Seaport Model," *SSR* 2 (July 1968): 4; "Walter Lord," *Seaport* 26 (Winter 1992): 43; Fitch, *Assassination of New York*, 95; Neil Smith, "Historic Preservation in a Neoliberal Age," *Housing Policy Debates* 9 (1998): 479–85.

11. Emily Dennis, "Seminar on Neighborhood Museums," *Museum News*, Jan. 1970, 19; Philip Yenawine to author, Apr. 27, 2009, email; "Destruction of Lower Manhattan," *SSR* 2 (May 1968): 1, 4; Daniel Wolff, "Razed: *The Destruction of Lower Manhattan*: A Conversation with Photographer Danny Lyon," *Village Voice*, July 12, 2005, http://www.villagevoice.com/2005-07-12/art/razed/full/; Danny Lyon, *The Destruction of Lower Manhattan* (New York: Macmillan, 1969), particularly illus. 2–11 and 57–67; Talbot Hamlin, *Greek Revival Architecture in America* (New York: Oxford University Press, 1944), 149 and fig. 35; Allon Schoener to author, Nov. 13, 2007, email.

12. Richard Rosenkranz, *Across the Barricades* (Philadelphia: Lippincott, 1971), postlog 2–3, 44–45; John Young to author, July 15, 28, 2008, email; "Architecture Firm Beyer Blinder Belle Rings in as Landmarks Lion," *District Lines* 18 (Autumn 2004): 7–8; David W. Dunlap, "The Preservation Band That Sets the Tone," *NYT*, June 7, 1998, RE1.

13. Peter Stanford to Seaport & Museum Trustees, July 16, 1968, SSSM History file, 1968–69; Huxtable to author, Mar. 25, 2009, email; Cotter, "Remembrance of Downtown Past"; Glenn Loney, "South Street Seaport," *NYDN*, n.d., in SSSM History, 1968–69, SSSM; John G. Waite, Paul R. Huey, and Geoffrey M. Stein, "A Preliminary Historical Study of Land Uses," in *A Compilation of Historical and Architectural Data on the New York State Maritime Museum Block in New York City* (1969; repr., New York: NYS Historic Trust, 1972), 10.

14. Jakob Isbrandtsen, undated fundraising letter, in Printings File, 1969, SSSM; Peter Stanford, " 'Street of Ships' Being Rebuilt," *Westender* 34 (Summer 1969): 60.

15. "Conference Charts Course for Seaport Development," *SSR* 2 (Nov. 1968): 1.

16. "South Street Planning Conference," Nov. 7, 1968, transcription of tape recording, made

by Office of State History, NY Dept. of Education, SSSM; Kent Barwick, interview, June 24, 2008.

17. T. R. Adam, *The Civic Value of Museums* (New York: American Association for Adult Education, 1937); Adam, *The Museum and Popular Culture* (New York: George Grady, 1939), 5; "South Street Planning Conference"; Peter and Norma Stanford, "South Street Besieged!," in "A Venture in South Street," ms. of book, 2007. For an overview, see Edward P. Alexander, *Museums in Motion* (Nashville: American Association for State and Local History, 1973); and Stephen E. Weill, "From Being *about* Something to Being *for* Somebody: The Ongoing Transformation of the American Museum," *Daedalus* 128 (Summer 1999): 236.

18. John O. Sands, "Small Craft Tradition in North American Maritime Museums," in *International Congress of Maritime Museums: Third Conference Proceedings, 1978* (Mystic, CT: Mystic Seaport Museum, 1979), 207; "South Street Planning Conference."

19. Peter Stanford, "South Street: The Street of Dreams," *Cue*, Sept. 20, 1969, 9; Stanford, "Progress Report," Sept. 24, 1970, in Annual Reports file, SSSM; Stanford to author, Apr. 24, 2007, email; Malcolm S. Knowles, *The Modern Practice of Adult Education* (New York: Association Press, 1970), 39; Stanford, "The South Street Seaport Plan Moves toward Full Achievement," *SSR* 5 (Spring 1972): 4–5; Schoener to author, Nov. 13, 2007, email; Thomas P. F. Hoving, "Branch Out!," *Museum News* 46 (Sept. 1968): 19; Stanford, "This Museum *Is* People," *Curator* 13, no. 4 (1970); Stanford, "South Street," 9; Duncan F. Cameron, "The Museum: A Temple or the Forum," *Journal of World History* 14 , no. 1 (1972): 189–202.

20. Peter and Norma Stanford, "South Street Besieged!" and "Planning the Future Seaport," in "A Venture in South Street"; Ada Louise Huxtable, "How to Impoverish a City at $400 a Square Foot," *NYT*, Sept. 29, 1968, D31; Bill Richards, "Making Waves on Old South Street," *Newsday*, May 10, 1969; "Ad Hoc Committee to Save South Street," *NYT*, Dec. 15, 1968, E5; Editorial: "Schermerhorn Row: Landmark," *NYT*, Dec. 19, 1968, 46; Eric Ridder, "What Kind of City?," *JoC*, Nov. 8, 1968.

21. Anthony C. Wood, "Pioneers of Preservation: Part II: An Interview with Harmon Goldstone," *Village Views* 4 (Summer 1987): 37; Roberta Brandes Gratz, *The Battle for Gotham: New York in the Shadow of Robert Moses and Jane Jacobs* (New York: Nation Books, 2010), 46; Roger Starr, "Must Landmarks Go?," *Horizon* 8 (Summer 1966): 53, 58.

22. Editorial: "Schermerhorn Row Saved," *NYT*, Dec. 21, 1968, 36; Jakob Isbrandtsen, telephone interview, Mar. 7, 2008; Ada Louise Huxtable, "A 'Landmark' Decision on Landmarks," *NYT*, July 9, 1978, D21.

23. Isbrandtsen, telephone interview, Mar. 7, 2008; Peter Stanford, *This Museum Is People* (New York: SSSM, 1973), 6; Stanford, "South Street Seaport Plan," 4; Percy Knauth, "South Street," *On the Sound* (Port Chester, NY), Jan. 1973, 38–39; Peter Manigault, vice chairman of NTHP, "A View of the Work in South Street," in *Report to the Membership, 1971* (New York: SSSM, 1971), inside cover.

24. "Mayor Launches Seaport Restoration," *SSR* 3 (July 1969): 1; Ada Louise Huxtable, "Stumbling toward Tomorrow: The Decline and Fall of the New York Vision," *Dissent*, Fall 1987, 458.

25. Weinstein, telephone interview, Oct. 16, 2009; Alan Frazer to Karl Kortum, Apr. 1, 1970, Kortum Collection, HDC 1084, Series 2:8, File 2, SFMNHP; Peter Stanford to Karl Kortum, July 14, 1969, Kortum Correspondence, SSSM.

26. Richard Phalon, "Isbrandtsen Resigns Here as American Export Head," *NYT*, June 18, 1971, 78; Peter and Norma Stanford, "The Seaport Plan," in "A Venture in South Street"; "The Fall of Jakob Isbrandtsen," *Forbes*, Mar. 15, 1972, 23; Frank J. Prial, "South St. Seaport Seen as Key to Manhattan Landing," *NYT*, Apr. 17, 1972, 65; Robert Carroll, "South Street Seaport Plan Hits a Financial Reef," *NYDN*, June 27, 1971; Editorial: "Salvation on the East River," *NYT*, July 17, 1971, 22.

27. Owen Moritz, "Plan a $1.2B Wonderful Town on East River Landfill," *NYDN*, Apr. 13, 1972; Prial, "South St. Seaport Seen as Key," 65; Peter Sanford to Karl Kortum, Feb. 10, 1973, SSSM.

28. "Roundtable on Rouse," *Progressive Architecture*, July 1981, 103; Stanford to author, June 21, 2006, email; "On April 11," *SSR* 6 (Summer 1972): 1; "Stop Press," *SSR* 6 (Fall 1972): 11; Editorial, *NYDN*, Feb. 8, 1973, in "We Share a Vision," *SSR* 7 (Spring 1973): 7. For the 1.4 million square feet of air rights that were transferred, the banks agreed to drop their mortgage liens on the museum properties. They eventually sold some 900,000 square feet but in 1989 were left with another 540,000 square footage that was perhaps unusable. Of the city's $8 million commitment, $4.5 million went to Atlas-McGrath for 74E and part of 74W and $3.5 million went to the banks that held mortgages on plots in Blocks 96W and 97 E-W. In 1974, the city transferred the Row and a portion of Burling Slip to the Seaport for $800,000, which resold the Row to New York State for $1.1 million. The $300,000 difference was intended to relocate the Row's tenants; instead, the museum placed it in its general operating fund, causing a later audit by and harsh criticism from the city comptroller. Additionally, the city leased with a ten-year option Block 74W to the telephone company, which expected to buy the land for $8 million (retiring the city's bonded debt) and build a high-rise. The city's annual lease of $580,000 would cover its debt service and carrying cost. The telephone company planned to include access to the proposed Second Avenue subway, which was canceled by Mayor Beame with the city's financial crisis.

29. Weinstein, telephone interview, Oct. 16, 2009; Stanford to author, Aug. 12, 2009, email.

30. Roberta B. Gratz, "Landmarks: A Rating after Ten Years," *NYP*, Jan. 12, 1973, 2, 50. National newspapers still praised the air-rights strategy, repeating the inflated predictions but missing the deflated realities (William Marlin, "New York Protects Rich Heritage," *CSM*, June 14, 1974, F1).

31. "East Side Plan," *NYT*, Apr. 14, 1972, 38; Marie Lore to the editor, *NYT*, Apr. 26, 1972, 44; Thomas Kinsolving to the editor, "Propaganda Sheet," *SSR* 7 (Summer 1973): 10; Frank Braynard to the editor, *SSR* 8 (Summer 1974): 22; Peter Stanford to Karl Kortum, May 7, 1972, Kortum file, SSSM.

32. Herbert J. Gans, "Preserving Everyone's Noo Yawk," *NYT*, Jan. 28, 1975, 33; Gans to the editor, "Of City Landmarks and Elitism," *NYT*, Feb. 25, 1975, 34; Ada Louise Huxtable, "Preserving Noo Yawk Landmarks," *NYT*, Feb. 4, 1975, 33; Barwick, interview, June 24, 2008. Placed on the National Register of Historic Places in 1972, the boundary of the

South Street Seaport Historic District was expanded by the LPC on May 10, 1977, and accepted by the National Register on Dec. 12, 1978. It included Piers 15–17. Fletcher Street (or Alley) was included to protect what became the Yankee Clipper Restaurant, earlier known as the Baker, Carver & Morrell Building (1840) at 170–76 John Street. In 1989, the city included Block 106 but excluded Pier 18 and the New Market Building of the FFM (see LPC, "South Street Seaport," http://www.nyc.gov/html/lpc/downloads/pdf/maps/s_st_seaport.pdf).

33. Karl Kortum to Peter Stanford, Dec. 27, 1968, SSSM.

NOTES TO CHAPTER 3

1. SSSM, *A Proposal to Recreate the Historic "Street of Ships" as a Major Recreational and Cultural Resource in the Heart of New York City* (New York: SSSM, 1967), 21; "Move to Save NY's 'Street of Ships,'" *SSR* 1 (Jan. 1967): 1; "Panel No. 1: The Heart of the Story," agenda for 1968 planning conference, in Kortum Collection, HDC 1084, Series 2:8, File 1, SFMNHP; Peter and Norma Stanford, "Racing the Clock," in "A Venture in South Street," ms. of book, 2007; Irving Johnson, *The* Peking *Battles Cape Horn* (New York: Sea History Press, 1977), 165; Peter Stanford to John Harbour, June 5, 1968, Kortum Collection, HDC 1084, Series 2:8, File 2, SFMNHP; Peter Stanford to Jakob Isbrandtsen, Sept. 11, 1970, ibid.; "Where People Come Together," *SSR* 5 (Jan. 1971): 1; Terry Walton, Editorial, *SSR* 9 (Summer 1975): 2.

2. Norman Brouwer, interview by C. A. Richards, typescript, May 23, [1979], SSSM; Peter Neill, "Developing a National Cultural Policy for Maritime Preservation," *APT Bulletin* 9, no. 1 (1987): 24; Karl Kortum to Peter Stanford, Mar. 9, 1967, Kortum Correspondence, SSSM.

3. "Report to Members," *SSR* 3 (Mar. 1969): 5; Peter Stanford, *The Ships That Brought Us So Far* (New York: NMHS, 1971), 5, 19; Peter Manigault, introduction to ibid.; Crosbie Smith et al., "'Avoiding Equally Extravagance and Parsimony': The Moral Economy of the Ocean Steamship," *Technology and Culture* 44, no. 3 (2003): 443; Peter Stanford, "The Ship as Museum," *Sea History* 46 (Winter 1987–88): 14; *South Street Seaport: A Plan for a Vital New Historic Center in Lower Manhattan* (New York: SSSM, 1969), 9, 11; Peter Stanford, *This Museum Is People* (New York: SSSM, 1973), 13; Peter Stanford, Minutes of Advisory Committee, SSS & MM, May 21, 1968, SSSM.

4. The history of US maritime preservation floats in relatively uncharted waters. Unlike the chronicle of landside preservationists, which was surveyed by Charles B. Hosmer Jr. in a handful of works and then critically assessed by numerous scholars, the story of maritime preservation awaits a full telling. Part of that will be found in my forthcoming "Preserving Maritime America: Public Culture and Memory in the Making of the Nation's Great Marine Museums," which will examine institutions that have a specific maritime focus, including the East India Marine Society (1799) in Salem (MA), the New Bedford (MA) Whaling Museum (1903), Mystic Seaport Museum (1929), the Mariners' Museum (1930) in Newport News (VA), the San Francisco Maritime Museum (1951), and South Street Seaport.

5. Stanford, *Ships That Brought Us So Far*, 13–17, 19; Norman Brouwer, "The Port of New

York, 1860–1985: Preserving the Past of the Port," *Seaport* 25 (Winter–Spring, 1991): 42–43; Peter Stanford, "How Historic Ships Live," in *First National Maritime Preservation Conference Proceedings* (Washington, DC: Preservation Press, 1977), 7; Robert B. Streeter, "George B. Douglas: A Passion for the *Packard*," *Sea History* 56 (Winter 1990): 9, 11.

6. Bob Ferraro, "Some Quick Memories, a Gathering of Friends, Honoring Peter and Norma Stanford," Oct. 17, 2006, SSSM (a packet of submitted materials); Helen Hayes and Anita Loos, *Twice Over Lightly: New York Then and Now* (New York: Harcourt Brace Jovanovich, 1972), 29–30.

7. "George W. Rogers, David Rockefeller Open *Ambrose* Lightship," *SSR* 4 (Mar. 1970): 1; Peter and Norma Stanford, "Sea Day Ushers in a Turn of the Tide," in "A Venture in South Street."

8. Joe Garland, "A Piece of Gloucester's in Old N.Y.," *Gloucester (MA) Daily Times*, Oct. 7, 1968; Peter Stanford, "*Ambrose* and *Caviare*," *SSR* 2 (Sept. 1968): 2; "*Caviare* Finds New Home at Pier 16," ibid., 1; Norman Brouwer, "The Many Lives of *Lettie*: A History of the Fishing Schooner *Lettie G. Howard*," *Seaport* 23 (Winter–Spring 1990): 19–24; Brouwer, "The Ships of South Street," *Seaport* 17 (Summer 1983): 23–24; Peter and Norma Stanford, "South Street Acquires Its First Ships!," in "A Venture in South Street"; Timothy Ferris, "South St. Museum Grows with the Incoming Tide," *NYP*, Mar. 30, 1970; Ferraro, "Some Quick Memories."

9. Brouwer, "Ships of South Street," 24; Meeting of [SSSM] Ship Committee, Oct. 8, 1970, Kortum Collection, HDC 1084, Series 2:8, File 2, SFMNHP; George Matteson to author, Oct. 17, 2008, email; Matteson, "A Centennial History of the *Pioneer*," *Seaport* 19 (Summer 1985): 26.

10. John Smith, *Condemned at Stanley* (London: Picton, 1986), 17; Robert Gallagher, "South Street Seaport," *American Heritage* 20 (Oct. 1969): 77; Karl Kortum to Peter Stanford, Aug. 1, 1967, Kortum Collection, HDC 1084, Series 2:8, File 2, SFMNHP; Suzanne Boorsch, "Charles Cooper," *SSR* 4 (Mar. 1970): 3; Peter Throckmorton, "The American Heritage in the Falklands," *Sea History* 4 (July 1976): 40–41. When restored in 2008–13, *Morgan* lost much of its original framing and those adze and broad-axe markings.

11. Karl Kortum to Peter Stanford, Apr. 7, 1967, Kortum Correspondence, SSSM; Kortum, "The Finding of *Wavertree*," *Sea History* 20 (Spring 1981): 20–22; Kortum to Stanford, June 26, 1967, Kortum Collection, HDC 1084, Series 2:8, File 2, SFMNHP.

12. Peter Neill, "Reflections on 20 Years—and Then Some," *Seaport* 21 (Summer 1987): 12; Peter Stanford to unknown, second page of undated letter, Kortum Collection, HDC 1084, Series 2:8, File 2, SFMNHP.

13. Stanford, "Ship as Museum," 13. On reintroducing sailors' culture into history, see Jesse Lemisch, "Jack Tar in the Streets: Merchant Seamen in the Politics of Revolutionary America," *William and Mary Quarterly* 25 (July 1968): 371–407; Peter Linebaugh, "Jack Tar in History," *History Workshop Journal* 32 (Autumn 1991): 217–21; and Marcus Rediker, *Between the Devil and the Deep Blue Sea: Merchant Seamen, Pirates, and the Anglo-American Maritime World, 1700–1750* (New York: Cambridge University Press, 1987).

14. Ellen F. Rosebrock, *Walking Around in South Street: Discoveries in New York's Old Shipping District* (New York: SSSM, 1974), 60; Chip Brown, "The *Wavertree* at One Hundred,"

Seaport 20 (Spring 1986): 14. For explosives, see Stephen R. Bown, *A Most Damnable Invention: Dynamite, Nitrates, and the Making of the Modern World* (New York: T. Dunne, 2005), 156–63.

15. Alan Villiers to the editor, "Aura of Sailing Ships," *NYT*, June 8, 1972, 46; Villiers to the editor, *SSR* 3 (July 1969): 2; "Capt. Villiers Campaigns for Ship," *SSR* 3 (May 1969): 1.

16. "Recollections," *SSR* 7 (Winter 1973–74): 11; Peter and Norma Stanford, "Beautiful Necessities of Life," in "A Venture in South Street"; "Old Salts Reminisce at Seaport Seminar," *SSR* 3 (Jan. 1969): 8; Nels O. Rasmussen to the editor, *SSR* 11 (Winter 1977– 78): 4; Stanford to author, June 21, 2006, email; Stanford, "Ship as Museum," 13.

17. Jakob Isbrandtsen, telephone interview, Mar. 7, 2008; Charles Deroko to author, Feb. 23, 2010, email; Karl Kortum to Fred Klebingat, July 24, 1969, Kortum Collection, HDC 1084, Series 2:2, SFMNHP; "Panel No. 1: The Heart of the Story"; Peter and Norma Stanford, "The Seaport Plan," in "A Venture in South Street."

18. Peter and Norma Stanford, "Leaning Forward" and "Seaport Plan," in "A Venture in South Street"; Stanford to Karl Kortum, May 20, 1970, Kortum Correspondence, SSSM.

19. Barbara Johnson, "Return of a Wanderer," *Nantucket Times Inquirer & Mirror*, Aug. 1970; "*Wavertree* Is Here!," *SSR* 4 (Sept. 1970): 1, 7. The cost of getting the ship to New York City ran as high as $136,000 (Isbrandtsen, telephone interview, Mar. 7, 2008).

20. Meeting of [SSSM] Ship Committee, Oct. 8, 1970, Kortum Collection, HDC 1084, Series 2:8, File 2, SFMNHP; "Villiers Visits *Wavertree*," *SSR* 4 (Nov. 1970): 4; "*Wavertree*: A Plan for 1973," [c. 1972], PSP. The museum later placed an exhibit aboard *Wavertree*, including rigging tools and artifacts on sailors' lives, until *Peking*'s tweendeck was reconfigured for exhibits ("South Street Today," *SSR* 10 [Summer 1976]: 10). Funded by a DCA capital grant, the Seaport committed to a shipyard installation of *Wavertree*'s tweendeck in 2014 (Jonathan Boulware, telephone interview, Sept. 20, 2013).

21. Norman Brouwer, "Nautical Autobiography," *Seaways* 2 (Mar.–Apr. 1991): 38–40; Brouwer to the editor, *SSR* 4 (July 1970): 2; Brouwer to author, Feb. 7, 8, 2007, email; Karl Kortum to Jane A. Fisher, Aug. 8, 1977, Kortum Collection, HDC 1084, Series 2:2, File 101, SFMNHP. See J. Revell Carr, review of *The International Register of Historic Ships*, by Norman Brouwer, *Seaport* 20 (Winter 1986–87): 44.

22. Richard Fewtrell to author, May 30, 2008, email; Edward H. Fitzelle, "*Peking & Wavertree*," *Oceans*, May 1977, 7; Karl Kortum to Peter Stanford, Nov. 27, 1970, Kortum Collection, HDC 1084, Series 2:8, File 2, SFMNHP.

23. Fewtrell to author, Apr. 18, May 30, 2008, email; Jeremiah Driscoll, interview transcript, Nov. 20, 1987, JBP; Walter Rybka to author, Sept. 12, 2006, email; Bob Atkinson, "Versatile Rigger Is South Street's Restoration Chief," *National Fisherman*, Feb. 1980; Michael Creamer to author, June 2, 2010, email.

24. Fewtrell to author, May 30, 2008, email; Fitzelle, "*Peking & Wavertree*," 8; Deroko to author, Feb. 11, 2011, email.

25. *The Street of Ships*, prod. Charles Richards, 1983, 16 mm film, NYPL; George Matteson to author, May 7, 2008, email.

26. Alan Frazer to Ship Committee, Sept. 21, 1970, Kortum Collection, HDC 1084, Series 2:8, File 2, SFMNHP; Steven C. Dubin, "Crossing 125th Street: *Harlem on My Mind*

Revisited," in *Displays of Power: Controversy in the American Museum from the* Enola Gay *to* Sensation (New York: NYU Press, 1999), 18–63.

27. John Hastings, "NY's Last Paddle-Wheel Steamer," *SSR* 1 (Oct. 1967): 3; Norman Brouwer, "The Port of New York, 1860–1985: Steamboats on the Hudson River," *Seaport* 21 (Summer 1987): 44; Laurie Johnston, "Hudson Sidewheeler Ties Up at Seaport," *NYT*, Apr. 4, 1972, 39; Driscoll, interview transcript, Nov. 20, 1987; Richard J. O'Shea to the editor, "Proud *Hamilton*," *SSR* 7 (Fall 1973): 19; "Membership," *SSR* 8 (Summer 1974): 11; Robert Hanley, "Fate of Sunken Alexander Hamilton Rests in Raising Funds," *NYT*, Dec. 5, 1977, 78.

28. Peter Stanford to Ralph Snow, Apr. 18, 1978, Kortum Collection, HDC 1084, Series 2:8, File 7, SFMNHP; Peter Spectre, "The Politics of Maritime Preservation," *WB* 44 (Jan.–Feb. 1982): 68; Rybka to author, Nov. 14, 2006, email; David Hull, "Unity in Maritime Preservation," *WB* 44 (Jan.–Feb. 1982): 71.

29. Karl Kortum to Peter Stanford, Apr. 7, 1967, Kortum Correspondence, SSSM; Stanford to Kortum, June 10, 1970, Kortum Collection, HDC 1084, Series 2:8, File 1, SFMNHP; Lars Bruzelius, "Kurt," *The Maritime History Virtual Archives*, n.d., http://www.bruzelius .info/Nautica/Ships/Fourmast_ships/Kurt(1904).html; "*Alexander Hamilton* and *Moshulu* Coming," *SSR* 5 (Spring 1972): 1; Norman Brouwer, "*Moshulu* Has Come," *SSR* 6 (Winter 1972–73): 5.

30. Peter Aron, telephone interview, Dec. 17, 2009; editor to David A. Cisney, *SSR* 9 (Winter 1975–76): 22; James L. White, "Accuracy vs. Safety vs. Profit, *Moshulu* Dress Rig," San Francisco Maritime Park Association, n.d., http://www.maritime.org/conf/conf-white .htm.

31. Peter Aron to Norman Brouwer, Nov. 18, 2002, JACF; Charles D. Ellis, *The Partnership: The Making of Goldman Sachs* (New York: Penguin, 2008), 255–56, 264.

32. "Savills: The Four-Masted Steel Barque *Aresthusa* [*sic*] (Formerly S.S. *Peking*)," *NYT*, Aug. 11, 1974, 195; Peter Aron to Norman Brouwer, Nov. 18 2002, JACF; Alan Villiers, *The Set of the Sails: The Story of a Cape Horn Seaman* (New York: Charles Scribner's Sons, 1949), 248; Peter Aron, voice-mail message, May 27, 2010, and telephone interview, May 28, 2010; Isbrandtsen, telephone interview, Mar. 7, 2008.

33. "Basic Understandings between JACF and SSSM," amended Oct. 15, 1974, included in Executive Committee, Minutes, Appendix A, Oct. 18, 1974, JACF; Peter Aron to Norman Brouwer, Nov. 18, 2002, JACF; Hans-Joachim Gersdorf to the editor, *SSR* 9 (Fall 1975): 16.

34. Deroko to author, Feb. 26, 2010, email; Norman Brouwer, "The Life and Rebirth of the *Peking*," in Johnson, Peking *Battles Cape Horn*, 180; Peter Aron to author, Jan. 27, 2010, email; "Seaport Museum Given a Square-Rigger," *NYT*, Nov. 23, 1975, 60. Jack Aron's claim of "largest sailing vessel" was a stretch; while *Moshulu* was twenty feet longer than *Peking*, other ships had a greater overall length.

35. Brouwer to author, Jan. 29, 2010, email; Peter Aron to author, Jan. 27, 2010, email.

36. Peter Aron to author, Jan. 27, 2010, email, and telephone interview, Dec. 17, 2009, May 28, 2010; Fitzelle, "*Peking* & *Wavertree*," 5, 8.

37. Isbrandtsen, telephone interview, Mar. 7, 2008; Fewtrell to author, Mar. 18, 2009, email; Peter Aron, voice mail, May 27, 2010; Bob Herbert to Karl Kortum, Apr. 5, 1976, Kortum

Collection, HDC 1084, Series 2:2, File 143, SFMNHP; Howard Slotnick, telephone interview, Sept. 9, 2008; Jennifer Stanley to author, May 4, 2009, email.

38. David Berson, review of film *Around Cape Horn*, *Seaport* 22 (Fall 1988): 46–47; Johnson, *Peking Battles Cape Horn*, 164–65; Johnson, "Remarks," in *First National Maritime Preservation Conference*, 49.

39. "Seaport Notes," *SSR* 7 (Fall 1973): 16; Peter Aron, telephone interview, Dec. 17, 2009; Peter Stanford to Karl Kortum, Feb. 10, 1976, Kortum Collection, HDC 1084, Series 2:8, File 6, SFMNHP

40. John Noble, "The Coming of the *Aqua*," *SSR* 7 (Fall 1973): 4; Norman Brouwer, *New York Central No. 29*, *SSR* 11 (Winter 1977–78): 20. Later, in 1986, the newly founded Hudson Waterfront Museum in Brooklyn exhibited an unaltered wooden covered lighter barge (Brouwer, "Port of New York, 1860–1985: Preserving the Past," 44).

41. Michael Creamer to author, June 2, 2010, email (he was referring to the MCNY uptown); Neill, "Reflections on 20 Years," 11–12; Peter Stanford to Jakob Isbrandtsen, Feb. 1, 1976, Kortum Collection, HDC 1084, Series 2:8, File 6, SFMNHP.

NOTES TO CHAPTER 4

1. "Galbraith and Lodge Speak for Seaport," *SSR* 3 (Nov. 1969): 1; "Opens Poetry Series," *NYT*, Apr. 26, 1974, 41 (photo with *Black Pearl* and Ginsberg); Peter Stanford, "How Historic Ships Live," in *First National Maritime Preservation Conference Proceedings* (Washington, DC: Preservation Press, 1977), 9.

2. Peter and Norma Stanford, "South Street Besieged!," in "A Venture in South Street," ms. of book, 2007; Stanford, Minutes of Advisory Committee, SSS & MM, May 21, 1968, SSSM; Stanford, *This Museum Is People* (New York: SSSM, 1973), 13; *South Street Seaport: A Plan for a Vital New Historic Center in Lower Manhattan* (New York: SSSM, 1969), 23; Stanford, "Why We Started a New History Museum Right Now," remarks at the American Association of Museums Convention, June 2, 1970, in Publications file, SSSM (revised for publication as "One Man's View of the Emergence of New York's New Sea Museum," *Curator* 13, no. 4 [1970]: 267–81); Stanford, "The South Street Seaport Plan Moves toward Full Achievement," *SSR* 5 (Spring 1972): 4; "Landmarks Guardian: Harmon Hendricks Goldstone," *NYT*, Aug. 27, 1969, 46; "The Seaport in the City: Summary Report," Dec. 3, 1970, 2, in Printings file, 1970, SSSM; Robert Ferraro to author, June 6, 2007, email; James Sanders, "Adventure Playground," in *America's Mayor: John V. Lindsay and the Reinvention of New York*, ed. Sam Roberts (New York: Columbia University Press, 2010), 96.

3. Anonymous to the editor, *SSR* 3 (July 1969): 2; Michael Creamer to author, Apr. 23, 2010, email; Bob Ferraro, "Some Quick Memories, a Gathering of Friends, Honoring Peter and Norma Stanford," Oct. 17, 2006, SSSM (a packet of submitted materials); Helen Hayes and Anita Loos, *Twice Over Lightly: New York Then and Now* (New York: Harcourt Brace Jovanovich, 1972), 30.

4. Peter and Norma Stanford, "The Seaport Established, Year-end 1970," in "A Venture in South Street"; Allon Schoener to author, Nov. 13, 2007, email; "Where People Come Together," *SSR* 5 (Jan. 1971): 1; Philip Yenawine to author, Apr. 27, 2009, email.

5. "Community Enthusiasm Sparks Seaport Museum Projects in Urban Renewal Area," *History News* 26 (Apr. 1971): 82–83; "Development of Urban Museum Center," *Museum News*, Sept. 1971, 338; Emily Dennis, "Seminar on Neighborhood Museums," *Museum News*, Jan. 1970, 16; Alex Fournier to the editor, in "We Share a Vision," *SSR* 7 (Spring 1973): 7; Barbara Mensch, interview, Mar. 19, 2010; William W. Warner, "At the Fulton Market," *Atlantic Monthly* 236 (Nov. 1975): 59.

6. Whitney North Seymour Jr., *Making a Difference* (New York: William Morrow, 1984), 111–12; Ann L. Buttenwieser, *Manhattan Water-Bound: Planning and Developing Manhattan's Waterfront from the Seventeenth Century to the Present* (New York: NYU Press, 1986), 202–3; "Eagle," *SSR* 2 (Mar. 1968): 3; Russell Drumm, *The Barque of Saviors: Eagle's Passage from the Nazi Navy to the U.S. Coast Guard* (Boston: Houghton Mifflin, 2001), 49.

7. Joseph Mitchell, "The Bottom of the Harbor," *New Yorker*, 1951, in Mitchell, *Up in the Old Hotel and Other Stories* (New York: Pantheon, 1992), 465; Marilyn Hoffman, "Renewing a Neglected Waterfront," *CSM*, Nov. 6, 1967; Peter Stanford, *Look at Our Waterfront! Just Look* (New York: SSSM, 1970); Stanford, "Why We Started a New History Museum"; Robert Lifset, "Storm King Mountain and the Emergence of Modern American Environmentalism, 1962–1980" (Ph.D. dissertation, Columbia University, 2005), 408; Robert D. McFadden, "Young and Old Labor to Make Parts of City Gleam in Earth Day Prelude," *NYT*, Apr. 19, 1970, 1, 84.

8. Pete Seeger, telephone interview, Nov. 16, 2007; Seeger, foreword to *Songs and Sketches of the First Clearwater Crew*, comp. and ed. Don McLean (Croton-on-Hudson, NY: North River, 1970), 3; Peter Stanford to author, Apr. 24, 2007, email; David King Dunaway, *How Can I Keep from Singing? The Ballad of Pete Seeger* (New York: McGraw-Hill, 1981), 277–87; Burl Ives, *Songs They Sang in South Street*, SPT-101, 33 rpm vinyl (New York: SSSM, 1970); Ives to Fellow Members of South Street, Nov. 1969, mimeographed fundraising letter, SSSM.

9. *Songs and Sketches*; Douglas Robinson, "Sloop Will Sail Up the Hudson in Campaign for Clean Water," *NYT*, Aug. 2, 1969, 53; "Sails, Songs, Jazz & a Yellow Submarine," *SSR* 3 (Sept. 1969): 3; Lifset, "Storm King Mountain," 384; Environmental Committee, American Association of Museums, *Museums and the Environment: A Handbook for Education* (New York: Arkville, 1971), 115.

10. "Sewage Mars Pier Songfest," *NYSN*, Aug. 23, 1970; Robert Carroll, "It's a Scrubadubdub Day at Fulton Fish Market," *NYDN*, Sept. 13, 1970; Graydon Carter, "Lucky George," *NYT*, Nov. 16, 2008, BR1. For Patton, see D. K. Patton, "New York City," *Historic Preservation* 21 (Oct.–Dec. 1969): 15–18; Miriam Goldberg, *Branding New York: How a City in Crisis Was Sold to the World* (New York: Routledge, 2008), 99.

11. "If You Love Your Uncle Sam (Bring Them Home)" (words and music by Pete Seeger), *Songs and Sketches*, 81; Stanford, interview, May 11, 2006; Rhodri Jeffreys-Jones, *Peace Now! American Society and the Ending of the Vietnam War* (New Haven: Yale University Press, 1999), 15; Seeger, telephone interview, Nov. 16, 2007; Seeger to the editor, *Seaport* 14 (Spring 1980): 48.

12. Peter Stanford to Karl Kortum, May 20, 1970, Kortum Correspondence, SSSM (a carbon

copy was sent to Seeger); David Katzive, "Up against the Waldorf-Astoria," *Museum News*, Sept. 1970, 12–17; Stanford, "Why We Started a New History Museum."

13. John S. Wilson, "Sloop Is Saluted in Program Here," *NYT*, May 30, 1971, 39; "*Clearwater* Concert," *Village Voice*, June 10, 1971; Creamer to author, June 2, 2010, email. *Clearwater* even took on cash-paying customers for cruises ("Six-Day Cruises on Hudson River Sloop," *NYT*, Oct. 21, 1973).

14. Seeger to the editor, "Out of a Common Past . . . a Future for Man," *Sea History* 7 (Spring 1977): 8.

15. Mitchell L. Moss, "The Urban Waterfront: Opportunities for Renewal," *National Civic Review* 65 (May 1976): 241–44; Moss, "Staging a Renaissance on the Waterfront," *New York Affairs* 6 (Nov. 2, 1980): 3–19; Peter and Norma Stanford, "Celebrating City Waterfronts," in "A Venture in South Street"; Ann Satterthwaite, "Methods of Planning for Protection and Enhancement of Historic Waterfronts," in *Selected Papers: Conference on Conserving the Historic and Cultural Landscape, Denver, Colorado, May 2–3, 1975* (Washington, DC: Preservation Press, 1975), 19; Yenawine to author, Apr. 27, 2009, email.

16. John Hightower, "Report from the President," *Seaport* 13 (Summer 1979): 3; Report of the Graphics Committee, Dec. 1973, PSP; "Earth Day to Be a Bell-Ringer," *NYP*, Mar. 16, 1972; "Mead: Mother the Earth," *Columbia (University) Press*, Mar. 21, 1973; Laurie Johnston, "It's Spring Again, a Bit Early This Year," *NYT*, Mar. 20, 1972, 39.

17. Lifset, "Storm King Mountain," 398–401; "Earth Day Brings Ringing of Bells," *SSR* 7 (Spring 1973): 14; "30 Volunteers Put Fulton St. Block in Shipshape for Sea Day Tomorrow," *NYT*, May 19, 1973, 41.

18. Vivien Leone, "Adrift on a Holy Sea: Literary Luminaries Dine Topside," *Manhattan Tribune*, June 6, 1970, 4, 19; Paul L. Montgomery, "National Maritime Day," *NYT*, May 23, 1970, 24; Peter Stanford, "Report from the President," *SSR* 9 (Spring 1975): 10, 12.

19. Norman Brouwer, "The Port of New York, 1860–1985: New York's Floating Classrooms," *Seaport* 24 (Fall 1990): 36–41; Ship Committee, Minutes, May 27, 1971, Kortum Collection, HDC 1084, Series 2:8, File 1, SFMNHP; George Matteson to author, May 7, Oct. 17, 2008, email; Dick Rath, "Sail Training: A Movement Comes of Age," *Sea History* 57 (Spring 1991): 15–18. The New York City school closed in 1982. After *Brown* was transferred by congressional act to Project Liberty Ship, it was towed to Baltimore in 1988.

20. Richard Rath, "City's Youth Sail *Pioneer*," *SSR* 5 (May 1971): 4; Matteson to author, May 7, 2008, email; Shari Galligan Johnson to author, July 8, 2008, email; Peter Stanford, *Pioneer Lives* (New York: SSSM, c. 1971): 12–13, 19 ("Lives" is a verb, not a noun, in the pamphlet's title).

21. Johnson to author, July 8, 2008, email; Walter Rybka to author, Sept. 12, 2006, email; Matteson to author, May 7, 2008, email.

22. Matteson to author, May 7, 2008, email; Johnson to author, July 8, 2008, email; Tom Condon, "Life without Drugs: New York Men 'Find It' at Sea," *Hartford Courant*, Sept. 3, 1971; Percy Knauth, "South Street," *On the Sound* 3 (Jan. 1973): 33–48; "Pioneer Marine School," an eight-page leaflet for prospective students (New York: SSSM, n.d.).

23. Rath, "City's Youth Sail *Pioneer*," 4, 8; Matteson to author, May 7 and July 21, 2008, email; Peter and Norma Stanford, "Beautiful Necessities of Life," in "A Venture in South Street."

24. Richard Fewtrell to author, Apr. 18, 2008, email; Johnson to author, Apr. 17, 2008, email; Creamer to author, June 2, 2010, email.

25. Joanne A. Fishman, "Work Key Ingredient in Marine School Course," *NYT*, Jan. 13, 1974, 227; Marilyn Berger, "Being Brooke Astor," *NYT Magazine*, May 20, 1984: 72; Berger, "Brooke Astor, 105, Aristocrat of the People, Dies," *NYT*, Aug. 14, 2007; Matteson to author, May 7, 2008, email; Johnson to author, July 8, 2008, email.

26. Matteson to author, May 7, 2008, email; "Special Ferryboat," *AP Newsfeatures* No. 538 (Dec. 26, 1972), Johnson Private Collection; Steve Cady, "Rehabilitated Addicts Earn Marine School Diplomas," *NYT*, Feb. 1, 1973, 28; SSSM, *Pioneer Marine School*, a four-page brochure (New York: SSSM, 1972); "Pioneers in Service," *Marine Service News*, release dated Jan. 31, 1973, Johnson Private Collection.

27. Clive Lawrence, "Museum Devoted to Sea, Opportunity," *CSM*, Oct. 31, 1972, 15; Creamer to author, June 2, 2010, email; Matteson to author, May 7, 2008, email; David Brink, telephone interview, Sept. 14, 2006; David Brink, "Marine School Class to Graduate in March," *SSR* 6 (Winter 1972–73): 3; Editorial: "Someone's Using His Head," *NYDN*, Dec. 14, 1972.

28. Susan Stephenson, "*Pioneer*, Wildcat Begin Ship Restoration," *SSR* 7 (Fall 1973): 11; Matteson to author, May 7, 2008, email; Joanne A. Fishman, "Mechanics and Methadone: Pioneer School Sinks in Sea of Bureaucracy," *Soundings*, Jan. 1975, 5.

29. Fishman, "Mechanics and Methadone," 5; Fishman, "Ferry That Doesn't Move Helps Youth Get Ahead," *NYT*, Jan. 9, 1977, 206; Rybka to author, Nov. 14, 2006, email; Brink, telephone interview, Sept. 14, 2006.

NOTES TO CHAPTER 5

1. Marty Twersky, "South Street Seaport: The Best of Yesterday for Today," *NYT*, Jan. 28, 1973, 518; Report of the Graphics Committee, Dec. 1973, PSP.

2. "New Seaport Model," *SSR* 2 (July 1968): 4; "South Street Seaport—A Vital New Historic Center in Progress," *Re: Port* (Port Authority, Public Affairs Dept.), May 1971, 1; Bronson Binger to author, Mar. 7, 2008; Binger to Marie Lore, *Scuttlebut* 1 (Oct. 1974): 5; Landmarks Preservation Commission, "Proposed Brooklyn Bridge Southeast URA, Showing Construction Dates," May 1, 1968, South Street Seaport file, SFMNHP.

3. Charles Evans Hughes, "The Water Street That Was," *SSR* 6 (Summer 1972): 8–9; Robert Lifset, "Storm King Mountain and the Emergence of Modern American Environmentalism, 1962–1980" (Ph.D. dissertation, Columbia University, 2005), 409; Ada Louise Huxtable, "'Development' at the Seaport," *NYT*, Feb. 25, 1979, D31–D32; Paul Goldberger, "The Lesson of Peck Slip," *Seaport* 12 (Winter 1979): 8; "A Bit of Peck Slip Elegance, but It's All Trompe l'Oeil," *NYT*, Feb. 7, 1979, B3.

4. Richard Joseph, "South St. Seaport," *NYP*, Feb. 9, 1971; Ada Louise Huxtable, "Where Ghosts Can Be at Home," *NYT*, Apr. 7, 1968, D25; Huxtable, "Farewell Old New York," *NYT*, Nov. 18, 1973, 103–4; Peter Aron, telephone interview, Dec. 17, 2009; Terry Walton, "Art Around South Street," *SSR* 10 (Spring 1976): 3–5; Marie Lore to Karl Kortum, June 15, 1977, Kortum Collection, HDC 1084, Series 2:2, SFMNHP; Lewis Mumford, "Mother Jacobs' Home Remedies," *New Yorker*, Dec. 1, 1962, 158. For attitudes toward the

disheveled past, see David Lowenthal, *The Past Is a Foreign Country* (New York: Cambridge University Press, 1985); and Lowenthal, *Possessed by the Past: The Heritage Crusade and the Spoils of History* (New York: Free Press, 1996).

5. "Panel Two: A Lively Center for the City," agenda for 1968 planning conference, in Kortum Collection, HDC 1084, Series 2:8, File 1, SFMNHP.

6. Peter Stanford to unknown, second page of undated letter, Kortum Collection, HDC 1084, Series 2:8, File 2, SFMNHP; Stanford, "Digging into Our Unholy Past . . . Traffics and Discoveries," *SSR* 8 (Fall 1974): 8; Stanford, "One Man's View of the Emergence of New York's New Sea Museum," *Curator* 13, no. 4 (1970): 281; Peter and Norma Stanford, "South Street Besieged!," in "A Venture in South Street," ms. of book, 2007. For Mystic Seaport's self-described indoctrination program, see Edouard A. Stackpole, *Interpretation at Mystic Seaport* (Mystic, CT: Marine Historical Association, 1960).

7. Ellen F. Rosebrock and Faith Harris, "Who Cares about a Lot of Old Warehouses?," *SSR* 8 (Fall 1974): 3; Neville Thompson, review of *Counting-house Days in South Street*, by Ellen F. Rosebrock, *SSR* 8 (Winter 1974–75): 26; Rosebrock, *Counting-house Days in South Street: New York's Early Brick Seaport Buildings* (New York: SSSM, 1975), 8; Rosebrock, *Farewell to Old England: New York in Revolution* (New York: SSSM, 1976), 7–8.

8. Peter Stanford, *This Museum Is People* (New York: SSSM, 1973), 8; Joanna Dean, "The Sidewalk History Project," *SSR* 10 (Winter 1976–77): 10; Thomas Bender, review of *The Sidewalk History Portfolio*, by Susan S. Connor and Ellen F. Rosebrock, *SSR* 11 (Fall 1977): 22; "The Street of Ships," *Irving World* 2 (Mar.–Apr. 1970): 6. Sidewalk History relied on the research of Columbia University's Floyd M. Shumway, who went on to write *Seaport City: New York in 1776* (1975). For some contrast, see Ada Louise Huxtable, "Washington Never Slept Here," *NYT*, Mar. 25, 1973, 163–64; and Mike Wallace, "History Museums and the Prison of the Past," *Culturefront* 1 (May 1992): 29.

9. "From Manhattan to Mid-America—A 'Grass Roots' Bicentennial," *U.S. News & World Report*, Aug. 19, 1974, 65–66; "From Mr. Mahoney's Remarks," *SSR* 6 (Winter 1972–73): 1; "There Is to Be a Bicentennial," *SSR* 5 (Spring 1972): 8–9; Karal Ann Marling, *George Washington Slept Here: Colonial Revivals and American Culture, 1876–1986* (Cambridge: Harvard University Press, 1988), 381; Richard F. Shepard, "Tea-Party Observances Make a Splash Here," *NYT*, Apr. 23, 1974, 86; "NYC Tea Party Held," *SSR* 8 (Summer 1974): 12–13; David Rockefeller to the editor, "BiCentennial Distinction," *SSR* 6 (Winter 1972–73): 11; David Canright, "Farewell to Old England," *SSR* 10 (Spring 1976): 9.

10. John S. Martin Jr., Sentencing Memorandum, *United States v. Carmine Romano, et al.*, United States District Court, Southern District of New York, Jan. 4, 1981 (SS 81 Cr. 514 LPG); Peter Stanford to author, Feb. 12, 2007, email.

11. Ellen F. Rosebrock, *Walking Around in South Street: Discoveries in New York's Old Shipping District* (New York: SSSM, 1974); Rosebrock, *South Street: A Photographic Guide to New York City's Historic Seaport*, photographs by Edmund V. Gillon Jr. (New York: Dover, 1977); Lynne Waller, *South Street: The Story of the "Street of Ships" in Pictures and Words* (New York: SSSM, 1977), 3, 12, 16, 18.

12. Ellen F. Rosebrock, "211 Water Street," *SSR* 8 (Spring 1974): 17; Rosebrock, *Walking Around in South Street*, 14–17, 24–26; Waller, *South Street*, 14, 19; Barbaralee Diamonstein,

The Landmarks of New York (New York: Harry N. Abrams 1988), 110; Peter and Norma Stanford, "South Street Besieged!," in "A Venture in South Street"; Marshall B. Davidson, "New York City and the China Trade Years, 1784–1860," *Seaport* 14 (Summer 1980): 14; US Census Bureau, "Trade in Goods (Imports, Exports and Trade Balance) with China," http://www.census.gov/foreign-trade/balance/c5700.html#1985.

13. Ada Louise Huxtable, *Classic New York: Georgian Gentility to Greek Elegance* (Garden City, NY: Doubleday, 1964), 117; Rosebrock, *Walking Around in South Street*, 15; Rosebrock, *South Street*, 17, 20–21; Alvin Toffler, *Future Shock* (New York: Random House, 1970).

14. Stan Hugill, *Sailortown* (New York: Dutton, 1967), 157–67; Rosebrock, *Walking Around in South Street*, 4, 31–34; "The Captain Rose House," *Seaport* 34 (Spring 1999): 4–5; Daniel Czitrom, "The Wickedest Ward in New York," *Seaport* 20 (Winter 1986–87): 20, 26; Ellen Fletcher (Rosebrock), "Saved from the Wrecker's Ball," *Seaport* 17 (Summer 1983): 36–37. For the district's saloons, opium and cocaine dens, and prostitution, see Luc Sante, *Low Life: Lures and Snares of Old New York* (New York: Farrar, Straus & Giroux, 1991), 104–51, 177–93. In 1997, developer Frank Sciame, who later became Seaport chairman, purchased the Joseph Rose house for one dollar and transformed the building into four luxury apartments that were selling for over $1 million apiece in 2010 (" 'The Rat Pit' —Captain Joseph Rose House," *Daytonian in Manhattan* [blog], June 15, 2010, http://daytoninmanhattan.blogspot.com /2010/06/rat-pit-captain-joseph-rose-house.html).

15. David Streitfeld, "The Subjective Observer," *Newsday*, Aug. 27, 1992, sec. 2, 60; John Hightower to author, Oct. 23, 2010, email; Joseph Mitchell, "Old Mr. Flood," *Seaport* 21 (Summer 1987): 24–26; Phillip Lopate, *Waterfront: A Journey around Manhattan* (New York: Crown, 2004), 245, 255; "Panel Two: A Lively Center for the City."

16. Bronson Binger, "Project Report," *SSR* 8 (Winter 1974–75): 11; Barry Hesselson, "Presses Roll for T.V.," *Scuttlebut* 2 (Mar. 1975): 1; "South Street Notes," *SSR* 9 (Summer 1975): 15; Jakob Isbrandtsen, "The South Street Seaport Museum," *Historic Preservation* 21 (Oct.–Dec. 1969): 8; Alan D. Frazer, *North West Passage: The Manhattan on the Tides of History* (New York: SSSM, 1970), 15–20. Seaport trustee Melvin Conant was an associate of Henry Kissinger and an authority on the geopolitics of oil.

17. Norman Brouwer, "The Titanic Memorial Lighthouse," *Seaport* 18 (Fall 1984): 38; Francis James Duffy, "When Coal Was King," *Seaport* 24 (Fall 1990): 43.

18. "Fun Renewal," *Downtown Idea Exchange* 17 (May 15, 1970): 2; Howard Klein, "Fish Market Concert Flounders a Bit," *NYT*, June 30, 1967, 27; "Museum Programs," "1981 Annual Report," an insert in *Seaport* 16 (Fall 1982): 23.

19. X Seamens Institute, *Sings at South Street Seaport*, 33 rpm, vinyl (Smithsonian Folkways FTS-32418); "Sings Salty Sea Songs at South Street Seaport," *Public Employees Press* 12 (June 18, 1971): 11; Stanford to author, Nov. 17, 2006, email; "South Street Seaport: A Museum That Floats," *TV Guide*, Aug. 18, 1973, A25; "Ford to City: Drop Dead," *NYDN*, Oct. 30, 1975. Ford never uttered those exact words.

20. Norma Stanford, interview, May 11, 2006; Rhoda Amon, "Frank Braynard, 'OpSail' Originator, Dies at 91," *Newsday*, Dec. 13, 2007; Tom Buckley, "Electrified Spaghetti on Avant Garde Fete Menu," *NYT*, Oct. 29, 1972, 70; Annette Kuhn, "The Underwater Cellist:

'Push Her Further Down!,' " *Village Voice*, Nov. 2, 1972; Carman Moore, "The Avant-Garde in Dry Dock," *Village Voice*, Nov. 9, 1972.

21. "Autumn Fetes Tomorrow in Manhattan," *SIA*, Oct. 27, 1972; "South Street Seaport," handbill, n.d. [1973?], appendix in "Report of the Graphics Committee," Dec. 1973, SSSM (translation by Shao Xia Liu); Twersky, "South Street Seaport," 518.

22. "*Kaiulani*," *SSR* 1 (May 1967): 3; Karl Kortum to Abe Mellinkoff, Apr. 10, 1967, Kortum Collection, HDC 1084, Series 2:8, File 2, SFMNHP; Peter Stanford to William F. Buckley Jr., Apr. 3, 1973, ibid.; Stanford to Charles W. Wittholz, Aug. 10, 1971, ibid.; Stanford to author, Jan. 13, 2007, email; Minutes of an Exploratory Meeting Which Resulted in the Formation of the Council of American Maritime Museums, Jan. 8, 1973, PSP; Terry Walton, "CAMM'S First 25 Years: An Invitation on Millennium's Eve," *CAMM Gamming* (Spring–Summer 1999): Anniversary Insert, 1; Stanford, "The *Kaiulani*, Last of the Yankee Square-Riggers," *United States Naval Institute Proceedings* 100 (Mar. 1974): 73; Stanford, "President's Report," *SSR* 7 (Fall 1973): 9; Jakob Isbrandtsen, telephone interview, Mar. 7, 2008. The Sea Museums Council included museums in Honolulu, San Diego, San Francisco, Seattle, Newport News (VA), Philadelphia, New York, Cold Spring Harbor (NY), and St. Michael's (MD). Formed in 1974, CAMM grew to twenty-seven maritime museums and historic seaports by 1977 (Philip Karl Lundeberg, introduction to *First National Maritime Preservation Conference Proceedings* [Washington, DC: Preservation Press, 1977], 21).

23. Frank G. G. Carr, "Toward a World Ship Trust," *Sea History* 13 (Winter 1979): 22; John Corry, "Preserving a Nautical Heritage," *NYT*, Oct. 11, 1974, 18; Peter Stanford, *Take Good Care of Her, Mister . . . : Frank Carr and the Ship Trust Movement* (New York: NMHS, [1974]), 13; Karl Kortum to Sen. Edward M. Kennedy, Jan. 29, 1974, Kortum Correspondence, SSSM; Peter Stanford to Walter Schlech, Sept. 8, 1976, Kortum Collection, HDC 1084, Series 2:8, File 7, SFMNHP; Leon Schertler, "The Advisory Council and Federal Funds for Preservation," in *First National Maritime Preservation Conference Proceedings*, 63; William J. Murtagh, telephone interview, Aug. 27, 2008; "The Maritime Heritage Fund of 1979," *Sea History* 18 (Fall 1980): 14; Marcia L. Myers, *Maritime America: A Legacy at Risk* (Washington, DC: NTHP, 1988), 11, 13; James P. Delgado, "The National Register of Historic Places and Maritime Preservation," *APT Bulletin* 19, no. 1 (1987): 35.

24. Peter Stanford to Peter Manigault, July 8, 1971, Kortum Collection, HDC 1084, Series 2:8, File 1, SFMNHP; Stanford to Lance Lee, Oct. 23, 1978, ibid., File 7; S. 228, *Congressional Record*, 94th Cong., 1st sess. (1975), vol. 121, pt. 1, 692–93 (Murphy's bill was H.R. 8722); Waldo C. M. Johnston to Karl Kortum, Jan. 30, 1975, Kortum Collection, HDC 1084, Series 2:2, SFMNHP; Johnson to Members of CAMM, Sept. 10, 1975, ibid.; Harry Allendorfer, "Forging Ahead at Flank Speed," *Preservation News* 21 (Feb. 1981): 8.

25. Peter Stanford, interview, May 11, 2006; Frank Braynard, *The Tall Ships: Official Op Sail '76 Portfolio* (New York: Sabine, 1976), x–xii; Marilyn Hoffman, "Schooners Stretch Their Sails," *CSM*, Nov. 6, 1967, Family sec., 15; Peter Stanford, "Schooners at South Street," *Scuttlebut* 1 (Oct. 1974): 2.

26. "The Talk of the Town: Schooners," *New Yorker*, Oct. 21, 1985, 31–32; Norman Brouwer, "The Port of New York, 1860–1985: Recreation on New York's Waters," *Seaport* 23

(Summer 1989): 39; Brouwer, "Port Enthralled: New York Harbor as Theater," *Seaport* 25 (Summer 1991): 16–17.

27. "'Admiral' Behind Show," Frank Osborn Braynard," *NYT*, July 5, 1976, 18; Josef Konvitz, "Changing Concepts of the Sea, 1550–1950," *Terra Incognitae* 11 (1979): 1; Stanford to author, Aug. 18, 2008, email; Amon, "Frank Braynard."

28. Braynard, *Tall Ships: Official Op Sail '76 Portfolio*, n.p.; Braynard, *The Tall Ships of Today in Photographs* (New York: Dover, 1993), xiii–xiv; Dennis Hevesi, "Frank O. Braynard, Ship Maven, Dies at 91," *NYT*, Dec. 14, 2007, A39; Jack Miner, "Bicentennial: Sailing Out of History," *CSM*, Feb. 24, 1976, 12.

29. Walter Rybka to author, Aug. 20, 2008, email; Leslie Maitland, "Four-Master from Chile Is Called 'Torture Ship,'" *NYT*, June 20, 1976, 34.

30. Howard Slotnick, telephone interview, Sept. 9, 2008; Arnold H. Lubasch, "Four in Jewish Defense League Held in 2 U.N. Mission Attacks," *NYT*, Aug. 20, 1976, 34; James Ring Adams, "No Goodbyes Yet for the Tall Ships," *WSJ*, July 15, 1976, 16; Barclay Warburton, "Sail Training," in *First National Maritime Preservation Conference Proceedings*, 37; Mitchell L. Moss, "The Lost Waterfront of New York," *Coastal Zone Management Journal* 6, nos. 2–3 (1979); Richard Fewtrell to author, Aug. 13, 2009, email.

31. Karl Kortum to Peter Stanford, Oct. 2, 1970, Kortum Correspondence, SSSM; Stanford to Kortum, Oct. 14, 1970, Aug. 15, 1971, and undated draft copy (May 1972), SSSM; Board of Trustees, Minutes, May 10, 1972, Kortum Collection, HDC 1084, Series 2:8, File 1, SFMNHP; Stanford to author, June 21, 2007, email; "Friends Meeting Questions Ships, Seaport Organization," *SSR* 5 (May 1971): 9.

32. Barry Lewis and Virginia Dajani, "The South Street Seaport Museum," *Livable City* (Municipal Art Society) 8 (June 1981): 4; Peter Sanford to Karl Kortum, Mar. 6, 1973, SSSM; Twersky, "South Street Seaport," 518.

33. Christopher Lowery to author, Sept. 21, 2010, email; Aron, telephone interview, Dec. 17, 2009; Peter Stanford to author, July 24, 2008, email; Peter Stanford, interview, May 11, 2006; Richard Weinstein, telephone interview, Oct. 16, 2009; Isbrandtsen, telephone interview, Mar. 7, 2008.

34. Peter Stanford to Trustees, July 10, 1972, Kortum Collection, HDC 1084, Series 2:8, File 1, SFMNHP; Executive Committee, Minutes, May 8, 1972, ibid.; Stanford to Karl Kortum, Sept. 19, 1972, Bicentennial file, SSSM; Ann Satterthwaite, "Methods of Planning for Protection and Enhancement of Historic Waterfronts," in *Selected Papers: Conference on Conserving the Historic and Cultural Landscape, Denver, Colorado, May 2–3, 1975* (Washington, DC: Preservation Press, 1975), 21, 24; Lewis and Dajani, "South Street Seaport Museum," 4.

35. Isbrandtsen, telephone interview, Mar. 7, 2008; Kent Barwick, interview, June 24, 2008; Norma Stanford to Richard Buford, Apr. 4, 1975, PSP; Norma Stanford to author, Feb. 27, 2009, email.

36. Peter Aron to Norman Brouwer, Nov. 18, 2002, JACF; Aron, telephone interview, Dec. 17, 2009; Barwick, interview, June 24, 2008; Lewis and Dajani, "South Street Seaport Museum," 4; David Brink, telephone interview, Sept. 14, 2006; Peter Stanford, interview, May 11, 2006; Peter Stanford to author, Feb. 17, 2007; Norma Stanford to author, Feb. 27,

2009, email; Bronson Binger to author, Mar. 7, 2008, email; "Robert Thomas Bonham," *WP*, Jan. 1, 2012.

37. Philip Yenawine to author, Apr. 27, 2009, email; Norma Stanford to Yenawine, Sept. 30, 1974, PSP; Norma Stanford to author, Feb. 27, 2009, email; Marie Lore to [Robert] Bonham, in *Scuttlebut* 1 (Aug. 1974): 7. The populist newsletter was short-lived.

38. Dick Rath to [Melvin Conant], [June 1974], a copy in Peter Stanford to author, Oct. 25, 2006, email; Yenawine to author, Apr. 27, 2009, email; Jennifer Stanley to author, May 4, 2009, email; "A View on the Annual Meeting," *Scuttlebut* 1 (May 1974).

39. Peter Aron to Norman Brouwer, Nov. 18, 2002, JACF; Lewis and Dajani, "South Street Seaport Museum," 4; Weinstein, telephone interview, Oct. 16, 2009; Yenawine to author, Apr. 27, 2009, email.

40. Peter Stanford to Jakob Isbrandtsen, June 7, 1975, Trustees file, SSSM; Dick Rath to Isbrandtsen, June 20, 1975, ibid.

41. Peter Stanford to Jakob Isbrandtsen, Feb. 1, 1976, Kortum Collection, HDC 1084, Series 2:8, File 6, SFMNHP; Stanford to Kortum, Feb. 10, 1976, ibid.; Executive Committee, Minutes, Feb. 18, 1976, Trustees file, SSSM; Yenawine to author, Apr. 27, 2009, email.

42. Peter Stanford to author, July 24, 2008, email; Dick Sheridan, "Port of Missing Ships: Whatever Happened to the South Street Dream?," *NYSN*, Mar. 26, 1989, Magazine sec., 11; Pete Seeger to Andrea Anderson, Apr. 29, 2001, PSP; Seeger, telephone interview, Nov. 16, 2007.

43. *The Street of Ships*, prod. Charles Richards, 1983, 16 mm film, NYPL; Michael Creamer to author, Apr. 23, 2010, email; Aron, telephone interview, Dec. 17, 2009; Yenawine to author, Apr. 27, 2009, email; Thomas Gochberg, telephone interview, Apr. 28, 2010; Isbrandtsen, telephone interview, Mar. 7, 2008.

44. "Head of Seaport Museum Resigns in Policy Dispute," *NYT*, Mar. 2, 1976, 33; Richard F. Shepard, "Museum without Walls," *NYT*, Oct. 13, 1975, 44; Peter Stanford to Karl Kortum, Nov. 3, 1976, Apr. 23, 1979, Kortum Collection, HDC 1084, Series 2:8, File 7, SFMNHP; Yenawine to author, Apr. 27, 2009, email. Stanford's NMHS stayed in Brooklyn for six years until the city refused to renew its lease.

45. Executive Committee, Minutes, Aug. 17, 1976, JACF; David F. White, "Seaport Museum Forced to Reduce Staff," *NYT*, Sept. 1, 1976, 52; Rybka to author, Sept. 12, Nov. 11, 2006, email.

46. Executive Committee, Minutes, Nov. 30, 1976, JACF; Melvin Conant, "Comments on Goals, Priorities & Management Issues before the Trustees of South Street," Jan. 1, 1977, Trustees file, SSSM.

47. Ada Louise Huxtable, "Stumbling toward Tomorrow: The Decline and Fall of the New York Vision," *Dissent*, Fall 1987, 453–61; Yenawine to author, Apr. 27, 2009, email.

NOTES TO CHAPTER 6

1. Douglas Davis, "David and Goliath in Gotham," *Newsweek*, Aug. 15, 1983, 51; Christopher Lowery, "Report to the Membership," in *SSSM Annual Report, 1982–83* (New York: SSSM, 1984), 7; Wayne De La Roche, "Preserving without History," in *Historic Preservation: Forging a Discipline: Proceedings of a Symposium in Honor of James Marston Fitch*, ed.

Beth Sullebarger (New York: Preservation Alumni, 1989), 34 (the symposium was held Jan. 26, 1985).

2. Peter Stanford to Karl Kortum, Dec. 30, 1967, Kortum Collection, HDC 1084, Series 2:8, File 2, SFMNHP; Bronson Binger to author, Mar. 7, 2008, email; Binger, "Report from the Project Director: The South Street Plan," *SSR* 7 (Winter 1973–74): 14; Stanford, "East River Renaissance," *Sea History* 13 (Winter 1979): 17. See also Robin Winks, *Laurance S. Rockefeller: Catalyst for Conservation* (Washington, DC: Island Press, 1997), 78, 105, 186, 207.

3. Jonathan Barnett, *Urban Design as Public Policy: Practical Methods for Improving Cities* (New York: Architectural Record Books, 1974), 78; Barnett, "The Development Plan for South Street Seaport Museum," *SSR* 7 (Oct. 1973): 9–13; David R. Simmons to the editor, *SSR* 8 (Summer 1974): 2, 21; Bronson Binger, "Project Report: The Plan," *SSR* 8 (Spring 1974): 10–11; Binger, "Project Report," *SSR* 8 (Winter 1974–75): 11; Alison Isenberg, *Downtown America: A History of the Place and the People Who Made It* (Chicago: University of Chicago Press, 2004), 256.

4. "Visit the New Fulton Market," a trifold leaflet (New York: SSSM, c. 1975); William S. Kowinski, *The Malling of America: An Inside Look at the Great Consumer Paradise* (New York: William Morrow, 1985), 330–31; Thomas P. Dowd to the editor, *SSR* 8 (Winter 1974–75): 20; Ada Louise Huxtable, "A Delightful Walk Downtown," *NYT*, July 20, 1975, D23.

5. Ada Louise Huxtable, "Why You Always Win and Lose in Urban Renewal," *NYT*, Sept. 19, 1976, 106; Dick Ryan, "Countdown on Fulton Street," *NYSN*, Oct. 19, 1975; William W. Warner, "At the Fulton Market," *Atlantic Monthly* 236 (Nov. 1975): 64; Ann Satterthwaite, "Methods of Planning for Protection and Enhancement of Historic Waterfronts," in *Selected Papers: Conference on Conserving the Historic and Cultural Landscape, Denver, Colorado, May 2–3, 1975* (Washington, DC: Preservation Press, 1975), 21, 24.

6. Nina Roberts, "Raising Anchor," *NYT*, Dec. 12, 2004; Joe Doyle, "Sal Celona: 16 Hours Is a Normal Day," *Seaport* 23 (Winter–Spring 1990): 64; "Interview with Barbara Mensch," Columbia University Press website, http://cup.columbia.edu/static/Interview-mensch-barbara; Mensch, interview, Mar. 19, 2010; "South Street Notes," *SSR* 8 (Spring 1974): 21; "Fish Market," *SSR* 8 (Winter 1974–75): 13.

7. John Hightower to author, Oct. 23, 2010, email; Stanley Penn, "New York Fish Market Points Up a Pattern of Extortion and Fear," *WSJ*, Apr. 14, 1982, 1; Fred Siegel, with Harry Siegel, *The Prince of the City: Giuliani, New York, and the Genius of American Life* (San Francisco: Encounter Books, 2005), 169. The Romano group was also named the Committee to Preserve the Fulton Fish Market.

8. John S. Martin Jr., Sentencing Memorandum, *United States v. Carmine Romano, et al.*, United States District Court, Southern District of New York, Jan. 4, 1981 (SS 81 Cr. 514 LPG); Penn, "New York Fish Market," 16; Hightower to author, Oct. 23, 2010, email; Christopher Lowery to author, Sept. 21, 2010, email; Peter Stanford to author, Feb. 13, 2007, email; Thomas J. Maier, "Mob-Seaport Tie Alleged," *Newsday*, Aug. 30, 1988.

9. Peter Aron, telephone interview, Dec. 17, 2009; Douglas C. McGill, "In Search of Versatile Museum Leaders," *NYT*, Mar. 7, 1987, 11; Slotnick, telephone interview, Sept. 9, 2008.

10. James J. Farrell, *One Nation under Goods: Malls and the Seduction of American Shopping* (Washington, DC: Smithsonian Institution Press, 2003), 174; Jon C. Teaford, *The Rough Road to Renaissance: Urban Revitalization in America, 1940–1985* (Baltimore: Johns Hopkins University Press, 1990), 253–54; Peter H. Spectre, "The Issues of Maritime Preservation," *WB* 38 (Jan.–Feb. 1981): 37.

11. Tom Long, "Faneuil Hall's Designer Dies at 85 [*sic*]" (Thompson was actually eighty-four), *Boston Globe*, Aug. 19, 2002, B1; Jim Powell, *Risk, Ruin, and Riches: Inside the World of Big-Time Real Estate* (New York: Macmillan, 1986), 105; James W. Rouse to Richard Buford, Mar. 18, 1977, SSSM; Calvin Trillin, "Thoughts Brought On by Prolonged Exposure to Exposed Brick," *New Yorker*, Mar. 22, 1977, 107; Harmon Goldstone, "The Future of the Past," *Village Views* 4 (Summer 1987): 15. Finished in 1978, Faneuil Hall Marketplace is more popularly called Quincy Market.

12. Peter Aron to Norman Brouwer, Nov. 18, 2002, JACF; Grace Glueck, "Hightower Meets Museum Critics," *NYT*, Mar. 4, 1970, 38; Glueck, "Museum Rift Was Developing a Year," *NYT*, Jan. 10, 1972, 28; "John B(rantley) Hightower," *Current Biography* 31 (July 1970): 180–82; Aron, notes on hiring of John B. Hightower, Apr. 21, 1977, JACF; Paul Vitello, "John Hightower, Besieged Art Museum Director, Dies at 80," *NYT*, July 14, 2013, A22.

13. Stan Kulp, "Seaport in Hot Water with City," *Soundings*, Aug. 1978; Aron to Brouwer, Nov. 18, 2002, JACF; Aron, telephone interview, May 28, 2010; "Report to the Membership: Financial Development," *Annual Report, 1982–1983*, an insert in *Seaport* 18 (Fall 1984): 28.

14. Gregory F. Gilmartin, *Shaping the City: New York and the Municipal Art Society* (New York: Clarkson Potter, 1995), 404; City of New York, Planning Commission, "A Development Proposal for South Street Seaport," July 1977, 3, 9–10 (maps), in Printings file, 1977, SSSM; Jonathan Barnett, "Onward and Upward with the Art of Zoning," *New York Affairs* 6, no. 3 (1980): 7. See also Miriam Goldberg, *Branding New York: How a City in Crisis Was Sold to the World* (New York: Routledge, 2008), 19–39.

15. Whitney North Seymour Jr., telephone interview, Apr. 10, 2009; Aron, telephone interview, Dec. 17, 2009; Annette Kuhn, "Big Bucks for South Street," *Village Voice*, Nov. 7, 1977, 75; Lowery to author, Sept. 21, 2010, email; Karen Rothmyer, "Seaport the Focus of Push for Development," *NYT*, Feb. 12, 1978, R4; Challenge Grant Application, Jan. 1980, funded by NEH, in Operations file, SSSM; Hightower, "The President's Report," *SSR* 12 (Spring 1978): 6–7.

16. George Matteson to author, May 30, 2008, email; Rothmeyer, "Seaport the Focus," R4; Aron, telephone interview, Dec. 17, 2009.

17. Peter Stanford to Jakob Isbrandtsen, Feb. 1, 1976, Kortum Collection, HDC 1084, Series 2:8, File 6, SFMNHP; Bill Tuttle, "South Street Growth Plan Pains Ship Restorer," *Soundings*, Nov. 1979, A2; Peter H. Spectre, in "Preservation Forum," *WB* 41 (July–Aug. 1981): 40–41.

18. Richard Fewtrell to author, Mar. 18, 2009, email; Matteson to author, Feb. 11, 2010, email; Edward H. Fitzelle, "*Peking* & *Wavertree*," *Oceans*, May 1977, 7; Peter Aron to Larry Huntington et al., Sept. 5, 2006, Task Force 2006 file, JACF; Aron, telephone interview, Dec. 17, 2009.

19. Philip Levy to author, Nov. 17, 2010, email; Michael Creamer to author, June 2, 2010, email; Hightower to author, Oct. 23, 2010, email.

20. Hightower to author, Oct. 23, 2010, email; Stanford to author, Nov. 17, 2006, email; Fewtrell to author, Aug. 13, 2009, email; Walter Rybka to author, Sept. 12, 2006, email.

21. John Hightower to James Shepley, July 18, 1978, ExCom file, SSSM; Tuttle, "South Street Growth Plan," A2; Charles Deroko to author, Nov. 24, 25, 2009, Sept. 23, 2013, email; Kenneth D. Reynard, "Restoration of an Iron Star," in *International Congress of Maritime Museums: Third Conference Proceedings, 1978* (Mystic, CT: Mystic Seaport Museum, 1979), 18; Fewtrell to author, Apr. 20, 2009, email.

22. Richard Johnson and James Norman, "Seaport Museum in Rough Waters," *NYP*, Sept. 25, 1979; Aron, telephone interview, Dec. 17, 2009; Stanford to author, Nov. 17, 2006, email; Deroko to author, Mar. 3, 2010, email.

23. Lowery to author, Sept. 21, 2010, email; Kent Barwick, interview, June 24, 2008; "Christopher Lowery: New Vice President for Operations," *South Street Packet* 3 (Apr. 1978): 2; Hightower to author, Oct. 23, 2010, email; Peter Neill to author, Nov. 9, 2008, email.

24. Board of Trustees, Minutes, June 10, 1980, Oct. 14, 1981, Trustees file, SSSM; "Museum Development," in "1981 Annual Report," an insert in *Seaport* 16 (Fall 1982): 25; Jack Newfield and Paul Du Brul, *The Abuse of Power: The Permanent Government and the Fall of New York* (New York: Viking, 1977), 86; Michael Oreskes, "The Webs They Weave after Leaving City Hall," *NYT*, Mar. 9, 1986.

25. Peter Stanford to John Hightower, Feb. 27, 1978, Operations file, SSSM; Jeremiah Driscoll, interview transcript, Nov. 20 and Dec. 6, 1987, JBP; Neil Barsky, "A Casualty in the Wake of the Seaport's Rebirth," *Newsday*, Sept. 30, 1985; Norman Brouwer to author, Mar. 1, 2010, email; Decision and Partial Final Award, In the Matter of Arbitration between SSSM and Marine Ship Chadlery Co., Inc., et alia., Oct. 30, 1984, VISOSSSM; Aron, telephone interview, Dec. 18, 2009. *Robert Fulton* was later abandoned near the Baltimore Harbor Tunnel (Brouwer to author, Oct. 22, 2009, email).

26. John G. Waite, L. John Shank, Frederick D. Carvley, and Doris J. Manley, New York State Maritime Museum, draft report (New York: NYS Historic Trust, Jan. 1972), n.p., in Clippings File, SSSM; "Walter Lord," *Seaport* 26 (Winter 1992): 43; Giorgio Cavaglieri and A. D. Ateshoglou, *New York State Maritime Museum at the South Street Seaport and Renovation of Schermerhorn Row* (Albany: New York State Urban Development Corp., 1973), 9–15; Aaron M. Rennert to Board of Trustees, Nov. 9, 1973, SSSM; Marie Lore to Board of Trustees, Nov. 14, 1973, SSSM.

27. Leonard C. Rennie, *New York State Maritime Museum: Museum Consultant's Narrative Report* (Albany: New York State Office of Parks and Recreation, 1974), 5, 48; Clifford Lord, "N.Y.S. Maritime Museum," *SSR* 9 (Winter 1975–76): 14; John Bunker, "New York State to Launch Maritime Museum," *CSM*, Nov. 18, 1975, 13.

28. John Hightower to Orin Lehman, Sept. 8, 1978, Operations file, SSSM; Aron, telephone interview, Dec. 17, 2009.

29. Ada Louise Huxtable, "Albany's Threat to New York's Planning," *NYT*, May 20, 1968, 46; Hightower to author, Oct. 23, 2010, email; Aron, telephone interview, Dec. 17, 2009.

30. "Robert Rauschenberg," *Telegraph* (UK), May 13, 2008; Phillip Lopate, "Introduction:

The Fulton Fish Market," in *South Street*, by Barbara G. Mensch (New York: Columbia University Press, 2007), 32; Creamer to author, June 2, 2010, email.

31. John Young to author, July 28, 2008, email; Stanford to author, Sept. 1 and 4, 2006, email.

32. Barry Lewis and Virginia Dajani, "The South Street Seaport Museum," *Livable City* (Municipal Art Society) 8 (June 1981): 5–6; Orin Lehman to Robert McCullough, Sept. 27, 1977, Trustees file, SSSM; Miriam Friedlander to John Hightower, Dec. 8, 1977, ExCom file, SSSM.

33. "The State and the Seaport: Cultural Center or Two Headed Monster?," *Villager*, Oct. 12, 1978, 5; Creamer to author, June 2, 2010, email. See also Sharon Zukin, *Landscapes of Power from Detroit to Disney World* (Berkeley: University of California Press, 1991), 191–94.

34. Peter Freiberg, "Seaport Row Heats Up," *SoHo Weekly News*, n.d., in Clippings file, 1978, SSSM; Laurie Johnston, "Plan for South Street Market Leaves a Wake of Dissension," *NYT*, Nov. 28, 1979, B20; "South Street Community," a one-page broadside, n.d., in Clippings file, 1978, SSSM; John Hightower and Christopher Lowery to the Board of Trustees, Sept. 22, 1979, JACF.

35. "Will the Seaport Become Another Amusement Park?," *WMR*, Nov. 1979, cover; Paul M. Bray, "Urban Cultural Parks," *Planning News* 41, no. 5 (1977): 5; Rothmeyer, "Seaport the Focus," R4; Nicholas Dagen Bloom, *Merchant of Illusion: James Rouse, America's Salesman of the Businessman's Utopia* (Columbus: Ohio State University Press, 2004), 156–57; De La Roche, "Preserving without History," 37; Judy Mattivi Morley, *Historic Preservation and the Imagined West: Albuquerque, Denver, and Seattle* (Lawrence: University Press of Kansas, 2006), 91–126, 152. See also Alice Shorett and Murray Morgan, *Soul of the City: The Pike Place Public Market* (Seattle: University of Washington Press, 2007).

36. Peter Neill, "Why Supermall Is Superbad," *NYT*, Aug. 5, 1979, CN20; Roberta S. Friedman to the editor, *NYT*, Aug. 19, 1979, CN20.

37. Lowery to author, Sept. 21, 2010, email; Aron, telephone interview, Dec. 17, 2009; Wayne Hoffman, "Mickey & the Peep Show," *Nation*, Oct. 18, 1999, 30; Michael Hechtman, "Pact Signed for $210M Seaport Marketplace," *NYP*, Sept. 28, 1979; Stephanie Ball, "Seaport Tenants Kept from Merger Meeting," *WMR*, Feb. 1979, 6, 10.

38. Powell, *Risk, Ruin, and Riches*, 181–200; Nory Miller and Suzanne Stephens, in "Roundtable on Rouse," *Progressive Architecture*, July 1981, 100–101; Jane Thompson, "In Search of the 'Real City,'" *Space and Society* 7 (June 1984): 32; Ron Stepneski, "South Street Seaport Finds Its Future in Its Past," *Bergen (County, NJ) Record*, June 12, 1983; Richard Goldstein, "The Most Important Retail Project in America," *Village Voice*, Oct. 15, 1979.

39. Paul Goldberger, "The Lesson of Peck Slip," *Seaport* 12 (Winter 1979): 5, 7; Lewis and Dajani, "South Street Seaport Museum," 8.

40. John Hightower, "Report from the President," *Seaport* 13 (Fall 1979): 5; Hightower to author, Oct. 23, 2010, email; *The Street of Ships*, prod. Charles Richards, 1983, 16 mm film, NYPL; Sally Yerkovich, "Corporations, Museums, and Culture: An Unlikely Ménage à Trois," paper presented at the annual meeting of the American Studies Association, 1987; Sharon Zukin, *The Culture of Cities* (Cambridge, MA: Blackwell, 1995), 130–32.

41. "City and State Approve Rouse Plans for Seaport, Area Groups Skeptical," *WMR*, Nov.

1979, 14–16; WCBS, Channel 2, Editorial: "South Street Seaport," Dec. 20, 1979, 6:00 p.m.
news, in Clippings file, 1979, SSSM; Robert Fitch, *The Assassination of New York* (New
York: Verso, 1993), 29; Robert Atkinson, "Plans to Revamp New York City's Seaport
Get Mixed Reviews," *National Fisherman*, Jan. 1980, 51; Claudia Lorber, "The Seaport
Development Plan 1980," a supplement to *Seaport* 14 (Spring 1980), 26–33; Michael
Demarest, "He Digs Downtown," *Time*, Aug. 24, 1981, 42, 48; Teaford, *Rough Road to
Renaissance*, 273; "Harborplace," *Seaport* 14 (Fall 1980): 31; Goldstein, "Most Important
Retail Project."

NOTES TO CHAPTER 7

1. Ada Louise Huxtable, "'Development' at the Seaport," *NYT*, Feb. 25, 1979, D32; John
   Morris Dixon, in "Roundtable on Rouse," *Progressive Architecture*, July 1981, 100; Wolf
   Von Eckardt, "Reclaiming Our Waterfronts," in *Urban Open Spaces*, ed. Lisa Taylor (New
   York: Cooper-Hewitt Museum, 1979), 49; John Hightower, "The President's Report,"
   SSR 11 (Winter 1977–78): 6; Hightower to author, Oct. 23, 2010, email; Hightower to the
   editor, *NYT*, Mar. 11, 1979, D8; Hightower to the editor, *NYT*, Jan. 30, 1981, A26; Hightower to Stanford, Apr. 7, 1978, Operations file, SSSM. A historian credited Huxtable as
   "the undisputed champion" of the preservation movement (William Seale, "On Building's Past Pleasures," *WP*, Dec. 29, 1986, D3), but she believed that "a critic or reporter
   who becomes involved beyond the story crosses the line into advocacy and compromises his or her proper role" (Huxtable to author, Mar. 26, 2009, email). She wrote for
   the *Times* editorial board between 1973 and 1981 but without a byline. She most likely
   authored a critical editorial, "Selling the Seaport," *NYT*, Jan. 8, 1981, A22.
2. "City and State Approve Rouse Plans for Seaport, Area Groups Skeptical," *WMR*, Nov.
   1979, 16; Ada Louise Huxtable, "A Squint at South Street," *NYT*, Oct. 17, 1979, A26; Editorial: "Selling the Seaport," A22; William S. Kowinski, "A Mall Covers the Waterfront,"
   NYT, Dec. 13, 1981, SM27; Paul Goldberger, "Baltimore Marketplace: An Urban Success," *NYT*, Feb. 18, 1981, A18; Nicholas Dagen Bloom, *Merchant of Illusion: James Rouse,
   America's Salesman of the Businessman's Utopia* (Columbus: Ohio State University Press,
   2004), 158.
3. E. Blaine Cliver, in "A Tribute to James Marston Fitch (1909–2000)," *APT Bulletin* 31,
   nos. 2–3 (2000): 4; David W. Dunlap, "The Preservation Band That Sets the Tone," *NYT*,
   June 7, 1998, RE22.
4. Board of Trustees, Minutes, Feb. 11 and May 6, 1980, JACF; Carol Morgan to Stan Mack,
   July 10, 1981, in Correspondence, SSSM; James A. Glass, "The National Historic Preservation Act: A 40th Anniversary Appraisal," *Forum Journal* 21 (Fall 2006): 14; Patricia Leigh
   Brown, "Is South Street Seaport on the Right Tack?," *Historic Preservation* 33 (July–Aug.
   1981): 10–19. See also Thomas Bender, *Community and Social Change in America* (New
   Brunswick: Rutgers University Press, 1978), 146.
5. Barry Lewis and Virginia Dajani, "The South Street Seaport Museum," *Livable City*
   (Municipal Art Society) 8 (June 1981): 3, 7.
6. James DeFilippis, "From a Public Re-Creation to Private Recreation: The Transformation of Public Space in South Street Seaport," *Journal of Urban Affairs* 19, no. 4 (1997):

414; "Roundtable on Rouse," *Progressive Architecture*, July 1981, 103; Peter Stanford, "At Hearings in City Hall on November 13, 1980," *Seaport* 14 (Winter 1981): 25–26; Richard Goldstein, "The Most Important Retail Project in America," *Village Voice*, Oct. 15, 1979.

7. John Hightower, "From the President," *SSSM Annual Report, 1981* (New York: SSSM, 1982), 9–10; [Peter Aron], SSSM—Points for Discussion, Jan. 28, 1985, JACF.

8. John Hightower to Peter Stanford, Apr. 7, 1978, Operations file, SSSM; R. D. Wall, "Commentary," in *International Congress of Maritime Museums: Third Conference Proceedings, 1978* (Mystic, CT: Mystic Seaport Museum, 1979), 32–33; "CETA Jobs Program Spared Budget Cuts," *NYT*, Mar. 29, 1981, 44; "A Shining Example," *NYDN*, Apr. 3, 1981.

9. Chris Oliver, "Scandal Makes Waves at South St. Seaport," *NYP*, Apr. 8, 1981; Oliver, "Payroll Piracy Forces 'Em to Walk the Plank," *NYP*, June 16, 1981; George Matteson to author, May 7, 2008, email; "Our Maritime Heritage," *Preservation News* 18 (Dec. 1978): S2; David Brink, telephone interview, Sept. 14, 2006; Peter Stanford to author, Nov. 17, 2006, Oct. 24, 2007, email; Pete Seeger, telephone interview, Nov. 16, 2007; Marshall Berman, "Take It to the Streets," *Dissent* 33 (1986): 483; Jon Goss, "Disquiet on the Waterfront: Reflections on Nostalgia and Utopia in the Urban Archetypes of Festival Marketplaces," *Urban Geography* 17, no. 3 (1996): 231.

10. David Stonehill to the editor, *Seaport* 15 (Fall 1981): 42; Ward Morehouse III, "A Prince, a First Lady, and 1,300 Men in Blue," *CSM*, June 19, 1981, 3.

11. Peter Aron, telephone interview, Dec. 17, 2009; Jeremiah Driscoll, interview transcript, Nov. 20, 1987, JPB; William J. Murtagh, *Keeping Time: The History and Theory of Preservation in America* (Pittstown, NJ: Main Street, 1988), 46; Murtagh, telephone interview, Aug. 27, 2008; Hightower to author, Oct. 23, 2010, email.

12. Barbara G. Mensch, interview, Mar. 19, 2010; Christopher Lowery to author, Sept. 21, 2010, email; Neil Barsky, "Ominous Odor at Fulton Fish Market," *New York City Business*, Mar. 25, 1985; "City and State Approve Rouse Plans," 14; Deirdre Carmody, "Rejuvenated Seaport Is Due to Open July 28," *NYT*, July 15, 1983, B1, B3.

13. Kent Barwick, interview, June 24, 2008; Chris Oliver and Arthur Greenspan, "South Street Seaport Anchors Away!," *NYP*, July 28, 1983.

14. "Down to the Sea in Shops," *Architectural Record*, Jan. 1984, 102; Jan Hoffman, "South Street Seaport: A Restoration Comedy," *Village Voice*, Aug. 9, 1983, 8–10; P. Brown, "Is South Street Seaport on the Right Tack?," 19; Ron Stepneski, "South Street Seaport Finds Its Future in Its Past," *Bergen (County, NJ) Record*, June 12, 1983; Editorial: "New Seaport Poses Problems," *WMR*, Aug. 10, 1983, 8.

15. Ada Louise Huxtable, "Where Ghosts Can Be at Home," *NYT*, Apr. 7, 1968, D25; "History Sans Dictionary," *SSR* 5 (Mar. 1971): 2; Charles Evans Hughes, "The Water Street That Was," *SSR* 6 (Summer 1972): 9; Norman Brouwer, interview by C. A. Richards, May 23, [1979], typescript, SSSM; "Proposal for an East River Seaport," in Norma Stanford to Anita Ventura, Aug. 16, 1966, Kortum Collection, HDC 1084, Series 2:8, File 4, SFMNHP; Bronson Binger, "Project Report: The Plan," *SSR* 8 (Spring 1974): 11.

16. James Marston Fitch, preface to *Counting-house Days in South Street: New York's Early Brick Seaport Buildings*, by Ellen F. Rosebrock (New York: SSSM, 1975), 7; Fitch, *Historic*

Preservation: Curatorial Management of the Built World (New York: McGraw-Hill, 1982), 86–87; Ellen F. Rosebrock, Minutes of Restoration and Planning and Development Committees, Oct. 10, 1973, SSSM; David W. Dunlap, "James Marston Fitch, 90, Architect and Preservationist," *NYT*, Apr. 12, 2000, A29. Fitch claimed in his popular textbook that the Row should "have been restored to its original configuration; instead, an 1869 remodeling into a hotel will be preserved while the remainder of the block will be returned to a status c. 1840" (*Historic Preservation*, 86–87).

17. Matthew L. Wald, "Downtown Dig Sifts New York's Past," *NYT*, Aug. 19, 1977, B18; Joy Cook, "History & Histrionics on Fulton St.," *NYP*, Dec. 3, 1977; John T. Metzger, "The Failed Promise of a Festival Marketplace: South Street Seaport in Lower Manhattan," *Planning Perspectives* 16, no. 1 (2001): 42; Mark Lovewell, "Seaport Sets Sail for Rebirth," *NYP*, Feb. 14, 1978; Erin Drake Gray, "The Schermerhorn Row Block Preservation Project: It's Begun," *Seaport* 15 (Winter 1982): 10–17.

18. Paul Goldberger, "At Seaport, Old New York with a New Look," *NYT*, July 29, 1983, C17; Thomas Hine, "The Gilding of N.Y.C.," *Philadelphia Inquirer*, n.d., in Clippings file, 1983, SSSM; Jane Holtz Kay, "Rouse-ification of Lower Manhattan," *CSM*, Sept. 16, 1983, 9. See also John D. Stewart, ed., *The Schermerhorn Row Block: A Study in Nineteenth-Century Building Technology in New York City* (Waterford, NY: New York State Parks, Recreation and Historic Preservation, 1981), 1.

19. Kay, "Rouse-ification of Lower Manhattan," 9; Donald Canty, "New Meets Old in a Museum That Is a Neighborhood," *Architecture* 72 (Nov. 1983): 44; Joan Davidson, "Looking Back at South Street," *Seaport* 21 (Summer 1987): 14; "One Seaport Plaza," advertisement, *Seaport* 19 (Fall 1985): 41. See also Anthony M. Tung, *Preserving the World's Great Cities: The Destruction and Renewal of the Historic Metropolis* (New York: Clarkson Potter, 2001), 361.

20. John Hightower, "The President's Report," *SSR* 11 (Winter 1977–78): 6–7; Bronson Binger to author, Mar. 7, 2008, email; Peter Blake, "The Bogardus Heist," *New York* 7 (Aug. 5, 1974): 59; Ada Louise Huxtable, "The Case of the Stolen Landmarks," *NYT*, July 11, 1977, 18; James Marston Fitch, "The Case of the Purloined Building," *Architectural Record* (Jan. 1984): 117.

21. Goldberger, "At Seaport," C17; Wolf Von Eckardt, "South Street Seaport Opens," *Time*, Aug. 8, 1983, 68; Douglas Davis, "David and Goliath in Gotham," *Newsweek*, Aug. 15, 1983, 51 (the David was Battery Park City); Carmody, "Rejuvenated Seaport," B1, B3; David S. Bruce (pseudonym), "Our Nonvintage Ports: Snug (Smug?) Harbors," *NYT*, June 4, 1983, 23. In this context, *nostalgie de la boue* meant a bourgeois affection for the ruins of an older landscape and the romanticization of its more authentic culture, accompanied by a varying degree of dissatisfaction with the trappings of modernity (Tom Wolfe, *Radical Chic and Mau-Mauing the Flak Catchers* [New York: Farrar, Straus & Giroux, 1970], 32–33).

22. Barbara G. Mensch, "A South Street Story," in *South Street* (New York: Columbia University Press, 2007), 119; Hoffman, "South Street Seaport," 8–10.

23. Jonathan Yardley, "Muddling through the Urban Maze," *WP*, Aug. 19, 1984, BR 3, 14; Editorial: "New Seaport Poses Problems," *WMR*, Aug. 10, 1983, 8; Metzger, "Failed Promise

of a Festival Marketplace," 26, 40–41; Robert Fitch, *The Assassination of New York* (New York: Verso, 1993), 145; Margaret Stix, "The New South Street Seaport," *WMR*, Aug. 10, 1983, 7; Michael C. D. Macdonald, *America's Cities: A Report on the Myth of Urban Renaissance* (New York: Simon & Schuster, 1984), 332.

24. Peter Stanford, "A Restoration of Spirit Indeed!," *Sea History* 34 (Winter 1984–85): 8–9; Chip Brown, "The *Wavertree* at One Hundred," *Seaport* 20 (Spring 1986): 17; Aron, telephone interview, Dec. 17, 2009; Jakob Isbrandtsen to James Shepley et al., Nov. 15, 1982, JACF; Isbrandtsen, telephone interview, Mar. 7, 2008; Peter Neill to author, Sept. 23, 2009, email.

25. Maggie Lewis, "*Wavertree*: The Restoration of a Great Sailing Ship," *CSM*, May 5, 1983; "Report to the Membership: Ships, Buildings, and Collections," in "1981 Annual Report," an insert in *Seaport* 16 (Fall 1982): 20; Laurie Johnston, "At Seaport, a Restoration of Spirit," *NYT*, Oct. 16, 1981, B1–B2; Zdena Nemeckova, "Love on the Waterfront," *New Manhattan Review*, June 26, 1985: 14; Volunteer Proposals, in Susan Fowler to Peter Neill, June 4, 1985, VISOSSSM; C. Brown, "*Wavertree* at One Hundred," 19; Isbrandtsen, telephone interview, Mar. 7, 2008.

26. Lewis, "*Wavertree*"; Eric J. Sundberg, "Lending a Hand," *Seaport* 17 (Winter 1984): 6; Lowery to author, Sept. 21, 2010, email.

27. Peter Stanford to John Hightower, Feb. 27, 1978, Operations file, SSSM; David Lowenthal, *The Past Is a Foreign Country* (New York: Cambridge University Press, 1985); Lowenthal, *Possessed by the Past: The Heritage Crusade and the Spoils of History* (New York: Free Press, 1996); Robert Hewison, "Commerce and Culture," in *Enterprise and Heritage: Crosscurrents of National Culture*, ed. John Corner and Sylvia Harvey (New York: Routledge, 1991), 162–77; Hewison, *The Heritage Industry: Britain in a Climate of Decline* (London: Methuen, 1987). Along with actual heritage tourism, the scholarly study of the history of US heritage and its meaning skyrocketed in the 1990s and after. Any review should begin with Michael Kammen, *Mystic Chords of Memory: The Transformation of Tradition in American Culture* (New York: Knopf, 1991).

28. "How Others See Us," in Printings, 1975, SSSM; Emily Dennis, "Seminar on Neighborhood Museums," *Museum News*, Jan. 1970, 19; Stephen Canright, "The Black Man and the Sea," *SSR* 7 (Winter 1973–74): 5; Herbert Aptheker to the editor, *SSR* 8 (Spring 1974): 22; Pete Seeger to the editor, ibid. 22. For a more nuanced picture, see W. Jeffrey Bolster, *Black Jacks: African American Seamen in the Age of Sail* (Cambridge: Harvard University Press, 1997).

29. Peter Stanford to John Hightower, Feb. 27, 1978, and Hightower's reply, Apr. 7, 1978, Operations file, SSSM; Ellen F. Rosebrock to the editor, *Seaport* 13 (Spring 1979): 26; Dick Hoover to the editor, *Seaport* 13 (Summer 1979): 29.

30. Howard Thompson, "Vigorous Playing Buoys Waterfront 'Moby Dick,'" *NYT*, Aug. 14, 1974, 26; John Hightower, "Report from the President," *Seaport* 12 (Winter 1979): 3; "South Street Venture," *Seaport* 17 (Summer 1983): 48; Board of Trustees, Minutes, Mar. 17 and Dec. 15, 1982, Trustees file, SSSM.

31. "Down to the Sea in Shops," 102; Alice Rubinstein Gochman, "South Street Seaport," *Gourmet*, July 1985, 40; "South Street Venture," *Seaport* 17 (Summer 1983): 48; John

Hannigan, *Fantasy City: Pleasure and Profit in the Postmodern Metropolis* (New York: Routledge, 1998), 98.

32. Bill Reel, "Set Your Sails for South Street," *NYDN*, July 29, 1983; "South Street Venture," *Newsday*, Nov. 11, 1983; "Arts & Entertainment Guide," *NYT*, Mar. 27, 1987, 125; Richard Brandt to author, Aug. 11, 2006, email. For an advertisement, see "South Street Venture," *NYT*, Nov. 25, 1983, C16.

33. Linda Moss, "Trans-Lux's Reel after Reel of Trouble," *Crain's New York Business*, May 12, 1986, 3; Brandt to author, Aug. 11, 2006, email; Neill to author, Nov. 9, 2008, email; Sally Yerkovich to author, May 19, 2009, email; David Berson, review of *The Street of Ships*, *Seaport* 22 (Fall 1988): 47–48.

34. Ann Breen and Dick Rigby, "Festival Markets: Show-Stealers of the Waterfront," *EPA Journal* 14 (May 1988): 20; Kevin Walsh, *The Representation of the Past: Museums and Heritage in the Post-Modern World* (New York: Routledge, 1992), 143.

35. Lowery to author, Sept. 21, 2010, email; Lewis and Dajani, "South Street Seaport Museum," 11; Michael Sorkin, ed., *Variations on a Theme Park: The New American City and the End of Public Space* (New York: Hill and Wang, 1992); Sorkin to author, July 28, 2008, email; Neil Barsky, "Fishy Business at Pier 17," *New York City Business*, Mar. 11, 1985; "Seaport Cranks Up Plan B," *Crain's New York Business*, Mar. 1, 1985.

36. Lowery to author, Sept. 21, 2010, email; Joanne Lipman, "For a New Small Business in New York, Corruption Is One Obstacle to Success," *WSJ*, May 7, 1986, 22; Robert Guenther, "Construction Industry in New York Is a Hotbed of Extortion, Bribery," *WSJ*, May 7, 1986, 1; John S. Martin Jr., Sentencing Memorandum, *United States v. Carmine Romano et al.*, United States District Court, Southern District of New York, Jan. 4, 1981 (SS 81 Cr. 514 LPG).

37. Crystal Nix, "Pier 17 Opens at Seaport with Fanfare of Trumpets and Fireworks," *NYT*, Sept. 12, 1985, B3; "Seaport," *New Yorker*, Sept. 23, 1985, 28–29; John R. MacArthur, "Give Me Old-Time America without the Gloss," *WSJ*, Jan. 14, 1986, 1; Arnold M. Berke, "Pier Pressure," *Preservation News* 26 (June 1986): 3, 20.

38. Susan Doubilet, "Professor Preservation," *Historic Preservation* 44 (Nov.–Dec. 1992): 90; Jerilou Hammett and Kingsley Hammett, preface to *The Suburbanization of New York: Is the World's Greatest City Becoming Just Another Town?*, ed. Jerilou Hammett and Kingsley Hammett (New York: Princeton Architectural Press, 2007), 20; Kurt Andersen, "Americanizing the Singular City," *Architectural Digest* 45 (Nov. 1988): 78, 86–90; Susan LaRosa, "James Marston Fitch," *Seaport* 26 (Winter 1992): 50.

39. Enid Nemy, "Museum Benefit Is a Seaworthy Affair," *NYT*, May 25, 1978, C6; "Visiting the Seaport," *East Side Express*, Sept. 19, 1984; Jean Waller, "Ship Soiree Launches Perfume," *Soundings*, Dec. 1978, 11; Louise Sweeney, "Giving Perfume a Bad Name: Glamorizing of a Deadening Addiction Provokes Protest," *CSM*, May 15, 1979, B4–B5.

40. Lewis and Dajani, "South Street Seaport Museum," 13; Leslie Lindenauer, review of *The Last Waterfront: The People of South Street*, by Barbara Mensch, *Seaport* 19 (Summer 1985): 41–42; Matteson to author, May 30, 2008, email; William E. Geist, "An Old Salt Wonders Why People Pay $20 a Fish," *NYT*, Sept. 20, 1986, 30.

41. *New Yorker*, Apr. 30, 1984, cover; "South Street Seaport 1983 Marketing Program,"

Operations file, SSSM; Carmody, "Rejuvenated Seaport," B1, B3; "Visiting the Seaport"; William S. Kowinski, *The Malling of America: An Inside Look at the Great Consumer Paradise* (New York: William Morrow, 1985), 329, 333.

42. "At Seaport, Twilight of a Jazz Summer," *NYT*, Aug. 28, 1981, C24; Marc Kristal, "On the Waterfront: The Seaport in the Movies," *Seaport* 20 (Spring 1987): 22, 24.

43. Helen Hayes and Anita Loos, *Twice Over Lightly: New York Then and Now* (New York: Harcourt Brace Jovanovich, 1972), 30; Mensch, "South Street Story," 54; Thomas Walker to author, Sept. 30, 2009, email; Barwick, interview, June 24, 2008; "The South Street Seaport, a Sleepy Hollow Come Alive," *WP*, Feb. 12, 1984.

44. Ariel Kaminer, "Lower Manhattan," *NYT*, Mar. 17, 2006, F3; "Panel Two: A Lively Center for the City," agenda for 1968 planning conference, in Kortum Collection, HDC 1084, Series 2:08, File 1, SFMNHP; Chris Oliver, "Sordid Days on the High Sleaze," *NYP*, Oct. 23, 1985.

45. Carol Dix, "Yuppies Drop Anchor at Seaport," *NYP*, July 19, 1985; George Anders, "Wall Street's Boom Is Breaking Up the Old Gang in Hanover Square," *WSJ*, Apr. 11, 1986, 1; Yerkovich to author, May 19, 2009, email; Goss, "Disquiet on the Waterfront," 238; "Do You Know Us?," *NYT*, Sept. 19, 1986, C22; Patrick Reilly, "Port Museum Is Floundering in Sea of Debt," *Crain's New York Business*, Mar. 11, 1985; Neill to author, Jan. 23, 2009, email; Meg Cox, "Seaport Clears Deck for a Brighter Future," *WSJ*, Aug. 27, 1987, 31. While New Jersey changed its drinking age to twenty-one in 1983, New York changed from age eighteen to nineteen in 1982 and to twenty-one in 1985.

46. Ada Louise Huxtable, "Selling Out the South Street Seaport," in *Architecture Anyone?* (New York: Random House, 1986), 159 (revised in 1985, the essay was originally published in the *NYT* on Feb. 25, 1979); Goldstein, "Most Important Retail Project"; Board of Trustees, Minutes, Mar. 8 and Sept. 27, 1983, Trustees file, SSSM; J. Revell Carr, "Ship Preservation in the Cities of the United States," in *Proceedings of the 5th International Congress of Maritime Museums*, ed. Joachim Haarmann (Hamburg: Museum für Hamburgische Geschichte, 1985), 137.

47. Board of Trustees, Minutes, Sept. 19, 1984, JACF; Stanford to author, June 19, 2006; Meg Cox, "All at Sea: New York Museum's Problems Show Snares in Mixing Commerce, Culture," *WSJ*, Apr. 12, 1985.

48. Sally Yerkovich, review of *Sabotage*, by Alice Harron Orr (1986), *Seaport* 20 (Spring 1987): 38–39; Charles Deroko to author, Apr. 16, 2010, email; Peter Aron, SSSM—Points for Discussion, Jan. 28, 1985, JACF; Aron, South Street Seaport, Feb. 22, 1985, JACF.

49. Huxtable, *Architecture Anyone?*, xii; Peter Stanford to Christopher Lowery, Feb. 14, 1985, PSP; Sharon Churcher, "A Sea of Trouble for South Street's Museum," *New York*, Apr. 1, 1985, 11; Lowery to author, Sept. 21, 2010, email; Peter Stanford, "Report to the Ship's Company: What Happened in South Street?," unpublished editorial for *Sea History*, 1985, PSP; Stanford to author, June 22, 2006, email.

50. Hightower to author, Oct. 23, 29, 2010, email; Stanford to author, Aug. 12, 2009, email.

51. Norman Brouwer to author, Aug. 28, 2009, email; Stanford to author, Aug. 12, 2009, email; Lowery to author, Sept. 21, 2010, email; Donald Elliott to author, Mar. 27, 2009, email (in which he initially agreed to answer my questions but did not respond to my

subsequent email inquiries in 2009 and 2010); Board of Trustees, Minutes, Mar. 13, 1985, Trustees Meeting file, SSSM.

52. Susan Fowler, telephone interview, Aug. 12, 2009; Martin Gottlieb, "Trump Says He Wants to Build World's Tallest Tower at East River Site," *NYT*, July 31, 1984, B1, B3; Jim Powell, *Risk, Ruin, and Riches: Inside the World of Big-Time Real Estate* (New York: Macmillan, 1986), 277; Nemeckova, "Love on the Waterfront," 15; Sundberg, "Lending a Hand," 9; [Joseph Baiamonte], handwritten draft of statement, n.d. [Apr. 1985], VISOSSSM.

53. Board of Trustees, Minutes, Feb. 26, 1985, Trustees file, SSSM; Gerald Boardman, Notes on SSSM, Jan. 24, 1985, SSSM; Chris Oliver, "Seaport 'Skipper' Resigns," *NYP*, Feb. 27, 1985; Oliver, "Seaport Staffers Sacked," *NYP*, Mar. 5, 1985; Lowery to author, Sept. 21, 2010, email; Stanford to author, June 19, 22, 2006; Stanford to Edward I. Koch, Mar. 2, 1985, PSP; Peter Aron to Lawrence A. Silverstein, Mar. 14, 1985, JACF.

54. Board of Trustees, Minutes, Mar. 13, 1985, in Trustees file, SSSM; Stanford to author, June 19, 21, 22, 2006, Nov. 9, 2007, email; Peter Aron, Pledge, Mar. 13, 1985, JACF; Aron, telephone interview, Dec. 17, 2009; Aron to Norman Brouwer, Nov. 18, 2002, JACF; Cox, "All at Sea"; Joseph Halpern, "Commodore Takes Helm of Seaport Museum," *Greenwich (CT) Time*, Feb. 9, 1986.

55. Cox, "Seaport Clears Deck," 31; Cox, "All at Sea"; Churcher, "Sea of Trouble," 11; Deirdre Carmody, "Seaport Museum in Dispute on Goals," *NYT*, Apr. 1, 1985, B3.

NOTES TO CHAPTER 8

1. William Grimes, "As Museum and Mall, a Seaport Lives On," *NYT*, May 1, 1992, C6; Peter Neill, "The State of the Museum, 1986," *Seaport* 20 (Spring 1987): 8; Christopher Lowery to author, Sept. 21, 2010, email; Peter Aron to unknown, n.d., JACF; Aron, telephone interview, Dec. 17, 2009; Aron, South Street Search Committee Meeting with Peter Neill, Jan. 15, 1985, JACF; Douglas C. McGill, "In Search of Versatile Museum Leaders," *NYT*, Mar. 7, 1987, 11. Also on the search committee were Walter Lord, Pat Mosbacher, and Whitney North Seymour Jr.

2. Whitney North Seymour Jr., telephone interview, Apr. 10, 2009; Peter Neill, "A Saving Bit: Irving Johnson," *Seaport* 20 (Spring 1987): 6–7; Neill to the editor, "Why Supermall Is Superbad," *NYT*, Aug. 5, 1979, CN20; Joe Doyle, "Melvin Madison: Madison Men's Wear, 26 Eleventh Avenue," *Seaport* 20 (Winter 1986–87): 52. See also Catherine Lutz and Jane Lou Collins, *Reading National Geographic* (Chicago: University of Chicago Press, 1993); Alison Isenberg, *Downtown America: A History of the Place and the People Who Made It* (Chicago: University of Chicago Press, 2004), 272–83.

3. Marcia L. Myers, *Maritime America: A Legacy at Risk* (Washington, DC: NTHP, 1988), 35; Peter Neill to author, Nov. 8, 2008, email; David McKay Wilson, "The Sound Becomes a Classroom," *NYT*, June 17, 1984, CN11; Carl L. Nelson, "At the Helm with Peter Neill," *Historic Preservation* 36, no. 5 (1984): 64–68. See also Neill, "Lance Lee & His Icon Boats: The Personification of an Ethos," *WB* 209 (July–Aug. 2009): 66–75; Peter Dobkin Hall, *Inventing the Nonprofit Sector and Other Essays on Philanthropy, Voluntarism, and Nonprofit Organizations* (Baltimore: Johns Hopkins University

Press, 1992), particularly chap. 5: "Conflicting Managerial Cultures in Nonprofit Organizations."

4. Peter Neill, "We Must Draw the Circle Larger," *Sea History* 33 (Autumn 1984): 4; Neill, "A Past in Search of a Future," *WB* 62 (Jan.–Feb. 1985): 13–15; White Elephant Management, *Summary of Results of the Maritime Heritage Survey Conducted for the National Trust for Historic Preservation* (Galveston, TX: White Elephant Management, 1985), 21–22.

5. Neill, "A Past in Search of a Future," 13–15; Nelson, "At the Helm," 64–68; "Peter Neill Named President," SSSM press release, Apr. 23, 1985, SSSM; Ray Isle, "On the Waterfront: Peter Neill Runs the South Street Seaport Museum," *Stanford Magazine*, May–June 2004, 58; Michael Naab to author, Apr. 3, 2007, email.

6. Glenn Collins, "Living the Life of the Sea from a 5th-Floor Walk-up," *NYT*, Aug. 5, 2003, B2; Isle, "On the Waterfront," 58; Peter Stanford to author, Feb. 2, 2009, email; Peter Aron to Norman Brouwer, Nov. 18, 2002, JACF; Peter Neill, "Developing a National Cultural Policy for Maritime Preservation," *APT Bulletin* 19, no. 1 (1987): 24.

7. Neill to author, Nov. 9, 2008, email; Howard Slotnick, telephone interview, Sept. 9, 2008; Meg Cox, "Seaport Clears Deck for a Brighter Future," *WSJ*, Aug. 27, 1987, 31; David Berson, "Museum Chief Wants It All," *Soundings*, July 1986, B52; Lowery to author, Sept. 21, 2010, email.

8. Neill to author, Nov. 9, 2008, email; Andrea Houtkin, "Sail into the Last Century and Escape the City," *Crain's New York Business*, June 29, 1987, 9; George Matteson to author, Feb. 11, 2010, email.

9. Neill to author, Nov. 9, 2008, email; Houtkin, "Sail into the Last Century," 9; Matteson to author, Feb. 11, 2010, email; *SSSM Volunteer News* 1 [July 1985]: 1; Meeting Notes, July 20, 1985, and Executive Committee Notes, July 17, 1985, VISOSSSM; Susan Fowler to Membership, Sept. 9, 1985, VISOSSSM; Fowler to Mayor Ed Koch, Mar. 14, 1986, VISOSSSM; Fowler to Guy Molinari, Mar. 14, 1986, VISOSSSM; "Charting New Course for Maritime Museum," *Newsday*, Apr. 12, 1986, 11.

10. Wayne De La Roche to author, Jan. 24, 2007, email; De La Roche, "Preserving without History," in *Historic Preservation: Forging a Discipline: Proceedings of a Symposium in Honor of James Marston Fitch*, ed. Beth Sullebarger (New York: Preservation Alumni, 1989), 34 (the symposium was held Jan. 26, 1985). See also James J. Farrell, *One Nation under Goods: Malls and the Seduction of American Shopping* (Washington, DC: Smithsonian Institution Press, 2003).

11. De La Roche, "Preserving without History," 35; Suzanne Stephens, in "Roundtable on Rouse," *Progressive Architecture*, July 1981, 102; Jon C. Teaford, *The Rough Road to Renaissance: Urban Revitalization in America, 1940–1985* (Baltimore: Johns Hopkins University Press, 1990), 273–74; Thomas Bender, *New York Intellect: A History of Intellectual Life in New York City, from 1750 to the Beginnings of Our Own Time* (New York: Knopf, 1987), 341. See also Miriam Goldberg, *Branding New York: How a City in Crisis Was Sold to the World* (New York: Routledge, 2008), chap. 7: "Purging New York through I ♥ NY," 193–234.

12. De La Roche, "Preserving without History," 35; Barry Lewis and Virginia Dajani, "The South Street Seaport Museum," *Livable City* (Municipal Art Society) 8 (June 1981): 7;

Peter Neill, "Reflections on 20 Years—And Then Some," *Seaport* 21 (Summer 1987): 13; Berson, "Museum Chief," B52; Douglas Martin, "Margot Gayle, Urban Preservationist and Crusader with Style, Dies at 100," *NYT*, Sept. 30, 2008, B6; Richard Weinstein, telephone interview, Oct. 16, 2009; Allen Salkin, "Lower East Side Is under a Groove," *NYT*, June 3, 2007. In 2008, the National Trust placed the Lower East Side on its list of the eleven most endangered historic sites because of the rising property values resulting from gentrification. See also Neil Smith, "New City, New Frontier: The Lower East Side as Wild, Wild West," in *Variations on a Theme Park*, ed. Michael Sorkin (New York: Hill and Wang, 1992), 77; Smith, "Historic Preservation in a Neoliberal Age," *Housing Policy Debates* 9, no. 3 (1998): 479–85.

13. City of New York, Planning Commission, "A Development Proposal for South Street Seaport," July 1977, 9–10 (maps), in Printings file, 1977, SSSM; Kathy Larkin, "South Street Rebirth," *NYDN*, June 26, 1983.

14. Lowery to author, Sept. 21, 2010, email; Robert Fitch, *The Assassination of New York* (New York: Verso, 1993), xiii, xv; Neil Smith and James DeFilippis, "The Reassertion of Economics: 1990s Gentrification in the Lower East Side," *International Journal of Urban and Regional Research* 23 (Dec. 1999): 639; Bernard Stamler, "Rough Sailing for South Street Seaport," *NYT*, Mar. 29, 1998, CY12; Robert Guskind and Neal R. Pierce, "Faltering Festivals," *National Journal*, Sept. 17, 1988, 2307–11.

15. Historic Preservation Program, *Reviving Lower Manhattan: Preserving the Past to Ensure the Future* (New York: Columbia University, 1996), 35; Peter Neill, "The Cultural Power of Fish," *Seaport* 23 (Winter–Spring 1990): 6; Neill to author, Jan. 23, 2009, and Mar. 1, 2010, email; Gary Fagin to author, Mar. 5, 2010, email.

16. Neill to author, Nov. 9, 2008, email; Barbara Mensch, interview, Mar. 19, 2010; Selwyn Raab, "Fish Market's Problems Revert to New York City," *NYT*, Mar. 27, 1994, 1, 30; "Fish Market Fire a Critical Turning Point," *SCC Action Agenda* 2 (Spring 1995): 1–2. See also Michael Conn, "Final Years of the New York Fisheries," *Seaport* 23 (Winter–Spring 1990): 35; John Waldman, *Heartbeats in the Muck: The History, Sea Life, and Environment of New York Harbor* (New York: Lyons, 1999), 67. Fishport later became a New York Police Department dumping ground for towed cars.

17. Peter Neill, "A Place for Teaching and Learning," *Seaport* 20 (Summer 1986): 10; Neill to author, Nov. 9, 2008, email; AAM, *Museums for a New Century: A Report* (Washington, DC: AAM, 1984), 112; Joe Doyle to author, July 26, 2009, email.

18. John T. Metzger, "The Failed Promise of a Festival Marketplace: South Street Seaport in Lower Manhattan," *Planning Perspectives* 16, no. 1 (2001): 42; Board of Trustees, Minutes, Apr. 21, 1987, JACF; Aron, telephone interview, Dec. 17, 2009; Minda Zeitin, "Rouse Formula Serves Seaport Retailers Well," *Crain's New York Business*, Apr. 27, 1987, 14; Peter and Norma Stanford, Dec. 31, 1973, "Timeline," in "A Venture in South Street," ms. of book, 2007; "Coalition Defends Pier 16 Open Space Encroachment," *SCC Action Agenda* 2 (Spring 1995): 2.

19. Peter H. Spectre, "On the Waterfront," *WB* 89 (July–Aug. 1989): 27; M. Christine Boyer, *The City of Collective Memory: Its Historical Imagery and Architectural Entertainments* (Cambridge: MIT Press, 1994): 438–39; Richard Handler and Eric Gable, *The New*

History in an Old Museum: Creating the Past at Colonial Williamsburg (Durham: Duke University Press, 1997).

20. Bernard J. Frieden and Lynne B. Sagalyn, *Downtown, Inc.: How America Rebuilds Cities* (Cambridge: MIT Press, 1990), 312; Zeitin, "Rouse Formula," 14; Clara Hemphill, "Seaport Is Tops in New Yorkers' Plans," *Newsday*, Oct. 28, 1988, 25; Board of Trustees, Minutes, Nov. 1, 1988, JACF; Peter Grant, "A Watertight Seaport Deal," *Crain's New York Business*, Jan. 9, 1989, 1.

21. Jere Hester, "Lost at Seaport," *DE*, Feb. 13, 1991; Hester, "Malls Who've Been Misunderstood," *DE*, June 12, 1991; Michael McAuliff, "Abandoning Ships," *DE*, July 19, 1993; Myers, *Maritime America*, 28; Joelle Attinger, "The Decline of New York," *Time* 136 (Sept. 17, 1990): 36; William Grimes, "Seaport Museum Reduces Operation," *NYT*, Aug. 9, 1994, C13, C16; Neill to author, Mar. 2, 2010, email.

22. Hester, "Lost at Seaport"; McAuliff, "Abandoning Ships"; Stamler, "Rough Sailing," CY12–CY13; Douglas Martin, "South Street Seaport: Just Another Mall?," *NYT*, Oct. 17, 1993, CY4; "Warner Bros. in the Seaport?," *SCC Action Agenda* 2 (Spring 1995): 3; Stephen Kloepfer to author, Nov. 12, 2010, email; Kloepfer to Michael Carey et al., Aug. 24, 1999, JACF. See also Margaret Crawford, "The World in a Shopping Mall," in Sorkin, *Variations on a Theme Park*, 3–30.

23. Hester, "Lost at Seaport"; Peter Aron to Joseph E. Ochs, May 6, 1994, JACF; Melanie Warner, "Takeout Real Estate," *Crain's New York Business*, Oct. 16, 1995, 36; Sharon Zukin, *Landscapes of Power from Detroit to Disney World* (Berkeley: University of California Press, 1991), 51; Nicholas Dagen Bloom, *Merchant of Illusion: James Rouse, America's Salesman of the Businessman's Utopia* (Columbus: Ohio State University Press, 2004), 151; Joan Lebow, "Nature Specialty Chain Appreciates Greenery," *Crain's New York Business*, Sept. 21, 1987, 14. See also Michael Sorkin, "The Great Mall of New York," in *Suburbanization of New York: Is the World's Greatest City Becoming Just Another Town?*, ed. Jerilou Hammett and Kingsley Hammett (New York: Princeton Architectural Press, 2007), 113–27.

24. Neill to author, Nov. 9, 2008, email; Jakob Isbrandtsen, telephone interview, Mar. 7, 2008; Joe Doyle, "George the Waiter: Twenty Years at Sloppy Louie's," *Seaport* 20 (Spring 1986): 48; James DeFilippis, "From a Public Re-Creation to Private Recreation: The Transformation of Public Space in South Street Seaport," *Journal of Urban Affairs* 19, no. 4 (1997): 411.

25. Joanna Molloy, "The Case of the Hanging Boats," *Battery News*, Oct. 10, 1988; Neill to author, Feb. 8, 2010, email; Jakob Isbrandtsen, "Memo for the Files," Jan. 26, 1998, in Peter Aron to Isbrandtsen, Jan. 29, 1998, JACF; Michael Kimmelman, "What Price Love? Museums Sell Out," *NYT*, July 17, 2005.

26. Richard F. Shepard, "Summer of Music Anchors at Seaport," *NYT*, May 30, 1980, C20; Martin, "South Street Seaport," CY4; Douglas Martin, "Urban Pirate Is Sailing East with His Loot," *NYT*, Dec. 18, 1998, B17; Warner, "Takeout Real Estate," 36; Stamler, "Rough Sailing," CY12–CY13.

27. Stephen Kloepfer to Michael Carey et al., Aug. 24, 1999, JACF; Kloepfer to author, Nov. 12, 2010, email.

28. Jim Sleeper, "Boodling, Bigotry, and Cosmopolitanism: The Transformation of a Civic

Culture," *Dissent* 34 (Fall 1987): 413; Smith, "New City, New Frontier," 61, 66–67, 90; Lucy W. Lippard, "Seven Stops in Lower Manhattan: A Geographic Memoir," in Hammett and Hammett, *Suburbanization of New York*, 82; Jason Hackworth, *The Neoliberal City: Governance, Ideology, and Development in American Urbanism* (Ithaca: Cornell University Press, 2007), 121.

29. Fagin to author, Mar. 5, 2010, email; Dan Barry, "A Last Whiff of Fulton's Fish, Bringing a Tear," *NYT*, July 10, 2005; Barry, "Death of a Fulton Fish Market Fixture," *NYT*, Oct. 15, 2010, MB1; Neill to author, Nov. 9, 2008, email. Winning five Oscars, *The French Connection* (1971, dir. William Friedkin) pictured the real grit of Water and Dover Streets and Peck Slip, but it excised the nighttime fishmongers and inserted a gang of teens playing street hockey. Fish Market Annie was also known as South Street Annie or Shopping Bag Annie.

30. Anthony M. Tung, *Preserving the World's Great Cities: The Destruction and Renewal of the Historic Metropolis* (New York: Clarkson Potter, 2001), 351–62; "Seaport in a Storm," *NYT*, Jan. 12, 1987, A26; Fagin to author, Mar. 5, 2010, email; David W. Dunlap, "Seaport May Regain Block City Excised," *NYT*, Dec. 20, 1987, R2. Of the original 1.4 million square feet of air rights, some nine hundred thousand had already been transferred; the remaining were restricted to the district (Dunlap, "Seaport May Regain," R2).

31. Mitchell Moss, "The Long and Short of Developers' Plan," *Newsday*, Jan. 9, 1990, 27; Fagin to author, Mar. 5, 2010, email; Lowery to author, Sept. 21, 2010, email; David W. Dunlap, "Seaport Project Again Opposed by Its Neighbors," *NYT*, Mar. 1, 1989, B3.

32. MAS, *Zoning and Historic Districts* (New York: Abeles, Phillips, Preiss & Shapiro, 1990); Alan S. Oser, "Controlling Scale Near Historic Districts," *NYT*, Oct. 28, 1990, R7; Nick Ravo, "Crusader for New York City Landmarks Moves On," *NYT*, July 16, 1995, RNJ7; Amy Feldman, "Real Estate Watch," *Crain's New York Business*, July 15, 1996, 11; Bernard Stamler, "Latest Plan Joined by Counterplan in Landmarks Fight at 250 Water St.," *NYT*, June 8, 1997, CY9; Fagin to author, Mar. 5, 2010, email; Lowery to author, Sept. 21, 2010, email.

33. Hope Cooke, *Seeing New York: History Walks for Armchair and Footloose Travelers* (Philadelphia: Temple University Press, 1995), 45; Richard F. Shepard, "Ahoy, Mates, the Institute's Back at the Seaport," *NYT*, May 6, 1991; Jotham Sederstrom, "Seamen's Institute to Sell Its Building and Leave Manhattan," *NYT*, Oct. 6, 2010, B6.

34. Constance L. Hays, "Restoration Encounters Head Winds," *NYT*, July 22, 1990, 25; McAuliff, "Abandoning Ships"; Laura L. Castro and Paul Marinaccio, "Port Authority Talks Link Fulton Market with Fishport," *Newsday*, Aug. 26, 1988, 51; Attachment A, Dec. 31, 1995, JACF.

35. "New York's Fulton Fish Marker Suffers Partial Collapse in Fire," *JoC*, Mar. 30, 1995, 12A; Selwyn Raab, "For Half Century, Tradition Has Foiled Attempts to Clean Up Fulton Fish Market," *NYT*, Apr. 1, 1995, 22; Fred Siegel, with Harry Siegel, *The Prince of the City: Giuliani, New York, and the Genius of American Life* (San Francisco: Encounter Books, 2005), 169–70; Phillip Lopate, *Waterfront: A Journey around Manhattan* (New York: Crown, 2004), 236.

36. Attachment A, Dec. 31, 1995, JACF; "EDC Moves to Enforce Lease on Historic

Buildings," *SCC Action Agenda* 2 (Spring 1995): 1, 3; Selwyn Raab, "New Fulton Market Lease Includes Big Rent Increase," *NYT*, May 4, 1995, B3; Board of Trustees, Minutes, Sept. 30, 1997, Dec. 1, 1998, JACF; Stanford to author, Sept. 6, 2006, email.

37. Carleste Hughes, "Fulton Move Hits Snag: Fishmongers Say City Never Struck a Deal," *Newsday*, Feb. 15, 2001, A3; Hester, "Malls Who've Been Misunderstood."

NOTES TO CHAPTER 9

1. Peter Stanford, *This Museum Is People* (New York: SSSM, 1973), 8; Philip Yenawine to author, Apr. 27, 2009, email; Paul Goldberger, "Touring Little Old New York," *NYT*, July 2, 1976, 62. André Malraux coined the phrase "museum without walls" about an excess of images without historical contexts, but the phrase's meaning shifted dramatically as writers adapted it to real-life experiences, as in Richard F. Shepard, "Museum without Walls," *NYT*, Oct. 13, 1975, 44. The international museum community later embraced the concept (Stephen E. Weill, "From Being *about* Something to Being *for* Somebody: The Ongoing Transformation of the American Museum," *Daedalus* 128 [Summer 1999]: 236).

2. Peter Aron, "South Street Seaport Museum," Apr. 16, 1985, JACF; Aron, telephone interview, Dec. 17, 2009; Peter Neill, "A Museum like No Other," *Seaport* 19 (Fall 1985): 4; Neill, "The State of the Museum, 1986," *Seaport* 20 (Spring 1987): 9.

3. Neill, "Museum like No Other," 5–7; Neill, "Master Plan: 1985–1990," draft, Aug. 1985, SSSM; "Volunteer Proposals," in Susan Fowler to Neill, June 4, 1985, VISOSSSM; A. H. Saxon, "P. T. Barnum's American Museum," *Seaport* 20 (Winter 1986–87): 28–29, 33. As of 2014, the plans for the seamen's hotel had not been implemented.

4. Editorial: "Not Yet a Nautical Museum," *NYT*, Dec. 28, 1985, 22; Editorial: "Expanding South Street Seaport," *Newsday*, Jan. 2, 1986.

5. Maureen Dowd, "Pigeons, Elvises, Immigrants: Staging Patriotism for the 4th," *NYT*, June 24, 1986, A1; Joseph McLellan and Lloyd Grove, "Liberty's Hot Finale," *WP*, July 7, 1986, A1; Cass Peterson, "Celebrating Liberty Weekend in Manhattan Not for Claus- trophobics," *WP*, July 5, 1986, A10; Carl L. Nelson, "OpSail '86," *Preservation News* 26 (June 1986): 3. See also Mike Wallace, "Boat People: Immigration History at the Statue of Liberty and Ellis Island," in *Mickey Mouse History* (Philadelphia: Temple University Press, 1996), 57.

6. "Stars of the Harbor: A Roster," *NYT*, June 29, 1986, A39. The definition of "tall ships" varies, but it generally includes Class A and B ships. Class C vessels were included in the 1986 parade, but berthed at Liberty State Park in New Jersey.

7. "The Interloper at Liberty's Party," *NYT*, June 9, 1986, A22; Steven V. Roberts, "Festival Group Is Urged to Bar 'Notorious' Ship," *NYT*, June 14, 1986, 30; Howard Slotnick, telephone interview, Sept. 9, 2008; Peter Stanford to the editor, "Let *Esmeralda* Sail in Liberty's Flotilla," *NYT*, June 18, 1986, A34; Stanford to author, Aug. 18, 2008, email; Virginia M. Bouvier to the editor, "Chilean Torture Ships Mocks Liberty Gala," *NYT*, June 30, 1986, A18; Norma Stanford to author, Aug. 19, 2008, email; Walter Rybka to author, Aug. 20, 2008, email; David Berson, "TV Anchor Pulled by Tall Ships," [*Sound- ings?*], n.d., in Clippings file, 1986, SSSM.

8. Ward Morehouse III, "Developers for Ellis Island," *CSM*, Jan. 14, 1982, 6; Howard Fast,

"The World within a Nation," *Seaport* 20 (Summer 1986): 20–21; Mario Cuomo, "Message from the Governor: Preserving Our Heritage," *Seaport* 21 (Summer 1987): 8; Mike Wallace, "The Politics of Public History," in *Past Meets Present*, ed. Jo Blatti (Washington, DC: Smithsonian Institution Press, 1987), 49.

9. Neill to author, June 3, 2009, email.

10. Deirdre Carmody, "Norwegian Tall Ship Arrives and Op Sail Begins," *NYT*, June 26, 1986, B2; "Counties in the USA with More than One Percent Norwegian Ancestry," *Sogn og Fjordane Emigration*, http://www.emigration.no/sff/emigration3.nsf/o/A3DFE3958 F4DD8F9C1256F460045FC0C?OpenDocument; Joe Doyle, "Daniel Fjelldall of Bay Ridge," *Seaport* 20 (Summer 1986): 60.

11. Neill, "State of the Museum, 1986," 9; Neill, "Small Boats," *Seaport* 22 (Summer 1988): 9, 10; Marvine Howe and Alexander Reid, "Norse Restake Claim," *NYT*, Sept. 27, 1986, 1, 35; Paul Bisberg, "New Museum President Forecasts Expansion, Restoration," *Soundings*, July 1985, sec. 2, 12–13.

12. Peter Neill, "Connections," *Seaport* 19 (Winter 1986): 6; "Exhibition: Dogwatch and Liberty Days," *SSSM Volunteer News* 3 (Aug. 24, 1985): 3; "Progress in Pictures," *Seaport* 19 (Winter 1986): 9; "Do You Know Us?," *NYT*, Sept. 19, 1986, C22.

13. Stuart E. Jones, "Here's New York Harbor," *National Geographic*, Dec. 1954, 808; "At Joe Dirsa's Bar," *SSR* 6 (Summer 1972): 8 (photo); Walter Ritter, "Marine Art," *SSR* 8 (Spring 1974): 9; Erin Urban, *John A. Noble: The Rowboat Drawings* (New York: John A. Noble Collection and SSSM, 1988), 7–10; Urban, "John A. Noble: *The Rowboat Drawings*," *Seaport* 23 (Summer 1989): 8; Urban to author, Apr. 20, 2007, email; Neill, "Connections," 7; Jim O'Grady, "Paying Proper Tribute to the Burly Guy on the Far Stool," *NYT*, Apr. 21, 2002, CY7; Howard W. Serig Jr., "Derelict Ships: Treasure or Eyesore?," *NYT*, Sept. 15, 1985; "New Home for Maritime Art," *NYT*, Oct. 29, 2000, CY19.

14. Jacqueline Trescott, "Exhibiting a New Enthusiasm: Across U.S., Museum Construction, Attendance Are on the Rise," *WP*, June 21, 1998, A1; Peter Neill, "A Place for Teaching and Learning," *Seaport* 20 (Summer 1986): 10; Neill, "The Whole Museum," *Seaport* 24 (Summer 1990): 6; Catherine M. Lewis, *The Changing Face of Public History: The Chicago Historical Society and the Transformation of an American Museum* (DeKalb: Northern Illinois University Press, 2005), 22; Gerald Boardman, Notes on SSSM, Sept. 20, 1985, SSSM.

15. Norman Brouwer, "The Port of New York, 1860–1985: The Passenger Liner Era," *Seaport* 22 (Fall 1988): 36; Neill, "Place for Teaching and Learning," 10, 12; Anindita Dasgupta, "Museum Acquires Thousands of Ocean Liner Artifacts," *DE*, Aug. 18, 2006; Lawrence S. Huntington and Paula M. Mayo, presentation to the New York City Economic Development Corporation, Oct. 18, 2006, JACF; Alisha Berger, "Bidder $weet," *NYP*, June 11, 2004, 23.

16. "$2.2 Million Trustee Challenge Met," *Beacon*, Spring 1987, 1; William Goscener Jr., "The State of the Museum, 1986: An Alternative View," in Operations file, SSSM; Meg Cox, "Seaport Clears Deck for a Brighter Future," *WSJ*, Aug. 27, 1987, 31; James Defilippis, "From a Public Re-Creation to Private Recreation: The Transformation of Public Space in South Street Seaport," *Journal of Urban Affairs* 19, no. 4 (1997): 411; Sally Yerkovich to author, May 19, 2009, email; SSSM, "Long-Range Interpretive Plan," Jan. 1989,

Yerkovich personal files. The consultants also included Candace Matelic, director of the Cooperstown Graduate Program; Ronald Grele, director of Columbia University's Oral History Research Office; Richard Lieberman, director of the Fiorello La Guardia Archives; and John Kuo Wei Tchen, associate director of the Asian/American Center at Queens College.

17. Steven Jaffe to author, Jan. 27, 2009, email; Wallace, "Politics of Public History," 52; Peter Neill, "History, by, and for, the People," *Seaport* 21 (Spring 1988): 6; Dena Kleiman, "Behind Inflated Attendance Figures," *NYT*, Feb. 21, 1987. The 425,000 included those who came for exhibits, excursions, school functions, Elderhostels, and crafts programs.

18. Peter Matthiessen, *Men's Lives: The Surfmen and Baymen of the South Fork* (New York: Random House, 1986), 4. See also Michael Conn, "Final Years of the New York Fisheries," *Seaport* 23 (Winter–Spring 1990): 35.

19. Kathleen Condon, "Men, Models, and Memory," *Seaport* 26 (Winter 1992): 16–17; Catherine Comar Quintana, "Legacy of the Clipper *Hornet*," ibid., 44–45.

20. Sarah Boxer, "The Great Seamen's Fleet: A Failed Bank's Maritime Collection Faced Disruption," *Sports Illustrated*, Dec. 17, 1990; Neill to author, Jan. 8, 9, 2009, email; Neill to Board of Trustees, Aug. 20, 1990, in Board of Trustees, Minutes, JACF; Board of Trustees, Minutes, Sept. 11, 1990, JACF.

21. Boxer, "Great Seamen's Fleet"; James Barron, "Museum and a Collector Vie for the Treasures of the Seas," *NYT*, Mar. 25, 1991; A. J. Peluso Jr., "Collector Sues FDIC," *Maine Antique Digest*, May 1991, 6C; *Thomas H. Gosnell v. FDIC and South Street Seaport Museum*, U.S. Court of Appeals, Second Circuit, 938 F.2d 372, 1991, http://cases.justia .com; Peter Neill to Prescott S. Bush Jr., Nov. 12, 1990, JACF; Neill to author, Jan. 8, 2009, email; Jere Hester, "Seaport Hauls in Maritime Collection," *DE*, Nov. 21, 1990.

22. Richard B. Grassby, *Ship, Sea and Sky: The Marine Art of James Edward Buttersworth* (New York: SSSM in association with Rizzoli International, 1994); Grassby, "The Marine Paintings of James Edward Buttersworth," *Magazine Antiques* 146 (July 1994): 62–69; Alan Cameron, "A Rewarding Volume for Historians and Art Lovers," *Lloyd's List*, Sept. 17, 1994, 5; Nick Karas, "Romancing Sailing's Past," *Newsday*, Apr. 17, 1994, Sports sec., 24; Peter Neill, "A Year of Triumphs and Tough Choices," *Seaport* 28 (Fall 1994): 2.

23. Michael A. Jehle, "Captain James Cary and Nantucket's China Trade," *Magazine Antiques* 146 (July 1994): 75.

24. Board of Trustees, Minutes, Feb. 23, 1988, Nov. 1, 1988, Feb. 1, 1989, June 15, 1989, Jan. 31, 1990, June 12, 1991, Dec. 14, 1994, JACF; Weill, "From Being *about* Something," 238; Kenneth Hudson, "The Museum Refuses to Stand Still," *Museum International* 50 (Jan.–Mar. 1998): 43–50; Robin Pogrebin and Glenn Collins, "Shift at Historical Society Raises Concerns," *NYT*, July 19, 2004.

25. "Ten Reasons for City Support of the SSSM," Mar. 8, 1989, JACF; Board of Trustees, Minutes, Feb. 1, 1989, Sept. 13, 1989, JACF.

26. Board of Trustees, Minutes, Apr. 1, 1992, June 10, 1992, Sept. 9, 1992, Oct. 14, 1992, Oct. 13, 1993, JACF.

27. Board of Trustees, Minutes, June 8, 1994, June 14, 1995, June 16, 1997, Sept. 30, 1997, JACF; Alex Witchel, "Schuyler Chapin: Getting Ulcers for Art's Sake," *NYT*, Feb. 8, 1995; Paul

Goldberger, "Shifting Course on the Arts, Aiming for the Mainstream," *NYT*, Apr. 13, 1995. New York City's fiscal year runs from July 1 to June 30.

28. Aron, telephone interview, Aug. 18, 2010; Stephen Kloepfer to author, Nov. 12, 2010, email; Board of Trustees, Minutes, June 16, 1997, Sept. 30, 1997, Dec. 2, 1997, Dec. 1, 1998, JACF; Aron to Rudolph W. Giuliani, June 14, 1999, JACF; Neill to author, Aug. 18, 2010, email; "Funding for Cultural Organizations," http://www.nyc.gov/html/dcla/html/funding/institutions.shtml.

29. "Scotch, and Water," *NYT*, June 18, 1995; SSSM, *The Campaign for the SSSM: Immediate Goals $27.5 Million* (New York: SSSM, 1997), 5.

30. Peter Neill, "Our Five-Year Imperative," *Seaport* 27 (Spring 1993): 6; Board of Trustees, Minutes, Feb. 10, 1993, Apr. 13, 1994, JACF; Charles Sachs, interview, Mar. 19, 2009; Yerkovich to author, May 19, 2009, email; William Grimes, "As Museum and Mall, a Seaport Lives On," *NYT*, May 1, 1992, C1.

31. William Murtagh, "Janus Never Sleeps," in *Past Meets Future: Saving America's Historic Environments*, ed. Antoinette J. Lee (Washington, DC: Preservation Press, 1992), 56; Board of Trustees, Minutes, Apr. 1, 1992, Dec. 9, 1992, JACF; Peter Neill, "Personal Dialogues with Ghosts," in *Past Meets Future*, 43–44.

32. Umberto Eco, *Travels in Hyper Reality: Essays* (San Diego: Harcourt Brace Jovanovich, 1986): 8, 19; Yerkovich to author, May 19, 2009, email; Peter Howard, "Editorial—Heritage Challenges in the New Century," *International Journal of Heritage Studies* 6, no. 1 (2000): 8; "Maritime New York," *New York Folklore Newsletter* 11 (Summer 1990): 3; "Maritime Traditions in Wood," 1990 program, brochure, in Printings file, 1990, SSSM.

33. Kathleen Condon, "Twelve Ties to Tradition: Model Making in New York City," *New York Folk Lore Newsletter* 14 (Winter 1993): 6; "A Model Event," *NYT*, July 31, 1998, E40; Peter Neill, "Voices of the People," *Seaport* 28 (Summer 1994): 10–11; Dulcie Leimbach, "For Children," *NYT*, Sept. 3, 1993, C12; Donald Yannella, "The Water-Gazer: Herman Melville and His City," *Seaport* 25 (Fall 1991): 22, 25; John Putnam, "My Search for Herman," *Seaport* 25 (Fall 1991): 18.

34. I. Sheldon Posen, "And Big Fish," *Seaport* 29 (Summer 1995): 5; Peter Neill, "Threatened by Opportunity," *Seaport* 29 (Summer 1995): 3; Michael J. Chiarappa, "When Cod Was King," *Public Historian* 19 (Winter 1997): 127, 131; "Celebrating Cod and Its Royal Ancestry," *NYT*, Feb. 21, 1996, C2. For a less sanguine view, see Mansel G. Blackford, *Making Seafood Sustainable: American Experiences in Global Perspective* (Philadelphia: University of Pennsylvania Press, 2012), 34–37.

35. Neill, "Threatened by Opportunity," 2–3; Neill to author, Jan. 15, 2009, email; Steve Gilbert, "Tattoo," *Seaport* 29 (Summer 1995): 12; Michael Kimmelman, "Tattoo Moves from Fringes to Fashion. But Is It Art?," *NYT*, Sept. 15, 1995, C1, C27; Amy Krakow, telephone interview, Jan. 15, 2009; Mary Talbot, "Beneath the Skin of Tattoos, Seaport Museum Harbors Exhibit on a New York Folk Art," *NYDN*, June 12, 1995, 31; "Celebrating the Tattoo, Past and Present," *NYT*, May 14, 1995, CY11; Daniel Barron, "The Devil's Blue," *Seaport* 29 (Spring 1995): 4.

36. Peter Neill, "Past Imperfect," *Seaport* 30 (Spring 1996): 2–3; Jaffe to author, Jan. 31, 2009, email; Robert Dominguez, "Rooting through the History Books," *NYDN*, June 23, 1996.

For one example of a "politically manipulated" assault, Neill was referring to a controversy at the Smithsonian; see Mike Wallace, "The Battle of the *Enola Gay*," in *Mickey Mouse History*, 269–318.

37. Peter Neill to the Trustees, "Year End Report," Dec. 24, 1995, SSSM Board, JACF; *Seaport* 31 (Fall 1997), cover; Naomi Serviss, "Sailing into Dark, Pirate Waters," *Newsday*, Apr. 20, 1997, C33.

38. "Off the High Seas, a Look at Piracy," *NYT*, Apr. 6, 1997, CY14; "Desperate Men," *Seaport* 31 (Fall 1997): 30–31.

39. Teresa Annas, "Mariners' Museum Joins N.Y. Seaport Museum as Partner," *Virginian-Pilot*, June 17, 1997.

40. Board of Trustees, Minutes, Dec. 14, 1994, Feb. 25, 1997, JACF; Peter Neill, "A More Per-fect Union," *Seaport* 31 (Fall 1997): 3; Neill, "The Value of Belonging," *Seaport* 31 (Winter 1997): 2; Stephanie Elizondo Griest, "A Match Made in Museum Heaven," *NYT*, July 10, 1997, C15; Annas, "Mariners' Museum."

41. Thomas Wilcox, telephone interview, Mar. 13, 2009; John Hightower to author, Oct. 23, 2010, email; Michael Naab to author, Apr. 3, 2007, Feb. 23, 2009, Mar. 2, 2009, email; Aron, telephone interview, Dec. 18, 2009; Aron to Norman Brouwer, Nov. 18, 2002, JACF; Rybka to author, Feb. 23, 2009, email; Neill to author, Sept. 23, 2009, email. See section 1068 of the Strom Thurmond National Defense Authorization Act for Fiscal Year 1999 (Public Law 105-261; 112 Stat. 2135; 16 U.S.C. 5409); section (c) does not preclude other institutions from being added. As in S.2804 of 2002 and S.674 of 2003, the proposed "America's National Maritime Museum Designation Act" is referenced as 16 U.S.C. 5409.

42. Board of Trustees, Minutes, Apr. 14, 1993, JACF.

43. Board of Trustees, Minutes, Dec. 2, 1997, JACF; Peter Neill, "Search Your Closets, Barns & Basements," *Seaport* 25 (Fall 1991): 9. Fearing the closure of the SSSM in 2013, Peter Aron, who was president of the SSSM Foundation, voiced a possible plan to donate the foundation's holdings to the MCNY to ensure their protection, which would close the South Street Seaport Museum Foundation (Aron, telephone interview, Mar. 25, 2013).

44. Mark Sherman, "Office Development Unearthing City's Buried History," *NYT*, Aug. 5, 1984, R7; Board of Trustees, Minutes, Apr. 21, 1982, JACF; John O. Sands, "The Journey to the Mariner's Museum," *Mariners' Museum Journal* 12, no. 3 (1985): 7; Warren Riess and Sheli O. Smith, "The Ronson Ship," *Sea History* 28 (Summer 1983): 22; Kent Barwick, interview, June 24, 2008; Riess to author, Mar. 8, 2009, email; Riess, telephone interview, Mar. 13, 2009; Neill to author, Mar. 7, 2009, email; Hightower to author, Oct. 23, 2010, email; Anne-Marie Cantwell and Diana diZerega Wall, *Unearthing Gotham: The Archae-ology of New York City* (New Haven: Yale University Press, 2001), 234.

45. Peter Neill, "New York Unearthed," *Seaport* 24 (Fall 1990): 6–7; David W. Dunlap, "250,000 Glimpses of 18th-Century New York," *NYT*, Apr. 7, 1988, B1; Dunlap, "State Street Penitent: A Taste of the Past to Emend a Builder's Blunder," *NYT*, May 6, 1990; Board of Trustees, Minutes, Dec. 6, 1989, JACF; Jakob Isbrandtsen, Memo for the Files, Jan. 26, 1998, in Peter Aron to Isbrandtsen, Jan. 29, 1998, JACF; Diane Dallal to the editor, *NYT*, June 27, 1999, CY15.

46. "Unearthing Memories," *NYT*, Feb. 5, 1999, E41; Antoinette J. Lee, "The Social and

Ethnic Dimensions of Historic Preservation," in *A Richer Heritage: Historic Preservation in the Twenty-First Century*, ed. Robert E. Stipe (Chapel Hill: University of North Carolina Press, 2003), 393.

47. AAM, *Museums for a New Century: A Report* (Washington, DC: AAM, 1984); Peter Neill, "A Festival Museum," *Seaport* 22 (Fall 1988): 8, 10; Neill, "A Special Place for Children," *Seaport* 23 (Fall 1989): 10; David Berson, "*Pioneer* Skipper Chosen to Crew Aboard *Te Vega*," *Soundings*, July 1989, B12; Neill to author, Oct. 28, 2009, email; Seymour, telephone interview, Apr. 10, 2009; Board of Trustees, Minutes, Apr. 1, 1992, JACF.

48. Daniel S. Parrott, *Tall Ships Down* (Camden, ME: International Marine / McGraw-Hill, 2003), 7; Dick Rath, "Sail Training," *Sea History* 57 (Spring 1991): 15; Barclay H. Warburton III, "Sail Training," in *First National Maritime Preservation Conference Proceedings* (Washington, DC: Preservation Press, 1977), 36–37; Berson, "*Pioneer* Skipper," B12; Richard Huff, "Walter Cronkite, 'Most Trusted Man in America' and CBS Anchor, Dead at 92," *NYDN*, July 17, 2009; Justine M. Ahlstrom, "Launching the Maritime Education Initiative, Part I," *Sea History* 62 (Summer 1992): 7–9.

49. Paul M. Barrett, "Harbor as Classroom," *WSJ*, Sept. 4, 2003, B1; Kathleen Carroll, "A Voyage with an Ulterior Purpose," *NYT*, Sept. 5, 2001, B7.

50. Goscener, "State of the Museum, 1986"; Board of Trustees, Minutes, Oct. 11, 1989, JACF; "Lincoln Harbor Yacht Club," *Seaport* 24 (Summer 1990): 1; Yerkovich to author, May 19, 2009, email.

51. Peter Neill, "New York's Past and *Seaport*'s Future," *Seaport* 19 (Winter 1986): 5; Neill, "History, by, and for, the People," 8; Anne D. Neal and Jerry L. Martin, *Restoring America's Legacy* (Washington, DC: American Council of Trustees and Alumni, 2002); Robert E. Stipe, "Where Do We Go from Here?," in Stipe, *Richer Heritage*, 532n11.

52. Joe Doyle to author, July 26, 2009, email; Kenneth Jackson, interview, June 23, 2010; Daniel Czitrom, "The Wickedest Ward in New York," *Seaport* 20 (Winter 1986–87): 20–26; SSSM, "Tours: Vice on South Street," *Broadside*, Apr.–June 1994, 18; Steven Jaffe, "The New York Sailors' Strike of 1869," *Seaport* 34 (Spring 1999): 15–16; John Steele Gordon, "Seaport Commerce: The Case of the *Obo Buzzard*," *Seaport* 24 (Summer 1990): 42–43. In addition to the Bridge Café, the most notable extant building was 273 Water Street, where Kit Burns ran his Sportsman's Hall.

53. Doyle to author, July 26, 2009, email; Doyle, "John Singleton, 'The Lonely Life,'" *Seaport* 19 (Winter 1986): 48; Doyle, "Small Craft Craftsman," *Seaport* 25 (Summer 1991): 14–15; Doyle, "Rose Chevell, 'Glory Hole Sailor,'" *Seaport* 21 (Winter 1987–88): 48; Doyle, "George the Waiter: Twenty Years at Sloppy Louie's," *Seaport* 20 (Spring 1986): 48; Doyle, "Sal Celona: 16 Hours Is a Normal Day," *Seaport* 23 (Winter–Spring 1990): 64; Doyle, "Ernest Chambré: Custom House 'Trash' Is His Treasure," *Seaport* 22 (Summer 1988): 52; Doyle, "Melvin Madison: Madison Men's Wear, 26 Eleventh Avenue," *Seaport* 20 (Winter 1986–87): 52; Neil Smith, "New City, New Frontier: The Lower East Side as Wild, Wild West," in *Variations on a Theme Park: The New American City and the End of Public Space*, ed. Michael Sorkin (New York: Hill and Wang, 1992), 89–90; Luc Sante, *Low Life: Lures and Snares of Old New York* (New York: Farrar, Straus & Giroux, 1991), xi–xii.

54. Talbot, "Beneath the Skin of Tattoos," 31.

NOTES TO CHAPTER 10

1. Laurie Johnston, "At Seaport, a Restoration of Spirit," *NYT*, Oct. 16, 1981, B1–B2; Board of Trustees, Minutes, Dec. 13, 1983, SSSM; Peter Neill, "A Museum like No Other," *Seaport* 19 (Fall 1985): 8; Neill, "Reflections on 20 Years—And Then Some," *Seaport* 21 (Summer 1987): 11–12. See also James P. Delgado, "Grim Realities, High Hopes, Moderate Gains: The State of Historic Ship Preservation," *CRM Bulletin* 12, no. 4 (1989): 3.

2. Neill, "Reflections on 20 Years," 11; Neill, "Developing a National Cultural Policy for Maritime Preservation," *APT Bulletin* 19, no. 1 (1987): 24, 27; Peter Spectre, "The Issues of Maritime Preservation," *WB* 38 (Jan.–Feb. 1981): 44–45.

3. Editorial: "Not Yet a Nautical Museum," *NYT*, Dec. 28, 1985, 22; Peter Neill, "A Confusion of Ships," *Seaport* 20 (Spring 1986): 6; Neill, "The Whole Museum," *Seaport* 24 (Summer 1990): 6; Neill, "Reflections on 20 Years," 12; Carl Notke, "Historic Ships Are Rotting Away in S. F. Bay," *San Francisco Chronicle*, Nov. 23, 1987, A2. See also appendixes A and D, in Alex Roland, W. Jeffrey Bolster, and Alexander Keyssar, *The Way of the Ship: America's Maritime History Reenvisioned, 1600–2000* (Hoboken, NJ: Wiley, 2008), 419–43. Then holding the barque *Star of India* (1863) and ferry *Berkeley* (1898), the Maritime Museum of San Diego later acquired additional ships.

4. James W. Loewen, *Lies across America: What Our Historic Sites Get Wrong* (New York: New Press, 1999), 404; Peter Neill, "Save Our Ships!," *Seaport* 22 (Fall 1988): 6; Neill, "Reflections on 20 Years," 12; Dick Sheridan, "Port of Missing Ships: Whatever Happened to the South Street Dream?," *NYSN*, Mar. 26, 1989, Magazine sec., 12.

5. SSSM, "Long-Range Interpretive Plan," Jan. 1989, Sally Yerkovich personal files; Steven Jaffe to author, Jan. 26, 27, 2009, email; Lee T. Pearcy to the editor, "South St. Seaport Ignoring Its Museum Role," *NYT*, July 18, 1988, A16; Sheridan, "Port of Missing Ships," 11; Peter Spectre, "On the Waterfront," *WB* 89 (July–Aug. 1989): 27; Peter Neill to Peter Spectre, "Duck Again, Peter," *WB* 90 (Sept.–Oct. 1989): 4, 6; Jere Hester, "Lost at Seaport," *DE*, Feb. 13, 1991.

6. Carl L. Nelson, "At the Helm with Peter Neill," *Historic Preservation* 36, no. 5 (1984): 65; Norman Brouwer, "The Port of New York, 1860–1985: Recreation on New York's Waters," *Seaport* 23 (Summer 1989): 41; Peter Neill to author, Feb. 19, 2010, Mar. 1, 2010, email; Ed Koch, "Message from the Mayor: Happy Anniversary, South Street," *Seaport* 21 (Summer 1987): 9; William E. Geist, "An Old Salt Wonder Why People Pay $20 a Fish," *NYT*, Sept. 20, 1986, 30; Stephen Kloepfer to author, Nov. 12, 2010, email; "Seaport," *New Yorker*, Sept. 23, 1985, 28–29; Jon Goss, "Disquiet on the Waterfront: Reflections on Nostalgia and Utopia in the Urban Archetypes of Festival Marketplaces," *Urban Geography* 17, no. 3 (1996): 238.

7. Neill, "Confusion of Ships," 6; Neill to author, Dec. 5, 2011, email; Board of Trustees, Minutes, Feb. 10, 1993, Oct. 13, 1993, JACF; Joe Baiamonte to Dan Kurtz (EDC vice president), Jan. 9, 1995, JACF.

8. Board of Trustees, Minutes, Dec. 2, 1997, Feb. 3, 1998, JACF; Neill to author, Oct. 22, 23, 2009, Nov. 10, 2010, email; David Firestone, "Giuliani Says City Must Plan for Gambling," *NYT*, Dec. 6, 1997, A1.

9. Paul Restuccia, "Contest Puts Design in Focus," *Boston Herald*, Nov. 27, 1998, 56; Bernard

Stamler, "Museum Looks Ahead," *NYT*, Mar. 29, 1998, CY13; George Matteson to author, Oct. 19, 2009, email; Board of Trustees, Minutes, Oct. 13, 1993, JACF. Matteson anonymously funded the barge's purchase. City Hall had already demolished Piers 9, 13, 14, 18, and 22 and refused to replace them.

10. Joe Doyle, "Lars Henning Hansen: The Rigger of South Street," *Seaport* 23 (Summer 1989): 52; Phillip Lopate, *Waterfront: A Journey around Manhattan* (New York: Crown, 2004), 60; Eric Lipton, "New York Port Hums Again, with Asian Trade," *NYT*, Nov. 22, 2004, A1; Roland, Bolster, and Keyssar, *Way of the Ship*, 358, 419–21; Sharon Zukin, *Naked City: The Death and Life of Authentic Urban Places* (New York: Oxford University Press, 2010), chap. 5.

11. Chris Black, "Mr. Kennedy's Trophy Goes to Washington," *Boston Globe*, Feb. 14, 1998, A3; Brouwer, "Port of New York, 1860–1985," 39; "A Day When Wooden Boats Rule the Waters Once Again," *NYT*, Sept. 13, 1998.

12. "*Wavertree* Is Here!" *SSR* 4 (Sept. 1970): 1, 7; John Hightower to author, Oct. 23, 2010, email; Meeting Notes, June 29, 1985, VISOSSSM; Peter Spectre, Editorial, *WB* 84 (Sept.–Oct. 1988): 2; Neill, "Save Our Ships!," 6–7. In 2006, the largest container ship, *Emma Mærsk*, measured 1,304 feet.

13. J. J. Thompson to the editor, "Value of Ship Restoration," *Sea Breezes*, n.d., in Clippings file, 1983, SSSM; Chris [Lowery] to Ellen [Fletcher], n.d., appended to ibid.

14. Walter Rybka, comments during "Getting Visitors to Do More than Listen: Training Docents to Foster Dialogue" panel at "Opening Historic Sites to Civic Engagement" conference, Apr. 1–2, 2004, http://www.nps.gov/nero/greatplaces/GettingVisitors.htm.

15. Thompson, "Value of Ship Restoration"; Walter Rybka, "*Elissa*: Now Real and Beautiful," *Sea History* 26 (Winter 1982–83): 21–22; Charles Deroko to author, Nov. 25, 2009, email; Zdena Nemeckova, "Love on the Waterfront," *New Manhattan Review*, June 26, 1985, 13–15; Spectre, "Issues of Maritime Preservation," 38.

16. Barrett T. Beard Sr., "American Maritime Historic Preservation; Practice and Policy" (M.A. thesis in history, Western Washington University, 1986), 58; Neill, "Confusion of Ships," 9; Richard Fewtrell to author, Jan. 27, 2010, email; Spectre, "Issues of Maritime Preservation," 38.

17. Donald P. Robinson, "Commentary," in *International Congress of Maritime Museums: Third Conference Proceedings, 1978* (Mystic, CT: Mystic Seaport Museum, 1979), 28–29; Walter Rybka, "Preserving Historic Vessels: A Long View of History," *APT Bulletin* 19, no. 1 (1987): 46; Judith Cummings and Albin Krebs, "Prince's Tack May Draw Shots across the Bow," *NYT*, Oct. 3, 1980, B5.

18. Peter Stanford to Ralph L. Snow, Apr. 18, 1978, Kortum Collection, HDC 1084, Series 2:8, File 7, SFMNHP; Norman Brouwer, "Con: Some Are 'Deceptions,' " *Preservation News* 26 (June 1986): 5; Brouwer to author, Jan. 12, 2010, email; Brower, "The Role of Historical Research in Documenting Historic Vessels," *APT Bulletin* 19, no. 1 (1987): 42; "Major Restoration Projects Underway on Two Historic Sailing Ships," *Eastern Boating*, Apr. 1984, 6.

19. Chip Brown, "The *Wavertree* at One Hundred," *Seaport* 20 (Spring 1986): 18; Clem Richardson, "Sal Polisi Carves Out a Nice Career at South Street Seaport's Maritime Craft Center," *NYDN*, May 17, 2010; Neill to author, May 20, 2010, email; "Superstitions

of Sailors," in *The Oxford Companion to Ships and the Sea*, ed. Peter Kemp (New York: Oxford University Press, 1976), 847. The figurehead was later removed. For Mystic's "Saucy Sally," see my " 'Stout Hearts Make a Safe Ship': Individual and Community at Mystic Seaport," in "Preserving Maritime America: Public Culture and Memory in the Making of the Nation's Great Marine Museums" (forthcoming).

20. Michael Naab, *The Secretary of the Interior's Standards for Historic Vessel Preservation Projects, with Guidelines for Applying Standards* (Washington, DC: NPS, 1990), 69; Naab to author, Jan. 28, 2010, email; Joe Baiamonte to Carlos M. Rivera, May 21, 1990, VISOSSSM; John J. Toohey to Joe Baiamonte, Jan. 15, 1991, VISOSSSM.

21. Doyle, "Lars Henning Hansen," 52; "South Street Seaport's Beauty Receives Major Drydock Overhaul," *Via Port of New York–New Jersey*, Aug. 1987, 17; Peter Aron to author, Jan. 27, 2010, email; Howard Slotnick, telephone interview, Sept. 9, 2008; Spectre, "Issues of Maritime Preservation," 44; Charles Deroko, "Re-rigging the *Peking*," http://charlescderokoinc.com/writing/index.htm; Deroko to author, Oct. 15, 2009, email; Naab to author, Jan. 28, 2010, email.

22. Joe Doyle to author, July 26, 2009, email; Meg Cox, "Seaport Clears Deck for a Brighter Future," *WSJ*, Aug. 27, 1987, 31; "Spooky Shakespeare at Sea," *NYT*, Oct. 31, 1999, CY15; Lawrence Van Gelder, "A Ship Full of Pop References," *NYT*, June 21, 2001, E1.

23. Doyle, "Lars Henning Hansen," 52; Deroko to author, Feb. 1, 2010, email; Elizabeth Giddens, "Captain of the Low Seas," *NYT*, Apr. 8, 2007, 4.

24. Spectre, "Issues of Maritime Preservation," 38–39; Spectre, "The Politics of Maritime Preservation," *WB* 44 (Jan.–Feb. 1982): 68; Norman Brouwer, "The Sailing Ships of the Falkland Islands," *SSR* 10 (Fall 1976): 11; "*Charles Cooper* Ordered Out," *Sea History* 61 (Spring 1992): 38. In 2003, *Cooper* became an exhibit, but the Falklands Museum later determined that the bow might be the only part that can be preserved (http://www.falklands-museum.com/index.php/history/maritime/wrecks-a-hulks/214-charles-cooper11).

25. John B. Forbes, "Schooners Transport Sailors into Another Era," *NYT*, Oct. 10, 1988, C12; Dianne Glennon, "At the Museum: A *Pioneer* for All Seasons," *Seaport* 19 (Summer 1985): 6; George Matteson, "A Centennial History of the *Pioneer*," *Seaport* 19 (Summer 1985): 24–26; Doyle to author, July 26, 2009, email.

26. Waterfront Committee, Minutes, Dec. 10, 1984, JACF; Nora McAuley-Gitin to author, Sept. 3, 2010, email; Nemeckova, "Love on the Waterfront," 13–15; Jack R. Aron to Peter Neill, [1985], JACF; Peter Aron, "5-Year Plan Memo," Apr. 16, 1985, JACF; Eric J. Sundberg, "Lending a Hand," *Seaport* 17 (Winter 1984): 7, 9.

27. Terry Walton, "CAMM'S First 25 Years," *CAMM Gamming*, Spring-Summer 1999, Insert sec., 2; James P. Delgado, "The National Maritime Initiative: An Interdisciplinary Approach to Maritime Preservation," *Public Historian* 13 (Summer 1991): 76; Delgado, "Introduction," *APT Bulletin* 19, no. 1 (1987): 20–21; Neill, "Developing a National Cultural Policy," 26–27; Madeline Rogers, "Ship Keeper: Meet South Street's New Man on the Waterfront," *Seaport* 26 (Summer 1992): 12. For the difficult issues associated with professionalizing the study of history, see Michael Kammen, *Mystic Chords of Memory: The Transformation of Tradition in American Culture* (New York: Knopf, 1991); and my " 'A

New Departure in Historic, Patriotic Work': Personalism, Professionalism, and Conflicting Concepts of Material Culture in the Late Nineteenth and Early Twentieth Centuries,"
Public Historian 18 (Spring 1996): 41–60.

28. "Volunteer Proposals, Ongoing Projects, and Volunteer Backgrounds and Skills," in
Susan Fowler to Peter Neill, June 4, 1985, VISOSSSM; Neill to author, Feb. 6, 8, 2010,
email; Thomas C. McAuliffe to Neill, July 16, 1985, VISOSSSM; Brouwer to author,
Feb. 10, 2010, email.

29. Neill to author, Feb. 8, 2010, email; Neill to Joe Baiamonte, July 14, 1989, JACF; Neill to
William Goscener Jr., July 14, 1989, JACF; Yerkovich to author, Feb. 19, 2010, email; Susan
Fowler, telephone interview, Aug. 12, 2009; Baiamonte, telephone interview, Feb. 22,
2010; McAuley-Gitin to author, Sept. 3, 2010, email.

30. Neill, "Save Our Ships!," 6; Neill, "Save the *Lettie!*," *Seaport* 23 (Summer 1989): 6. Drawings and photographs from HABS and HAER are available at the Library of Congress,
http://memory.loc.gov.

31. Board of Trustees, Minutes, Sept. 13, 1989, JACF; Jere Hester, "Seaport Civil War,"
Battery News, Aug. 28, 1989, 1, 3; Hester, "Delayed Boat Plan Sets Sail," *DE*, Jan. 2, 1991;
Matteson to author, Feb. 11, 2010, email; Constance L. Hays, "Restoration Encounters
Head Winds," *NYT*, July 22, 1990, 25; Joe Baiamonte to Carlos M. Rivera, May 21, 1990,
VISOSSSM; Neill to author, Feb. 8, 2010, email.

32. Peter Neill, "Personal Dialogues with Ghosts," in *Past Meets Future: Saving America's
Historic Environments*, ed. Antoinette J. Lee (Washington, DC: Preservation Press, 1992),
45, 46; Richard Dorfman, telephone interview, June 16, 2010; Matteson to author, Feb. 11,
2010, email.

33. Peter Aron to Mathias J. DeVito, Dec. 13, 1991, JACF; Baiamonte, telephone interview,
Feb. 22, 2010; "NY Fishing Schooner Gets New Masts," *JoC*, Mar. 26, 1993, 1B; Neill to
author, Jan. 27, 2010, email.

34. "Lettie's New Course," *Seaport* 28 (Winter 1994): 5; Neill to author Feb. 17, 2010, email;
"*Lettie G. Howard* Sets Sail as Our New Classroom at Sea," *Beacon*, Spring 1995, 2.

35. Jakob Isbrandtsen to James Shepley et al., Nov. 15, 1982, JACF; "Seaport Leaves Hart in
Bridgeport," *DE*, Feb. 3, 1992; Brouwer to author Sept. 25, 2006, email; "Urban Kayak
Camping," *flickr*, Apr. 9, 2009, http://www.flickr.com/photos/findkam/3462664684/.

36. Neill, "Save Our Ships!," 7; Rybka, "Preserving Historic Vessels," 52; Rybka to author,
Feb. 19, 2010, email; William Grimes, "Celebrating Columbus and the Age of Sail," *NYT*,
July 3, 1992, C1, C21; Richard E. Mooney, "Not Just a Mobile Museum," *NYT*, July 4, 1992, 18.

37. Bernard Stamler, "$12 Million Helps Restart Plan for Pier," *NYT*, July 13, 1997, CY7;
Stamler, "Ill Wind Blows Tall Ships to Wrong Side of Pier," *NYT*, Sept. 7, 1997, CY6;
Stamler, "Rough Sailing for South Street Seaport," *NYT*, Mar. 29, 1998, CY12–CY13; Neill
to author, Feb. 19, 2010, email.

38. Deroko to author, Feb. 17, 2010, email; Donald Birkholz, telephone interview, Oct. 16,
2009; Attachment A, Dec. 31, 1995, JACF; Jakob Isbrandtsen, "Memo for the Files,"
Jan. 26, 1998, in Peter Aron to Isbrandtsen, Jan. 29, 1998, JACF; Stanford to author,
Oct. 24, 2007, email. In 2006, Isbrandtsen's financial adviser, Paul Nordberg, filed suit to
reclaim the assets, but the case was dismissed because of the statute of limitations.

39. Bill Bleyer, "Ship Shapes Up," *Newsday*, June 6, 2000, B3; Amanda Gardner, "Getting All Decked Out," *NYDN*, Jan. 24, 2000, 38–39; Peter Neill, "A Tall Ship for New York and the Nation," *JoC*, Nov. 29, 1999, 8; "Historic Properties Repaired with State Bond Act Money," *Syracuse Post-Standard*, Dec. 18, 2000, A5; Paul Goldberger, "In Honor of the Fund That Loves New York," *NYT*, June 9, 1997, C12. Important funds were provided by the Daniel K. Thorne Foundation, which was headed by the eponymous chairman of the museum's Waterfront Committee.

40. Deroko to author, Feb. 23, 2010, email; Ashley Hall, "N.Y. Shipshape, Historic Armada Converges on Waterways," *NYDN*, July 4, 2000; Neil Graves, "Glorious Old Freighter Gets Its Second Wind," *NYP*, June 30, 2000, 5; Bill Bleyer, "Ship Misses Call," *Newsday*, July 4, 2000, A5.

41. Bleyer, "Ship Misses Call," A5; Neill to author, Apr. 7, 2010, email; Neill to Board of Trustees, July 5, 2000, JACF; David Noonan, "Armada Sailing in for July 4th," *NYDN*, Mar. 19, 2000, 18; Richard Dorfman to author, Oct. 2, 2013, email; Angela C. Allen, "Hard-Luck Ship Returns to Glory," *NYP*, July 5, 2000, 5; Hall, "N.Y. Shipshape," 3. As the *NYT* reported, there were 27 Class A vessels starting with the *Esmeralda* of 371 feet, "to 25 Class B ships of 161 to 100 feet, to 61 Class C Vessels of 90 to 18 feet" (Ralph Blumenthal, "Down to the Sea Again, in Ships Tall and Fleet," *NYT*, June 30, 2000, E41).

42. Deroko to author, Oct. 15, 2009, Feb. 17, 23, 2010, email; Neill to author, Apr. 7, 2010, email; Neill, "Dollars and Dreams," *Seaport* 35 (Fall 2000): 2; Thomas Gochberg, telephone interview, Apr. 28, 2010; Bleyer, "Ship Shapes Up," B3.

NOTES TO CHAPTER 11

1. "$5 Million Port Authority Grant," *SSSMN* (Fall 2002): 1; Peter Aron, telephone interview, Dec. 18, 2009. The port of New York / New Jersey followed numerically behind those of South Louisiana and Houston, as measured in metric tons (Mário Soares, *The Ocean Our Future* [Cambridge: Cambridge University Press, 1998], 101).

2. Richard Dorfman, telephone interview, June 16, 2010; Peter Neill to author, June 2, 2010, email; Stephen Kloepfer to author, Nov. 12, 2010, email; Yvonne Simons to author, June 11, 2010, email; Rebecca Solnit, *A Paradise Built in Hell: The Extraordinary Communities That Arise in Disaster* (New York: Viking, 2009), 188.

3. Dorfman, telephone interview, June 16, 2010; Neill to author, June 2, 2010, email; Colin Freeze, " 'Souvenir Ghouls' Hustle Trade Center Memorabilia," *Globe and Mail*, Sept. 14, 2001; Joanne Wasserman, "Ailing at Ground Zero," *NYDN*, Jan. 12, 2002, 7; Simons to author, June 11, 13, 2010, email; Steven Jaffe to author, Feb. 4, 2009, email. See also Nancy Foner, ed., *Wounded City: The Social Impact of 9/11* (New York: Russell Sage Foundation, 2005).

4. Hugo Kugiya, "Showing Support for the Big Apple," *Newsday*, Oct. 6, 2001, A23; Simons to author, June 11, 2010, email; James B. Gardner and Sarah M. Henry, "September 11 and the Morning After: Reflections on Collecting and Interpreting the History of Tragedy," *Public Historian* 24 (Summer 2002): 38; Neill to author, Sept. 28, 2010, email; Greg Gittrich, "Group: Save Historic Downtown," *NYDN*, Oct. 12, 2001, 40.

5. Andrew Friedman, "'Five Points' Artifacts Outlast Time but Not Terrorism," *NYT*, Nov. 18, 2001, 4; Peter Neill to Peter Aron, Dec. 18, 2001, JACF; Neill to author, Sept. 28, 2010, email; Neill, "Water, Water, Everywhere," *Seaport* 37 (Winter 2002): 2; Solnit, *Paradise*, 184, 191; Madeline Rogers, "Salt of the Earth," *Seaport* 37 (Spring–Summer 2002): 42. See also David Harvey, "Cracks in the Edifice of the Empire State," in *After the World Trade Center: Rethinking New York City*, ed. Michael Sorkin and Sharon Zukin (New York: Routledge, 2002), 65; Ruth Hargraves, *Cataclysm and Challenge: Impact of September 11, 2001, on Our Nation's Cultural Heritage* (Washington, DC: Heritage Preservation, 2002), 3; Diane Dallal, "The Five Points Collection: An Obituary," *Seaport* 37 (Spring–Summer 2002): 44.

6. Norman Brouwer, "All Available Boats," *Seaport* 37 (Spring–Summer 2002): 6; "Museum Exhibition and Book Honored by U.S. House of Representatives," *SSSMN*, Spring–Summer 2003, 2A–3A; "All Available Boats Exhibition to Travel to Costa Rica," ibid., 3A; Peter Neill, prologue to *All Available Boats: The Evacuation of Manhattan Island on September 11, 2001*, ed. Mike Magee (New York: Spencer Books, 2002), 2; Neill to author, June 2, 2010, email; "Harbor Voices & Images 9.11.01: Tom Sullivan," *Seaport* 37 (Spring–Summer 2002): 26; Jaffe to author, Feb. 4, 2009, email.

7. Denny Lee, "South Street Seaport's Vital Fuel, Its Foot Traffic, Slows to a Near Halt," *NYT*, Nov. 18, 2001; Neill to author, June 2, 2010, email.

8. Kloepfer to author, Nov. 12, 2010, email; Neill to author, June 2, 3, 2010, email; Peter Aron to Rudolph Giuliani, June 14 1999, JACF; Aron to Brouwer, Nov. 18, 2002, JACF; "Consolidated Financial Statements, 1999, 2000, 2001," *SSSMN*, Fall 2002, 12.

9. Peter Neill, "Thirty-Five Years Young . . . and the Future Is Ours," *Seaport* 37, no. 4 (Fall 2002): 3; Neill to author, Jan. 14, 2009, June 7, 2010, email; Glenn Collins, "New Body for a Seaport's Soul: At Maritime Museum's Remade Home, Old Walls Talk," *NYT*, July 3, 2003, B8; Celia McGee, "Arts Casualties of 9/11 Get $6.6M in Grants," *NYDN*, Jan. 31, 2002, 43; "Aron $5 Million Pledge," JACF; "$5 Million Port Authority Grant," *SSSMN*, Fall 2002, 1.

10. Zev Chafets, "Facing Ground Zero," *NYDN*, Feb. 10, 2002, 39; G. Jeffrey MacDonald, "At Ground Zero, Uncertainty over How to Pay Respects," *CSM*, Jan. 4, 2002; Simons to author, June 11, 2010, email; Debbie Lisle, "Gazing at Ground Zero: Tourism, Voyeurism and Spectacle," *Journal for Cultural Research* 8 (Jan. 2004): 4, 9–10; Lore Croghan, "Downtown Is Ruled by Tourists While Offices Stay Empty," *Crain's New York Business*, Mar. 4, 2002; Dorfman, telephone interview, June 16, 2010; Marita Sturken, *Tourists of History: Memory, Kitsch, and Consumerism from Oklahoma City to Ground Zero* (Durham: Duke University Press, 2007), 183.

11. Gardner and Henry, "September 11," 52; Ed Robinson and Kate Sheehy, "'Liar!' Firestorm; FDNY Rally Hits Writer's 'Loot' Claim," *NYP*, Nov. 19, 2002; David Carr, "Rebutting a Claim of Tarnished Valor," *NYT*, Mar. 23, 2003, A31, A33; Neill to author, June 7, 2010, email; Dana Heller, "Introduction: Consuming 9/11," in *The Selling of 9/11: How a National Tragedy Became a Commodity*, ed. Dana Heller (New York: Palgrave Macmillan, 2005), 13–15. Of the major dailies, the only reference to "All Available Boats" was "Spare Times: For Children," *NYT*, Apr. 12, 2002, E41 (note the subtitle).

12. Gardner and Henry, "September 11," 40; Caryn James, "Beyond Comforting the Afflicted," *NYT*, Sept. 12, 2005, E1; Russell Shorto, "The Future of the Past," *NYT*, Sept. 12, 2004, 1; Douglas Feiden, "Painting a Controversy, 9-11 Art Exhibit Trashing War on Terror to Debut near WTC," *NYDN*, Sept. 1, 2005, 8; Ronda Kaysen, "9/11 Art Flap on 9/11," *DE*, Sept. 16, 2005.

13. Neill to author, Nov. 9, 2008, email; Thomas Gochberg, telephone interview, Apr. 28, 2010; Al Amateau, "Seaport Museum Plans a $20 Million Center," *DE*, Oct. 5, 1998; Collins, "New Body for a Seaport's Soul"; Miriam Kreinin Souccar, "Seaport Leads Way to Area's Recovery, but Visitors Scarce," *Crain's New York Business*, Oct. 28, 2002, 4.

14. Neill to author, Apr. 23, 2010, Nov. 1, 2010, email; Paul Clancy, "Captive Passage," *Virginian-Pilot*, Apr. 30, 2002; Elizabeth Olson, "Getting Rich off Human Cargo: The Grim Details," *NYT*, Feb. 7, 2003; Beverly C. McMillan, ed., *Captive Passage: The Transatlantic Slave Trade and the Making of the Americas* (Washington, DC: Smithsonian Institution and the Mariners' Museum, 2002); Tariq Mehmood, "Trophies of Plunder," *Museums Journal* 90 (Sept. 1990): 27; Celeste-Marie Bernier, review of "Transatlantic Slavery: Against Human Dignity," *Journal of American History* 88 (Dec. 2001): 1008.

15. Jaffe to author, Jan. 29, 2009, email; Neill to author, Apr. 23, 2010, email; Kenneth Jackson, interview, June 23, 2010; John Hightower to author, Oct. 23, 2010, email; Kloepfer to author, Nov. 12, 2010, email; Jeanne Willoz-Egnor to author, Nov. 10, 2010, email.

16. "Resistance, Creativity, and Survival: The Janina Rubinowitz Collection of Maroon Arts," gallery talk, Schermerhorn Row, Oct. 20, 2003, http://www.gothamcenter.org/events/detail.cfm?id=1669; Elizabeth O'Brien, "Museum's New Wing Linked to Seaport's History," *DE*, Oct. 14, 2003; Peter Neill, "Schermerhorn Row Opens with a Landmark Exhibition," *Seaport* 39 (Winter–Spring 2004): 2–3; Kloepfer to author, Nov. 12, 2010, email.

17. Willoz-Egnor to author, Nov. 10, 2010, email; Hightower to author, Oct. 29, 2010, Nov. 1, 2010, email; Jaffe to author, Jan. 29, 2009, email; Jackson, interview, June 23, 2010; Elizabeth O'Brien, "Sparse Turnout for Seaport Museum's New Galleries," *DE*, Dec. 16, 2003; Sharon Holt to author, May 25, 2010, email; "Spare Times," *NYT*, Jan. 16, 2004, E44; Olson, "Getting Rich off Human Cargo."

18. Margaret Coady, "Slave Trade Exhibition Inaugurates South Street Seaport Museum's New Space," *Broadsheet* (SSSM), Nov. 8, 2003; Neill to author, Apr. 23, 2010, email; Paul Clancy, "Captive Passage Mariners' Museum Exhibit Depicts the Cruelty of the Trans-Atlantic Slave Trade," *Virginian-Pilot*, Apr. 30, 2002; Daniel C. Littlefield, review of "Captive Passage: The Transatlantic Slave Trade and the Making of the Americas," *Public Historian* 25 (Summer 2003): 134.

19. Glenn Collins, "Living the Life of the Sea from a 5th-Floor Walk-Up," *NYT*, Aug. 5, 2003, B2; Neill to author, Nov. 9, 2008, June 10, 2010, email; Neill to Larry Huntington et al., May 5, 2004, JACF; "Neill to Step Down at Seaport Museum," *DE*, Mar. 26, 2004; "World Ocean Observatory," http://thew2o.net/content/history-world-ocean-observatory.

20. Aron, telephone interview, Dec. 18, 2009, Mar. 25, 2013; Neill to author, Jan. 14, 2009, email; Howard Slotnick, telephone interview, Sept. 9, 2008; Hightower to author, Oct. 23, 2010, email.

21. Simons to author, June 13, 2010, email; Dorfman, telephone interview, May 16, 2011; Gochberg, telephone interview, Apr. 28, 2010; Neill to author, May 21, 2010, email; Kloepfer to author, Nov. 12, 2010, email; Robin Pogrebin, "Museum at South St. Reduces Staff to Cut Budget," *NYT*, July 8, 2004, B6.

22. Simons to author, June 13, 2010, email; panel discussion on museum research, May 15, 2010, annual meeting of CAMM/NMHS at the University of Connecticut, Avery Point; Nora McAuley-Gitin to author, Sept. 3, 2010, email; Peter Spectre, Editorial, *WB* 84 (Sept.–Oct. 1988): 2; Christine Lilyquist to author, Apr. 15, 2011, email; Pogrebin, "Museum at South St.," B6; Joe Doyle to author, July 26, 2009, email; Neill to author, Oct. 8, 2010, email; Ileen Gallagher to author, May 19, 2011, email.

23. Simons to author, June 13, 2010, email; Pogrebin, "Museum at South St.," B6; Diane Dallal, "The Dutch Legacy," *Seaport* 39 (Summer 2004): 34–40; Steven Jaffe, "Discovering History Beneath Our Feet," *Seaport* 36 (Fall 2001): 40; Lisa Schiffman, "No Money for Archaeology," *Archaeology*, Jan. 10, 2005, http://www.archaeology.org/online/features/seaport/update.html; Mark Rose, "Seaport Museum Artifacts Ship Out," June 22, 2005, http://archive.archaeology.org/online/features/seaport/update2.html; Alexander Nazaryan, "City History Locked Away: The Short Unhappy Life of New York Unearthed," *NYDN*, Dec. 18, 2011.

24. Holt to author, May 25, 2010, email; [Holt], "World Port New York: Sixteen Gallery Version," Sept. 2003, in ibid.; Holt, "The Port of New York: Lost and Found," *SSSMN*, Winter–Spring 2004, 4A; Jaffe to author, Jan. 26, 2009, email.

25. Holt to author, May 25, 2010, email; Peter Aron to Paula Mayo, Mar. 16, 2004, JACF; "Treasures of South Street," n.d., JACF; "Special Exhibition Catalog," *Seaport* 39 (Summer 2004); Neill to author, Jan. 16, 2009, email.

26. Simons to author, June 13, 2010, email; Dennis O'Toole to author, Nov. 7, 2011, email; Gochberg, telephone interview, Apr. 28, 2010; Aron, telephone interview, Apr. 14, 2010. See also SSSM, "Request for Qualifications for Exhibition Design Services for a New Permanent Collection Exhibition," Mar. 3, 2003, http://www.renewnyc.com/content/rfps/NonProfit/SouthStreetSeaportRFQDesignServices.pdf, in which the Seaport announced its intention of converting the Row's fourth and fifth floors for a permanent exhibit. It did not deliver.

27. Harold Skramstad, "An Agenda for American Museums in the Twenty-First Century," *Daedalus* 128 (Summer 1999): 127. Huntington did not respond to my requests for information.

28. Lawrence Huntington and Paula Mayo, "Presentation to the New York City Economic Development Corporation," Oct. 18, 2006, JACF; Pete Seeger to author, Nov. 13, 2007 (Seeger borrowed the line from Eric Hoffer); Pogrebin, "Museum at South St.," B6; Mayo, interview, Nov. 16, 1998 (Mayo did not respond to requests a decade later); George Matteson, interview, June 24, 2008; Matteson to author, Sept. 24, 2009, email; Matteson, *Tugboats of New York: An Illustrated History* (New York: NYU Press, 2005), 96–97. Sold for one dollar in 2012, *Marion M.* is being restored on Chesapeake Bay, while *Helen McAllister* was returned to its original owners.

29. Martin Sokolinsky, "Swinging with the Young Ones, Fixing an Old Ship," *DE*, Nov. 14,

2008; Norman Brouwer to author, Nov. 9, 2010, email; Peter Stanford to author, Nov. 9, 2010, email; Terry Walton to Brouwer et al., Nov. 9, 2010, email; Charles Deroko to author, May 19, 2011, email; Ileen Gallagher to author, May 19, 2011, email.

30. Eric Wolff, "*Peking* May Duck Out of City: Schooner [*sic*] for Sale," *New York Sun*, May 1, 2003; Kelly Crow, "After 27 Years, with Money Tight, a Tall-Masted Classic Must Go," *NYT*, May 18, 2003, CY6; Neill to author, Nov. 12, 2010, email; SSSM, "*Peking* Proposal," n.d. [Oct. 8, 2004], JACF; Lionel Amos to Paula Mayo, Nov. 20, 2004, and Mayo's reply, Nov. 22, 2004, email, JACF; Jill Trazino to the South Street Seaport Museum, "Keep the *Peking*," *DE*, Mar. 26, 2004; Julie Shapiro, "Museum Looks to Save Ship by Selling Some," *DE*, Mar. 28, 2008; Stanford to author, June 21, 2007, email. Lionel Amos did not respond to my request for information.

31. "Packing up Peking," *DE*, Jan. 11, 2008; Gochberg, telephone interview, Jan. 4, 2011; David Berson, "The Barque *Peking* and the P-Line Ships," *Ocean Navigator* 206 (Nov.–Dec. 2012); Terese Loeb Kreuzer, "A Giant among Tall Ships, Seaport's *Peking* Reopens for Select Saturdays," *DE*, Sept. 18, 2013. As of early 2014, the Hamburg museum was still fundraising, leaving *Peking* at Pier 16 and at *Wavertree*'s future berth.

32. Shapiro, "Museum Looks to Save Ship"; Ben Fractenberg and Julie Shapiro, "Seaport Museum May Look to Sell Off Historic Schooner," *DNAinfo New York*, Dec. 24, 2010, http://www.dnainfo.com/new-york/20101224/downtown/seaport-museum-may-look -sell-off-historic-schooner; Deroko to author, Jan. 1, 2011, email; Aron to author, Jan. 1, 2011, email.

33. Bronson Binger to author, Mar. 7, 2008, email; Phillip Lopate, "Introduction: The Fulton Fish Market," in *South Street*, by Barbara G. Mensch (New York: Columbia University Press, 2007), 37; Sara Jane, comment on Sewell Chan, "Loaders, Lumpers and the Smell of Fish," *City Room* (blog), *NYT*, Apr. 28, 2008, and G. Stone, comment on ibid.; Selwyn Raab, "City Considering a Modern Fulton Fish Market at a New Site," *NYT*, May 14, 1999, B6; Sharon Zukin, *Naked City: The Death and Life of Authentic Urban Places* (New York: Oxford University Press, 2010); Neill to author, Mar. 2, 2010, email; Naima Rauam to author, Nov. 2, 2010, email; Janel Bladow, "Seaport Report," *DE*, Nov. 21, 2008; "The Photographs of Barbara Mensch," http://www.southstreetseaportmuseum.org (no longer available); Dan Barry, "That Smell? Fish and Sweat, Fading into a Sanitized Future," *NYT*, Apr. 3, 2004.

34. Liz Willen, "South Street Sizzles," *Newsday*, July 3, 2000, A4; David Freedlander, "Changes in Store for South Street Seaport," *Newsday*, Nov. 12, 2007; Gary Fagin to author, Mar. 5, 2010, email; Julie Satow, "Redevelopment Activity in South Street Seaport Area Picks Up Momentum," *New York Sun*, Oct. 28, 2004, 13; Satow, "The Fish Market Cleans Up Good," *NYT*, Sept. 18, 2011, RE1.

35. Vivian S. Toy, "The Financial District Attracts Families," *NYT*, Feb. 22, 2009, RE1; Mark Caldwell, "The Scent of the Past," *NYT*, Mar. 26, 2006, 3.

36. Susan Dominus, "Trying to Find the Right Balance for the Seaport," *NYT*, June 27, 2008, B4; Phillip Lopate, telephone interview, Apr. 22, 2011; Andrew Jacobs, "Cadaver Exhibition Raises Questions Beyond Taste," *NYT*, Nov. 18, 2005 (editors' note appended, Jan. 7, 2006).

37. Skye H. McFarlane, "Seaport Residents Say Peck Plan Won't Sail," *DE*, Mar. 16, 2007; Julie Shapiro, "Museum Hopes for Historic Ships on Pier 15," *DE*, Mar. 29, 2008; Phillip Lopate, *Waterfront: A Journey around Manhattan* (New York: Crown, 2004), 105; Josh Rogers, "City Floats Tower-Park Idea for the East River," *DE*, Oct. 8, 2004. Because of the city's Manhattan Landing Plan in the early '70s, it only leased the north side of Pier 15 to the Seaport, which appropriated the whole pier after the scheme failed.

38. Robert, "Boat-Free, Yoga Visions for East River Waterfront," *Curbed New York*, Oct. 26, 2007, http://ny.curbed.com/archives/2007/10/26/boatfree_yoga_visions_for_east_river_waterfront.php; Robert, "East River Esplanade for Couch Potatoes?," *Curbed New York*, Oct. 24, 2007, http://ny.curbed.com/archives/2007/10/24/east_river_esplanade_plan_for_couch_potatoes.php; Julie Shapiro, "Boat Lovers Say City Plan Abandons Ship," *DE*, Oct. 26, 2007; Shapiro, "Museum Hopes for Historic Ships"; Robert LaValva to author, June 13, 2010, email; Nicole Dooskin (assistant vice president, EDC), telephone interview, Jan. 20, 2011; Aline Reynolds, "Pier 15's New Look Wows Visitors," *DE*, Jan. 4, 2012.

39. Ronda Kaysen, "Firm Dips Its Toes in Seaport Waters," *DE*, Mar. 18, 2005; William Neuman, "A Mall in Decline Eyes Fish-Market Space," *NYT*, July 3, 2005; Megan Costello, "Community Boards," *New York Observer*, Dec. 2, 2002, 10; Steven Jaffe to the editor, "The South Street Seaport's Heritage," *NYT*, June 24, 2008; "Too Tall, Too Private," *DE*, June 27, 2008; Stanford to author, Dec. 29, 2008, email; Patrick Hedlund, "Calatrava's Cubes on Deck?," *DE*, Mar. 28, 2008. The 120-foot limitation applied only to nine blocks and left out Block 72 south of John Street, one-half of which had been placed on the National Register to protect the Yankee Clipper (a City Landmark) and its adjacent lot.

40. Joey Arak, "Proposed New South Street Seaport Fully Revealed," *Curbed New York*, June 18, 2008, http://ny.curbed.com/archives/2008/06/18/proposed_new_south_street_seaport_fully_revealed.php; David W. Dunlap, "Seaport Plan Faces a Major Roadblock," *NYT*, June 18, 2008; "South Street Seaport Historic District and Extension," http://www.nyc.gov/html/lpc/downloads/pdf/maps/s_st_seaport.pdf; Terry Pristin, "After Storm, Moving to Update a Mall at the South Street Seaport," *NYT*, Dec. 26, 2012, B5; Terese Loeb Kreuzer, "Hidden No More, Seaport Developer's Desire for Hotels & Housing Revealed," *DE*, Apr. 3, 2013; Josh Rogers, "Seaport Museum Must Stay, Pols Tell Developer," *DE*, May 2, 2013; David Fisher, "Interest-Rate Fears Drag Down Howard Hughes Corp.: Buying Opportunity?," *Forbes.com*, Aug. 16, 2008, http://www.forbes.com/sites/danielfisher/2013/08/16/interest-rate-fears-drag-down-howard-hughes-corp-buying-opportunity/. Paying only $1.2 million in annual base rent at the seaport, the HHC expected to "turn a $111 million annual profit" (Kate Briquelet, "South '$weet' Lease Deal," *NYP*, Feb. 24, 2013).

41. SeaportSpeaks, *Seaport Speaks, Your Charrette Resource* (New York: SeaportSpeaks, 2006), 2, 7, 14, 18; Neill to author, Jan. 10, 2011, email. For the "Briefing Book" and "Final Report," see http://www.seaportspeaks.org.

42. Peter and Norma Stanford, *The Once and Future Seaport: A Proposal to Rededicate South Street Seaport as a Vital Center for History and for People* (Peekskill, NY: NMHS, 2006); P. Stanford to author, June 21, 2006, email; P. Stanford interview, June 21, 2010.

43. Aron, telephone interview, Apr. 14, 2010, Mar. 25, 2013; "The Museum is *in extremis*," in Aron to Frank Sciame, Nov. 2, 2006, JACF; Aron to [Task Force], Oct. 9, 2006, JACF; Matteson to author, Sept. 24, 2009, email; Aron to Sciame, Nov. 2, 2006, JACF; "A possible solution . . . ," in ibid.

44. Huntington and Mayo, "Presentation to the NYC EDC"; Dooskin, telephone interview, Jan. 20, 2011; Gochberg, telephone interview, Apr. 28, 2010; Robin Pogrebin, "Finances Could Sink Seaport Museum," *NYT*, Feb. 19, 2011, C1.

45. Ed Litvak, "LaValva's Seaport Market Vision Coming into Focus," *The Lo-Down*, Apr. 1, 2010, http://www.thelodownny.com/leslog/2010/04/lavalvas-seaport-vision -coming-into-focus.html#more-8298; Robert LaValva to author, June 13, 2010, email; "Press Conference for New Amsterdam Market Tomorrow," *Lighthearted Locavore* (blog), Apr. 14, 2010, http://lightheartedlocavore.blogspot.com/2010/04; Mark Bittman, "A Food Market for New York," *Opinionator* (blog), *NYT*, Mar. 12, 2013, http:// opinionator.blogs.nytimes.com/2013/03/12/a-food-market-for-new-york/?_r=0; Terese Loeb Kreuzer, "Council OKs Seaport Plan with Markets," *DE*, Mar. 20, 2013, and online comments, http://www.downtownexpress.com/2013/03/20/council-oks-seaport-plan -with-food-markets/; Kreuzer, "City Says No to Landmarking Seaport Building, Leaving Door Open to Demolition," *DE*, Sept. 9, 2013; NAM to author, Mar. 25, 2013, email. See also Alice Shorett and Murray Morgan, *Soul of the City: The Pike Place Public Market* (Seattle: University of Washington Press, 2007), 166–69.

NOTES TO THE CONCLUSION

1. Richard Fewtrell to author, Feb. 10, 2010, email; Phillip Lopate, "Her New York," *NYT*, Nov. 9, 2008, CY1.

2. Harold Skramstad, "An Agenda for American Museums in the Twenty-First Century," *Daedalus* 128 (Summer 1999): 128; Gloria Goodale, "Museums' New Mantra: Connect with Community," *CSM*, July 20, 2009.

3. Christopher Lowery to author, Sept. 21, 2010, email; Peter Neill to author, Feb. 8, 2010, email.

4. Thomas Gochberg, telephone interview, Apr. 28, 2010; Bob Ferraro, "Some Quick Memories, a Gathering of Friends, Honoring Peter and Norma Stanford," Oct. 17, 2006, SSSM (a packet of submitted materials); Walter Rybka to author, Sept. 12, 2006, email; Joe Doyle to author, July 26, 2009, email.

5. Whitney North Seymour Jr., telephone interview, Apr. 10, 2009; Lopate, "Her New York," CY1; Richard Weinstein, telephone interview, Oct. 16, 2009; "A Brief Sampling of Hoffer Aphorisms," *Life* (Mar. 24, 1967): 38; Huxtable to author, Mar. 26, 2009, email.

6. John Hightower to Peter Stanford, Apr. 7, 1978, Operations file, SSSM; Allon Schoener to author, Nov. 13, 2007, email; Steven Jaffe to author, Jan. 29, 2009, email; Phillip Lopate, telephone interview, Apr. 22, 2011.

7. Peter Neill, "Personal Dialogues with Ghosts," in *Past Meets Future: Saving America's Historic Environments*, ed. Antoinette J. Lee (Washington, DC: Preservation Press, 1992), 45.

8. Neill to author, Mar. 2, 2010, email; Luc Sante, *Low Life: Lures and Snares of Old New*

York (New York: Farrar, Straus & Giroux, 1991), xi; Phillip Lopate, introduction to *South Street*, by Barbara G. Mensch (New York: Columbia University Press, 2007), 32.

9. Stephen Kloepfer to author, Nov. 12, 2010, email.

10. Donald Birkholz, telephone interview, Oct. 16, 2009; Anthony C. Wood, "Celebrating Preservation's Story: 'It's Your Memory. It's Our History. It's Worth Saving," *Preservation Forum* 20 (Winter 2006): 50. The museum's new name, Seaport Museum New York, was trademarked on Aug. 4, 2010, but the trademark is now dead after the museum's reversion to its traditional name in 2012 (Trademark Search, http://www.trademarks411.com).

11. SSSM, *The Campaign for the SSSM: Immediate Goals $27.5 Million* (New York: SSSM, 1997); Peter Neill, "Save Our Ships!," *Seaport* 22 (Fall 1988): 6; Eric Darton, *Divided We Stand: A Biography of New York's World Trade Center* (New York: Basic Books, 1999), 20.

12. Patricia Leigh Brown, "Joe Cantalupo, 1906–1979," *Soho Weekly News*, Aug. 23, 1979, 5; Lopate, "Her New York," CY1; Kloepfer to author, Nov. 12, 2010, email.

13. Lopate, telephone interview, Apr. 22, 2011; Julie Shapiro, "Seaport Museum Struggles to Stay Afloat," *DNAinfo New York*, Feb. 10, 2011, http://www.dnainfo.com/new-york/20110210/downtown/seaport-museum-struggles-stay-afloat; Richard Dorfman, telephone interview, May 16, 2011; Robin Pogrebin, "Finances Could Sink Seaport Museum," *NYT*, Feb. 19, 2011 C1; Kate Taylor, "Founding President of Seaport Museum Calls for Resignations," *Arts Beat* (blog), *NYT*, Feb. 24, 2011; Julie Shapiro, "Seaport Museum 'Vastly' Overspent, New Manager Says," *DNAinfo New York*, Sept. 28, 2011, http://www.dnainfo.com/new-york/20110928/downtown/seaport-museum-vastly-overspent-new-manager-says.

14. Stanford to author, Apr. 7, 2011, email; Julie Shapiro, "Struggling Seaport Museum Will Dump Leaders to Stay Afloat," *DNAinfo New York*, May 16, 2011, http://www.dnainfo.com/new-york/20110516/downtown/struggling-seaport-museum-will-dump-leaders-stay-afloat; Abbie Fentress Swanson, "Museum of City of New York to Acquire Seaport Museum," WNYC website, Sept. 8, 2011, http://culture.wnyc.org/articles/features/2011/sep/08/museum-city-new-york-acquire-seaport-museum/; Terese Loeb Kreuzer, "It's Full Steam Ahead for Seaport Museum's New Director," *DE*, Nov. 9, 2011; Robin Finn, "At Harbor, Answering an S.O.S.," *NYT*, Nov. 2, 2011, MB1; Jessica Terrell, "CB1 Committee Calls for Council Hearing on Museum's Woes," *Tribeca Trib*, July 2011; Aline Reynolds, "Seaport Museum Lease Outdated, Says Jones," *DE*, Dec. 28, 2011; Reynolds, "Seaport Museum Prepares for Imminent Reopening," *DE*, Jan. 18, 2012; Reynolds, "Photo Exhibit 'Occupies' Seaport," *DE*, Feb. 2, 2012. The MCNY committed $600,000 to repairing the hull and deck of *Ambrose*, and another $250,000 to rebuilding *Lettie* (Kreuzer, "Anchors Aweigh: Seaport Museum Loses Its Operator," *DE*, July 3, 2013). *Lettie* will return to sailing in 2014.

15. Robin Pogrebin, "Seaport Museum Works to Dry Out," *NYT*, Nov. 13, 2012, C1; Terry Pristin, "After Storm, Moving to Update a Mall at the South Street Seaport," *NYT*, Dec. 26, 2012, B5; Terese Loeb Kreuzer, "Hidden No More, Seaport Developer's Desire for Hotels & Housing Revealed," *DE*, Apr. 3, 2013; Kreuzer, "S.O.S. Seaport Museum Says It's Getting Pushed Out," *DE*, Apr. 16, 2013; Kreuzer, "Liu and City Say Seaport Operator

Owes $1.3 Million," *DE*, May 1, 2013; Josh Rogers, "Seaport Museum Must Stay, Pols Tell Developer," *DE*, May 2, 2013.

16. Kreuzer, "S.O.S. Seaport Museum Says"; Kreuzer, "Liu and City Say"; Rogers, "Seaport Museum Must Stay." On Oct. 31, 2013, Silver, Squadron, Chin, and Manhattan Borough President Scott Stringer wrote the EDC, deploring its secrecy and urging it to employ a "collaborative, community-based planning process" for the seaport (Kreuzer, "Elected Officials Pressure EDC and Howard Hughes to Open Up on Seaport Planning," *DE*, Nov. 3, 2013).

17. Susan Henshaw Jones, telephone interview, May 28, 2013; Robin Pogrebin, "Cut Adrift by Its Would-Be Rescuer, Seaport Museum Seeks a Lifeline," *NYT*, June 25, 2013, C1; Terese Loeb Kreuzer, "Department of Cultural Affairs Steps in to Rescue South Street Seaport Museum," *DE*, July 9, 2013.

18. Terese Loeb Kreuzer, "City Is Keeping Seaport Museum Afloat," *DE*, July 17, 2013; Kreuzer, "Seaport Developer Quietly Moves to Transform the Area," *DE*, Sept. 5, 2013; Kreuzer, "City Says No to Landmarking Seaport Building, Leaving Door Open to Demolition," *DE*, Sept. 9, 2013; Kreuzer, "Seeking a View into the Seaport's Future," *DE*, Sept. 25, 2013; Josh Rogers with Terese Loeb Kreuzer, "Hughes Corp. & City Agree on Plan for Seaport Museum," *DE*, Oct. 23, 2013; Jonathan Boulware, telephone interview, Sept. 20, 2013, Dec. 11, 2013.

19. HABS, South Street Seaport, Survey NY-5632, 1976; Kreuzer, "It's Full Steam Ahead"; Editorial: "On the Seaport Museum's Reopening," *DE*, Jan. 25, 2012.

20. Peter H. Miller, "NTHP Enters a New Era," *Traditional Building* 25 (Aug. 2012).

INDEX

Page numbers in italics refer to illustrations.

Author of *Preserving the Old Dominion: Historic Preservation and Virginia Traditionalism* (1993), *Preserving Historic New England: Preservation, Progressivism, and the Remaking of Memory* (1995), and over two dozen published essays, James M. Lindgren is Professor of History at SUNY Plattsburgh, where he teaches courses on the history of US museums, historic sites, and preservation. He is now close to completing "Preserving Maritime America: Public Culture and Memory in the Making of the Nation's Great Marine Museums."